The Book of Resolutions
of
The United Methodist Church
1984

The
Book of Resolutions
of
The United Methodist
Church

———◆———

1984

The United Methodist Publishing House
Nashville, Tennessee

MANUFACTURED BY THE PARTHENON PRESS AT
NASHVILLE, TENNESSEE, UNITED STATES OF AMERICA

Preface

The Book of Resolutions has been published after each General Conference since 1968. This edition includes all valid resolutions since that time. Resolutions which are no longer timely or have been rescinded or superceded have been omitted. This volume also contains a complete topical index.

The resolutions, when approved by the General Conference, state the policy of The United Methodist Church on some of the current social issues and concerns.

The Book of Resolutions is published by The United Methodist Publishing House, Robert K. Feaster, Publisher. Ronald P. Patterson, Book Editor of The United Methodist Church, is responsible for editing the resolutions. Peggy Augustine, editor of United Methodist Resources, along with Maxine McKinney and Lee Ranck, staff members of the General Board of Church and Society, served as the editorial team.

Contents

1980 Resolutions

1984 Resolutions

11

SOCIAL PRINCIPLES

Preface

The United Methodist Church has a long history of concern for social justice. Its members have often taken forthright positions on controversial issues involving Christian principles. Early Methodists expressed their opposition to the slave trade, to smuggling, and to the cruel treatment of prisoners.

A social creed was adopted by the Methodist Episcopal Church (North) in 1908. Within the next decade similar statements were adopted by the Methodist Episcopal Church, South, and by the Methodist Protestant Church. The Evangelical United Brethren Church adopted a statement of social principles in 1946 at the time of the uniting of the United Brethren and The Evangelical Church. In 1972, four years after the uniting in 1968 of the Methodist Church and the Evangelical United Brethren Church, the General Conference of the United Methodist Church adopted a new statement of Social Principles, which was revised in 1976.

The Social Principles are a prayerful and thoughtful effort on the part of the General Conference to speak to the human issues in the contemporary world from a sound biblical and theological foundation as historically demonstrated in United Methodist traditions. They are intended to be instructive and persuasive in the best of the prophetic spirit. The Social Principles are a call to all members of The United Methodist Church to a prayerful, studied dialogue of faith and practice. (¶ 610.)

Preamble

We, the people called United Methodists, affirm our faith in God our Father, in Jesus Christ our Savior, and in the Holy Spirit, our Guide and Guard.

We acknowledge our complete dependence upon God in birth, in life, in death, and in life eternal. Secure in God's love, we affirm the goodness of life and confess our many sins against God's will for us as we find it in Jesus Christ. We have not always been faithful stewards of all that has been committed to us by God the Creator. We have been reluctant followers of Jesus Christ in his mission to bring all persons into a community of love. Though called by the Holy Spirit to become new creatures in Christ, we have resisted the further call to become the people of God in our dealings with each other and the earth on which we live.

Grateful for God's forgiving love, in which we live and by which we are judged, and affirming our belief in the inestimable worth of each individual, we renew our commitment to become faithful witnesses to the gospel, not alone to the ends of earth, but also to the depths of our common life and work.

¶ 70. I. The Natural World

All creation is the Lord's and we are responsible for the ways in which we use and abuse it. Water, air, soil, minerals, energy resources, plants, animal life, and space are to be valued and conserved because they are God's creation and not solely because they are useful to human beings. Therefore, we repent of our devastation of the physical and nonhuman world. Further, we recognize the responsibility of the Church toward life style and systemic changes in society that will promote a more ecologically just world and a better quality of life for all creation.

A) Water, Air, Soil, Minerals, Plants.—We support and encourage social policies that serve to reduce and control the creation of industrial by-products and waste; facilitate the safe processing and disposal of toxic and nuclear waste; provide for appropriate disposal of municipal waste; and enhance the rejuvenation of polluted air, water, and soil. We support measures which will halt the spread of deserts into formerly productive lands. We support regulations designed to protect plant life, including those that provide for reforestation and for conservation of grasslands. We support policies that retard the *indiscriminate* use of chemicals, including those used for growing, processing, and preserving food, and encourage adequate research into their effects upon God's creation prior to utilization. We urge development of international agreements concerning equitable utilization of the ocean's resources for human benefit so long as the integrity of the seas is maintained. Moreover, we support policies on the part of governments and industries that conserve fossil and other fuels, and that eliminate methods of securing minerals that destroy plants, animals, and soil. We encourage creation of new sources for food and power, while maintaining the goodness of the earth.

B) Energy Resources Utilization.—We support and encourage social policies that are directed toward rational and restrained transformation of parts of the nonhuman world into energy for human usage, and which de-emphasize or eliminate energy-producing technologies that endanger the health, safety, and even existence of the present and future human and nonhuman creation. Further, we urge wholehearted support of the conservation of energy and responsible development of all energy resources, with special concern for the development of renewable energy sources, that the goodness of the earth may be affirmed.

C) Animal Life.—We support regulations that protect the life and health of animals, including those ensuring the humane treatment of pets and other domestic animals, and the painless slaughtering of meat animals, fish, and fowl. Furthermore, we encourage the preservation of animal species now threatened with extinction.

D) Space.—The moon, planets, stars, and the space between and among them are the creation of God and are due the respect we are called to give the earth. We support the extension of knowledge through space exploration, but only when that knowledge is used for the welfare of humanity.

¶ 71. II. The Nurturing Community

The community provides the potential for nurturing human beings into the fullness of their humanity. We believe we have a responsibility to innovate, sponsor, and evaluate new forms of community that will encourage development of the fullest potential in individuals. Primary for us is the gospel understanding that all persons are important—because they are human beings and not because they have merited significance. We therefore support social climates in which human communities are maintained and strengthened for the sake of every person.

A) The Family.—We believe the family to be the basic human community through which persons are nurtured and sustained in mutual love, responsibility, respect, and fidelity. We understand the family as encompassing a wider range of options than that of the two-generational unit of parents and children (the nuclear family), including the extended family, families with adopted children, single parents, couples without children. We affirm shared responsibility for parenting by men and women and encourage social, economic, and religious efforts to maintain and strengthen relationships within families in order that every member may be assisted toward complete personhood.

B) Other Christian Communities.—We further recognize the movement to find new patterns of Christian nurturing communities such as Koinonia Farms, certain monastic and other religious orders, and some types of corporate church life. We urge the Church to seek ways of understanding the needs and concerns of such Christian groups and to find ways of ministering to them and through them.

C) Marriage.—We affirm the sanctity of the marriage covenant which is expressed in love, mutual support, personal commitment, and shared fidelity between a man and a woman. We believe that God's blessing rests upon such marriage, whether or not there are children of the

16

union. We reject social norms that assume different standards for women than for men in marriage.

D) Divorce.—Where marriage partners, even after thoughtful consideration and counsel, are estranged beyond reconciliation, we recognize divorce as regrettable but recognize the right of divorced persons to remarry. We express our deep concern for the care and nurture of the children of divorced and/or remarried persons. We encourage that either or both of the divorced parents be considered for custody of the minor children of the marriage. We encourage an active, accepting, and enabling commitment of the church and our society to minister to the members of divorced families.

E) Single Persons.—We affirm the integrity of single persons, and we reject all social practices that discriminate or social attitudes that are prejudicial against persons because they are unmarried.

F) Human Sexuality.—We recognize that sexuality is a good gift of God, and we believe persons may be fully human only when that gift is acknowledged and affirmed by themselves, the Church, and society. We call all persons to disciplines that lead to the fulfillment of themselves, others, and society in the stewardship of this gift. We encourage the medical, theological, and humanistic disciplines to combine in a determined effort to understand human sexuality more completely.

Although men and women are sexual beings whether or not they are married, sex between a man and a woman is only to be clearly affirmed in the marriage bond. Sex may become exploitative within as well as outside marriage. We reject all sexual expressions which damage or destroy the humanity God has given us as birthright, and we affirm only that sexual expression which enhances that same humanity, in the midst of diverse opinion as to what constitutes that enhancement.

We deplore all forms of the commercialization and exploitation of sex with their consequent cheapening and degradation of human personality. We call for stern enforcement of laws prohibiting the sexual exploitation or use of children by adults. We call for the establishment of

17

adequate protective services, guidance, and counseling opportunities for children thus abused.

We recognize the continuing need for full and frank sex education opportunities for children, youth, and adults.

Homosexual persons no less than heterosexual persons are individuals of sacred worth, who need the ministry and guidance of the Church in their struggles for human fulfillment, as well as the spiritual and emotional care of a fellowship which enables reconciling relationships with God, with others, and with self. Further we insist that all persons are entitled to have their human and civil rights ensured, though we do not condone the practice of homosexuality and consider this practice incompatible with Christian teaching.

G) Abortion.—The beginning of life and the ending of life are the God-given boundaries of human existence. While individuals have always had some degree of control over when they would die, they now have the awesome power to determine when and even whether new individuals will be born. Our belief in the sanctity of unborn human life makes us reluctant to approve abortion. But we are equally bound to respect the sacredness of the life and well-being of the mother, for whom devastating damage may result from an unacceptable pregnancy. In continuity with past Christian teaching, we recognize tragic conflicts of life with life that may justify abortion, and in such cases support the legal option of abortion under proper medical procedures. We call all Christians to a searching and prayerful inquiry into the sorts of conditions that may warrant abortion. Governmental laws and regulations do not provide all the guidance required by the informed Christian conscience. Therefore, a decision concerning abortion should be made only after thoughtful and prayerful consideration by the parties involved, with medical, pastoral, and other appropriate counsel.

H) Death with Dignity.—We applaud medical science for efforts to prevent disease and illness and for advances in treatment that extend the meaningful life of human beings. At the same time, in the varying stages of death and life that advances in medical science have occasioned, we recognize the agonizing personal and moral decisions faced by the dying, their physicians, their families, and their friends. Therefore, we assert the right of every person to die in dignity, with loving personal care and without efforts to prolong terminal illnesses merely because the technology is available to do so.

¶ 72. III. The Social Community

The rights and privileges a society bestows upon or withholds from those who comprise it indicate the relative esteem in which that society holds particular persons and groups of persons. We affirm all persons as equally valuable in the sight of God. We therefore work toward societies in which each person's value is recognized, maintained, and strengthened.

A) Rights of Racial and Ethnic Minorities.—Racism plagues and cripples our growth in Christ, inasmuch as it is antithetical to the gospel itself. Therefore, we reject racism in every form, and affirm the ultimate and temporal worth of all persons. We rejoice in the gifts which particular ethnic histories and cultures bring to our total life. We commend and encourage the self-awareness of all racial and ethnic minorities and oppressed people which leads them to demand their just and equal rights as members of society. We assert the obligation of society, and groups within the society, to implement compensatory programs that redress long-standing systemic social deprivation of racial and ethnic minorities. We further assert the right of members of racial and ethnic minorities to equal opportunities in employment and promotion; to education and training of the highest quality; to nondiscrimination in voting, in access to public accommodations, and in housing purchase or rental; and positions of leadership and power in all elements of our life together.

B) Rights of Religious Minorities.—Religious persecution has been common in the history of civilization. We urge politics and practices that ensure the right of every religious group to exercise its faith free from legal, political, or economic restrictions. In particular, we condemn anti-Semitism in both its overt and covert forms, and assert the right of all religions and their adherents to freedom from legal, economic, and social discrimination.

C) Rights of Children.—Once considered the property of their parents, children are now acknowledged to be full human beings in their own right, but beings to whom adults and society in general have special obligations. Thus, we support the development of school systems and innovative methods of education designed to assist every child toward full humanity. All children have the right to quality education, including a full sexual education appropriate to their stage of development that utilizes the best educational techniques and insights. Moreover, children have the rights to food, shelter, clothing, health care, and emotional well-being as do adults, and these rights we affirm as theirs regardless of actions or inactions of their parents or guardians. In particular, children must be protected from economic and sexual exploitation.

D) Rights of Youth and Young Adults.—Our society is characterized by a large population of youth and young adults who frequently find full participation in society difficult. Therefore, we urge development of policies that encourage inclusion of youth and young adults in decision-making processes and that eliminate discrimination and exploitation. Creative and appropriate employment opportunities should be legally and socially available for youth and young adults.

E) Rights of the Aging.—In a society that places primary emphasis upon youth, those growing old in years are frequently isolated from the mainstream of social existence. We support social policies that integrate the aging into the life of the total community, including sufficient incomes, increased and non-discriminatory employment opportunities, educational and service opportunities, and adequate medical care and housing within existing communities. We urge social policies and programs, with emphasis on the unique concerns of older women and ethnic minority persons, that ensure to the aging the respect and dignity that is their right as senior members of the human community. Further, we urge increased consideration for adequate pension systems by employers with provisions for the surviving spouse.

F) Rights of Women.—We affirm women and men to be equal in every aspect of their common life. We, therefore, urge that every effort be made to eliminate sex role stereotypes in activity and portrayal of family life and in all aspects of voluntary and compensatory participation in the church and society. We affirm the right of women to equal treatment in employment, responsibility, promotion, and compensation. We affirm the importance of women in decision-making positions at all levels of church life and urge such bodies to guarantee their presence through policies of employment and recruitment. We urge employers of persons in dual career families, both in the church and society, to apply proper consideration of both parties when relocation is considered.

G) Rights of Persons with Handicapping Conditions.—We recognize and affirm the full humanity and personhood of all individuals as members of the family of God. We affirm the responsibility of the church and society to be in ministry with all persons, including those persons with mentally, physically and/or psychologically handicapping conditions whose disabilities or differences in appearance or behavior create a problem in mobility, communication, intellectual comprehension, or personal relationships, which interfere with their participation or that of their families in the life of the church and the community. We urge the church and society to receive the gifts of persons with handicapping conditions to enable them to be full participants in the community of faith. We call the church and society to be sensitive to, and advocate programs of rehabilitation, services, employment, education, appropriate housing and transportation.

H) Population.—Since growing populations will increasingly strain the world's supply of food, minerals, and water, and sharpen international tensions, the reduction of the rate of consumption of resources by the affluent and the

21

reduction of current population growth rates have become imperative. People have the duty to consider the impact on the total society of their decisions regarding childbearing, and should have access to information and appropriate means to limit their fertility, including voluntary sterilization. We affirm that programs to achieve a stabilized population should be placed in a context of total economic and social development, including an equitable use and control of resources; improvement in the status of women in all cultures; a human level of economic security, health care, and literacy for all.

I) Alcohol and Other Drugs.—We affirm our long-standing support of abstinence from alcohol as a faithful witness to God's liberating and redeeming love for persons. We also recommend abstinence from the use of marijuana and any illegal drugs. As the use of alcohol or tobacco is a major factor in both disease and death, we support educational programs encouraging abstinence from such use.

Millions of living human beings are testimony to the beneficial consequences of therapeutic drug use, and millions of others are testimony to the detrimental consequences of drug misuse. We encourage wise policies relating to the availability of potentially beneficial or potentially damaging prescription and over-the-counter drugs; we urge that complete information about their use and misuse be readily available to both doctor and patient. We support the strict administration of laws regulating the sale and distribution of all opiates. We support regulations that protect society from users of drugs of any kind where it can be shown that a clear and present social danger exists. The drug dependent person is an individual of infinite human worth in need of treatment and rehabilitation, and misuse should be viewed as a symptom of underlying disorders for which remedies should be sought.

J) Medical Experimentation.—Physical and mental health has been greatly enhanced through discoveries by medical science. It is imperative, however, that governments and the medical profession carefully enforce the requirements of the prevailing medical research standard, maintaining rigid controls in testing new technologies and drugs utilizing human beings. The standard requires that those engaged in research shall use human beings as research subjects only after obtaining full, rational, and uncoerced consent.

K) Rural Life.—We support the right of persons and families to live and prosper as farmers, farm workers, merchants, professionals, and others outside of the cities and metropolitan centers. We believe our culture is impoverished and our people deprived of a meaningful way of life when rural and small-town living becomes difficult or impossible. We recognize that the improvement of this way of life may sometimes necessitate the use of some lands for nonagricultural purposes. We oppose the indiscriminate diversion of agricultural land for nonagricultural uses when nonagricultural land is available. Further, we encourage the preservation of appropriate lands for agriculture and open space uses through thoughtful land use programs. We support governmental and private programs designed to benefit the resident farmer rather than the factory farm, and programs that encourage industry to locate in nonurban areas.

L) Urban-Suburban Life.—Urban-suburban living has become a dominant style of life for more and more persons. For many it furnishes economic, educational, social, and cultural opportunities. For others, it has brought alienation, poverty, and depersonalization. We in the Church have an opportunity and responsibility to help shape the future of urban-suburban life. Massive programs of renewal and social planning are needed to bring a greater degree of humanization into urban-suburban life styles. Christians must judge all programs, including economic and community development, new towns, and urban renewal by the extent to which they protect and enhance human values, permit personal and political involvement, and make possible neighborhoods open to persons of all races, ages, and income levels. We affirm the efforts of all developers who place human values at the heart of their planning. We must help shape urban-suburban development so it provides for the human need to identify with and find meaning in smaller social communities. At the same time such smaller communities must be encouraged to assume responsibilities for the total urban-suburban community instead of isolating themselves from it.

¶ 73.   IV. The Economic Community

We claim all economic systems to be under the judgment of God no less than other facets of the created order. Therefore, we recognize the responsibility of governments to develop and implement sound fiscal and monetary policies that provide for the economic life of individuals and corporate entities, and that ensure full employment and adequate incomes with a minimum of inflation. We believe private and public economic enterprises are responsible for the social costs of doing business, such as unemployment and environmental pollution, and that they should be held accountable for these costs. We support measures that would reduce the concentration of wealth in the hands of a few. We further support efforts to revise tax structures and eliminate governmental support programs that now benefit the wealthy at the expense of other persons.

A) Property.—We believe private ownership of property is a trusteeship under God, both in those societies where it is encouraged and where it is discouraged, but is limited by the over-riding needs of society. We believe that Christian faith denies to any person or group of persons exclusive and arbitrary control of any other part of the created universe. Socially and culturally conditioned ownership of property is, therefore, to be considered a responsibility to God. We believe, therefore, governments have the responsibility, in the pursuit of justice and order under law, to provide procedures that protect the rights of the whole society, as well as those of private ownership.

B) Collective Bargaining.—We support the right of public and private (including farm, government, institutional, and domestic) employees and employers to organize for collective bargaining into unions and other groups of their

24

own choosing. Further, we support the right of both parties to protection in so doing, and their responsibility to bargain in good faith within the framework of the public interest. In order that the rights of all members of the society may be maintained and promoted, we support innovative bargaining procedures that include representatives of the public interest in negotiation and settlement of labor-management contracts including some that may lead to forms of judicial resolution of issues.

C) Work and Leisure.—Every person has the right and rsponsibility to work for the benefit of himself or herself and the enhancement of human life and community and to receive adequate remuneration. We support social measures that ensure the physical and mental safety of workers, that provide for the equitable division of products and services and that encourage an increasing freedom in the way individuals may use their leisure time. We recognize the opportunity leisure provides for creative contributions to society and encourage methods that allow workers additional blocks of discretionary time. We support educational, cultural, and recreational outlets that enhance the use of such time. We believe that persons come before profits. We deplore the selfish spirit which often pervades our economic life. We support policies which encourage workplace democracy, cooperative and collective work arrangements. We support rights of workers to refuse to work in situations that endanger health and/or life, without jeopardy to their jobs. We support policies which would reverse the increasing concentration of business and industry into monopolies.

D) Consumption.—We support efforts to ensure truth in pricing, packaging, lending, and advertising. We assert that the consumers' primary responsibility is to provide themselves with needed goods and services of high quality at the lowest cost consistent with economic practices. They should exercise their economic power to encourage the manufacture of goods that are necessary and beneficial to humanity while avoiding the desecration of the environment in either production or consumption. Those who manufacture goods and offer services serve society best when they aid consumers in fulfilling these responsibilities. Consumers should evaluate their consumption of goods and services in the light of the need for enhanced quality of life rather than unlimited production of material goods. We call upon consumers to organize to achieve these goals.

E) Poverty.—In spite of general affluence in the industrialized nations, the majority of persons in the world live in poverty. In order to provide basic needs such as food, clothing, shelter, education, health care, and other necessities, ways must be found to share more equitably the resources of the world. Increasing technology and exploitative economic practices impoverish many persons and make poverty self-perpetuating. Therefore, we do not hold poor people morally responsible for their economic state. To begin to alleviate poverty, we support such policies as: adequate income maintenance, quality education, decent housing, job training, meaningful employment opportunities, adequate medical and hospital care, and humanization and radical revisions of welfare programs.

F) Migrant Workers.—Migratory and other farm workers, who have long been a special concern of the Church's ministry, are by the nature of their way of life excluded from many of the economic and social benefits enjoyed by other workers. We advocate their right to, and applaud their efforts toward, responsible self-organization and self-determination. We call upon governments and all employers to ensure for migratory workers the same economic, educational, and social benefits enjoyed by other citizens. We call upon our churches to seek to develop programs of service to such migrant people as come within their parish.

G) Gambling.—Gambling is a menace to society, deadly to the best interests of moral, social, economic, and spiritual life, and destructive of good government. As an act of faith and love, Christians should abstain from gambling, and should strive to minister to those victimized by the practice. Where gambling has become addictive, the Church will encourage such individuals to receive therapeutic assistance so that the individual's energies may be redirected into positive and constructive ends. Community standards and personal life styles should be such as would make unnecessary and undesirable the resort to commercial gambling, including public lotteries, as a recreation, as an escape, or as a means of producing public revenue or funds for support of charities or government.

¶ 74. V. The Political Community

While our allegiance to God takes precedence over our allegiance to any state, we acknowledge the vital function of government as a principal vehicle for the ordering of society. Because we know ourselves to be responsible to God for social and political life, we declare the following relative to governments:

A) Basic Freedoms.—We hold governments responsible for the protection of the rights of the people to the freedoms of speech, religion, assembly, and communications media, and petition for redress of grievances without fear of reprisal; to the right to privacy; and to the guarantee of the rights to adequate food, clothing, shelter, education, and health care. We also strongly reject domestic surveillance and intimidation of political opponents by governments in power, and all other misuses of elective or appointive offices. The use of detention and imprisonment for the harassment and elimination of political opponents or other dissidents violates fundamental human rights. Furthermore, the mistreatment or torture of persons by governments for any purpose violates Christian teaching and must be condemned and/or opposed by Christians and churches wherever and whenever it occurs.

The Church regards the institution of slavery as an infamous evil. All forms of enslavement are totally prohibited and shall in no way be tolerated by the Church.

B) Political Responsibility.—The strength of a political system depends upon the full and willing participation of its citizens. We believe that the state should not attempt to control the Church, nor should the Church seek to

27

dominate the state. "Separation of church and state" means no organic union of the two, but does permit interaction. The Church should continually exert a strong ethical influence upon the state, supporting policies and programs deemed to be just and compassionate and opposing policies and programs which are not.

C) Freedom of Information.—Citizens of all countries should have access to all essential information regarding their government and its policies. Illegal and unconscionable activities directed against persons or groups by their own governments must not be justified or kept secret even under the guise of national security.

D) Education.—We believe responsibility for education of the young rests with the family, the Church, and the government. In our society this function can best be fulfilled through public policies which ensure access for all persons to free public elementary and secondary schools and to post-secondary schools of their choice. Persons in our society should not be precluded by financial barriers from access to church-related and other independent institutions of higher education. We affirm the right of public and independent colleges and universities to exist, and we endorse public policies which ensure access and choice and which do not create unconstitutional entanglements between Church and state. The state should not use its authority to inculcate particular religious beliefs (including atheism) nor should it require prayer or worship in the public schools, but should leave students free to practice their own religious convictions.

E) Civil Obedience and Civil Disobedience.—Governments and laws should be servants of God and of human beings. Citizens have a duty to abide by laws duly adopted by orderly and just process of government. But governments, no less than individuals, are subject to the judgment of God. Therefore, we recognize the right of individuals to dissent when acting under the constraint of conscience and after exhausting all legal recourse, to disobey laws deemed to be unjust. Even then, respect for law should be shown by refraining from violence and by accepting the costs of disobedience. We offer our prayers for those in rightful authority who serve the public and we support their efforts to afford justice and equal opportunity for all people. We assert the duty of churches to support everyone who suffers for the cause of conscience, and urge governments seriously to consider restoration of rights to such persons while also maintaining respect for those who obey.

F) Crime and Rehabilitation.—To protect all citizens from those who would encroach upon personal and property rights, it is the duty of governments to establish police forces, courts, and facilities for rehabilitation of offenders. We support governmental measures designed to reduce and eliminate crime, consistent with respect for the basic freedom of persons. We reject all misuse of these necessary mechanisms, including their use for the purpose of persecuting or intimidating those whose race, appearance, life style, economic condition, or beliefs differ from those in authority, and we reject all careless, callous, or discriminatory enforcement of law. We further support measures designed to remove the social conditions that lead to crime, and we encourage continued positive interaction between law enforcement officials and members of the community at large. In the love of Christ who came to save those who are lost and vulnerable, we urge the creation of genuinely new systems of rehabilitation that will restore, preserve, and nurture the humanity of the imprisoned. For the same reason, we oppose capital punishment and urge its elimination from all criminal codes.

G) Military Service.—Though coercion, violence, and war are presently the ultimate sanctions in international relations, we reject them as incompatible with the gospel and spirit of Christ. We therefore urge the establishment of the rule of law in international affairs as a means of elimination of war, violence, and coercion in these affairs.

We reject national policies of enforced military service as incompatible with the gospel. We acknowledge the agonizing tension created by the demand for military service by national governments. We urge all young adults to seek the counsel of the Church as they reach a conscientious decision concerning the nature of their responsibility as citizens. Pastors are called upon to be available for counseling with all young adults who face conscription, including those who conscientiously refuse to cooperate with a system of conscription.

We support and extend the ministry of the Church to those persons who conscientiously oppose all war, or any particular war, and who therefore refuse to serve in the armed forces or to cooperate with systems of military conscription. We also support and extend the Church's ministry to those persons who conscientiously choose to serve in the armed forces or to accept alternative service.

¶ 75. VI. The World Community

God's world is one world. The unity now being thrust upon us by technological revolution has far outrun our moral and spiritual capacity to achieve a stable world. The enforced unity of humanity, increasingly evident on all levels of life, presents the Church as well as all people with problems that will not wait for answer: injustice, war, exploitation, privilege, population, international ecological crisis, proliferation of arsenals of nuclear weapons, development of transnational business organizations that operate beyond the effective control of any governmental structure, and the increase of tyranny in all its forms. This generation must find viable answers to these and related questions if humanity is to continue on this earth. We commit ourselves, as a Church, to the achievement of a world community that is a fellowship of persons who honestly love one another. We pledge ourselves to seek the meaning of the gospel in all issues that divide people and threaten the growth of world community.

A) Nations and Cultures.—As individuals are affirmed by God in their diversity, so are nations and cultures. We recognize that no nation or culture is absolutely just and right in its treatment of its own people, nor is any nation totally without regard for the welfare of its citizens. The

30

Church must regard nations as accountable for unjust treatment of their citizens and others living within their borders. While recognizing valid differences in culture and political philosophy, we stand for justice and peace in every nation.

B) *National Power and Responsibility.*—Some nations possess more military and economic power than do others. Upon the powerful rests responsibility to exercise their wealth and influence with restraint. We affirm the right and duty of the people of developing nations to determine their own destiny. We urge the major political powers to use their power to maximize the political, social, and economic self-determination of developing nations, rather than to further their own special interests. We applaud international efforts to develop a more just international economic order, in which the limited resources of the earth will be used to the maximum benefit of all nations and peoples. We urge Christians, in every society, to encourage the governments under which they live, and the economic entities within their societies, to aid and to work for the development of more just economic orders.

C) *War and Peace.*—We believe war is incompatible with the teachings and example of Christ. We therefore reject war as an instrument of national foreign policy and insist that the first moral duty of all nations is to resolve by peaceful means every dispute that arises between or among them; that human values must outweigh military claims as governments determine their priorities; that the militarization of society must be challenged and stopped; that the manufacture, sale, and deployment of armaments must be reduced and controlled; and that the production, possession, or use of nuclear weapons be condemned.

D) *Justice and Law.*—Persons and groups must feel secure in their life and right to live within a society if order is to be achieved and maintained by law. We denounce as immoral an ordering of life that perpetuates injustice. Nations, too, must feel secure in the world if world community is to become a fact.

Believing that international justice requires the participa-

31

tion of all peoples, we endorse the United Nations and its related bodies and the International Court of Justice as the best instruments now in existence to achieve a world of justice and law. We commend the efforts of all people in all countries who pursue world peace through law. We endorse international aid and cooperation on all matters of need and conflict. We urge acceptance for membership in the United Nations of all nations who wish such membership and who accept United Nations responsibility. We urge the United Nations to take a more aggressive role in the development of international arbitration of disputes and actual conflicts among nations by developing binding third-party arbitration. Bilateral or multilateral efforts outside of the United Nations should work in concert with, and not contrary to, its purposes. We reaffirm our historic concern for the world as our parish and seek for all persons and peoples full and equal membership in a truly world community.

¶ 76.   VII.   Our Social Creed

We believe in God, Creator of the world; and in Jesus Christ the Redeemer of creation. We believe in the Holy Spirit, through whom we acknowledge God's gifts, and we repent of our sin in misusing these gifts to idolatrous ends.

We affirm the natural world as God's handiwork and dedicate ourselves to its preservation, enhancement, and faithful use by humankind.

We joyfully receive, for ourselves and others, the blessings of community, sexuality, marriage, and the family.

We commit ourselves to the rights of men, women, children, youth, young adults, the aging, and those with handicapping conditions; to improvement of the quality of life; and to the rights and dignity of racial, ethnic, and religious minorities.

We believe in the right and duty of persons to work for the good of themselves and others, and in the protection of their welfare in so doing; in the rights to property as a trust from God, collective bargaining, and responsible consumption; and in the elimination of economic and social distress.

We dedicate ourselves to peace throughout the world, to freedom for all peoples, and to the rule of justice and law among nations.

We believe in the present and final triumph of God's Word in human affairs, and gladly accept our commission to manifest the life of the gospel in the world. Amen.

(It is recommended that this statement of Social Principles be continually available to United Methodist Christians and that it be emphasized regularly in every congregation. It is further recommended that our Social Creed be frequently used in Sunday worship.)

1968

Project Equality

In consideration of long established support, by The United Methodist Church, for fair employment practices;

in consideration of national policy for fair employment practices in the United States, which policy embraces legislation against employment discrimination;

in recognition of The United Methodist Church's responsibility to make ethical use of its own financial resources;

in the conviction that "Project Equality," a voluntary cooperative interdenominational enterprise of churches, synagogues, and related institutions, sponsored by the National Catholic Conference on Interracial Justice, provides a responsible, consistent, ethical, practical, effective, and positive means whereby The United Methodist Church and other churches can support fair employment practices in the United States:

The United Methodist Church endorses "Project Equality," and recommends cooperation, both through participation and financial support, on the part of all United Methodist Annual Conferences, local churches, local or national institutions, agencies, and organization.

Racial Equality in The United Methodist Church

WHEREAS, Article IV of the Constitution of The United Methodist Church provides that "In the United Methodist Church no conference or other organizational unit of the church shall be structured so as to exclude any member or any constituent body of the church because of race, color, national origin, or economic condition," and

WHEREAS, the Judicial Council has ruled in Decision No. 242, that during a transitional period of indeterminant length "Article IV is not to be read so as to forbid the continued existence of annual conferences, the membership of which may be predominantly, or even exclusively racial in composition," and

WHEREAS, in the formation of The Methodist Church in 1939 and 1940 expedient arrangements were made in the expectation that basic issues should be resolved in due course, and in fact these issues have not been satisfactorily resolved within an elapsed time of some twenty-eight years; therefore

The General Conference is urgently petitioned to declare that Article IV of the Constitution is an essential part of the basic law of The United Methodist Church, and that arrangements shall be made forthwith for its implementation.[1]

The United Methodist Church and Church-Government Relations

A STATEMENT CONCERNING CHURCH-GOVERNMENT RELATIONS AND SOCIAL WELFARE
I

The United Methodist Church is concerned about the health and well-being of all persons because it recognizes

---

[1]See Social Principles III-A; "The United Methodist Church and Race" (1976)

that physical health and social well-being are necessary pre-conditions to the complete fulfillment of man's personal and social possibilities in this world. Our Master himself cared for the sick and fed the multitudes in recognition that man's physical well-being cannot be divorced from his spiritual health.

Service to persons in need, along with social education and action to eliminate forces and structures that create or perpetuate conditions of need, is integral to the life and witness of Christians, both as individuals and as churches. However, there are no fixed institutional patterns for the rendering of such service. It may be rendered effectively as a Christian vocation or avocation, and through the channels of either a governmental or a private agency.

We recognize that churches are not the only institutions exercising a critical and prophetic role in the community and in society. They share that responsibility with many other institutions and agencies in such fields as law, education, social work, medicine, and the sciences. Yet churches cannot escape their special obligation to nurture and encourage a critical and prophetic quality in their own institutional life. That quality should be expressed also through their members—as they act as citizens, trustees of agencies and persons with professional skills. It should be understood that the performance of such roles by church members will often involve them in revaluing the norms avowed by churches as well as using such norms as a basis for judgment.

II

We recognize that governments at all levels in the United States have increasingly assumed responsibility for the performance of social welfare functions. There is reason to believe that this trend will continue and, perhaps, be accelerated. We assume that governments will continue to use private nonprofit agencies as instrumentalities for the implementation of publicly formulated social welfare policies. This means that private agencies will continue to face unprecedented demand for their services and have unprecedented access to government resources.

It is now evident that a variety of contributions is required to achieve a comprehensive social welfare policy for the nation, for the states, and for each community. Such a policy includes identification of the range of human needs, transformation of needs into effective demands, and development of programs to meet those demands. We believe that all the organizations and resources of the private sector, as well as those of governments, should be taken into account in the formulation and execution of social welfare policies.

We recognize that appropriate government bodies have the right to prescribe minimum standards for all private social welfare agencies. We believe that no private agency, because of its religious affiliations, ought to be exempted from any of the requirements of such standards.

III

Governmental provision of material support for church-related agencies inevitably raises important questions of religious establishment. In recognition, however, that some health, education, and welfare agencies have been founded by churches without regard to religious proselytizing, we consider that such agencies may, under certain circumstances, be proper channels for public programs in these fields. When government provides support for programs administered by private agencies, it has the most serious obligation to establish and enforce standards guaranteeing the equitable administration of such programs and the accountability of such agencies to the public authority. In particular, we believe that no government resources should be provided to any church-related agency for such purposes unless:

1. The services to be provided by the agency shall meet a genuine community need.

2. The services of the agency shall be designed and administered in such a way as to avoid serving a sectarian purpose or interest.

3. The services to be provided by the agency shall be available to all persons without regard to race, color, national origin, creed, or political persuasion.

4. The services to be rendered by the agency shall be performed in accordance with accepted professional and administrative standards.

5. Skill, competence, and integrity in the performance of duties shall be the principal considerations in the employment of personnel and shall not be superseded by any requirement of religious affiliation.

6. The right to collective bargaining shall be recognized by the agency.

IV

We recognize that all of the values involved in the sponsorship of a social welfare agency by a church may not be fully expressed if that agency has to rely permanently on access to government resources for its existence. We are also aware that under certain circumstances sponsorship of a social welfare agency by a church may inhibit the development of comprehensive welfare services in the community. Therefore, the church and the agency should choose which pattern of service to offer: (1) channeling standardized and conventional services supplied or supported by government, or (2) attempting experimental or unconventional ministries and criticizing government programs when they prove inadequate. We believe that these two patterns are difficult, if not impossible, to combine in the same agency, and that the choice between them should be made before dependence upon government resources makes commitment to the first pattern irreversible.

V

We believe that persons in both public and private institutions of social welfare should have adequate opportunities for religious services and ministries of their own choosing. Such services and ministries should be available to all, but they should not be compulsory. Under certain circumstances, failure to provide such services and ministries may have a serious adverse effect on the free exercise of religion. Where, for medical or legal reasons, the free movement of individuals is curtailed, the institutions of social welfare involved ought to provide opportunities for religious worship.

VI

There is a new awareness of the need for welfare services to be complemented by action for social change. We believe that agencies of social welfare to churches have an obligation to provide data and insights concerning the causes of specific social problems. It should be recognized that both remedial and preventive programs may require legislation, changes in political structures, and cooperation in direct action and community organization.

In their efforts to meet human needs, churches should never allow their preoccupation with remedial programs under their own direction to divert them or the larger community from a common search for basic solutions. In dealing with conditions of poverty, churches should have no stake in programs which continue dependency or which embody attitudes and practices which may be described as "welfare colonialism."

We believe that churches have a moral obligation to challenge violations of the civil rights of the poor. They ought to direct their efforts toward helping the poor overcome the powerlessness which makes such violations of civil rights possible. Specifically, churches ought to protest such policies and practices by welfare personnel as unwarranted invasions of privacy and requirement of attendance at church activities in order to qualify for social welfare services.

1970

Use of Church Facilities by Community Groups

Encouragement shall be given for the use of local church facilities by community groups and agencies which serve social and service needs of the total community.

Use of Church Facilities for Operating Private Schools

The General Conference is urged to adopt appropriate legislation designed to make unlawful the formation and operation within the physical facilities of the local United Methodist Churches of private elementary and secondary schools where a major purpose of the formation and organization of such private schools is to preserve racially segregated education.

41

1972

Bishops' Call for Peace and the Self-Development of Peoples

The "basic beliefs" of the former Evangelical United Brethren Church stated forthrightly "that war and bloodshed . . . are not compatible with the gospel and spirit of Christ." The Methodist Social Creed said, "We must actively and constantly create the conditions of peace." World peace, a requisite for human survival, is a fundamental objective of Christians everywhere.

In a recent survey, United Methodists expressed their profound concern about the cheapness with which human life is treated and the possibility of the total extinction of the race; they revealed an overriding concern about world peace and the morality of war.[1] In response to this concern, in the light of traditional denominational teachings and on the basis of a biblical faith, the Council of Bishops of The United Methodist Church issues this call for peace and the self-development of people.

The Nature of Peace

Peace is not simply the absence of war—a nuclear stalemate or combination of uneasy cease-fires. It is that

[1] Virgil Wesley Sexton, *Listening to the Church* (Abingdon Press, 1971), pp. 55, 62-68.

emerging dynamic reality envisioned by prophets where spears and swords give way to implements of peace (Isa. 2:1-4); where historic antagonists dwell together in trust (Isa. 11:4-11); and where righteousness and justice prevail. There will be no peace with justice until unselfish and informed love are structured into political processes and international arrangements.

The enemies of peace are many. War results from a complex of personal, social, economic, and political forces. If war is to be overcome, its root causes must be isolated and dealt with.

The Enemies of Peace

1. Blind self-interest is an enemy of peace. The history of war is a history of unbridled greed, ambition, and self-centeredness. Nations have been willing to gain their own security and advantage at the expense of other weaker nations. Persons obsessed with their "rightness" and power have sought to impose their wills on their surroundings. Self-aggrandizement has too often prevailed over human rights and international justice. Vain self-assertion has been the "nature" of persons, and in no small measure, it has shaped their "destiny."

The self-interest that gives birth to war is both personal and social. Policy-makers are individuals. Their decisions are moral decisions. Whether they live in a tribal culture, a representative democracy, or a totalitarian police state, they are individually responsible. By their greed and cowardice, silence and truculence, arrogance and apathy, they contribute to the dismemberment of true community.

But self-interest is also institutionalized. Nation-states, economic systems, political and military forces, and the structures of our corporate life, serving their own interests, become self-seeking antagonists destroying the unity of humankind.

2. Economic exploitation is an enemy of peace. No economic system is divinely inspired and every economic

44

system should be judged by the ethical imperatives of the gospel of Jesus Christ. Personal fulfillment and international stability are impossible in a world where two out of three people go to bed hungry every night and where the chasm between "haves" and "have nots" grows wider day by day.

One cannot understand current events without taking into account the colonial policies of an earlier era. World powers carved up continents and divided the spoils. Third World nations and underdeveloped peoples are now reacting with bitterness and suspicion toward those forces that systematically exploited their personal and natural resources.

The Third World is understandably concerned about American domination of the world market, is wary of strings-attached aid programs, and is determined to assert its independent selfhood. The "superpowers" are the new imperialists. With networks of economic and military interests intruding into almost every land, they frustrate authentic self-determination, manipulate power relationships, and disturb the essential ingredients of international community.

3. Racism is an enemy of peace. Whether its attitudes and institutions disturb domestic tranquility, contravene justice, or erupt in bloody skirmishes, racism stands opposed to every humanizing process. Racist presuppositions are implicit in Western attitudes and policies toward Asia, Africa, the Middle East, and Latin America, as well as toward black, brown, yellow, and red persons in subcultures controlled by white majorities.

4. Population explosion is an enemy of peace. Nations often justify expansionist policies on the basis of overcrowded homelands.

Human congestion, linked with poverty, hunger, and filth, gives rise to frustration, despair, and violence.

In affluent societies, an increasing population intensifies the ecological crisis as wealth multiplies industrial waste, pollutes air and water, and jeopardizes the delicate balance of nature.

Both poverty and wealth, when complicated by over-population, aggravate hostilities and negate human values.

5. Nation worship is an enemy of peace. Insulated, self-serving nationalism must yield to genuine international cooperation if people are to survive. The unilateral intervention of superpowers in the affairs of smaller nations (Hungary, Vietnam, Laos, Cambodia, Czechoslovakia, the Dominican Republic, and Guatemala) must be ended. International anarchy is the most dangerous form of lawlessness confronting the human family today.

6. Continued reliance upon military violence is an enemy of peace. There have been more war casualties in the twentieth century than in all previous centuries of recorded history combined. Nuclear and biochemical weaponry and new technological war-making equipment have thrust the human race into an indefensible posture. It is alleged that 90 percent of the war casualties in Indochina have been civilian. Old "just war" theories need to be carefully rethought in the light of present reality. Wars fought in the national interest will doubtless continue, but violence begets violence, and in today's world extinction could result from irrational accident or momentary madness.

7. The arms race is an enemy of peace. Arms races have always resulted in the utilization of their products. In spite of Strategic Arms Limitation Talks, the superpowers have continued with the development of ABM and anti-ABM hardware, and MIRV has been deployed. The current overkill capacities of the Soviet Union and the United States, coupled with the fact that there are now five nuclear powers, make future prospects for world harmony bleak indeed.

Dehumanization, a special threat in a materialistic, technocratic society, is implicit in almost all the "enemies of peace" we have outlined. The gospel of Jesus Christ proclaims the inestimable worth of each individual. It is "personal" in the most radical sense of the word. It seeks to humanize, and would make common cause with those values and forces that are working for the fulfillment of the human potential in today's world.

The Sources of Peace

Peace is the gift of God, a gift that comes when persons meet the conditions of God.

The God who gives us peace is the Father of all peoples and the Judge of all nations. He has revealed his perfect will through Jesus Christ, the Lord of history and the Prince of Peace. God's Holy Spirit, the cleansing and unifying presence in our midst, is able to work through current conflict and disruption that the divine will might be done on earth.

And what are God's "conditions" for peace? There are many. They are personal and cultural; theological and practical; attitudinal and systemic.

God calls us to penitence and new life. In the light of present crisis we are called upon to be "heartily sorry for these our misdoings." We have been vain and self-serving, indifferent to poverty and hunger, insensitive in the face of exploitation and suffering; we have enthroned the values of a materialistic society; we have reflected racist attitudes and participated in racist systems; we have worshipped our native land, had undue faith in military violence, and permitted concepts of "national honor" to take precedence over the well-being of brutalized persons in distant places. Each of us, in the light of misguided loyalties and present apathy, is called upon to pray earnestly the familiar prayer, "O God, be merciful to me a sinner."

Genuine repentance can lead to new life. One of the central injunctions of a biblical faith is, "Repent, and believe . . ." (Mark 1:15). "When anyone is united to Christ, there is a new world; the old order has gone, and a new order has already begun" (II Cor. 5:17). New life based upon an honest awareness of past failures and sins is a requisite for peace within and world peace. Old values and allegiances are replaced by a new ethic in "the new being."

If God's "conditions" for peace include penitence and new life, they can also be summarized with one word: love. Mature love is neither sensuality nor sentimentality. It is not a refuge for the naïve. It is an unswerving and uncompro-

47

mising way of life. It goes a second mile, turns the other cheek, and accepts and offers itself for friend and enemy alike. It feeds the hungry, clothes the naked, seeks out the rejected, and liberates the oppressed. Freedom is love's expression. Justice is love's demand. Believing that those who live by the sword will perish by the sword, and that those who find their security in nuclear stockpiles may well be destroyed by that weaponry, love seeks to overcome evil with good. "God was in Christ reconciling the world to himself . . . and . . . he has entrusted us with the message of reconciliation" (II Cor. 5:19).

Even as God is the source of our peace, he has called us to be his servants; custodians of his message; "peacemakers."

We have mentioned "the enemies of peace." Each of these enemies needs to be dealt with specifically.

If war results from greed, ambition, and sinful self-interest, peace requires the literal conversion of person, of attitudes and values. It also requires a radical redefinition of institutional goals and priorities. Self-interest must be seen in relationship to love for God and our brothers and sisters (Luke 10:25-28).

If extremes of poverty and hunger are to be overcome, development programs must be based upon principles of global need and accountability. They should not be designed to reinforce particular economic systems or protect the markets of privileged nations. Development, however, involves more than economic improvement. It refers to self-reliance and self-determination. The self-development of people requires equality of opportunity, full participation in decision-making processes, and a diffusion of political power from the few to the many.

There will be no peace with justice unless liberation is gained by those who have been manipulated and victimized by interests that have been willing to profit from the continued deprivation of the weak and the powerless. But the oppressor needs to be liberated as truly as the oppressed. Liberation affects the whole person. It is salvation; it is humanization. It is social, economic, political, and spiritual. It calls for the structural implementation of those values announced by our Lord when he said he had come that the "broken victims" of life might "go free" (Luke 4:18).

Racism must give way to justice if peace is to become a reality. This justice, based upon new attitudes, understandings, and relationships, will be reflected in the laws, policies, structures, and practices of both church and state.

If dignity and self-determination are human rights, then respect for and the preservation of particular ethnic, cultural, and racial traditions and values should be encouraged and assured. It is not the function of Christian witness to "westernize," "easternize," "Americanize," or in other ways acculturate human attitudes and responses. It is the function of the Christian to bring the full dimensions of a gospel of love and justice to bear upon the human situation.

Concerned and adequate population control programs must be developed if the planet is not to be crowded beyond its capacity to support human life.

If peace is to come, nation worship must be supplanted by the loyalty implicit in the declaration, "God so loved the world. . . ." Persons are normally patriots. They love the soil of their native land and the heritage that has shaped their days. Grateful for home and heritage they are now called to a higher patriotism. Once people were forced to organize as tribes for self-protection, then tribes as city-states and city-states as nation-states. Today we are called to look beyond the limited and competing boundaries of nation-states to the larger and more inclusive community of persons.

This movement from narrow nationalism to global loyalties requires both international law and international organization. The development of international law has included landmark treaties resulting from conferences at The Hague, Dumbarton Oaks, and the Geneva Conventions. Structures of international order have been anticipated by the ill-fated League of Nations and the United Nations. If peace with justice is to come, nation-states should utilize the United Nations and the International Court of

49

Justice, as well as international trade, relief and scientific institutions, while seeking to perfect the instruments of international organization.

If peace is to come, our present reliance upon military institutions and domination by a military-industrial complex must be replaced by civilian control of the military. An ordered society must be policed by forces responsible to that same society. Self-serving national military forces must eventually give way to duly constituted international peacekeeping units.

The tradition of nonviolent love is a fundamental dimension of the Christian faith. Christians are challenged to consider and embrace this personal stance, thus providing a redemptive witness in society.

There must be eventual disarmament. We cannot be certain of the causes of a particular war. "Causes" may be simply pretexts. In the final analysis, it is the presence of military institutions in the nations of the world that makes wars possible and arms races probable. The tide must be turned. Recognizing the strategic dangers of unilateral disarmament, nations can begin processes of military disengagement and move toward bilateral and multilateral disarmament agreements within the framework of the United Nations. Our suicidal confidence in arms and military systems must give way to a radical reordering of priorities and an awareness of overriding human values.

The ingredients of peace are indivisible. Its realization cannot be achieved apart from theological, ethical, and practical sources. Individuals must assume their full responsibility for peacemaking. The Church must be far more faithful to its Lord, the Prince of Peace, than it has been willing to be in the past. And nations must become more deeply involved in the continuing processes of the self-development of people and the creation of a just and peaceful world order. Unless the most powerful and responsible members of the human family are willing to deal with the root causes of war, running the essential risks and making the necessary sacrifices, the human family will destroy itself.

"[Christ Jesus] is himself our peace . . . and in his own

50

body of flesh and blood has broken down the enmity which stood like a dividing wall. . . . For he [came] to create . . . a single new humanity in himself, thereby making peace." —Ephesians 2:13-16[2]

Children and Their Welfare and Health Care

The least powerful group in the world today are children. What they are today determines what tomorrow will be. The Church is called to minister in behalf of all children. We must nurture and protect their rights as persons created by God and in his image.

The hungry child, the abused child, the emotionally disturbed child—these, and many others, are the future. Wherever there is need, the Church has a ministry. The children of the world need the ministries of the Church.

The United States has dropped to thirteenth place in infant mortality. Physical brutality, i.e., child abuse, is increasingly widespread. Children have little chance in courts, where the child is the "property" of his parents. The practice of juvenile law has a position of low prestige in the profession.

The result of such victimizing is a generation of youth and adults who struggle for identity, trust, and the basic values of responsible citizenship. The Church can and must speak out in behalf of children. It can order an environment in which children's rights are protected.

Only in a home where love abounds may a child experience God's love for him and for all persons. Insecurity, unhappiness, and distrust develop where there is no expression of humility, acceptance, reconciliation, or accountability in the presence of the child. The rights of children for love, health, security, and emotional well-being must be recognized in the home, in the Church, and in the ordering of priorities in government planning.

[2]Social Principles VI; "United Methodist Church and Peace" (1984); Christian Faith and Disarmament (1984)

We therefore seek a creative partnership with national government agencies concerned with children, including utilization of federal funds and services.

a. *Child-Development Program.* We urge the recognition of child care as a developmental service with tremendous potential for influencing and strengthening the lives of children and families; therefore, we recommend that our local churches initiate and participate in comprehensive family-oriented child-development programs including health services, day care, and early childhood education.

b. *Child Advocacy.* We strongly urge our local churches to become advocates for children in the community so that safeguarding the rights of children may be recognized as a primary responsibility of the Church.

Local church action in this regard might entail: (1) establishing task forces on critical issues and problems; (2) insuring effective delivery of services with special emphasis on child mental health. Attention to the rights of children surely includes adequate housing, health services, nutrition, education, transportation, safety, and environment.

We further urge that The United Methodist Church take the lead in implementing the following mandate from the White House Conference on Children: "All institutions and programs that affect children must involve children as active participants in the decisionmaking process."

c. *People in the Lives of Children.* The extended family of the past is no longer available to many children. Children often are deprived of someone outside their immediate family who cares for them and enjoys being with them. Too few have experiences with kindly adults. The Church also has lonely older people who need the warmth and joy of children. The Church can bring the two together.

d. *Elimination of Prejudice.* Children have a right to grow up in a society which practices love for all God's creations. Racism does its most serious damage to children who already have much against them—poverty, broken homes, hunger, crowded living conditions.

We call upon the appropriate United Methodist boards and agencies:

1. To study the recommendations from the four White House Conferences on Food and Nutrition, Children, Youth, and Aging with relation to ethnic and racial issues as guides for further planning and action in the development of programs to eliminate the racism which cripples all children.

2. To sponsor demonstration projects to serve as models in implementing the goal of eliminating racism.

3. To produce quality educational materials in the language of national minorities.[3]

Goals and Recommendations on Participation of Women

Goals

The United Methodist Church in serious consideration of the issue of the role of women in the Christian community and their participation in the life and work of The United Methodist Church believes that it should direct its energies and resources:

1. To move toward the liberation of all persons so that all may achieve full humanity.

2. To bring about attitudinal changes in relation to (a) theological, philosophical, and biblical interpretations and understandings of the role of women and (b) expectations for achievement and contributions of women.

3. To make all United Methodists sensitive to the issues involved in the rights of women.

4. To overcome rigid sex-role distinctions which have traditionally characterized church structures and society.

5. To eliminate all discriminatory language, images, and practices in the life and work of The United Methodist Church.

6. To create an openness and receptivity for women in the professional ministry of The United Methodist Church.

7. To utilize the full potential of both men and women in

[3]*See* Social Principles III-C

elections and appointments at all levels in The United Methodist Church.

8. To establish a process for evaluation of the performance of The United Methodist Church regarding the role and participation of women in its life and work.

Recommendations for the Enhancement of the Participation of Women

1. That every programming agency in the denomination give serious attention to developing new avenues of participation for younger adult members of the denomination, particularly women in the 20-35 age range; and further that this attention be in the form of staff time and financial resources needed to explore varied styles of family life, that alternative life styles be considered, and that new styles (e.g., single women, employed women) be made more acceptable in the overall church population; and

2. That, inasmuch as the Study Commission has been preoccupied with the study of the problems of women's roles in general, to the exclusion of the particular problems of women in racial and ethnic groups, the study should be continued with special attention given to the roles of women of minority racial groups and ethnic groups within The United Methodist Church; and

3. That experimental ministries be developed to and by women, in order to increase awareness of roles and potential of women through consciousness-raising, counseling, education, and political action; and

4. That the media development agencies of the church produce and disseminate materials which would aid a sensitization process concerning the role of women with consideration being given to all forms of media presentation; and

5. That there be a development of curriculum which would help United Methodists avoid sustaining an inadequate image of male and female roles and understand how our rigidly held sexual roles deprive us of our full humanity,

and which would assist in the exploration and development of new and alternative life styles; and

6. That careful consideration be given to the professional ministry, beginning with the traditional practices of entering the profession, continuing through recruitment and acceptance at the schools of theology, educational programs for women in the schools of theology, the processes and attitudes of annual conference boards of ministry and the attitudes of local congregations toward women clergy; and

7. That the Theological Study Commission on Doctrine and Doctrinal Standards be requested to study and report on the role of women from a theological and doctrinal perspective; and

8. That all nominating committees in local churches, annual, jurisdictional, and general conferences give attention to the nomination of women for membership on committees, commissions, boards, councils, and other organizations, so that women are included in all of these units in significant numbers (bearing in mind that at least 50 percent of the membership of The United Methodist Church is made up of women); and

9. That the General Conference take whatever action is necessary to

a. assure an increased proportion of women in all levels of professional staff in general boards and agencies; and

b. create a more favorable setting for the recruitment, education, and appointment of women clergy; and

c. encourage local churches to be open to the acceptance of women as clergy (senior ministers, associate ministers, and ministers in special appointments) and as lay employees; and

10. That the General Conference establish a Commission on the Role of Women in The United Methodist Church to foster an ongoing awareness of the problems and issues relating to the status of women and to stimulate progress reports on these issues from the various boards and agencies. (The legislation for the organization and work of the commission is in the *Discipline*.)[4]

[4]*See* Social Principles III-F; "Equal Rights of Women" (1984)

Investment Ethics

WHEREAS, Over the years church agencies at local, conference, and national levels to some degree expressed social consciousness in investments by their refusal to invest in liquor, tobacco, and munitions industries; and

WHEREAS, Recent years, and events related to them, have intensified interest in trying to correlate investment policies with expanding social consciousness; and

WHEREAS, The General Conference in 1970 adopted legislation urging the general boards and agencies to invest in "institutions and corporations which make a positive contribution toward the realization of goals outlined in the Social Principles of our Church . . ."; and

WHEREAS, The General Conference in 1972 in its adoption of the Bishops' Call to Peace and the Self-Development of Peoples called upon each local congregation "to analyze and review its investment policies (if it has investments), bringing them into conformity with the goals outlined in the Bishops' Call and in the Social Principles of The United Methodist Church" and called upon boards and agencies of the general Church and of annual conferences and local churches "to review and analyze their investments in corporations holding military contracts seeking an immediate influence upon policies from within corporate structures" and

WHEREAS, The complexities of the interrelationships of investments, stewardship, fiscal responsibilities, and social principles demand constant analysis and evaluation; and

FURTHER WHEREAS, Actions of the General Conference in 1970 and the Bishops' Call in 1972 need to be implemented;

Be It Resolved, That the Council on Finance and Administration is directed to appoint a committee to:

1. Review and correlate the guidelines for investments already developed by several boards and agencies of the church.

2. Develop guidelines and procedures for investment review to be used by local churches, annual conferences, general boards and agencies, and church-related institutions.

3. Report regularly concerning its work to the Program Council and its successor Council on Ministries.

4. Work faithfully with the Coordinating Committee on Peace and Self-Development of Peoples.[5]

School Busing

WHEREAS, The Supreme Court in 1954 ruled that segregated public schools are inherently unequal and that de jure segregation in such schools is unconstitutional; and

WHEREAS, Integrated schools provide the best means for reducing racial bias and may be useful in providing beneficial learning experiences; and

WHEREAS, The busing of pupils is often the only method available to achieve racial integration and quality education in the public schools;

Resolved, That we call upon The United Methodist Church to support the use of busing where appropriate for school integration and to oppose legislative action or constitutional amendments prohibiting such busing.[6]

Use of Reclaimed Paper

Be It Resolved, That the General Conference request the publisher, boards, agencies, and all local churches to diligently seek suppliers of recycled or reclaimed paper for all possible uses whenever practicable and possible.

Be It Further Resolved, That the General Conference request that all said agencies use only recycled or reclaimed paper whenever possible for all printing, mimeographing, correspondence, and other uses of paper.[7]

[5]*See* Social Principles IV-Preamble
[6]*See* Social Principles III-A
[7]*See* Social Principles I-A; "Environmental Stewardship" (1984)

1976

Community Life

At the heart of the Christian faith is an abiding concern for persons. This concern is evidenced by the Christian's sensitivity to all factors which affect a person's life. In our society the community has become known as a gathering of people who nurture one another and create for all an atmosphere for general enhancement. The community should be characterized by good schools, adequate housing, spirit-filled churches, and creative community organizations.

The Church has always been interested in communities as arenas where people engage in the common experiences of life. It is in community that men, women, and youth discover and enhance their identity. And it is in community that all persons learn to appreciate social, religious, and ethical values.

Communities are undergoing serious changes. Perhaps the most serious of these changes are destructive of the forces which have built communities in the past. Integrated housing patterns are beginning to prevail in many sections all across America. The previous pattern was accentuated by massive flight of white residents to the suburbs and an entrenchment of blacks in the inner city. This polarization along racial lines serves to destroy the idea of a democratic community and has brought into being hostile entities along political, social, and educational lines.

The development of federal and state housing authorities with a democratic pattern for housing development has restored the faith of many that the possibilities of a new community are there. We affirm the 1972 Statement on Housing.

The Local Church and the Local Public Schools

In innumerable and concrete ways, the local church serves as interpreter of and witness to the gospel in the life of its community. Therefore, it is the primary channel through which the demands of the gospel are made known in society. By virtue of the nature of the church, there is nothing in the community outside its concern or beyond its ability to affect.

The local public schools historically represent one of the fundamental focal points in American communities. This is as it should be because the democratic approach to education is the bedrock of democratic, political, and economic systems. The local public schools also represent one of the largest financial outlays in any given community. In these days many public school systems have been caught in the whirling social and educational changes of the times and have fallen victim to influences and powers which have not kept the fundamental purposes of the public schools as highest priorities.

Some of the many challenging issues confronting the schools are: financial inadequacies, historic racial attitudes, busing, curriculum, growing professionalism of teachers and administrators, and the lack of well informed and sensitive school board members. Many times these issues are combined, making the problems that much more acute.

The issues confronting public schools may be different in the respective communities, as the church is different in its respective communities. Yet, by the virtue of its calling, the church must lead the communities in exploring the issues, and in identifying and seeking solutions to their particular problems.

In each community, the local United Methodist Church is

responsible for being a catalyst in helping the entire community become sensitive to the issues of public education.

We encourage each local church to recognize the importance of the culture, history and important contributions of ethnic minorities to the educational process and the resulting loss when these are omitted from the curriculum. Local churches should take the initiative to be certain that local school boards in their area or communities at every level of education include in the total curricula all contributions of all peoples to the growth and development of the United States.

The lack of opportunities to learn and understand the history and cultures of all races is reflected in our present problems in human relations.

Our Judeo-Christian tradition reveals clearly our personal accountability to Almighty God in relation to our personal responsibility to and for our fellow human beings.

Where problems exist, it is especially important that the local United Methodist Church support and work with existing community groups and organizations in bringing solutions. It is also recommended that each local United Methodist church develop a committee or an informal group of members to keep the congregation and community aware of public school issues and their obligation to assist in finding meaningful solutions.[1]

Extension of the Right to Organize and Bargain Collectively

Historically, The United Methodist Church has recognized and supported the right of workers to organize into unions of their own choosing and to bargain collectively over wages, hours, and conditions of employment. National policy since 1935 has codified procedures for the election of

[1]*See* Social Principles III-K, L; V-D.

labor unions by industrial workers, for the recognition of those unions by management, and for collective bargaining with the result of lessened conflict in the private industrial sector of the economy.

However, a major category of employees was excluded from the coverage of the National Labor Relations Act. These are the employees working for the federal government and employees of any political subdivision such as a state or school district.

Unfortunately, social strife in the occupational markets of public employees has led to high social costs such as the interruption of vital community services and even the tragedy of death. In view of this continued unresolved strain and many attendant injustices, The United Methodist Church requests the Congress to amend the National Labor Relations Act to include under its coverage government employees, federal, state, and local and to institute methods, for example, various forms of arbitration, for resolving disputes that significantly affect the health and safety of the public.[2]

Full Personhood

WHEREAS, We, as a General Conference, have taken steps to ensure the participation of women in the church such as the establishing of a Commission on the Status and Role of Women; and

WHEREAS, The call to serve Christ with all our gifts, time and abilities is made to both men and women;

Therefore, be it resolved, That all persons, boards and agencies responsible for programming at every level of the church be encouraged to evaluate their programs as to their explicit and implicit impact on women and take such steps necessary to affirm programs which encourage full personhood for everyone.[3]

[2]*See* Social Principles IV-B.
[3]*See* Social Principles II-Preamble

Gun Control

With the mounting proliferation of firearms in American society, the safety of our citizens cannot be guaranteed. Crime in city streets climbs, accidents abound, and suicides soar.

Christians concerned about reverence for life care about what is happening to many victims of gun murders and assaults. In the name of Christ, who came that persons might know abundant life, we call upon the Church to affirm its faith through vigorous efforts to curb gun violence.

In 1974, the last year for which complete figures are available, there were some 32,000 firearms deaths in the United States. Of these approximately 15,000[1] were murders, 14,000 suicides[2] and about 3,000 accidents.[3] The handgun was used in the largest proportion of these deaths. We know, for example, that 54 percent of the murders occurring in 1974 were by handguns.[40]

Behind the statistics often lies great tragedy: children and teachers are being shot in school; depressed persons are taking their lives with guns left around the house; householders purchasing guns to protect their homes often end up using them to kill a loved one; police officers are being gunned down in increasing numbers in the course of duty.

As Christians who are deeply concerned about human life, we intend to do something about the unregulated access to guns in this shooting gallery called America.

We do not believe there is any constitutional personal right to bear arms. As the United Sates Supreme Court has ruled a number of times, the Second Amendment has to do with the militia, currently comparable to the National Guard.

The United States might well learn from the experience of other societies where stringent gun control laws are enforced. The gun murder rate per 100,000 population in the United States is 100 times greater than in England and Wales, where strict gun laws prevail; it is 200 times greater than in Japan, where it is impossible for the public to secure handguns legally. We believe that the time has come when the United States should move toward a less violent and more civilized society.

Therefore, The United Methodist Church declares its support for the licensing of all gun owners and the registration of all firearms. Licensing provisions should require adequate identification of gun owners and provide basic standards with respect to age, absence of mental illness, and lack of a serious criminal record. These and other objective standards should be applied in determining the granting or denial of any license.

In addition, special controls should be applied to the handgun, for it is the most deadly and least utilitarian weapon in American society. Because the handgun is concealable, it is the weapon of crime; because the handgun is available, it is the instrument used in suicides and crimes of passion.

Therefore, we call upon the United States government to establish a national ban on the importation, manufacture, sale, and possession of handguns and handgun ammunition with reasonable limited exceptions. Such exceptions should be restricted to: the police, the military, licensed security guards, antique dealers who maintain guns in unfireable condition, and licensed pistol clubs where firearms are kept on the premises under secure conditions.

In fairness to handgun owners, we propose that those who comply with the law and turn in their guns be compensated at fair value through a cash payment or tax credit.[4]

International Women's Decade

WHEREAS, The United National General Assembly proclaimed 1975 to 1985 as International Women's Decade with these emphases:

[4]*See* Social Principles V-F; "Criminal Justice" (1984).

to promote equality between men and women;

to ensure the full integration of women in the total development effort;

to recognize the importance of women's increasing contribution to peace, and

WHEREAS, The Women's Division of the Board of Global Ministries, the Board of Church and Society, and other church agencies have given active support to the goals of the United Nations International Women's Decade, and

WHEREAS, The World Plan of Action adopted by the World Conference of International Women's Year provides guidelines for national action over the ten year period from 1975 to 1985 as part of a sustained, long-term effort to achieve the objectives of International Women's Decade, and

WHEREAS, The Social Principles of The United Methodist Church assert the Church's commitment "to the rights of men, women, children and youth," and its dedication to "peace throughout the world,"

Be It Resolved, That the General Conference affirm the three emphases of International Women's decade, and

Be It Further Resolved, That The United Methodist Church including all its boards and agencies study and implement as appropriate the priorities of the United Nations World Plan of Action of the World Conference of International Women's Decade and urge United Methodists to encourage governments to commit themselves to appropriate action for implementation of the Plan within the framework of national development plans and programs.[5]

A Just World Order in an Age of Interdependence

One of the most important reasons for the lack of support in United States governmental offices for undertaking the systemic changes necessary for narrowing the gap between the rich and poor nations is the absence of a constituency in the American public committed to justice for all people.

[5]*See* Social Principles III-F; "The Status of Women" (1980).

There is an anomaly in American attitudes toward development. On the one hand, Americans support development on humanitarian grounds. At the same time, Americans tend to be negative concerning governmental aid programs because they feel they are inefficient, primarily benefit a rich elite, are tied to short-term political gains, and are integrated with wasteful military expenditures. At the governmental level, these mixed feelings are interpreted as being opposed to developmental programs in general.

What is missing is a strong constituency that is sensitive to the ethical values in development issues, knows the facts, and is committed to action for narrowing the gap between the rich and the poor. Within The United Methodist Church, the nucleus of such a constituency already exists. Programs designed to broaden this constituency into every local parish are required if the grounds for peace and a greater social justice are to be achieved.

In order to develop such a constituency, the various boards and agencies of The United Methodist Church with facilitation supplied by the Board of Church and Society are authorized to develop cooperatively a program of action designed to aid in the resolution of the problem of a just world order in an age of interdependency[6] by undertaking to build a constituency favoring immediate action in meeting global development needs.

A. Background

One of the persistent themes in the Old Testament is the value of foregoing what may contribute to one's own comfort for the sake of a neighbor in need. Isaiah noted the

[6]"The combination of an egalitarian ethic and reciprocal vulnerability within a framework of wider technological and intellectual frontiers provides the essence of mature interdependence." Ali A. Mazrui, "The New Interdependence; From Hierarchy to Symetry," in *The U.S. and World Development: Agenda for Action 1975* (New York: Praeger Publishers, 1975), p. 119.

grinding of the face of the poor with more indignity and called for justice against those who were crushing the people. In his vision of the great judgment, Jesus observed that the criteria for the inheritance of the Kingdom were the deeds of feeding the hungry, giving drink to the thirsty, welcoming the stranger, clothing the naked, and visiting the sick and those in prison. The early church continued this emphasis on ministering to the needs of the poor. In the *Preaching of Peter* we read: "Rich is the man who pities many, and in imitation of God bestows from what he hath: for God giveth all things to all from his own creatures. Understand, then, ye rich, that ye are in duty bound to do service, having received more than ye yourselves need. Learn that to others is lacking what wherein you superabound. Be ashamed of holding fast what belongs to others. Imitate God's equity, and none shall be poor."[7] It is this rich tradition that focuses the church's attention in the last quarter of the twentieth century upon the widening gap between the rich and the poor.

In the 1960s, "The Decade of Development," the gap between the rich nations and the poor nations grew wider. The ratio between incomes in the industrialized societies and in the rest of the world was about 10 to 1 in 1950, 15 to 1 in 1960, and about 20 to 1 in 1975.[8] Since the developed nations are located primarily in the northern hemisphere, the gap between the rich and poor has been called a north-south gap.

The southern tier of nations is composed of 105 countries with a population of approximately 2.5 billion. These countries are often described as developing nations, or as Third World and Fourth World nations. The Fourth World nations have the lowest standard of living and are comprised of some 42 countries with an average per capita gross national product of $145 annually and with a life expectancy of 46 years.

[7]Quoted in Walter G. Muelder, *Religion and Economic Responsibility* (New York: Charles Scribner's Sons, 1953) p. 146.

[8]Lester R. Brown, *World Without Borders* (New York: Vintage Books, 1972), p. 42.

The dissatisfactions growing out of the experience of the 1960s and continuing into the 1970s has led the developing nations to reappraise the functioning of the international economic system. In the spring of 1974 the United Nations took the initiative in declaring the need for the establishment of a new international economic order. The demands of the developing countries grew out of their new perception of their bargaining strength as a result of the experience of the oil exporting countries in achieving a remarkable change in the relative power and wealth between the developed and the developing nations. In September 1975, these demands were countered with a proposal by the United States that included an openness to consider a greater participation by the developing nations in the decision-making process affecting their interests.

The relative decrease in the standard of living of approximately 2.5 billion persons and their demand for redress through equitable treatment constitutes a strain on the socioeconomic and political fabric of the world. Control and guidance of this strain into channels which will correct the inequities present a challenge to the moral conscience of humankind. Lester Brown has observed that economists have been able to provide useful advice in creating more economic goods and services "but for help on this new problem society must turn to theologians, social philosophers, and ultimately politicians."[9] This issue is fairly placed on the agenda of the churches. The response of the churches in the next twenty-five years will be crucial for the welfare of all humankind.

B. What Is Development?

The gap between the north and south can be narrowed by an informed set of policies and action to achieve a just global development. In recent year, numerous volumes have been written on this concept, and a great amount of misunder-

[9]*Ibid.*, p. 24.

standing concerning the components of development has actually divided persons who should have been natural allies. Professor Samuel L. Parmar of India's Allahabad University has furnished a balanced definition of development: "The central goal of development should consist of three interrelated objectives: economic growth, self-reliance, and social justice, of which social justice should be accorded primacy."[10] Andre van Dam, a Dutch corporate planner, has defined global development "as the process of man's legitimate aspiration to the basic amenities of life with a minimum equity in the distribution. This is a long and deep mutation that comes inevitably at a price: change into the unknown perhaps accelerated change in the beginning."[11] Both definitions carry within them an emphasis on material sufficiency and distributive justice. It is because of the question of justice that many social planners look to the church for leadership and guidance. James P. Grant thinks "The role of the churches in these new and different times is particularly important. . . . The really difficult issues for the future are posed by the needs to improve the *distribution* [author's emphasis] of increasingly scarce resources and to change life-styles and values."[12]

C. How Serious Is the Development Gap?

The global economic growth rate approached 5 percent annually during the 1960s. Ordinarily, this would have resulted in a marked improvement in the world standard of living. But, this was not so. World population increased by

---

[10]Samuel L. Parmar, "The Limits to Growth Debate in Asian Perspective," *The Ecumenical Review,* January 1974, pp.33-53.

[11]Quoted in Denis A. Goulet, "Ethical Strategies in the Struggle for World Development," *Global Justice and Development* (Report of the Aspen Interreligious Consultation, Aspen, Colorado, June 1974, published by the Overseas Development Council, May 1975), p. 41.

[12]James P. Grant, "Development Today: In Search of Global Justice," in *Global Justice and Development* (Report of the Aspen Interreligious Consultation, Aspen, Colorado, June 1974, published by the Overseas Development Council, May 1975), p. 19.

700 million, and the amenities of life provided by nature declined at a rapid rate at the same time. Lester R. Brown suggests that for everyone "there was nearly one fifth less fresh water, mineral reserves, arable land, energy fuels, living space, waste absorptive capacity, marine protein and natural recreation areas in 1970 than in 1960."[13] During this same period, over one half of the human family was living on less than $100 per year per capita.

The most populous of the Fourth World countries are India, Bangladesh, Pakistan, Ethiopia, Afghanistan, Sudan, Tanzania, Sri Lanka, Kenya, Nepal, and Uganda. The birthrate averages about 45 per 1,000 and the death rate about 20 per 1,000. In the developed world the birthrate is 18 per 1,000 and the death rate is 9.7 per 1,000. The Fourth World represents one-fourth of the earth's population and consumes about 6 percent of the world's goods and services. The United States has about 6 percent of the earth's population and consumes almost 35 percent of the world's goods and services. The developed market economies and the centrally planned economies consume 86 percent of the world's good and services leaving 14 percent for two and one-half billion people.[14]

The result of this disparity in income is poverty for the Third and Fourth World countries which is ever widening. The symptoms are malnutrition, hunger, disease, illiteracy, and population increase. The social consequences are the instability of governments, the seeking of armaments at the expense of the poor, desperate behavior such as air piracy, the kidnapping of diplomats, sabotage, strained relationship between nation-states, and threats of violence and economic revenge. At a time when nuclear capability is spreading among smaller nations (some of them Third and Fourth World nations), the issue has become one of distributive justice or chaos.

For many years, United Nations studies have revealed that despite substantial private investment in and govern-

[13]Brown, *op. cit.*, p. 5.
[14]In *Global Justice and Development*, *op. cit.*, p. 159.

70

mental aid to Latin American nations, there has been a steady net flow of dollars from those countries to the United States and other developed countries. This has been accompanied by an enormous growth in the debt burden of these developing countries. It seems clear that the problem will not be solved by increasing the amount of intergovernmental aid and private investment. The essential ingredients must include substantial changes in the nature and terms of international economic relationships, freedom for developing nations to chart their own future, and the emergence of self-reliance in place of dependency as the chief characteristic of their economies.

In order for the poor countries to reach the standard of living of the rich countries, the gross world product would have to rise from 3 trillion dollars to 18 trillion annually. This would place such an overload on the ecosystem that the fragile fabric of life would be threatened. We live in a finite world in which the ecosystem has the capacity of supplying limited natural resources for all humankind. A more reasonable solution is for the rich nations to consciously reorder their life-styles to demand and consume less while strengthening the economies of the developing nations so that the disparities in life-styles would be narrowed. Professor Tinbergen thinks the gap could be narrowed to a ratio of 5 to 1 in some areas of the world and 3 to 1 in other areas. This would require a massive effort by virtually all nations, drastic changes in the present economic relationships between countries, and the creation of new international institutions.[15]

D. What Is Needed?

The development gap is related to a series of interacting global problems: the activities of unregulated multinational

[15]Mihajlo Mesarovie and Edward Pestel, *Mankind at the Turning Point: The Second Report to the Club of Rome* (New York: E. P. Dutton and Co., 1974), p. 58.

corporations, population, malnutrition, hunger, environment, military spending, energy, inflation, recession, depletion of natural resources, and unjust economic patterns. Any one of these problems overwhelms the institutional responses that have been generated in the voluntary groups or by unilateral or multilateral governmental action. If the historical pattern of aid to developing countries continues for the next fifty years, the Second Report to the Club of Rome concludes, "Trying to close this gap might as well be forgotten. . . . The crises inherent in the economic gap are clearly not only persistent but even worsening."

Solution must be sought at two levels. First, there is the need to ameliorate the conditions of malnutrition and starvation. Christian justice and love demand it. A recent report estimates that the average caloric intake of two-thirds of the world's population is insufficient for normal growth and activity. Over one-half of the earth's population has little or no medical care. These are problems that the Church has faced historically and has attempted to meet through various voluntary programs. There is need for the continuance of these programs. These efforts, however, have never adequately met the need nor dealt with the systemic causes of world poverty within a framework of justice.

Second, there is the need for a long-term attack on the systemic causes of underdevelopment. Underdevelopment grows out of powerlessness and a colonial heritage and is marked, in part, by low endowment of presently known resources, rudimentary transportation and communication systems, dependency on trade for manufactured goods, a large proportion of population living outside the monetary system, dependence on agricultural products for trading, migration from country to towns creating concentrated unemployment, and a wide gap between the incomes of a rich elite and the rest of the population.

Without power to control their own resources, their own labor, their own capital, poor nations or the poor majority within nations cannot move toward genuine development.

Without that basic power, the poor will be drawn into networks of interdependence only to be exploited by nations or groups with far greater resources of technology, capital, political control, and military might. Only when the poor gain some measure of control over their own human gifts and natural resource will economic and technical aid, from governments, international agencies, or voluntary associations, be used to create, in terms of a basic definition of development, "economic growth, self-reliance, and social justice." As the richest nation in the world, the United States has the moral responsibility both to provide economic and technical aid and to encourage those factors which develop power among the powerless. This will require new international institutions, more equitable systems for distributing world resources, and, above all, a new vision of a world where all peoples have the power to bring to fruition the full possibilities of their humanity.

A missing factor, however, is a strong American constituency that favors the sharing of power and the transfer of resources to the developing world. American political leaders are often frank to admit that they do not think their constituencies favor such actions. The Overseas Development Council in 1975 conducted a survey to discover what Americans thought about international poverty and development. Only a few Americans said that they looked to their churches or synagogues for information on the subjects of worldwide poverty and under-development. Those with little or no religious affiliation were just as sympathetic to the problems as those who were practicing Christians or Jews. In Europe this is not so. There is a higher correlation between belief and interest or practice. This survey has identified a weakness in the American churches. Greater emphasis is needed in liturgy, education, sermons, the church media on the conditions of poverty in the developing world in order to organize a constituency whose voices would be heard by the government.

To delay is to raise the costs in dollars and to multiply the costs in human suffering. The Second Report to the Club of

Rome summarizes these costs: the dollar cost of early action, beginning with an adequate response in 1975, is less than one fifth of the dollar cost if the action is delayed by proceeding at historic levels of funding followed by a greater effort in the year 2000. By immediate action, the developing nations could be self-sustaining by the year 2000.[16] More important, the sooner we begin, the sooner the hungry are fed, the naked are clothed, the ill are healed, and the thirsty are given drink.

E. The Timeliness of the Issue

Some specialists in world economies fear that recent experience with soaring prices and scarcities, especially for fuel, in the rich countries and the success of the OPEC nations in gaining better terms of trade has weakened the political will to allow genuine development to take place among the poor countries. This is particularly true when development is seen in terms of "self-reliance and social justice," not only "economic growth."

It is true that studies made just prior to the recent experience with scarcity in the United States indicated a majority of American people were willing to continue development support for the poor countries. But the real test will come when, like the rich young ruler, we are asked to share not just our marginal gifts but our basic power, when justice will require us not only to give from our surplus but to cut back our affluent life-style and wasteful economic growth. Then we will need informed and committed leadership, particularly from those who live out of the freedom and hope of the gospel, if the powerful nations are to be on the side of genuine development in the poor countries.

Such leadership will enable us to share in the new visions discernible in some development thinking and to move away from the policies of the 1960s when growth in the rate

[16]*Idem.*

of gross national product was the primary goal of development policies. The poor were not always helped by such growth; a narrow elite was often the beneficiary.

There is a growing consensus that the immediate needs of poor nations can be met and long-term systemic growth achieved by increasing the power of the poor to participate in development. This recent experience suggests that developmental policies which strengthen social equity may accelerate social and economic growth rather than acting as a deterrent. This is a message which must be sent from the voluntary agencies if a strong constituency favoring immediate action in meeting global development needs is to be created.

F. A Program of Action for The United Methodist Church

In order to encourage the development of a constituency favoring a greater justice in international social and economic development, the boards and agencies of The United Methodist Church with initiative supplied by the Board of Church and Society in regard to public policy/advocacy issues, are authorized to develop programs in the following areas:

1. Education and Public Information

The United Methodist Church has a history of effort in striving to educate its members on various social issues. This experience ranges from nursery school through graduate schools, from the very young to the very old; and it includes educating through the various media—books, newspapers, journals, curriculum materials, radio, television, and the classroom.

The coordination of all of these resources is required if a coherent national program designed to help The United Methodist Church and the nation to understand and to play an appropriate role in achieving a greater equity in the production and distribution of the earth's resources to meet all humankind's needs is to be achieved.

At the heart of this educational approach is a fundamental premise: the primary goal in achieving a just world order is the production and equitable distribution of goods and services in the face of dwindling nonrenewable world resources. The equities will become more clear as biblical scholars, ethicists, theologians, and pastors examine the empirical facts in the context of religious history, teaching, and beliefs. The religious community can make its greatest contribution to development thought and practice through sharing its insights concerning the justice questions.

The key concept in understanding the future relationships between rich and poor countries is interdependence. In 1950, the United States was virtually self-sufficient in terms of natural resources needed for industrial production. The National Materials Policy Commission has estimated that by the year 2000 the United States will depend on imports for 80 percent of these materials—from independency to interdependency in less than 50 years. At the same time, some of these resource-rich nations will be trading their resources and goods for food. Even self-interest requires coherent development policies and programs that will ultimately be mutually beneficial.

A varied approach to education is proposed which is sensitive to the fact that different persons with The United Methodist Church tradition perceive the problem of world development from different perspectives. This educational approach includes:

a) Mutual discovery through exploratory groups of the primary causes of world poverty at home and abroad with particular emphasis on those world problems which impinge on the local community.

b) The defining of "action-goals" for achieving the resolution of identified and agreed upon problems.

c) A decentralized style which emphasizes the role of the local church in supporting, stimulating, and resourcing such explorations and for generating a significant mass of public opinion to be linked through coalitions to impact local, state, and federal policy makers.

d) A summarization of findings and activities which can be directed toward the public media.

2. *Public Policy and Legislation*

As solutions are sought to the problems generated by scarcity and a shift in political balances, a central issue arises as to whether the approach will be based on a narrow ad hoc unilateral strategy or on one based on a comprehensive response grounded on a more global approach. The problems are international in scope; solutions tend to be national.

Offices of The United Methodist Church are strategically located for researching and monitoring United States developmental policies in both Washington and in New York City at the United Nations. When these policies are analyzed and communicated through the educational network, they become information for moral and theological reflection and Christian response. This response, when legitimated through the regular channels of the Church become the basis for legislative testimony and political action. Again, there are likely to be differences of opinion as to what public policy should be in regard to development. However, this model carefully takes these differences into account as a consensus is sought. Only legitimated policy statements are reflected by this program to the Congress and the Administration. These legitimizing processes are composed of official actions taken by the General Conference and policy statements taken by the boards and agencies.

Seminars developed around legislative matters would be a resource for the educational network and could be used as the basis for regional briefings or in Annual Conferences. The circuit would not be complete until this information was part of the factual material considered in the local church where the meaningful response is generated.

3. Pastoral Care

The pastoral ministry provides the most direct and universal contact of the church with its people. The new forms of ministry call for:

a) Worship and liturgy which makes real, through historic religious symbols, the message of justice and equity in dealing with the needs of the poor. The themes of interdependency, community life, bread, the good earth, and Christian responsibility can be woven into worshipping, prayer, and teaching which address the fundamental facts within the context of hope and expectation. Days of Simplicity could lead to less consumption and offerings for the poor which will be channeled through the fourth emphasis of the program.

b) Life-style. One of the major pressures upon the ecosystem is life-styles of the affluent. Covenant groups are being organized interdenominationally around the theme of hunger. Participation in such groups would create a fellowship in the local community where psychological reinforcement for a life-style of austerity could be generated. The revival of fasting, not primarily as a means for raising funds, but as a means of internalizing the needs of the poor would result in better health for the participant and deeper motivation for social justice. The change in life-style, however, may mean the acceptance of new market realities which limit our control of natural resources.

c) Feeding the Hungry. There is a close relationship between world hunger and underdevelopment. Malnutrition and starvation must be dealt with directly as we seek longer-term solutions by helping to develop an adequate agricultural economy in underdeveloped nations. The United Methodist Church Committee on Overseas Relief and other voluntary agencies have done much to express Christian love by dealing directly with the hunger problem. Giving should become a learning experience in the broader causes of hunger, looking to the need for basic changes in the world's economy. Included in this program is a concern for domestic hunger, especially among the young and the elderly. Since the local parish is closest to these problems, special programs identifying the need and seeking solutions through public policy will be emphasized.

d) Community Action. The development of true community at the local and regional levels is basic for realizing the potential of the Christian community in world social and economic development. This would include participation in and support for local people's organizations functioning to widen participation in the decision-making processes that affect their lives. Richard Dickinson reminds us in his *To Set at Liberty the Oppressed* that "Preoccupation with international aspects of the problems of development should not obscure the fundamental importance of changes at the local and regional levels. Change at these levels can be more strategic and have a long-lasting effect. Real development can no longer be conceived apart from a people's movement for liberation and social justice."[17] Pastoral leadership in developing true community and relating to local and regional development needs is integral to the development of a strong constituency for narrowing the gap between the rich and the poor.

The President of the World Bank recently placed the issue of world development before the American people in these words: "Which is ultimately more in a nation's interest: to funnel national resources into an endlessly spiraling consumer economy, in effect a pursuit of consumer gadgetry with all its senseless byproducts of waste and pollution, or to dedicate a more reasonable share of those same resources to improving the fundamental quality of life, both at home and abroad."[18] These words are suggestive of the direction of our thinking and living in the last quarter of the twentieth century.[19]

[17]*Ibid.*, p. 77.
[18]Richard D. N. Dickinson, *To Set at Liberty the Oppressed* (Geneva, Switzerland: World Council of Churches, Commission on the Churches' Participation in Development, 1975), p. 71.
[19]*See* Social Principles V-B; "Human Hunger" (1984).

Local Church Organization for the Needs of People

Because United Methodist people do not personally involve themselves in the mission of the church as much as we should, and

Because United Methodist people do not contribute to the Church as much money as we can, and

Because United Methodist people and The United Methodist Church do not relate to other Christian denominations in an ecumenical way as much as we should, and

Because United Methodist people do not fully share ourselves in a pluralistic church as much as we should, and

Because most United Methodist people live and learn at the local church level, and

Because United Methodist people have a greater opportunity to serve their neighbors' needs at the local church level, and

Because there is a growing tendency in The United Methodist Church for the clergy and professionals to minister to all the demands of the missions of the church, and

Because the laypeople in The United Methodist Church do not have as many structures and institutions at the local church level as are necessary to meet all the demands of the missions of the Church.

Therefore, Be It Resolved, That the General Conference of The United Methodist Church meeting in Portland, Oregon, USA, during the month of April 1976, recommend to all United Methodist congregations that they create structures and organizations to meet all the demands of the mission of the Church such as:

1. An organization (similar to the Society of St. Vincent de Paul of the Roman Catholic Church and the Society of St. Stephen of the Texas Methodist Conference) which has as its primary purpose the meeting of needs of people who are without the necessities of life;

2. An organization which has as its primary function the bringing together of laypeople of Black, White, Indian, and Hispanic congregations in a personal and social way;

3. An organization which is especially designed as a blood donor program which will make available blood for those who need it; and

4. A program where laypeople can share and witness more fully to their faith.

Medical Rights for Children and Youth

Out of long tradition our society has valued the family as its fundamental social institution. The family is seen as the primary locus for the nurture and protection of children and youth. To preserve, protect, and defend the family as a social unit, the family's right to privacy as been protected in almost absolute fashion by law and custom. The rights of parents to determine the conditions and circumstances of their children have known little limitation.

When children are abused or maltreated, therefore, the tragic facts are often hidden or little known. We must awaken now to the reality that some of our children, at some times and places, have been battered and beaten within their own families. It has been estimated that "10,000 children are severely battered every year, at least 50,000 to 75,000 are sexually abused, 100,000 are emotionally neglected, and another 100,000 are physically, morally, and educationally neglected."

In light of these tragic facts, we as church people should particularly bear witness to our conviction that parental rights over children are limited, that all children are gifts of God and belong to God, and that parents do not own their children. Children have fundamental rights as persons—rights that are to be protected by the community at large when the family system fails any particular child.

Medical care represents a particularly crucial area of the rights of children. We therefore call particular attention to the following statement of the medical rights due children and youth, and commend its principles for adoption:

81

The Pediatric Bill of Rights Preamble

Every child, regardless of race, religion, ethnic background, or economic standing, has the right to be regarded as a person and shall have the right to receive appropriate medical care and treatment. The Pediatric Bill of Rights shall not be construed as a bypassing of the family's right to personal privacy, but shall become operative when parental rights and the child's rights are in direct conflict and it becomes necessary to act in the best interests of the child. Provision shall be made for adequate counseling of the child as to his right to receive and deny medical care. To the extent that a child cannot demand his rights as a person, those involved in his health care shall move to protect that child's medical interests to the best of their ability.

Canon I. Every person, regardless of age, shall have the right of timely access to continuing and competent health care.

Canon II. Every person, regardless of age, shall have the right to seek out and to receive information concerning medically accepted contraceptive devices and birth-control services in doctor-patient confidentiality. Every person, regardless of age, shall have the right to receive medically prescribed contraceptive devices in doctor-patient confidentiality.

Canon III. Every person, regardless of age, shall have the right to seek out and to receive information concerning venereal disease, and every person, regardless of age, shall have the right to consent to and to receive any medically accepted treatment necessary to combat venereal disease in doctor-patient confidentiality.

Canon IV. Every person, regardless of age, shall have the right to seek out and to accept in doctor-patient confidentiality the diagnosis and treatment of any medical condition related to pregnancy. Every person, regardless of age, shall have the right to adequate and objective counseling relating to pregnancy and abortion in doctor-patient confidentiality and every person, regardless of age, shall have the right to request and to receive medically accepted treatment which will result in abortion in doctor-patient confidentiality.

Canon V. Every person, regardless of age, shall have the right to seek out and to receive psychiatric care and counseling in doctor-patient confidentiality.

Canon VI. Every person, regardless of age, shall have the right to seek out and to receive medically accepted counseling and treatment for drug or alcohol dependency in doctor-patient confidentiality.

Canon VII. Every person, regardless of age, shall have the right of immediate medical care when the life of such person is in imminent danger. The decision of imminent danger to the life of such person is a decision to be made solely by the attending physician; and the attending physician shall decide what treatment is medically indicated under the circumstances.

Canon VIII. Any person, regardless of age, who is of sufficient intelligence to appreciate the nature and consequences of the proposed medical care and if such medical care is for his own benefit, may effectively consent to such medical care in doctor-patient confidentiality. The same shall not apply to Canons II through VIII which are deemed to be absolute rights.

Canon IX. In every case in which a child is being examined by, treated by, or is under the medical care of a qualfied medical practitioner, and where, in the opinion of that qualified medical practitioner, the child is in need of immediate medical care and where the parent or the legal guardian of said child refuses to consent to such needed, immediate medical treatment, said medical practitioner shall notify the juvenile court or the district court with juvenile jurisdiction immediately. The juvenile court or the district court with juvenile jurisdiction shall immediately appoint a guardian ad litem, who shall represent the child's interests in all subsequent legal proceedings. The juvenile court or the district court with juvenile jurisdiction shall immediately set a date for hearing, not to exceed 96 hours from the receipt of the initial report. The court shall determine at the hearing, based upon medical and other revelant testimony and the best interests of the child, whether or not said medical treatment should be so ordered by the court.

Canon X. Every person, regardless of age, shall have the right to considered and respectful care. During examinations, every attempt shall be made to insure the privacy of every patient, regardless of age; and every person, regardless of age, has the right to know, if observers are present, what role the observer may have in regard to the patient's treatment and shall have the right to request that observers remove themselves from the immediate examining area.

Canon XI. Every person, regardless of age, shall have the right to know which physician is responsible for his care. Every person, regardless of age, shall have the right to be informed concerning his diagnosis, his treatment and his prognosis in language that is readily understandable to him. Every person, regardless of age, shall have the right to ask pertinent questions concerning the diagnosis, the treatment, tests and surgery done, on a day-to-day basis in a hospital setting; and every person, regardless of age, shall have the right to immediate response to the best of the attending physician's knowledge and in language that the patient clearly understands.[20]

Mental Health

No aspect of health care had greater claim upon the concerns of our Lord Jesus Christ than did the needs of persons to be mentally and spiritually whole. Repeatedly he was drawn to those whom society rejected, and to them he brought both empathy and healing. His ministry to them is impressively summarized in his encounter with the man of Gadara (Mark 5:1-20), who was self-destructive and isolated from his community. Jesus sought him out, understood his condition, listened to his needs, and brought him a healing ministry which restored him to spiritual wholeness.

[20]*See* Social Principles III-C.

We affirm an understanding of mental health that is firmly within such biblical concern as: forgiveness of self and others, redeeming broken relationships, recognition of alienation and isolation as dependent on social as well as personal causes, and the development of the whole person. Some degree of spiritual brokenness is the condition of all persons. We affirm the goal of spiritual wholeness of which the mental health movement is a part. While we reject the casual use of such labels as mental illness, we recognize that certain mental disturbances commonly described as psychoses may require hospitalization, chemotherapy, and other forms of medical treatment.

We affirm the need for public discussion and awareness of mental health concerns, so troubled persons can be more free to ask for help. Mental health problems probably claim more victims than any other health-related concern. Those who suffer from such conditions often are the object of misunderstanding and rejection by communities and even families. We affirm anew that the church is called to follow the priorities of Jesus by seeking to minister to problems of the mind as well as of the spirit.

We call upon the churches to inform their members in a responsible and comprehensive manner on the nature of the mental health problems facing our society today. We urge such specific preventive efforts through:

1. Expansion of counseling services.

2. Establishing crisis intervention ministries.

3. Providing workshops on family life, parent-child communication, sex education, alcohol and drug abuse, coping with stress, and prayer therapy.

4. Witnessing to the therapies of acceptance, confession, forgiveness, love, and peace which our faith affords.

We also urge such therapeutic efforts as:

1. Including hospitalized or residential mental patients in church visitation and correspondence.

2. Providing supportive one-to-one assistance through the churches in the transition from institution to inclusion in community and congregational life—for patients and for their families.

3. Creating opportunities for employment in the community and within church staffs.

Persons with mental or emotional difficulties often have either no treatment at all or only dehumanizing treatment available to them. We urge active participation by congregations in promotion of a community-based approach to mental health services which emphasizes:

1. Prevention.
2. Comprehensiveness.
3. Alternatives to institutional care.
4. Establishment of community mental health services.
5. Strong family and community involvement.
6. Sensitivity to the mental health needs of culturally or racially diverse groups in the population.

We note that, through the Community Mental Health Act of 1963, a system of comprehensive and coordinated services is being made available. It has been implemented through the establishment of community mental health centers in approximately 500 communities in the United States—yet almost two-thirds of the nation is without such centers. We urge that congregations, collectively and individually, cooperate with mental health associations and other local agencies to establish community mental health centers in each community, including working for the passage of enabling legislation where necessary.

The church should insist that public and private funding mechanisms be developed to assure the availability of these services to all who are in need of them, including adequate coverage for mental health services in any national health insurance program. We believe that any community mental health system should include public clinics, hospitals and other tax-supported facilities as components, ensuring the availability of medical care for all persons who may require it.

The New Testament concept of salvation means wholeness. We affirm that mind, body, and spirit are created gifts of God, united within each person. To be whole in mind is essential to being whole in spirit. The church is a community committed to assisting persons within and without its membership to continually grow toward spiritual wholeness. We call upon the church to affirm and create those resources which enhance the possibility of wholeness of mind as it seeks to bring about the wholeness of spirit.[21]

Ministries in Social Conflict

The laity and the clergy of The United Methodist Church are called to ministries in the midst of social conflict as expressions of the reconciling love of God in Christ. We are called to the moderation of social conflict by the offering of ministries of mediation and conflict resolution. We are called to be actively present in those settings where the grievances of the powerless are thrust before those who have influence, authority and control. We are called to an identification with those whose voices are unheard and whose hurts are unfelt, and into communication with those whose official responsibilities are often overwhelming and whose ability to respond frequently is limited. We are called to help in opening alternative channels of communication, furnishing acceptable options for action, and working conscientiously toward establishing a climate of trust between the parties in conflict.

This call is made with the understanding that when intolerable social conditions and immovable resistance to change cause potentially violent frustration, there must be a demand by the church for a redress of grievances rather than a repression of those who point to the injustices. It is a call to peace within our society, based neither upon the pacification of those who suffer nor upon the condemnation of those who serve. It is a call to peace based on justice, which we pray will emerge from arousing the public conscience, creating responsible discussion, and encouraging good-faith negotiations in conflict through the use of the church's resources, both human and material.[22]

[21]See Social Principles V-A; "Health and Wholeness" (1984)
[22]See Social Principles VI-C; "National Academy of Peace and Conflict Resolution" (1980).

National Incomes Policy

Many Americans live today under economic conditions which do not permit them to meet their basic needs. This situation is deplorable because it is not necessary. The economic productivity of our society, instead of meeting the needs of all its people, serves the interest of special groups. The present programs for increasing employment are inadequate to meet the need. Likewise, various income transfer programs, such as public welfare, unemployment insurance, and even Social Security itself, have failed to make possible an adequate minimum standard of existence. While a national program of income maintenance is not a substitute for a full employment policy, neither is a full employment policy a substitute for an incomes policy. Both programs are needed, and if one or both are missing, we shall continue to block the development of the maximum productive skills of a tragically large number of citizens. Wage standards are needed which provide a living wage for all workers. It is also necessary to broaden and improve social welfare services.

Our present economic system functions imperfectly. It is the responsibility of society to develop new institutions which more adequately fulfill human rights—jobs, food, clothing, housing, education, and health care. As Christians we have the obligation to work with others to develop the moral foundation for public policies which will provide every family with the minimum income needed to participate as responsible and productive members of society.

We, as Christians, also recognize our obligation to work with others to develop in each person an attitude of responsible stewardship of time, talent, and resources that will enable the maximum number of families to be self-reliant and economically independent to the greatest possible extent.

Some basic objectives of a strategy for economic justice are:

1. A return to a full employment policy with the federal,

state, and local government as the employers of the last resort.

2. A guaranteed minimum annual income sufficient for every family living in the United States based on the Bureau of Labor Statistics' lower budget.

3. Supportive social services in the fields of education, health, housing, job training, and particularly adequate, comprehensive child development and day-care services for all children, especially those of the poor and low-income groups.

4. Improvement and expansion of the food stamp program, school breakfast and lunch programs, and the creation of new means to ensure that no person be hungry in this society of abundance.

We call upon our churches and the general boards and agencies:

1. To study the various methods for providing every individual and family an income capable of supporting human life in dignity and decency.

2. To participate in the development and implementation of a national income policy which best fulfills the following criteria:

a) Designed to provide a means to an income adequate for living and available to all as a matter of right.

b) Adequate to maintain health and human well-being and adjusted to changes in the cost of living.

c) Administered so as to extend coverage to all persons in need.

d) Developed in a manner which will respect the freedom of persons to manage their own lives, increase their power to choose their own careers, and enable them to participate in meeting personal and community needs.

e) Designed to reward rather than penalize productive activity.

f) Designed in such a way that existing socially desirable programs and values are conserved and enhanced.

g) Federally standardized, taking into consideration local and regional differences in cost of living.[23]

[23]*See* Social Principles II-A, C, G.

Police Firearms Policies

We deplore the killing and injuring of police officers by citizens and the unnecessary and unwarranted killing of persons by police. We, therefore, not only call for the tightening of legal control over citizens' ownership of firearms or of guns, but we also call for the formulation of more clearly defined written firearms policies by every agency of law enforcement in the country.[24]

Reconciliation and Reconstruction in Indochina

The wounds caused by the war in Vietnam will be long in healing. Many persons may be tempted to ignore or forget, to avoid the burden of remembering. But Jesus Christ is the healer of broken lives, divided peoples, and devastated nations. Those who follow him are called to help heal the wounds left from that war. One mark of our own spiritual vitality and of our hope in a new life for others is our sensitivity in dealing with the human concerns that still remain. This, likewise, will be a measure of the spiritual renewal of the nations involved.

The United States poured out tremendous wealth in the course of the war which destroyed villages, ravaged farmlands, and resulted in death, suffering, and homelessness for millions of human beings in Indochina as well as thousands from the United States and other nations. Will the many who paid for that war be willing, in the name of Christ, to help pay for the peace?

Therefore, we urge a program of healing, reconciliation and reconstruction which would include:

1. The provision of humanitarian aid for such purposes as the restoration of agriculture and village life, indigenous industries, medical and educational facilities, and supplies through the efforts of Christian churches and related agencies, including UMCOR, Church World Service, and

[24]See Social Principles V-F; "Criminal Justice" (1984).

the Fund for Reconciliation and Reconstruction in Indochina of the World Council of Churches and the humanitarian aid programs of Friendshipment.

2. The normalization of relations with Vietnam including diplomatic recognition, trade, and membership in the United Nations.

3. The participation of the United States government, as in the case of Japan and Germany following World War II, in assisting the reconstruction of Vietnam by economic aid, preferably through international agencies.

4. The completion of other unfinished business, such as information on the missing in action and the possible recovery of their remains, and a program of broad amnesty, with the Church continuing a ministry to the families of all youth who were victims of the war.

Responsible Parenthood

We affirm the principle of responsible parenthood. The family in its varying forms constitutes the primary focus of love, acceptance, and nurture, bringing fulfillment to parents and child. Healthful and whole personhood develops as one is loved, responds to love, and in that relationship comes to wholeness as a child of God.

Each couple has the right and the duty prayerfully and responsibly to control conception according to their circumstances. They are in our view free to use those means of birth control considered medically safe. As developing technologies have moved conception and reproduction more and more out of the category of a chance happening and more closely to the realm of responsible choice, the decision whether or not to give birth to children must include acceptance of the responsibility to provide for their mental, physical, and spiritual growth, as well as consideration of the possible effect on quality of life for family and society.

To support the sacred dimensions of personhood, all possible efforts should be made by parents and the community to ensure that each child enters the world with a healthy body, and is born into an environment conducive to realization of his or her full potential.

When, through contraceptive or human failure, an unacceptable pregnancy occurs, we believe that a profound regard for unborn human life must be weighed alongside an equally profound regard for fully developed person- hood, particularly when the physical, mental, and emotional health of the pregnant woman and her family show reason to be seriously threatened by the new life just forming. We reject the simplistic answers to the problem of abortion which, on the one hand, regard all abortions as murders, or, on the other hand, regard abortions as medical procedures without moral significance.

When an unacceptable pregnancy occurs, a family, and most of all the pregnant woman, is confronted with the need to make a difficult decision. We believe that continuance of a pregnancy which endangers the life or health of the mother, or poses other serious problems concerning the life, health, or mental capability of the child to be, is not a moral necessity. In such cases, we believe the path of mature Christian judgment may indicate the advisability of abor- tion. We support the legal right to abortion as established by the 1973 Supreme Court decision. We encourage women in counsel with husbands, doctors, and pastors to make their own responsible decisions concerning the personal and moral questions surrounding the issue of abortion.

We therefore encourage our churches and common society to:

1. Provide to all education on human sexuality and family life in its varying forms, including means of marriage enrichment, rights of children, responsible and joyful expression of sexuality, and changing attitudes toward male and female roles in home and marketplace.

2. Provide counseling opportunities for married couples and those approaching marriage on the principles of responsible parenthood.

3. Build understanding of the problems posed to society by the rapidly growing population of the world, and of the

need to place personal decisions concerning childbearing in a context of the well-being of the community.

4. Provide to each pregnant woman accessibility to comprehensive health care and nutrition adequate to assure healthy children.

5. Make information and materials available so all can exercise responsible choice in the area of conception controls. We support the free flow of information on reputable, efficient and safe nonprescription contraceptive techniques through educational programs and through periodicals, radio, television, and other advertising media. We support adequate public funding and increased participation in family planning services by public and private agencies, including church-related institutions, with the goal of making such services accessible to all, regardless of economic status or geographic location.

6. Make provision in law and practice for voluntary sterilization as an appropriate means for some for conception control and family planning.

7. Safeguard the legal option of abortion under standards of sound medical practice, and make abortions available to women without regard to economic status.

8. Monitor carefully the growing genetic and biomedical research, and be prepared to offer sound ethical counsel to those facing birth-planning decisions affected by such research.

9. Assist the states to make provisions in law and practice for treating as adults minors who have, or think they have, venereal diseases, or female minors who are, or think they are, pregnant, thereby eliminating the legal necessity for notifying parents or guardians prior to care and treatment. Parental support is crucially important and most desirable on such occasions, but needed treatment ought not be contingent on such support.

10. Understand the family as encompassing a wider range of options than that of the two-generational unit of parents and children (the nuclear family); promote the development of all socially responsible and life-enhancing expressions of the extended family, including families with

93

adopted children, single parents, those with no children, and those who choose to be single.

11. View parenthood in the widest possible framework, recognizing that many children of the world today desperately need functioning parental figures, and also understanding that adults can realize the choice and fulfillment of parenthood through adoption or foster care.

12. Encourage men and women to demonstrate actively their responsibility by creating a family context of nurture and growth in which the children will have the opportunity to share in the mutual love and concern of their parents.

13. Be aware of the fears of many in poor and minority groups and in developing nations about imposed birth planning, oppose any coercive use of such policies and services, and strive to see that family-planning programs respect the dignity of each individual person as well as the cultural diversities of groups.[23]

Sale and Use of Alcohol and Tobacco on Church Property

The United Methodist Church opposes the sale and discourages the consumption or use of alcoholic beverages and tobacco products within the confines of Church buildings, including worship centers, halls, and educational areas.

Self-Help Efforts of Poor People

We note with satisfaction the recent upsurge of community-based, cooperative, self-help efforts on the part of groups of low-income rural people in all parts of the United States. However, we recognize that such efforts do not offer a total solution to the problem of rural poverty or obviate the necessity for massive efforts on the part of government and private sector to combat rural poverty in other ways.

[23]*See* Social Principles II-A, C, G.

94

The church of Jesus Christ is concerned for the fulfillment of whole persons in community. Economic development which produces human and community development is to be preferred over other forms of economic activity. In the cooperative and other community-based enterprise of poor people we find a combination of economic gain, personal fulfillment, and community development.

We applaud and we will support these indigenous and cooperative self-help efforts because we see in them social and spiritual as well as economic values of great consequence.

We call upon our general boards, jurisdictions, area offices, annual conferences, districts, local churches and members to seek ways to become acquainted with the self-help efforts of poor people in rural areas and to help them with grants, credit, technical assistance, and training facilities.

We call upon federal and state governments, private industry, banks, colleges and universities, foundations, and all other public and private agencies to provide massive resources, both financial and technical, to assist the valiant efforts of low-income rural people to solve their own problems through self-help.[24]

Social Welfare

Concern for the welfare of the poor, the widowed, the orphan, the alien, is deeply rooted within the prophetic tradition and the New Testament message. Historically, social welfare had received motivation and impetus from biblical faith.

Social welfare increasingly implies the concern of all persons, organized for the welfare of all persons. Continued unemployment and poverty highlight the need for public

[24]*See* Social Principles IV-E; "Advocacy for the Poor" (1984); "Concern for Persons in Poverty" (1980).

and private assistance to those unable to earn an adequate livelihood. We urge national social welfare programs which at least meet minimal human needs. Public and private programs of welfare are needed which would:

1. Provide physical necessities for all who need them.
2. Respect the integrity and the dignity of persons.
3. Encourage economic independence.

These principles are especially important in the face of punitive proposals aimed at getting people off welfare. The nation would do far better to concentrate first on providing job opportunities for the millions of unemployed who desire them than to set about requiring work from welfare recipients who in general possess the poorest health and the least skills of all those in the total potential labor force. Most welfare recipients do not or ought not come under a work requirement in any event—they are the aged, the disabled, the blind, or they are children.

As of September 1975, these groups represented 79 percent of the total federally supported welfare roll. (See Tables M-25 and M-33, *Social Security Bulletin,* January 1976, pages 67 and 72.) Under the Supplementary Security Income Program are the aged—2,309,910; the blind—73,-875; the disabled—1,854,545. Under the program of Aid to Families with Dependent Children are families—3,474,838; total recipients—11,269,670; children—8,038,055. Only 21 percent of the welfare roll is represented by the parents of small children. These parents represent the only possible target group for a work requirement. It is important to note that the great majority of this 21 percent are mothers in one-parent families.

Of this parental group, many are not able-bodied. Of the able-bodied persons, we strongly reject the demand that mothers of children under sixteen should be required to take jobs outside the home. They, like other American mothers, should be allowed to make their own decision as to where their life efforts are most needed—whether in making a home for their children, or in the commercial job market as well as in the home.

The real work failure in our society is the national failure

96

to provide jobs for those who want them. In this light, any work requirement for able-bodied welfare recipients should include at least the following standards:

1. Single parents of children under age sixteen should be exempted from any mandatory work requirement.

2. Welfare support should not be reduced because of earnings of welfare recipients except at rates which will allow significant improvements in the financial position of recipients because of their earnings.

3. When work is requested of the welfare recipient, any judgment as to the work capability of the recipient should be attested by an independent qualified medical professional, covering mental and emotional as well as physical aspects, with opportunity for professional review of such judgment.

4. When work capability is established, the work provided should meet the following standards:

a) Suitable to the physical, mental and emotional characteristics of the worker and suitable to his or her skills and experience.

b) Travel to and from work not beyond a reasonable distance.

c) Pay rates not less than those prevailing for similar work in the area, and in no case less than the national minimum wage.

d) The work to be of such nature as to make a contribution to the general welfare.

e) The work to be of such nature as not to violate the moral scruples of the worker.

Current welfare policies often contribute to the deterioration of major cities and their inhabitants. Needy persons are attracted to urban areas where housing and employment are sought, thus adding to the financial crises of the cities. Administrative policies of the welfare programs may contribute to the breakup of inner city families, as well as welfare depending from one generation to another.

We urge adequate federal funding of welfare programs, and revision of administrative policies to eliminate such destruction of persons and harm to our urban areas.[25]

[25]*See* Social Principles IV-E

Special Needs of Farm Workers

Calling for special attention is the situation of farm workers in the United States. Traditionally they have been among the most poorly paid, housed, educated, and poorly served by health, welfare, and other social agencies. They have been systematically excluded from all, or nearly all, the benefits of social legislation.

Specifically, they have been and are excluded from unemployment insurance and workmen's compensation. Their coverage by social security, minimum wage, and child labor laws has come belatedly and is still inferior to that of most workers in industry. We support legislation designed to correct these injustices and to handle the strain within the labor market of the agricultural sector so that public interest is protected.

For over fifty years the churches have sought to improve the lot of seasonal farm workers through the Migrant Ministry, an ecumenical program to which The United Methodist Church has given significant support. The Migrant Ministry sincerely sought to meet some of the most acute needs of these oppressed people.

In recent days, the churches have come to recognize that the most fundamental of all the needs of farm workers is the need for dignity, for self-determination and for self-organization. Benefits won by any other route are at best second-rate.

At last the ten-year struggle of the farm workers in California has led to a major legislative breakthrough that is designed to ensure seasonal and year-round farm workers an opportunity to vote in secret-ballot elections for the unions of their choice. The California Agricultural Labor Relation Act of 1975 provides a better framework for the working out of justice in the fields, but does not guarantee that justice will finally prevail. Farm workers in other states are struggling also to bargain as equals with their employers. We call upon the Congress to enact legislation which enables farm workers to organize into unions of their own choosing.

We commit The United Methodist Church to support

98

state legislation similar to the California law in other states when farm workers are pressing for such legislation.

The United Methodist Church will continue to press for better educational opportunity, housing, and welfare services, more adequate minimum wages, and full coverage by all social legislation designed for the protection of workers.

We also call upon the federal government to allocate more attention and resources to the task of retraining and adjustment or those farm workers who are being progressively displaced by mechanization of agricultural operations.

We urge all United Methodists to monitor situations where farm workers have won elections but have not been able to negotiate effective agreements and, to use their personal and institutional resources to encourage bargaining in good faith.

We urge the California legislature, without further delay, to appropriate the funds which would allow the provisions of the Farm Labor Act to be carried out.

We urge the support of Farm Workers Week with special bulletin inserts and the invitation by local churches and/or districts to workers to inform the people of the week and the aspirations of these persons.

The United Methodist Church affirms in principle the position of the recently formed National Farm Worker Ministry (a continuation of the Migrant Ministry) that the Church's most significant role must be as advocate and supporter of the efforts of farm workers toward their own responsible self-organization and self-determination.[26]

The United Methodist Church and Race

A. Principles

1. The gospel of our Lord Jesus Christ makes no room for the arbitrary distinctions and expressions of racial or

[26]See Social Principles IV-F; III-K.

group prejudice. Jesus' followers early came to see that "God has no favourites, but . . . in every nation the man who is godfearing and does what is right is acceptable to him" (Acts 10:34-35). ". . . Through faith you are all sons of God in union with Christ Jesus. . . . There is no such thing as Jew and Greek, slave and freeman, male and female; for you are all one person in Christ Jesus" (Galatians 3:26, 28).

2. The church is an instrument of God's purpose. It is ours only as stewards under his lordship. The House of God must be open to the whole family of God. If we discriminate against any persons, we deny the essential nature of the church as a fellowship in Christ.

3. By biblical and theological precept, by the law of the Church, by General Conference pronouncement, and by episcopal expression, the matter is clear. With respect to race, the aim of The United Methodist Church is nothing less than an inclusive church in an inclusive society. The United Methodist Church therefore calls upon all its people to perform those faithful deeds of love and justice in both the church and community that will bring this aim into full reality.

B. In the Church

4. We recognize that The United Methodist Church has erased many of the legal boundaries which previously divided the people by race. Conference mergers have served to draw all United Methodist members into a closer geographical unit. We call upon each local church to seek out congregations of different racial backgrounds and form such fellowship as will demonstrate the oneness of their hopes and spiritual aspirations.

5. We also recognize that racial ethnic minorities in The United Methodist Church, whether clergy or lay persons, are working to strengthen the ethnic minority church. This may require special caucusing of such groups in white-dominated meetings. This does not contradict the church's aim of becoming an inclusive church, but it requires

particular attention by all levels of the church to nurture ethnic minority leadership which has been rapidly lost since mergers have occurred.

6. We call upon all pastors and church officials to maintain local services and activities and local church membership open to persons of all races, with equal opportunity for all to participate fully in every aspect of local church life.

7. We call upon all district superintendents and bishops to encourage "open pulpits" and integrate cabinets, and to appoint pastors to churches and charges without respect to the racial opposition of the congregations or the race of the appointed minister.

8. Minority group empowerment within the Church as an honest effort to enhance the Church in minority life enables The United Methodist Church to sustain its commitment to end racism. The progress made in this regard is commendable. We recognize, however, that simply placing racial and ethnic minority persons in positions of leadership does not necessarily mean empowerment.

9. The church is guilty of fostering unjust systems. We call upon each local church to examine its class values in light of the different systems of discrimination affecting sex and race and to recognize the necessity of dealing with the two as part of a larger system of oppression.

C. In the Community and Nation

10. The United Methodist Church should also use its influence in assisting in the economic empowerment of racial minority groups by encouraging the development of plans for the support of minority-controlled schools and colleges, minority-owned banks, housing corporations, and other business enterprises. The Church should especially support those minority business enterprises which benefit the largest number of persons in a community rather than a few individuals.

11. We call upon all United Methodist bodies, organizations, officials, and individual church members to practice and use their influence to encourage fair employment policies and the rendering of service to the public without racial segregation or discrimination in the companies, and concerns where they do business and in those areas where they hold investments. Consistent with that, we ask the General Conference of The United Methodist Church meeting in Portland, Oregon, in April 1976, to endorse the program of National Project Equality.

12. The minimum requirements for justice in the social order include the recognition of equal rights and opportunities for all races in voting, law enforcement, education, employment, housing, public accommodations, and cultural advantages. We support the passage and enforcement of laws appropriate to every level of government for the establishment and maintenance of equal rights in each of these areas of our common life.[27]

13. We seek a fully free and open society as the only society consistent with our basic principle of kinship in Christ.

14. We call upon each local church to assume its Christian responsibility for the creation of a community atmosphere in which all people will have free access to all community advantages inherent in its educational, political, employment, housing, and public accommodations opportunities.

15. We affirm the legality and right of oppressed persons to protest, to assemble in public, and to agitate for redress of grievances. A public march or other demonstration as a democratic petition for attention and justice is in line with the principles and practices of a free society. When such orderly protests are undertaken, the goal should be clearly indentifiable.

When orderly, responsible, nonviolent public demonstrations by those engaged in the struggle for racial justice provoke violent retaliation on the part of police or

[27]See Social Principles III-A; "Global Racism" (1984); "A Charter for Racial Justice Policies" (1980).

onlookers, the blame for the violence should be placed on the violent, not on the peaceable, demonstrators. On the other hand, any demonstration that initiates violence takes to itself the same blame. Even peaceable demonstrations supporting entirely just causes must be restrained and limited by the recognition that no decent society can exist apart from the rule of just law. Thus limited, however, orderly and responsible demonstrations can serve to bring order into being.

We recognize that conflict often produces awareness of the problems when legitimate desire for honest participation in community life confronts legalized injustices, and the church must accept this opportunity for useful service afforded by the conflict situation. This deep realization of the problem is the first necessary step toward an understanding solution.

D. Commitment to Prayer and Involvement

16. We are thankful to Almighty God that we have come to recognize the injustices which come from racial segregation and discrimination. We also realize that a deep and total life commitment is needed to undergird our involvement in the transformation of society. To this end, we call our people to serious and intense prayer. We shall also seek a spirit of humble penitence through which we may hear a voice of new direction as we seek to do the will of God in human relations.

17. We call upon every United Methodist to discover a unique sense of joy in living in these days. We discern in the tensions of our times the stirrings of the kingdom of God, for which we pray in our Lord's Prayer.

18. We call upon the Church to seek aggressive involvement in those areas of tension which are related to the stated social goals of the Church.

Christians must at all times be conscious of the risk taken in involvement, but they should glory in the opportunity to

103

establish the validity of the faith in the reality of the problems of the times.

19. We call upon the Church actively to seek opportunities of service in the area of human relations and to challenge its people to express their faith in action and thereby be witnesses to the faith which the Church declares. A program of persistent involvement through projects, study, and service is needed today.

20. We call upon all churches to seek an expansion of their spiritual resources. We are fully aware of the necessity for spiritual power before the involvement and results we seek are forthcoming. It may be that new dimensions of prayer, fasting, and meditating should be sought as possible avenues to break the bonds which prevent us from the kind of thinking, feeling, and action demanded of us as followers of the Way.

1980

Afghanistan
(Episcopal Address)

The Episcopal Address called us "in the name of Christ to let the world be liberated from the sin of war" and urged that "our voices must be heard in opposition to war, for it is a contradiction to the principles of Christianity and ignores the Prince of Peace."

We are deeply troubled over recent events in Afghanistan. We object to the decision by leaders of the USSR to intervene militarily in a country that, like all countries, has the right to self-determination. We condemn their use of aggressive force.

We urge United Methodists to reflect carefully on developing events, weighing them in the light of the New Testament message and of Christian experience. Let our response always be one of human beings to human beings, under God.

We direct the Secretary of the General Conference to communicate this statement to the Secretary General of the United Nations, commending the UN for its efforts to achieve a peaceful settlement in the region and urging further continuing efforts to avert this growing threat to world peace.

We also direct the secretary of the General Conference to send this statement to the Ambassador of the USSR to the United States, urging the immediate withdrawal of Soviet forces from the sovereign nation of Afghanistan and to the President of the United States urging his serious consideration.

Against Sterilization Abuse

We recognize, especially in this country, that the choice of sterilization as a method of limiting family size is winning more acceptance. When voluntary, this practice is a matter of personal choice; however, when someone else makes the decision, the chances of abuse are great.

Sterilization abuse is recognized as a problem of low-income women, particularly Third World women. According to *Family Digest*, May 1972, 35 percent of married Puerto Rican women of child-bearing age were sterilized. In November 1977 the U.S. General Accounting Office issued a report indicating that Health Service had sterilized approximately 5.5 percent of all Indians between 1973 and 1976, the Indian women of child-bearing age in the Aberdeen, Phoenix, Albuquerque, and Oklahoma City areas. In 1979, a study conducted by the Women's Division in New York City found in face-to-face interviews with 600 women ages 18-45 that of the first 50 interviews, 26 women had had tubal ligations and 8 had had hysterectomies. Of those who had tubal ligations, 13 were black, 9 were Puerto Rican, and 4 were white. Ten of the 26 were receiving public assistance. In 13 cases a doctor suggested the operation and 12 of these women indicated that the doctor was the single most influential person in the decision. Only 8 of the 26 brought up the subject themselves; 3 women did not remember how the subject came up; and in one case the woman's mother influenced her. Fifty per cent of the women showed regret over having been sterilized.

WHEREAS the decision to be sterilized is unique in the area of reproductive freedom because it is irreversible, the dangers of coercion, deception, and misinformation and the desire of some for population control, particularly among the poor, Third World (in the U.S. and overseas) people, require safeguards against an uninformed and involuntary decision with such inexorable consequences;

WHEREAS the importance of the sterilization decision for most people cannot be overestimated, since reproductive ability is key to the identity of many people, both male and

106

female, the decision to become sterilized can have tremendous psychological as well as physical repercussions;

WHEREAS sterilization abuse—the sterilizing of people against their will or without their knowledge—is still occurring;

It Is Therefore Recommended That:

1. The United Methodist Church support the following principles:
   a. The patient, not her physician or any other party, should make the ultimate decision in accordance with law, as to whether she will be sterilized. Involuntary sterilizations (for minors or persons adjudged to be mentally incompetent) are justifiable only if ordered by a competent court after a hearing according to due process of law.
   b. Adequate and accurate information should be given to women concerning sterilization and its alternatives.
   c. The decision to be sterilized should not be made during a time of stress, particularly during hospitalization for abortion or childbirth.
2. In order that the sterilization decision be both informed and voluntary, there is a need that:
   a. women considering sterilization be given specific information in their own language using understandable terms about the nature and consequences of the sterilization procedure to be performed, as well as the risks and benefits of that procedure;
   b. they have adequate time in which to make this irreversible decision in a non-coercive atmosphere— thus a thirty-day waiting period which would enable them to leave the hospital and consult with family, friends, or other physicians.
3. Local churches monitor the implementation of the guidelines in local hospitals.
4. Local churches be encouraged to ascertain women's attitudes toward and experience with sterilization in their communities.
5. Education and information about sterilization and other

107

forms of contraception be included in family life programs with special note taken of the guidelines for voluntary consent.

6. The United Methodist Church oppose racist population control policies and practices aimed at Third World peoples (in the U.S. and overseas).

7. The United Methodist Church oppose all forms of sterilization abuse, including lack of informed consent, arbitrary measures for handicapped and institutionalized women and industrial exposure to radiation.[1]

Barrier-Free Construction
for the Handicapped

Be it resolved, that Church monies from agencies of The United Methodist Church beyond the local church be granted, loaned, or otherwise provided only for the construction of church sanctuaries, educational buildings, parsonages, camps, colleges, or other church-related agencies or facilities that meet minimum guidelines in their plans for barrier-free construction.

That local churches utilizing their own funds or funds secured through lending agencies and institutions beyond The United Methodist Church be urged to make adequate provision in their plans to insure that all new church buildings shall be of barrier-free construction.

That local churches be urged to adapt existing facilities, through such programs as widening doorways, installing ramps and elevators, eliminating stairs where possible, providing handrails, adequate parking facilities, and rest rooms so that handicapped persons may take their appropriate place in the fellowship of the church.

That the appropriate national agencies provide technical information for local churches to assist in providing barrier-free facilities.[2]

[1]*See* Social Principles III-F.
[2]*See* Social Principles III-G; "The Church and Persons with Mentally, Physically, and/or Psychologically Handicapping Conditions" (1984).

The Black Hills Alliance

The Black Hills, historically the sacred, ancestral lands of the Lakota people, is designated a "national sacrifice area" in a federal plan known as Project Independence. Large scale plans are underway for the mining of uranium, coal, and taconite iron deposits, using open pits, strip mines, and solution mines. It is estimated that within 35 years the water tables will be exhausted. Radioactive by-products will pollute the air. Unrestricted strip mining will devastate the land.

We therefore affirm: 1) the right of native people to keep sacred their ancestral burial grounds and their right to determine the responsible use of natural resources, 2) the necessity to consider the long-range consequences of depleting the water supply, as opposed to the short-range benefits of obtaining additional coal and other mineral resources, and 3) the position of the Black Hills Alliance, an organization of persons who live in the Black Hills region who are dedicated to a safe and healthy future for their children, and who maintain research, education, and action projects in support of their cause.[3]

Capital Punishment

In spite of a common assumption to the contrary, "an eye for an eye and a tooth for a tooth," does not give justification for the imposing of the penalty of death. Jesus explicitly repudiated the *lex tallionis* (Matthew 5:38-39) and the Talmud denies its literal meaning, and holds that it refers to financial indemnities.

When a woman was brought before Jesus, having committed a crime for which the death penalty was commonly imposed, our Lord so persisted in questioning the moral authority of those who were ready to conduct the

[3]*See* Social Principles III-A; "The United Methodist Church and America's Native People," (1980).

execution, that they finally dismissed the charges (John 8:31f).

The Social Principles of The United Methodist Church condemns ". . . torture of persons by governments for any purpose," and asserts that it violates Christian teachings. The church through its Social Principles further declares, "we oppose capital punishment and urge its elimination from all criminal codes."

After a moratorium of a full decade, the use of the death penalty in the United States has resumed. Other Western nations have largely abolished it during the 20th century. But a rapidly rising rate of crime and an even greater increase in the fear of crime has generated support within the American society for the institution of death as the punishment for certain forms of homicide. It is now being asserted, as it was often in the past, that capital punishment would deter criminals and would protect law-abiding citizens.

The United States Supreme Court, on *Gregg V. Georgia,* in permitting use of the death penalty, conceded the lack of evidence that it reduced violent crime, but permitted its use for purpose of sheer retribution.

The United Methodist Church cannot accept retribution or social vengeance as a reason for taking human life. It violates our deepest belief in God as the creator and the redeemer of humankind. In this respect, there can be no assertion that human life can be taken humanely by the state. Indeed, in the long run, the use of the death penalty by the state will increase the acceptance of revenge in our society and will give official sanction to a climate of violence.

The United Methodist Church is deeply concerned about the present high rate of crime in the United States, and about the value of a life taken in murder or homicide. When another life is taken through capital punishment, the life of the victim is further devalued. Moreover, the Church is convinced that the use of the death penalty would result in neither a net reduction of crime in general nor in a lessening of the particular kinds of crime against which it was directed. Homicide—the crime for which the death penalty has been used almost exclusively in recent decades—increased far less than other major crimes during the period of the moratorium. Progressively rigorous scientific studies, conducted over more than forty years, overwhelmingly failed to support the thesis that capital punishment deters homicide more effectively than does imprisonment. The most careful comparisons of homicide rates in similar states with and without use of the death penalty, and also of homicide rates in the same state in periods with and without it, have found as many or slightly more criminal homicides in states with use of the death penalty.

The death penalty also falls unfairly and unequally upon an outcast minority. Recent methods for selecting the few persons sentenced to die from among the larger number who are convicted of comparable offenses have not cured the arbitrariness and discrimination that have historically marked the administration of capital punishment in this country.

The United Methodist Church is convinced that the nation's leaders should give attention to the improvement of the total criminal justice system and to the elimination of social conditions which breed crime and cause disorder, rather than foster a false confidence in the effectiveness of the death penalty.

The United Methodist Church declares its opposition to the retention and use of capital punishment in any for or carried out by any means; the Church urges the abolition of capital punishment.[4]

Certification of Conscientious Objectors

The United Methodist Church today nurtures a substantial number of conscientious objectors among its members. Since 1936, The United Methodist Church or one of its predecessors has provided to those of its members who claim to be conscientious objectors the opportunity to register. Certified copies of such registration are supplied for use with the draft authorities.

[4]See Social Principles V-F; "Criminal Justice," (1984).

We support this procedure and propose that The United Methodist Church further develop a churchwide process that certifies the decision of its members who seek to be identified as conscientious objectors. That process should be created by the General Board of Church and Society in cooperation with the General Board of Discipleship.

The process may begin in the local church, where the pastor, in cooperation with the Pastor-Parish Relations Committee and the Council on Ministries, could select a person or committee to implement the process developed by the general agencies.

The United Methodist theological statements, Social Principles, and historic statements on war, peace, and conscription should be primary points of reference. It is the responsibility of the Church at all levels to inform its members of the fact that conscientious objection, as well as conscientious participation, is a valid option for Christians and is recognized in many countries as a legal alternative for persons liable to military conscription.

The local committee's action does not express agreement or disagreement with the convictions of the applicant member. Rather, the committee's task is to record which of the church's members are opposed to participation in military service on grounds of conscience and to assist them in securing proper counsel. When a member has registered and his/her registration has been certified to the proper authorities, that action should be recorded with the conference and General Board of Church and Society.[5]

A Charter for Racial Justice Policies
in an Interdependent Global Community

Racism is the belief that one race is innately superior to all other races. In the United States, this belief has justified the

[5]*See* Social Principles V-G; "The United Methodist Church and Peace," 1984; "Concerning Draft in the United States," "The United Methodist Church and Conscription," 1980.

conquest, enslavement, and evangelizing of non-Europeans. During the early history of this country, Europeans assumed that their civilization and religion were innately superior to those of both the original inhabitants of the United States and the Africans who were forcibly brought to these shores to be slaves. The myth of European superiority persisted and persists. Other people who came and who are still coming to the United States by choice or force encountered and encounter racism. Some of these people are the Chinese who built the railroads as indentured workers; the Mexicans whose lands were annexed; the Puerto Ricans, the Cubans, the Hawaiians, and the Eskimos who were colonized; and the Filipinos, the Jamaicans, and the Haitians who live on starvation wages as farm workers.

In principle, the United States has outlawed racial discrimination but, in practice, little has changed. Social, economic, and political institutions still discriminate, although some institutions have amended their behavior by eliminating obvious discriminatory practices and choosing their language carefully. The institutional church, despite sporadic attempts to the contrary, also still discriminates.

The damage of years of exploitation has not been erased. A system designed to meet the needs of one segment of the population cannot be the means to the development of a just society for all. The racist system in the United States today perpetuates the power and control of those of European ancestry. It is often called "white racism." The fruits of racism are prejudice, bigotry, discrimination, and dehumanization. Consistently, Blacks, Hispanics, Asians, Native Americans, and Pacific Islanders have been humiliated by being given inferior jobs, housing, education, medical services, transportation, and public accommodation. With hopes deferred and rights still denied, the deprived and oppressed fall prey to a colonial mentality which acquiesces to the inequities, occasionally with religious rationalization.

Racist presuppositions have been implicit in U.S. attitudes and policies toward Asia, Africa, the Middle East, and Latin America. While proclaiming democracy, freedom, and independence, the U.S. has been an ally and an accomplice to perpetuating inequality of the races and colonialism throughout the world. The history of The United Methodist Church and the history of the United States are intertwined. The "mission enterprise" of the churches in the United States and "westernization" went hand in hand, sustaining a belief in their superiority.

We are conscious that "we have sinned as our ancestors did: we have been wicked and evil" (Psalm 106:6, Today's English Version). We are called for a renewed commitment to the elimination of institutional racism. We affirm the 1976 General Conference Statement on The United Methodist Church and Race, which states unequivocally: "By biblical and theological precept, by the law of the Church, by General Conference pronouncement, and by episcopal expression, the matter is clear. With respect to race, the aim of The United Methodist Church is nothing less than an inclusive church in an inclusive society. The United Methodist Church, therefore, calls upon all its people to perform those faithful deeds of love and justice in both the church and community that will bring this aim into reality."

Because We Believe

1. that God is the Creator of all people and all are God's children in one family;
2. that racism is a rejection of the teachings of Jesus Christ;
3. that racism denies the redemption and reconciliation of Jesus Christ;
4. that racism robs all human beings of their wholeness and is used as a justification for social, economic, and political exploitation;
5. that we must declare before God and before each other that we have sinned against our sisters and brothers of other races in thought, in word, and in deed;
6. that in our common humanity in creation all women and men are made in God's image and all persons are equally valuable in the sight of God;

114

7. that our strength lies in our racial and cultural diversity and that we must work toward a world in which each person's value is respected and nurtured;
8. that our struggle for justice must be based on new attitudes, new understandings, and new relationships, and must be reflected in the laws, policies, structures, and practices of both church and state;

We commit ourselves as individuals and as a community to follow Jesus Christ in word and in deed and to struggle for the rights and the self-determination of every person and group of persons. Therefore, as United Methodists in every place across the land . . .

We will unite our efforts within The United Methodist Church

1. to eliminate all forms of institutional racism in the total ministry of the Church, giving special attention to those institutions which we support, beginning with their employment policies, purchasing practices, and availability of services and facilities;
2. to create opportunities in local churches to deal honestly with the existing racist attitudes and social distance between members, deepening the Christian commitment to be the Church where all racial groups and economic classes come together;
3. to increase efforts to recruit people of all races into the membership of The United Methodist Church and provide leadership development opportunities without discrimination;
4. to create workshops and seminars in local churches to study, understand, and appreciate the historical and cultural contributions of each race to the Church and community;
5. to increase local churches' awareness of the continuing needs for equal education, housing, employment, and medical care for all members of the community and to create opportunities to work for these things across racial lines;
6. to work for the development and implementation of national and international policies to protect the civil,

political, economic, social, and cultural rights of all
people such as through support for the ratification of
United Nations covenants on human rights;
7. to support and participate in the world-wide struggle for
liberation in the church and community;
8. to support nomination and election processes which
include all racial groups employing a quota system until
the time that our voluntary performance makes such
practice unnecessary.[6]

Church/Government Relations

Introduction

In response to a question about paying taxes, Jesus said:
"Render to Caesar the things that are Caesar's, and to God
the things that are God's" (Luke 20:25). Although this
statement refers specifically to taxation, its apparent
implications are that there are separate obligations and
responsibilities to government and to religion.

The Social Principles of The United Methodist Church
asserts: "We believe that the state should not attempt to
control the church, nor should the church seek to dominate
the state. 'Separation of church and state' means no organic
union of the two, but does permit interaction. The church
should continually exert a strong ethical influence upon the
state, supporting policies and programs deemed to be just
and compassionate and opposing policies and programs
which are not."

As we consider the religious protections of the First
Amendment—the free exercise and non-establishment of
religion—we are profoundly grateful for the major
statement made by the 1968 General Conference on
"Church/Government Relations." In recognizing that debt,
we reaffirm much of the substance of that declaration
prepared by two distinguished committees under the

[6]*See* Social Principles III-A; "Global Racism," 1984; "A Just World Order
in An Age of Interdependence," 1976.

authority of the General Conference and operating over two quadrenniums of the life of the Church.

Religious Liberty

1

Christians share commitment to the protection of human dignity and recognition of the right of every individual to freedom of thought, conscience, and religion. In the Christian tradition, in the heritage of Western philosophy, and in the emerging consensus of humankind, this freedom is deemed to be inherent in human personality. The United Methodist Church rejoices, therefore, to be in agreement with the principles of the Universal Declaration of Human Rights regarding religious liberty, and basic affirmations of other religious communities concerning religious liberty. We seek the universal observance, in law and in social practices, of fundamental freedoms for all persons everywhere.

In the modern world, every person—individually or in association with others—should be free to hold or change religious beliefs; to express religious beliefs in worship, teaching, and practice; and to proclaim and act upon the implications of religious beliefs for relationships in a social and political community.

We support the explicit constitutional safeguards which have long undergirded religious liberty in the United States of America. We believe it is of utmost importance for all persons, religious groups, and governments to maintain a continuing vigilance to insure that religious liberty be guaranteed. We respectfully request all national churches within the fellowship of the world United Methodist family to continue to work for the realization and support of religious liberty in the constitutions, governmental forms, and social practices of their respective countries.

2

Religious freedom is of three kinds. 1) The freedom to worship and believe with integrity—that is, without being

117

required by any external authority to affirm beliefs that one does not hold or to engage in acts of worship that do not conform to one's inner state of mind. This form of freedom must be considered absolute. 2) The freedom to communicate the meaning of one's religious convictions to others. This freedom should be considered a near absolute, subject only to the limitation that verbal injury to others and direct incitement to criminal actions cannot be permitted legal refuge on grounds of religious motivation. 3) The freedom to act on the basis of one's religious convictions. This freedom may sometimes be limited in the regulation of human affairs, for the sake of public health and safety, or to guarantee the rights of others. Nevertheless, the widest possible latitude should also be provided for the expression of this form of religious liberty.

3

Since objection to all war on conscientious grounds has fundamental implications for religious liberty, we believe that the policy of national governments to grant deferment from military service on grounds of conscience must be affirmed.

4

The constitutional provisions which preclude governments from taking any action "respecting an establishment of religion" has a positive effect on the maintenance of religious liberty. "Establishment of religion" places the power of all of society behind the religious expressions of some part of society. The United Methodist Church is opposed to all establishment of religion by government. Therefore, we are in agreement with the Supreme Court's decisions declaring unconstitutional required worship services as part of the public school program. We believe these decisions enhance and strengthen religious liberty within the pluralism that characterizes the United States of America.

We are opposed to any attempts by Congress to take away from the Supreme Court's jurisdiction decisions with respect to school prayer or any other matter that might threaten constitutional proscriptions against "the establishment of religion."

We recognize that religious liberty includes the freedom of an individual to be agnostic, a non-theist, an atheist, or even an anti-theist. Otherwise, the civil community would be invested with authority to establish orthodoxy in matters of belief. We are confident that such a state of affairs would constitute a threat to all religious interests. According to the ethical concept of a responsible society, government commits a morally indefensible act when it imposes upon its people—by force, fear, or other means—the profession or reputation of any belief. Theologically speaking, religious liberty is the freedom that God has given, in his creative act, to all persons to think and to choose belief in God for themselves, including the freedom to doubt and deny God.

5

We recognize that civil authorities have often been leaders in expanding religious liberty. Many times in history it has been constitutions, legislatures, and courts that have served as protectors of religious liberty against the misuse of governmental powers by religious bodies.

At the same time, we believe it is essential to recognize that decisions of the courts with respect to constitutional issues should not be taken as wholly defining desirable relations between churches and governments.

Therefore, while we affirm our support of basic constitutional principles, we believe that if a constitution contains provisions that offend values basic to religious faith or the freedom of religious expression, or if constitutional provisions are being interpreted with that result, it is the right and the duty of churches to speak out in opposition to them.

6

In keeping with our commitment to religious liberty, we are concerned over the recent Internal Revenue Service

119

regulations regarding "integrated auxiliaries" of churches. The IRS has attempted to define which of the Church's organizations are integrated with it functionally and which are not.

Those organizations officially viewed as not being "integrated auxiliaries" will have to fill out informational returns. In time their tax status may be in doubt. The Church's hospitals and children's homes, for example, would not qualify as "integrated auxiliaries."

We believe that it should not be the role of a government agency to determine which Church organizations are integrated into its life and which are not. The Church itself should be given the role of defining which organizations are integral to the Church's mission. If this cannot be accomplished through administrative remedy, then the churches should initiate legislative remedies.

7

In recent years the nation has considered the question of whether government action was needed in coping with "cults." In the context of what follows, the word "cults" means a small religious group with a distinguishing system of beliefs, ritual, and practices.

In protecting the free exercise of religion, the First Amendment does not distinguish between the rights of members of well-established and members of newly-founded religious groups. "Equal protection of the laws" applies to all adherents to religious beliefs. The government may neither support any particular religious group nor limit the freedom of any person to join or remain in any religious body. For constitutional protections to apply to mainline religious groups, they must also protect the most unpopular or despised religious group.

If any cult or religious group imprisons its members by physical force or the threat of such force, the criminal law should be applied to them evenhandedly. However, public officials must also prosecute those who kidnap, assault, and imprison others—under conservatorship orders or otherwise—as a means of compelling renunciation of, or adoption of, beliefs of any kind.

The United Methodist Church supports the right of citizens who have reached the age of majority to accept or reject whatever religious beliefs they choose without facing the charge of "brainwashing."

We are sympathetic to the emotional trauma faced by parents whose children have been drawn into cults whose beliefs most citizens may regard as bizarre or repulsive. At the same time we oppose the physical coercion techniques of deprogramming which seek to "correct" the beliefs of those who have joined cults. If one's adult child adopts religious principles or a life style repugnant to one's own, one should not resort to vigilante-type lawlessness and interference with constitutional liberties. Parental remedies lie in attempting to understand, sympathize, and persuade.

In assessing whether or not governmental action is called for with respects to cults, we propose that the following principles be applied:

1. Investigations of alleged criminal activity within cults should be considered legitimate by appropriate law enforcement officials only so long as they operate within the bounds of normal constitutional standards. Sufficient evidence must exist to justify such a criminal investigation.

2. There should be no legal distinction made between "cults" and "bona fide religious groups." Evidence of criminal or other illegal conduct, not the content of an unpopular belief system, should govern a decision to launch an investigation.

3. Limitations such as the above should also apply to what is considered an appropriate congressional investigation. Unless there is a bona fide legislative purpose, no such investigations should be conducted. The business of the Congress is not to regulate religion. It would be inappropriate for national legislative bodies to deal with religious groups by conducting investigations that are primarily accusatory or prosecutorial.

121

A Statement Concerning Church-Government Relations and Education

1

The fundamental purpose of universal public education at the elementary and secondary levels is to provide equal and adequate educational opportunities for all children and young people, and thereby insure the nation an enlightened citizenry.

We believe in the principle of universal public education, and we reaffirm our support of public educational institutions. At the same time, we recognize and pledge our continued allegiance to the U.S. constitutional principle that citizens have a right to establish and maintain private schools from private resources so long as such schools meet public standards of quality. Such schools have made a genuine contribution to society. We do not support the expansion or the strengthening of private schools with public funds. Furthermore, we oppose the establishment or strengthening of private schools that jeopardize the public school system or thwart valid public policy.

We specifically oppose tuition tax credits or any other mechanism which directly or indirectly allows government funds to support religious schools at the primary and secondary level. Persons of one particular faith should be free to use their own funds to strengthen the belief system of their particular religious group. But they should not expect all taxpayers, including those who adhere to other religious belief systems, to provide funds to teach religious views with which they do not agree.

To fulfill the government's responsibility in education, sometimes it and non-public educational institutions need to enter a cooperative relationship. But public funds should be used only in the best interests of the whole society. Extreme caution must be exercised to assure that religious institutions do not receive any aid directly or indirectly for the maintenance of their religious expression or the expansion of their institutional resources. Such funds must be used for the express purpose of fulfilling a strictly public responsibility, subject to public accountability.

Public schools have often been an important unifying force in modern pluralistic society by providing a setting for contact at an early age between children of vastly different backgrounds. We recognize in particular that persons of all religious backgrounds may have insight into the nature of ultimate reality which will help to enrich the common life. It is therefore essential that the public schools take seriously the religious integrity of each child entrusted to their care. Public schools may not properly establish any preferred form of religion for common exercises of worship, religious observance, or study. At the same time, however, education should provide an opportunity for the examination of the various religious traditions of humankind.

2

We believe that every person has a right to an education, including higher education, commensurate with his or her ability. It is society's responsibility to enable every person to enjoy this right. Public and private institutions should cooperate to provide for these educational opportunities.

3

Freedom of inquiry poses a risk for established ideas, beliefs, programs, and institutions. We accept that risk in the faith that all truth is of God. Colleges and universities can best perform their vital tasks of adding to knowledge and to the perception of truth in an atmosphere of genuine academic freedom.

We affirm the principle that freedom to inquire, to discuss, and to teach should be regulated by the self-discipline of scholarship and the critical examination of ideas in the context of free public dialogue, rather than by supervision, censorship, or any control imposed by churches, governments, or other organizations. In the educational process, individuals have the right to appropriate freely for themselves what they believe is real, important, useful, and satisfying.

4

Experience has demonstrated that freedom to inquire, to discuss, and to teach is best preserved when colleges and universities are not dependent upon a single base or a few sources of support. When an educational institution relies upon multiple sources of financial support, and where those sources tend to balance each other, the institution is in a position to resist undue pressures toward control exerted from any one source of support. In the case of church-related colleges and universities, we believe that tuitions, scholarships, investment returns, bequests, payments for services rendered, loans, government grants, and gifts from individuals, business corporations, foundations, and churches should be sought and accepted in as great a variety as possible. Care must be exercised to insure that all support from any of these sources is free from conditions which hinder the college or university in the maintenance of freedom of inquiry and expression for its faculty and students.

We are very much aware of the dangers of church-sponsored colleges and universities being overly dependent upon government funding. However, we are also aware that, given the independent thought of most college students today, there is little danger of using government funds to indoctrinate students with religious beliefs. Therefore, institutions of higher leaning should feel free to receive government funds (except for religious teaching and structures for worship). At the same time they should be eternally cognizant of the dangers of accompanying government oversight that might threaten the religious atmosphere or special independent character of church-sponsored educational institutions.

No church-sponsored higher education institution should become so dependent upon government grants, research projects, or support programs, that its academic freedom is jeopardized, its responsibility for social criticism (including criticism of governments) inhibited, or its spiritual values denied.

We recognize that the freedom necessary to the existence of a college or university in the classical sense may be threatened by forces other than those involved in the nature and source of the institution's financial support. Institutional freedom may be adversely affected by governmental requirements of loyalty oaths from teachers and students, by public interference with the free flow of information, or by accreditation and certification procedures and requirements aimed at dictating the content of college and university curricula.

With respect to church-related institutions of higher education, we deplore any ecclesiastical attempts to manipulate inquiry or the dissemination of knowledge, to use the academic community for the promotion of any particular point of view, to require ecclesiastical "loyalty oaths" designed to protect cherished truth claims, or to inhibit the social action activities of members of the academic community. We call upon all members of The United Methodist Church, in whatever capacity they may serve, to be especially sensitive to the need to protect individual and institutional freedom and responsibility in the context of the academic community.

5

We are persuaded that there may be circumstances or conditions in which the traditional forms of tax immunities granted to colleges and universities may be a necessary requirement for their freedom. Therefore, we urge a continuation of the public policy of granting reasonable and non-discriminatory tax immunities to all private colleges and universities, including those which are related to churches.

We believe that colleges and universities should consider the benefits, services, and protections which they receive from the community and its governmental agencies, and should examine their obligations to the community in the light of this support. We believe it is imperative that all church-related institutions of higher education determine on their own initiative what benefits, services, and opportunities they ought to provide for the community as a whole as distinct from their usual campus constituencies.

A Statement Concerning Church-Government Relations and Governmental Chaplaincies

1

We recognize that military and public institutional chaplaincies represent efforts to provide for the religious needs of people for whom both churches and governments are responsible. We recognize that in such a broad and complex undertaking there are bound to exist real and serious tensions which produce genuine uneasiness on the part of government officials as well as church leaders. Great patience and skill are required to effect necessary accommodations with understanding and without compromising religious liberty.

2

We believe that there are both ethical and constitutional standards which must be observed by governments in the establishment and operation of public chaplaincies. At a minimum, those standards are as follows:

First, the only obligation which governments have is to assure the provision of opportunities for military personnel, patients of hospitals, and inmates of correctional institutions to engage in religious worship or have access to religious nurture.

Second, participation in religious activities must be on a purely voluntary basis; there must be neither penalties for non-participation nor any rewards for participation.

Third, no preferential treatment should be given any particular church, denomination, or religious group in the establishment and administration of governmental chaplaincies.

Fourth, considerable care should be exercised in the role assignments of chaplains so they are not identified as the enforcers of morals. Precaution should also be taken to avoid chaplains being given duties not clearly related to their primary tasks.

Standards should be maintained to protect the integrity of both churches and governments. The practice of staffing governmental chaplaincies with clergy personnel who have ecclesiastical endorsement should be continued. The practice of terminating the services of such personnel in any instance where it becomes necessary for ecclesiastical endorsement to be withdrawn should also be continued. Supervision of clergy personnel in the performance of their religious services in governmental chaplaincies should be clearly effected through ecclesiastical channels with the cooperation of the public agencies and institutions involved. In the performance of these administrative functions, churches and agencies of government have an obligation to be fair and responsible, and to insure that due process is observed in all proceedings.

3

The role of a governmental chaplain should be primarily pastoral but with important priestly, prophetic, and teaching roles. The chaplain has an obligation to perform these ministries in as broad an ecumenical context as possible. A chaplain is responsible for the spiritual welfare and religious life of all the personnel of the military unit or the public institution to which he/she is assigned.

There are many persons, and some groups, whose personal religious practices or whose church's rules make it impossible for them to accept the direct ministry of a particular chaplain. In such instances, the chaplain, to the full extent of his/her powers, has an obligation to make provision for worship by these persons or groups. A chaplain is expected to answer specific questions by members of faith groups other than his/her own. Chaplains must know the basic tenets of their denominations in order to protect such members in the expression and development of their faith. The absence of parochialism on the part of a chaplain is more than an attitude; it necessitates specific, detailed, and accurate knowledge regarding many religions.

The churches should strive to make public chaplaincies integral expressions of their ministry and to face the implications of this for supervision and budget. The chaplain represents the church by affirming the dignity of all persons in military service through the chaplain's function in upholding their freedom of religion and conscience. Every person exists within a broader set of values than those of the military, and within a broader spectrum of responsibilities than those created by military orders. The chaplain is a bearer of the gospel to affirm the freedom of the individual and represents The United Methodist Church at that point of tension. Whether the freedom of the gospel is compromised or limited may be a result of either external pressures or internal submission, or both. Failure to sustain the freedom of the gospel lies within any human system or any individual. It is the task of the church to prophetically confront institutions or chaplains who compromise the gospel. The United Methodist Church provides presence, oversight, and support to chaplains who risk ministry in such a setting.

There are degrees of tension in present arrangements whereby a chaplain is a commissioned officer of the armed forces or an employee of a public institution. As such, he/she is a member of the staff of the military commander or of the director of the public institution involved. Government regulations and manuals describe him/her as "the advisor on religion, morals, morale, and welfare." Therefore, we believe it is the chaplain's duty in faithfulness to his/her religious commitments to act in accordance with his/her conscience and make such viewpoints known in organizational matters affecting the total welfare of the people for whom the chaplain has any responsibility. The chaplain has the obligation and should have the opportunity to express his/her dissent within the structures in which the chaplain works, in instances where he/she feels this is necessary. With respect to such matters it is the obligation of religious bodies to give the chaplain full support.

Churches must encourage chaplains who serve in the armed forces to resist the exaltation of power and its exercise for its own sake. They must also encourage chaplains who serve in public institutions to maintain sensitivity to human anguish. Churches and chaplains have an obligation to speak out conscientiously against the unforgiving and intransigent spirit in people and nations wherever and whenever it appears.

A Statement Concerning Church-Government Relations and Tax Exemption

1

We believe that governments recognize that unique category of religious institutions. To be in this unique category is not a privilege held by these institutions for their own benefit or self-glorification but is an acknowledgement of their special identity designed to protect their independence and to enable them to serve humankind in a way not expected of other types of institutions.

2

We urge churches to consider at least the following factors in determining their response to the granting of immunity from property taxes:
1. Responsibility to make appropriate contributions for essential services provided by government;
2. The danger that churches become so dependent upon government that they compromise their integrity or fail to exert their critical influence upon public policy.

3

We support the abolition of all special privileges accorded to members of the clergy in U.S. tax laws and regulations and call upon the churches to deal with the consequent financial implications for their ministers. Conversely, we believe that all forms of discrimination against members of the clergy in U.S. tax legislation and administrative regulations should be discontinued. We believe that the status of an individual under ecclesiastical law or practice ought not to be the basis of governmental action either granting or withholding a special tax benefit.

A Statement Concerning Church Participation in Public Affairs

1

We recognize that churches exist within the body politic along with numerous other forms of human association. Like other social groups their existence affects, and is affected by, governments. We believe that churches have the right and the duty to speak and act corporately on those matters of public policy which involve basic moral or ethical issues and questions. Any concept of, or action regarding, church-government relations which denies churches this role in the body politic strikes at the very core of religious liberty.

The attempt to influence the formation and execution of public policy at all levels of government is often the most effective means available to churches to keep before humanity the ideal of a society in which power and order are made to serve the ends of justice and freedom for all people. Through such social action churches generate new ideas, challenge certain goals and methods, and help rearrange the emphasis on particular values in ways that facilitate the adoption and implementation of specific policies and programs which promote the goals of a responsible society.

We believe that any action that would deny the church the right to act corporately on public policy matters threatens religious liberty. We therefore oppose inclusion of churches in any lobby disclosure legislation.

This does not mean that, in any way, we wish to hide actions taken by the church on public issues. On the contrary, we are usually proud of such actions. It does recognize, however, that the church is already responding to members who request information with respect to church action on public policy questions. In effect, in accordance with legislation enacted by the 1976 General Conference, The United Methodist Church already has its own lobby disclosure provisions in place.

It is quite another matter, however, for the government to insist that it must know everything about what a church is saying in its private communications with its own members. When the U.S. Supreme Court acted in the 1971 landmark case of Lemon v. Kurtzman (403 U.S. 602 at pp. 612, 613) the Court applied a test to determine the constitutionality of legislation on First Amendment grounds as it deals with religion. Among its three criteria were these two: (1) its principle or primary effect must neither advance nor inhibit religion; (2) the statute must not foster an excessive government entanglement with religion.

Lobby disclosure legislation before the U.S. Congress over the last several years has required (1) extremely burdensome recordkeeping and reporting of all legislative activity; (2) reporting of contributions of churches giving $3,000 or more annually to a national body if a part of this is used for legislative action; (3) criminal penalties with up to two years in jail for violations; (4) unwarranted subpoena powers to investigate church records.

Legislation which passed the House in 1978 would have required detailed records of expenditures of 22 items. As such, it would have been burdensome and would "inhibit religion" in that The United Methodist Church would have been severely handicapped in implementing its Social Principles due to being neutralized by minutia.

Furthermore, if the government insists on knowing everything the church is doing on public policy questions over a five-year period (as was required) and imposes a criminal sentence for violations, this could "inhibit religion" to the extent that the church might be tempted to limit severely its activity to avoid non-compliance.

If the government is going to require that religious groups keep burdensome records and make voluminous reports, and there is some question as to whether the churches are complying, federal authorities would be authorized to step in and check church records and files. Such action would undoubtedly represent an unconstitutional "excessive government entanglement with religion."

The United Methodist Church would have great difficulty in complying with the provision that all organizational contributions of $3,000 annually be reported if some of these funds are used for lobbying. Since local churches contribute generously to the World Service Dollar, and a small portion of those funds are used for legislative action, this brings our Church under coverage of this provision. Such a requirement could mean that reports of contributions of some 30,000 United Methodist churches would have to be made to the government shortly after the close of each year. This could not be done and we would be in violation having "knowingly" omitted material facts "required to be disclosed." As a result, Church officials would be subject to criminal penalties of up to two years in prison.

For these reasons, we oppose lobby disclosure measures for the churches. In its most stringent form this legislation would inhibit our free exercise of religion. It would be impossible for the Church to comply with certain provisions, thus subjecting our Church leaders to criminal penalties.

3

We believe that churches must behave responsibly in the arena of public affairs. Responsible behavior requires adherence to ethically sound substantive and procedural norms.

We live in a pluralistic society. In such a society, churches should not seek to use the authority of government to make the whole community conform to their particular moral codes. Rather, churches should seek to enlarge and clarify the ethical grounds of public discourse and to identify and define the foreseeable consequences of available choices of public policy.

In participating in the arena of public affairs, churches are not inherently superior to other participants; hence the stands which they take on particular issues of public policy are not above question or criticism.

Responsible behavior in the arena of public affairs requires churches to accept the fact that, in dealing with complex issues of public policy, good intentions and high ideals need to be combined with as much practical and technical knowledge of politics and economics as possible.

Another norm of responsible behavior derives from the fact that no particular public policy which may be endorsed by churches at a given point in time should be regarded as an ultimate expression of Christian ethics in society. Churches should not assume that any particular social pattern, political order, or economic ideology represents a complete embodiment of the Christian ethic.

When churches speak to government they also bear the responsibility to speak to their own memberships. Cultivation of ethically informed public opinion is particularly crucial in local congregations. It is essential to responsible behavior that procedures be established and maintained to insure full, frank, and informed discussion by members and constituents of churches of the decisions and actions of religious groups within the arena of public affairs. In the present period of human history, attention should be given to the dignity of every person and appeal should be made to the consciences of all persons of good will. Churches must acknowledge and respect the role of the laity as well as the clergy in determining their behavior in the arena of public affairs.

Because of their commitment to unity and in the interest of an effective strategy, churches should, to the maximum extent feasible, coordinate their own efforts and, where appropriate, cooperate with other organizations when they seek to influence properly the formation and execution of public policy at all levels of government.

Finally, churches should not seek to utilize the processes of public affairs to further their own institutional interests or to obtain special privileges for themselves.

4

United Methodism is a part of the universal Church. In the formulation and expression of the United Methodist voice in public affairs, we must listen to the concerns and insights of church members and churches in all nations. It is imperative that our expressions and actions be informed by participation in the universal Church.

With particular reference to The United Methodist Church and public affairs, we express the following convictions: Connectional units of the denomination (such as General Conference, Jurisdictional Conference, Annual Conference, local congregation, or general board or agency) should continue to exercise the right to advocate government policies which involve basic moral or ethical issues or questions. In exercising this right, each such connectional unit, or any other official group within The United Methodist Church, should always make explicit for whom or in whose name it speaks or acts in the arena of public affairs. Only the General Conference is competent to speak or act in the name of The United Methodist Church.[7]

The Church's Ministry to
Women in Crisis

New attention and concern have developed for the crisis needs of women. Historically, many of these needs have been overlooked because of the secondary status of women. The United Methodist Church is especially challenged to minister to the needs of women in crisis, because of its support for the self-development of peoples and the empowerment of women. This ministry takes shape in a variety of ways: supportive community of the Church's own fellowship, advocacy for legal justice, counseling that provides understanding without judgmental attitudes. The reconciling and empowering love of God is a fundamental ingredient of ministry to women in crisis.

A crisis occurs whenever life's experiences become overwhelming. As a result, a woman is sometimes locked into situations from which she cannot escape and faces problems which she cannot solve with her usual resources. In transition from inferior to equal status with men, women

[7]*See* Social Principles.

are finding strength to speak about crisis conditions that have existed for generations. Battered women and victims of rape are only two of the several problem areas defined as crisis for women today. Other manifestations are seen when women are widowed, deserted, imprisoned, unemployed, or dependent on alcohol or drugs. For many women, it is not one but several of these conditions that result in crisis.

Many crisis situations become chronic as economic hardship and shrinking natural resources intensify the pressures on women and their families. Women regularly and consistently fare worse economically in many areas of life in the United States such as education, housing, and employment. The 1977 U.S. statistical abstract states that only seven percent of U.S. women fit the "traditional" understanding of family as "non-working" women with an employed husband and two children.[8] Of the women who are employed outside the home, women earned only 59 percent of the median earnings of men for year-round, fulltime work (1977 and 1978 statistics).[9] 79.3 percent of all mothers receiving A.F.D.C. (Aid for Families of Dependent Children) are under 40 years of age.[10] Of these A.F.D.C. mothers, 37.5 percent have graduated from high school only. 30.1 million women who are age 18 or over are single, widowed, divorced, or separated from their spouse. 16.9 million or 59 percent of these have incomes less than $5000 yearly.[11]

Whether short-term or more chronic problems the needs of women and their families are serious. Among these are personal safety, coping with loss and grief, dealing with fear, alienation, and loneliness, financial management,

[8]Women and Work, National Commission on Working Women, Center for Women and Work, 1978, p. 5

[9]Department of Labor, Bureau of Labor Statistics.

[10]Aid to Families with Dependent Children Data, 1975. Recipient Characteristics Studies, Part I, "Demographic and Program Statistics." U.S. Dept. of H.E.W., Social Security Administration, Office of Research and Statistics. HEW Pub. No. A-77-11777.

[11]Current Population Reports, 1976 data. "Money Income and Poverty Status of Families and Persons in U.S." U.S. Dept of Commerce, Bureau of Census, Series P-60, No. 106.

employment, and a need for reliable transportation and child care services. Counseling that enables them to make decisions and find needed services is essential. Whether services are to be supplied by church, government, or community organizations, efforts should be made to secure sound financial and public policy undergirding. Women are best served when they participate in the design and leadership of services.

Therefore we urge:

1. That Annual Conferences and seminaries provide awareness training for pastors to sensitize them to the problems and needs of women in crisis, with special emphasis on counseling skills;

2. That local churches advocate for community services that respond specifically to the needs of battered women, victims of rape, displaced homemakers, and unemployed women;

3. That the Church at every level provide opportunities for both lay and clergy to deal with physical violence, economic exploitation, loss and dependency;

4. That The United Methodist Church work through appropriate channels to initiate and support government policies that provide needed social services to women in crisis;

5. That appropriate agencies support research and evaluation of the impact of social services on women and their families.[12]

Comity Agreements Affecting Development of Native American Ministries by The United Methodist Church

WHEREAS, certain Annual Conferences of The United Methodist Church have used the alleged Comity Agreement as the basis for their functional relationship among Native Americans, limiting their capability to develop

---

[12]*See* Social Principles III-F; "Equal Rights of Women," 1984; "The Status of Women," 1980.

Native American ministries in certain geographical areas, and

WHEREAS, the effects of practicing the concept of a Comity Agreement by The United Methodist Church have resulted in the failure of the Church to follow through with the biblical mandate of propagating the gospel to all nations and, further, caused the failure of the Church to create the climate for leadership development of Native Americans, and

WHEREAS, it is concluded, on the basis of data collected, that a Comity Agreement limiting The United Methodist Church to certain geographical areas of ministry to Native Americans, does not exist, and

WHEREAS, such a Comity Agreement would be discriminatory in that it would violate the right of Native Americans to associate with the denomination of their choice, now

Therefore Be It Resolved, that the 1980 General Conference be requested to approve the following resolution for inclusion in the 1980 Book of Resolutions and subsequent publications:

That The United Methodist Church states, as a matter of policy, that it is not a party to any interdenominational agreement that limits the ability of any Annual Conference in any jurisdiction to develop and resource programs of ministry of any kind among Native Americans, including the organization of local churches where necessary.[13]

Concern for Persons in Poverty

We are aware of the plight of many in our country who do not have enough of the necessities of life to live as human beings, and

We know that some are caught in a depressing cycle that makes it difficult for them to move out of their plight, and

We, as Christians, accept the responsibility of trying to

[13]*See* "The United Methodist Church and America's Native Peoples," 1980.

provide sustenance, encouragement, education, and motivation to the poor to join the mainstream of society, and

We recognize that if we are to accomplish these goals of raising persons' standards of living we

Must request that federal minimum standards be set that will more nearly equalize welfare support in various states,

Must challenge the welfare systems of the states, and the nation, to recognize that the poor have both rights and responsibilities, and

Must reaffirm the statement on "National Income Policy and Social Welfare" that was adopted by the 1976 General Conference, and

Must urge our United Methodist Church and members to learn first hand about their local welfare systems and encourage more effective use of the resources available to serve the poor.

Therefore be it resolved that we request the boards and agencies of The United Methodist Church to include concerns for the persons in poverty to the end that the Church will make every effort to influence public action so that the rights of all persons will be protected.[14]

Concerning the Draft
in the United States

The General Conference of 1980 in session in Indianapolis is to transmit by special messengers an urgent message to the President of the United States. Messengers for this mission shall be named by the Council of Bishops and include, in addition to the president of the Council, six persons: one laywoman, one clergywoman, one layman, one clergyman, and two youth members (one male and one female). At least two of the six members shall be of racial or ethnic minorities.

Such a plan for communicating with the President of the United States today, in a new kind of world and for a

[14]*See* Social Principles IV-E; "Advocacy for the Poor," 1984.

different purpose, is in keeping with a tradition of the early history of Methodism. Deputations of distinguished persons were sent from time to time to convey messages of support or commendation to the President from the General Conference. Among these communications, history records the visit to President George Washington in 1789, expressing gratitude to him "for the preservation of civil and religious liberties and for the glorious revolution." Again in 1864, when General Conference convened in Philadelphia, the first order of business after the flag raising was to name a delegation to call on President Lincoln to assure him of the unfaltering support of Methodists in the war against slavery. Lincoln's response expressed gratitude that "The Methodist Church sends more soldiers to the field, more nurses to the hospitals, and more prayers to heaven than any" (Charles Ferguson, *Organizing to Beat the Devil*).

The basic content and guidelines of the message to the President today shall be as follows:

The 1980 General Conference of The United Methodist Church, which includes 912 duly elected delegates from 73 annual conferences across the United States of America, respectfully calls upon the President of the United States to rescind his announced policy calling for registration of youths in this land. We believe this will lead to the possible renewal of the draft into military service. We also believe that such a presidential plan has already increased the war hysteria in our own nation and generated greater tension among the Middle East nations and their neighbors.

We acknowledge that the issues are complex in today's military-industrial economy, but we believe that a peace-minded nation, such as we claim to be, needs your leadership as a President committed to peace. Your State of the Union message and your call for a great and continuing increase in defense weaponry, renewed registration of youths for a potential draft, and greatly strengthened military power seem to rule out all means for peaceful negotiation and the resolution of the conflict through United Nations and/or in cooperation with other concerned nations.

139

In the words of the 1976 action of this governing body of The United Methodist Church, "One hard fact must be bluntly stated: The arms race goes on. The momentum never slackens, and the danger of a holocaust is imminent. Meanwhile, millions starve, development stagnates, and international cooperation is threatened." We, the policy-making body of this world-wide Church, pray that you will reverse your policy of dangerous military threats and fulfill your commitment to peace. We do not believe that one life, man's or woman's, should be sacrificed in a war in this period of history when the global community provides untapped means for negotiation and the reconciliation of differences.

Therefore it is with the deepest concern and the greatest urgency that we call upon you, as President of the United States, to end the threat in this nation of registration of the youths of this land. We believe that such an act is clearly a basic step toward reinstating the draft. The question before us at this time is not whether both men and women should be registered and drafted for military service. The issue, in this enlightened beginning of our third century as a nation, is leadership in a world where war seems imminent and where the peoples of the world cry out to be saved from nuclear holocaust. We pray that God will give you wisdom and courage to take the necessary action for peace on earth—now![15]

Declare Zoar United Methodist Church a Primary Historical Emphasis

WHEREAS the Eastern Pennsylvania Annual Conference has declared Zoar United Methodist Church of Philadelphia, Pennsylvania to be an historic site;

AND WHEREAS the Annual Conference has declared Zoar

[15]See Social Principles V-G; "The United Methodist Church and Peace," 1984; "Certification of Conscientious Objectors;" "The United Methodist Church and Conscription," 1980.

United Methodist Church to be its primary historical emphasis for the 1980s and has committed itself to provide funds toward the refurbishing of the church;

AND WHEREAS the Annual Conference has undertaken appropriate research and development of the church as an historical center for United Methodism;

Therefore, Be It Resolved, that the General Conference of The United Methodist Church likewise declares Zoar United Methodist Church of Philadelphia to be one of its primary historical emphases for the 1980s.

Democracy and Religious Freedom

We believe that respect for human rights has its roots in the biblical notion, made manifest by Christ's treatment of all those who experienced his teaching, that respect for human dignity is commanded by the divine presence within each individual human being. We believe that people have a right to live their lives free from fear of torture, cruel and degrading psychological and physical punishment, arbitrary arrest and imprisonment without trial, invasion of the home, forcible separation of family members, enforced starvation, denial of emigration and employment, forced labor, acts of terrorism, racial discrimination, and all other violations of the integrity of the person.

We believe that people have the right to freedom of expression and freedom of association. The denial of these rights represents a violation of the integrity of the community, destroying people's ability to communicate with each other and with people in other lands, to organize themselves in pursuit of common aspirations, to worship with each other in privacy, and to engage in other social and communal undertakings.

We believe that people have the right to choose their own government through democratic, competitive elections, free from internal or external coercion. Countries that respect these democratic rights are much more likely to respect the integrity of individual and communal rights as well.

141

We support the aspirations and struggles of people to achieve higher living standards, better health care, and greater access to education and economic opportunity. However, we reject the idea that these "economic and social rights," as they are sometimes called, take precedence over individual, communal, and democratic rights. We believe that the best guarantee that people will ultimately achieve economic and social betterment is a system that protects their freedom to organize for these purposes.

We believe in freedom of religion, and we recognize the special threat to missionary activity that is posed by the evil of totalitarianism.

We believe in a single standard of human rights. Evil must be recognized as evil, whether it occurs in "progressive" or "capitalist" regimes, and whether it is rationalized by right wing or left wing ideologies. We recognize that the important criterion in judging human rights is not the economic system, which people should be able to choose for themselves, but the degree of freedom.

We unalterably oppose all governmental systems that deny human rights to the people within their borders, including facism, communism, apartheid, and all forms of military and authoritarian dictatorship. And those which, in addition to internal repression, seek to impose their tyrannies beyond their borders by means of military force, terror, and subversion.[16]

Drug and Alcohol Concerns

I. *Introduction*

We recognize the widespread use and misuse of drugs which alter mood, perception, consciousness, and behavior of persons among all ages, classes, and segments of our society. We express deep concern for those persons who must depend on the effects of chemical substances to

[16]*See* Social Principles V-A; "Religious Freedom," 1980.

medicate emotional problems or to meet personal, social, and/or recreational needs to an extent that debilitates the individual's health or functioning.

The church can offer a religious and moral heritage which views each individual as a person of infinite worth and significance, sees meaning and purpose in all of life, supports the individual and the society in the quest for wholeness and fulfillment, and seeks healing for the afflicted and liberty for the oppressed. The church should act to develop and support conditions in which responsible decision-making by both individuals and corporate bodies can occur.

We are also deeply concerned about the widespread ignorance and fear of drugs and their effects on the part of the general public. Such lack of knowledge and understanding makes for hysterical and irrational responses. Humane and rational approaches to solutions require an enlightened public capable of making discriminating judgments.

We understand the drug problem to be a "people problem" rather than merely a chemical, medical, or legal problem. As such, a human problems approach is required, focusing on why people use drugs, the meaning and significance of drugs in their lives, and the social and cultural conditions which may contribute to or alleviate the destructive use of drugs. Such an approach sees drug use and misuse in the larger context of health care, inadequate education and inadequate substandard housing, poverty in the midst of plenty, affluence without meaning, rapid social change and technological development, changing moral values and growing alienation, hostility and war between peoples, environmental pollution, the waste of natural resources, the quest for purpose and meaning to life, and the lack of self-understanding, self-affirmation and self-reliance.

The human problems approach is interdisciplinary; i.e., it involves all relevant fields of human knowledge in the search for solutions. It requires community involvement from professionals, self-help groups, volunteer agencies, and concerned individuals in the public and private sectors. Such active mobilization of community resources makes possible the consideration of all relevant dimensions of the situation, personal and social.

With all the conflicting opinions and misinformation available, accurate definitions are essential to clear understanding and constructive action on human problems involving the use and misuse of drugs. Pharmacologically, a drug is "any substance which by its chemical nature alters the structure or function of the human organism." This broad definition encompasses a wide range of substances, including medicines, food additives, and household remedies such as aspirin, as well as psychoactive substances such as alcohol, tobacco, caffeine, heroin, barbiturates, amphetamines, *cannabis sativa* (marijuana), tranquilizers, LSD, and miscellaneous substances such as glue and paint thinner. Even the proper medical use of drugs under guidance of a competent physician carries risks to health and functioning, and nonmedical use increases those risks considerably.

We understand drug use to mean taking a substance responsibly in the appropriate amount, frequency, strength, and manner that is likely to result in physical, psychological, and social well-being. We understand drug misuse to mean taking a substance irresponsibly in an amount, frequency, strength, or manner that is likely to result in damage to the user's health or impair his or her ability to function psychologically, socially, or vocationally, or proves harmful to society. The meaning of drug abuse is covered in the definition of misuse and is thus omitted, since it has generally confused rather than clarified understanding. No drug may be considered harmless, but the effects of any given drug must be judged in the light of such variables as dosage, manner of ingestion, the user's personality and disposition, and the social setting in which the drug is taken.

The ministry of the Church should be directed both to the prevention and the treatment of problems related to drug use and misuse. All members of society, including churchmen and churchwomen, should become thoroughly informed about drug issues so that they can make intelligent

144

and responsible decisions about personal use and social policy controlling drug use. Therefore:

1. We encourage and seek funding for the Church and the larger community to develop various forms of drug education for children, youths, and adults that deal with drug issues in an honest, objective, and factual manner. Informed public discussion is essential to enlightened public action.

2. We urge churches and their members to join with others engaged in positive and constructive programs of prevention and treatment to form a comprehensive, ecumenical, interfaith, and multi-disciplinary approach to the wide range of drug problems. The total resources of the community need to be mobilized. Therefore, churches should become involved in prevention and rehabilitation efforts and should encourage and support community-wide efforts to provide services and facilities to the total population in need.

3. We call upon the helping professions in general to develop an increased awareness of drug problems and to utilize their various skills in the search for solutions to these problems. The pastor should serve as a member of this interprofessional community service team.

4. We encourage public schools to integrate drug education into the curriculum in such a way that children and youths of the total community may learn about drugs in an open and supportive atmosphere that facilitates personal growth and responsible decision-making.

5. We urge professional schools in theology, medicine, education, and other graduate schools to develop drug education courses for the training of their students. Opportunities for continuing education and in-service training should also be provided for these professionals.

6. We encourage the efforts by city, state, and national government to find ways and means to deal with people who have drug-related problems within the framework of social, health, and rehabilitation services, rather than in the framework of law and punishment. The fundamental role of law enforcement agencies should be to reduce the traffic

in drugs by apprehending the professional profiteers. We ask legislative bodies to provide sufficient funding for an adequate drug education program.

7. We call upon members of the medical profession to join with the church, all community agencies, and government in finding ways and means of preventing the misuse of those drugs intended to be therapeutic.

8. We urge research into the effects, the extent, the causes, the prevention, and the treatment of all aspects of the use and misuse of drugs, and believe that such research is urgent and should be pursued in an atmosphere of flexibility and freedom.

9. We support the efforts of the President, the Congress, and state legislative bodies to develop social policy about drugs that is rational, humane, based on factual evidence, and commensurate with the known dangers of the drugs to the individual and to society.

II. *Alcohol*

Alcohol presents a special case of drug abuse because of its widespread social acceptance. We affirm our long-standing conviction and recommendation that abstention from the use of alcoholic beverages is a faithful witness to God's liberating and redeeming love.

This witness is especially relevant in a pluralistic society where drinking is so uncritically accepted and practiced; where excessive, harmful, and dangerous drinking patterns are so common; where destructive reasons for drinking are so glamorized that youthful immaturity can be exploited for personal gain; where alcohol contributes to a great proportion of fatal traffic and industrial accidents; where millions of individuals and their families suffer from alcoholism and countless others from various drinking problems, and where alcohol is a factor in many other social problems such as crime, poverty, and family disorder.

Thus the recommendation of abstinence to members of The United Methodist Church is based on a critical appraisal of the personal and socio-cultural factors in and surrounding alcohol use, the detrimental effects of irresponsible drinking on the individual and society, and a concrete judgment regarding what love demands. The Church recognizes the freedom of the Christian to make responsible decisions and calls upon each member to consider seriously and prayerfully the witness of abstinence as a part of his or her equipment for Christian mission in the world. The understanding of the social forces that influence people either to drink or to abstain must be encouraged. Christian love in human relationships is primary, thereby making abstinence an instrument of love and always subject to the requirements of love. Persons who practice abstinence should avoid attitudes of self-righteousness which express moral superiority and condemnatory attitudes toward those who do not abstain.

We believe that concern for the problems of alcohol carries with it the inherent obligation to seek the healing and justice in society that will alleviate the social conditions which contribute to and issue from alcohol problems. Therefore:

1. We urge every local congregation and each member to demonstrate an active concern for alcoholics and their families and for all persons with drinking problems.

2. We urge all legislative bodies and health care systems to focus on and implement measures to meet the special needs of women, racial minorities, juveniles, and the elderly. Basic to this concern is an informed mind and compassionate heart which views the alcoholic without moralism and with empathy.

3. We urge churches to make education about alcohol problems and the value of abstinence an integral part of all drug education efforts.

4. We encourage churches to develop special action programs on alcohol problems which include prevention education in the family, church, and community; utilizing mass media to develop responsible attitudes toward alcohol-related problems; care, treatment, and rehabilitation of problem drinkers; measures to prevent persons from driving while under the influence of alcohol; the

achievement of appropriate and effective legal controls; and the stimulation of sound empirical research.

5. We favor laws to eliminate the advertising of alcoholic beverages. Working toward this end, we urge the Board of Church and Society and local churches to increase efforts to remove all advertising of alcoholic beverages from television (as was done with cigarette advertising). We urge special attention to curbing promotions on use of alcoholic beverages on college campuses.

6. We urge the health system, especially United Methodist-related hospitals, to accept alcoholism as a medical-social-behavioral problem and to treat the alcoholic person with the same attention and consideration as is given any other patient.

7. We urge the Federal Trade Commission to develop a health hazard warning statement concerning the use of alcohol as a beverage, and that it be affixed to all alcoholic beverages offered for sale.

8. We urge the federal government to coordinate its drug and alcohol abuse efforts in treatment and prevention.

9. We urge all United Methodist Churches in the United States to work for a minimum legal drinking age of 21 years in their respective states.

III. *Tobacco*

Tobacco presents another special case of drug abuse. Constrained by the overwhelming evidence linking cigarette smoking with lung cancer, cardio-vascular diseases, emphysema, chronic bronchitis, and related illnesses, and moved to seek the health and well-being of all persons, we urge private and public health organizations to initiate intensive programs to demonstrate the link between smoking and disease. The United Methodist Church discourages persons, particularly youths and young adults, from taking up this generally habit-forming practice.

We are especially concerned about the portrayal of smoking in connection with commercial advertising. We commend the suspension of cigarette advertising on radio and television. Smoking in other advertisements is still depicted in ways which identify it with physical and social maturity, attractiveness, and success. We support the Federal Trade Commission's rules requiring health warning statements in cigarette packaging.

1. We support expanded research to discover the specific agents in tobacco which damage health, to develop educational methods which effectively discourage smoking, to organize services to assist those who wish to stop smoking.

2. We urge the Department of Agriculture and other government agencies to plan for and assist the orderly economic transition of the tobacco industry—tobacco growers, processors, and distributors into other, more benign, lines of production.

3. We recommend that tobacco smoking in our churches and in other public facilities be discouraged in support of the right of non-smokers to clean air.

4. We recommend the prohibition of commercial advertising of tobacco products in order to reduce enticement toward use of a proven health hazard.

IV. *Marijuana*

Marijuana is one form of the common hemp plant, *cannabis sativa,* which consists of the dried and crushed leaves and flowering tops of the plants. High concentration of the plant resin alone is called hashish, and is six to eight times as potent as the usual marijuana.

Recent studies by the Department of Health, Education and Welfare show (1) increases in the use of marijuana, especially by youths between the ages of 12 and 17, (2) that as many as 43 million Americans have tried marijuana at least once and 16 million use it regularly, (3) that one marijuana cigarette produces as much airway obstruction as 16 tobacco cigarettes, and that despite marijuana decriminalization efforts on the part of many states, in excess of 400,000 persons were arrested for possession of marijuana in 1978. Researchers contend that marijuana use will continue to rise among youths and other age groups.

Research conducted at the Institute of Behavioral Science at the University of Colorado concluded that "Personal control variables—whether religiosity, moral standards, or attitudes about transgression—were shown to be powerful in regulating whether marijuana use occurred at all, how early, and with what degree of involvement."

We recommend the following:

1. Abstinence from the use of marijuana.

2. The elimination of criminal penalties for possession of small amounts of marijuana not to exceed one ounce, for personal use. The social costs of wrecked lives and careers, especially among young people, and of wasted law enforcement resources involved with continued criminal prohibition far outweigh the harm caused by the misuse of the drug. This recommendation in no way, however, implies approval or encouragement of marijuana use or its legalization.

3. Therefore, we urge that special attention be given to marijuana in drug education programs. It is necessary to deal with the fear and misinformation which surround attitudes about this drug in order that discussion can be conducted on a rational basis.

4. We continue to support strong law enforcement efforts against the illegal sale of all drugs.

5. We encourage a review of cases of persons already serving sentences for use or possession of marijuana committed prior to reforms which reduce penalties for such use or possession.

6. We encourage continued medical and scientific research to determine the potential dangers of marijuana use to the individual.

7. We urge development of a social policy regarding the use of marijuana based upon accurate knowledge and enlightened understanding.

V. *Narcotics*

Narcotics are a group of drugs whose analgesic action relieves pain and produces sleep or stupor. They include derivatives of the opium plant such as heroin, morphine, codeine, and percodan, and synthetic substances such as methadone and meperidine. Medically, narcotics are employed primarily for the relief of pain, but the risk of physical and psychological dependence is well established. Dependence of both kinds refers to compulsive behavior characterized by a preoccupation with procuring and using the drug. The exact number of persons, commonly called "addicts," dependent on self-administered doses is unknown, but estimates place the number as high as 456,000.

The action of the narcotic reduces hunger, pain, and aggressive and sexual drives; it is the desire or need for the drug rather than its effects which motivates criminal activity associated with compulsive narcotic abuse. While the availability of heroin has long been prevalent in many inner-city ghetto communities, it is a growing problem in all segments of our society. Therefore:

1. We urge members of the Church to consider the compulsive users of narcotics as persons in need of treatment and rehabilitation, and to show compassion and supportive concern for them and their families.

2. We urge that public, private, and Church funds be made available for prevention of drug abuse and for treatment and rehabilitation methods for compulsive narcotic users, including types of chemical therapy, which emphasize becoming productive and emotionally stable members of society.

3. We urge continual reform of the law to make it easier for the compulsive users to be treated not as criminals, but as persons in need of medical attention, psychiatric treatment, pastoral care, and social rehabilitation.

4. We support strong enforcement measures aimed at reducing the illegitimate organized production, manufacture, distribution and sale of narcotics for profit.

VI. *Sedatives and Stimulants*

Sedatives are used therapeutically to treat anxiety, induce sleep, control convulsions, and also as muscle relaxants.

151

Barbiturates and minor tranquilizers are the sedatives most commonly prescribed by physicians.

Although major tranquilizers may properly be prescribed to treat mental illnesses such as schizophrenia, the use of such drugs to relieve emotional stresses of everyday living constitutes misuse as well as irresponsible prescribing practice.

Severe physical dependence on barbiturates can develop at doses higher than therapeutic doses, and withdrawal is severe and dangerous. Overdose of barbiturates is currently one of the major methods of committing suicide. Accidental overdoses sometimes occur when sleeping pills are left by the side of the bed and an already sedated, confused person ingests a lethal dose. Alcohol and barbiturates combined multiply their effects so that drinking after taking medication is especially hazardous. Enough barbiturate capsules are manufactured by pharmaceutical companies annually to supply approximately thirty capsules for each person in the United States. A significant proportion of these legitimately produced pills are diverted into illegitimate channels.

Stimulants produce a sense of vitality, alertness, and energy plus the ability to do without sleep for long periods. Stimulants include amphetamines, cocaine, and mild stimulants such as caffeine and nicotine. Therapeutically they are used to treat obesity, narcolepsy, hyperkinesis, fatigue, and depression.

Recent studies by the Department of Health, Education and Welfare on amphetamines (uppers, speed, etc.) show their excessive use causing increased blood pressure, brain damage, kidney failure, severe weight loss and malnutrition, irritability, violence, and severe delusions of persecution.

The stimulant misuser cannot be stereotyped but ranges from the diet pill abuser to the "speed freak." Few people die from the direct overuse of stimulants, but long-term misuse may result in disorientation and paranoid psychosis. Stimulants are not a magic source of energy, but instead push the user to a greater expenditure of his or her own physical resources often to a hazardous point of fatigue. The body builds a tolerance so that larger doses are required to maintain the same "high." Stimulants such as amphetamines are available legally on a written prescription of a physician. These prescriptions cannot be refilled, but can be obtained from one or more physicians, and filled by one or more pharmacists. Therefore:

1. We urge members of the medical profession to exercise special care in their prescription of sedatives and stimulants and that they provide therapeutic nonchemical alternatives where available and possible, especially to those eligible for third party payments.

2. We urge the federal government to take the necessary protective steps to curtail excessive production and distribution of sedative and stimulant drugs by setting quotas, requiring precise record-keeping of receipts, and positions to be filed with the government periodically, and the insuring of adequate drug storage procedures by the manufacturer and wholesalers through licensing requirements.

3. We call upon both the governmental and private sectors of society to develop cooperatively a comprehensive regulatory system in which the drug industry, the drug distributors, advertisers, the medical profession and the consumers will be required to assume collective responsibility for the proper production, distribution, promotion, and the use of prescription and nonprescription drugs.

4. We call upon the mass media, advertising agencies, and the drug companies to frame advertisements which promote appropriate drug use rather than to encourage their indiscriminate use to solve personal problems.

5. Because mood-altering drugs have often been promoted and prescribed for uses beyond those that are medically indicated, we recommend (1) the development of an independent drug information/evaluation system; (2) the upgrading of medical school training in regard to the prescribing of mood-altering drugs as well as post-graduate education for already practicing physicians; (3) the education of the public to the inherent dangers and inappropriate uses of such substances.

6. We encourage and support the efforts of the federal government to continue to monitor and reduce the manufacture and distribution of amphetamines.

VII. *Psychedelics or Hallucinogens*

Psychedelics or hallucinogens are a class of drugs which include LSD, psilocibin, mescaline, PCP, and DMT. These drugs produce radical changes in perception and altered states of consciousness. "Hallucinogenic" refers to the illusion-producing properties of these drugs, and psychedelic means, literally, mind-opening. PCP (Phencyclidine, Angel Dust) has been determined by the Federal government to have no recommended human medical use. It is a depressant, although it is sold on the street as an hallucinogen. Depending on the dosage, PCP can cause increased heart rate, elevated blood pressure, flushing, sweating, impaired coordination, speech and vision, drooling, nausea, and vomiting. The simple manufacture and easy distribution of PCP enables its production by a vast number of persons, making it the current drug of choice of the 15 to 25 year old age group in the United States.

Scientific experimentation to determine therapeutic uses for LSD-type drugs includes treatment of alcoholism, narcotic addiction, and terminal cancer patients. As far as is now known, these drugs do not produce physical dependence. The full dangers are still under investigation.

Some persons take LSD in the search for self-knowledge and self-awareness, others in quest of mystical or religious consciousness, still others because of disillusionment with reality and rebellion. Casual or promiscuous use is particularly hazardous since serious adverse reactions are common where warm and supportive settings are absent. These dangers include fear and panic which can lead to bizarre and self-destructive behavior or temporary psychosis. Long-term risks include prolonged depression, paranoia, psychosis, and the "flashback"—the recurrence of some aspect of the drug experience after the influence of the drug has gone. Buying LSD-type drugs through illicit channels carries the additional large dangers of unknown dosage and impure forms. Therefore:

1. We urge individuals to refrain from the use of psychedelics.

2. We urge modification of current legal controls of psychedelic drugs in order to make possible more controlled professional therapeutic research with these drugs.

3. We call upon the churches to demonstrate actively their concern for those who use such drugs.[17]

El Salvador

In El Salvador, Archbishop Oscar Romero stood out in the midst of his country's strife as a prophetic Christian leader, concerned for the poor and committed to an end of oppression and violence. His assassination should move Christians everywhere to action for economic justice and human rights that will provide the conditions for internal peace.

Shortly before his assassination, the Archbishop addressed a letter to the President of the United States asking that no further military aid be sent to the government of El Salvador while the repression and violence there continued. His appeal went unheeded, and the funding for military supplies was readily granted.

In view of our Christian commitment, it is recommended:

A. United States to reconsider and cancel the shipment of military supplies to El Salvador as pleaded by Archbishop Romero; and

B. That this General Conference express regret, sympathy, and solidarity with the people of El Salvador for the loss of their spiritual leader and champion who spoke on behalf of their human rights;

[17]See Social Principles III-I; "Alcohol as a Health Problem," 1984.

C. That the Secretary of the General Conference be instructed to send a letter to our Christian brothers and sisters of the Roman Catholic Church of El Salvador conveying our concern and expressing support for their continued ministry as exemplified by Archbishop Romero;

D. That a copy of this resolution be sent to appropriate Congressional leaders and to the Vatican.[18]

Energy Policy Statement

Preamble

In 1979 our nation experienced two shocks which are compelling us to reassess our energy future: the revolution in Iran and the accident at Three Mile Island. It is already clear that by the turn of this century our sources of power will be radically altered. Just as the first half of this century was marked by a rapid shift from wood, water, and coal to the fossil fuels that currently supply 90 percent of the U.S. energy needs, so we today are at the beginning of a rapid transition from these fuels, which are running out, to the renewable sources which must supply our energy future. Because society runs on its energy and is shaped by the fuels it uses and the way it uses them, we will, in effect, be shaping a new world by the energy policies we adopt in the next few decades. The stakes are high: the decisions which human societies are now making will either enhance or degrade the quality of life on our planet; they will either more closely approximate the vision of the reign of God which fires the Christian imagination or they will make that vision more remote from actual human existence. Furthermore, as our world comes up against limits and undergoes the stress of rapid change, fears will be raised and conflicts will become inevitable. Our responses to these stresses can either produce more repressive societies or ones in which liberty is enhanced.

[18]*See* "Concern for Human Rights in Central America," 1984.

Stewards of the Spaceship Earth

The recognition that a new world is emerging and that the Church of Jesus Christ may have a role to play in shaping that world calls us to re-examine the biblical sources out of which we as Christians live our lives.

Humankind enjoys a unique place in God's universe. On the one hand we are simply one of God's many finite creatures, made from the "dust of the earth," bounded in time and space, fallible in judgment, limited in control, dependent upon our Creator, and interdependent with all other creatures. On the other hand we are created in the very image of God, with the divine spirit breathed into us, and entrusted with "dominion" over God's creation (Gen. 1:26, 28; 2:7, Ps. 8:6). We are simultaneously co-creatures with all creation, and, because of the divine summons, co-creators with God of the world in which we live. This hybrid human condition produces both the opportunity and the twin dangers for humans on this planet.

The first danger is arrogance: that we may overestimate the extent of human control over our environment and the soundness of human judgments concerning it (after all, we still know very little about the ecosystem in which we live); that we may underestimate the limits of the planet where we live; and that we may misunderstand "dominion" to mean exploitation instead of stewardship.

The second danger is irresponsibility: that we may fail to be the responsible stewards of the earth that God has called us to be, choosing instead to bury our "talents" while awaiting the Master's return (Mt. 25:24-28). As stewards entrusted with dominion, then, we will demonstrate our faith in God by becoming God's avante garde in shaping the new human society which will emerge in the twenty-first century. We cannot, therefore, eschew the task of seeking to embody in the new-world-aborning the values which we hold in covenant with God. At the same time, however, we dare not overlook the limits of our control; nor can we forget the forgiving grace in Jesus Christ which alone makes us bold enough or the hope in Christ which alone keeps us from despair.

The Values Involved in Energy Policy

The scripture which provides the motive for our action in the present energy crisis also lays the foundation for the values which we seek to realize. These values underlying the policies we advocate are justice and sustainability.

1. *Justice.* Ever since the first covenant between God and Israel, and especially since the eighth century prophets, the people of God have understood that they bear a special concern for justice. "Let justice roll down like waters, and righteousness like an everflowing stream" (Amos 5:24) is a cry echoed in hundreds of contexts throughout the Old and New Testaments. Biblical righteousness includes a special concern for the least and the last: the poor, the captive, the oppressed (Lk. 4:18; cf. Isa. 61:1-2). Energy policies which Christians can support, then, will seek to actualize the multifaceted biblical vision of justice. They will be policies which close rather than widen the gap dividing wealth and poverty, rich nations and poor. They will be measures which liberate rather than oppress. They will be programs which distribute fairly the benefits, burdens, and hazards of energy production and consumption, taking into consideration those not yet born as well as the living. They will thus be strategies which give priority to meeting basic human needs, such as air, water, food, clothing, and shelter.

2. *Sustainability.* Only recently have we humans come to recognize that creation (finitude) entails limits to the resources entrusted to us as stewards of the earth. In particular we have come up against limits to the non-renewable fuels available for our consumption and limits to our environment's capacity to absorb poisonous wastes. These double limits mean that humans can betray their stewardship either by using up resources faster than they can be replaced or by releasing wastes in excess of the planet's capacity to absorb them. We now know that humans have the capacity to destroy human life and perhaps even life itself on this planet, and to do so in a very short period of time. Energy policy decisions, therefore, must be measured by sustainability as a criterion in addition to justice. In terms

of energy policy, sustainability means energy use which will not (a) deplete the earth's resources in such a way that our descendents will not be able to continue human society at the level which is adequate for a good quality of life, and (b) pollute the environment to such an extent that human life cannot be sustained in the future. These guidelines for sustainability must include considerations of quality of life as well as mere biological continuance.

Until such time as a truly inexhaustible source of power is developed, we must create and expand all of the energy resources available to us with special emphasis on renewable energy resources. We enjoy a highly sophisticated, industrialized world. It is not a realistic option for us to retrogress to a world where people read by candlelight and heat with wood. Also we should be aware of the tragic effects that steadily increasing energy costs will have, especially upon the aged and poor members of our society. All options available in the United States are not open to peoples in other parts of the world; hence we should endeavor to develop all available energy sources. We must creatively explore all of the energy options available to us.

There are environmental problems connected with these energy options that cause people to raise objections to their development and use. We believe that the objections to each energy source should be calmly assessed and then the risks and benefits of its use compared with the use of the other energy options. For example, the large-scale use of our coal resources poses many problems. Underground mining, in addition to operational accidents, causes disabling illness or death from black lung. Strip mining can despoil an area and ruin it for further use if restoration measures are not practiced. The actual burning of coal causes large-scale pollution and could seriously alter the environment by increasing the CO_2 content of the atmospheric envelope.

Hydroelectric power also has its problems. In addition to deaths from industrial accidents, many dam sites are (or were) attractive scenic areas. Destroying (or diminishing) such natural beauty areas as the Grand Canyon would be objectionable to most of us. Possible dam failure with the

159

resultant flood damage must also be considered in evaluation of this source of power.

The use of petroleum products creates environmental problems which are on the increase. Tankers and off-shore wells have created spills which have devastated sea coast areas; the damage is long-lasting or permanent. Atmospheric pollution, far from being under control, is a most serious health problem in centers of dense population.

Our nuclear energy option also has many problems to be faced. The hazards in storing radioactive wastes for thousands of years and the destructive potential of a catastrophic accident involve a great risk of irreversible damage to the environment or to the human genetic pool.

1. We support a strenuous national effort to conserve energy. Economists have concluded that in the next decade a greater increase in end-use energy can be gained through conservation than through any single new source of fuel. Furthermore, conservation is non-polluting and job-producing. We include under conservation: insulation, cogeneration, recycling, public transportation, more efficient motors in appliances and automobiles, as well as the elimination of waste and more simplified lifestyle. The technology for such steps is already known and commercially available; it requires only dissemination of information and stronger public support, including larger tax incentives than are presently available.

2. All United Methodist churches are encouraged to be models for energy conservation by doing such things as: installing dampers in furnaces, insulating adequately all church properties, heating and lighting only rooms that are in use, using air circulation, and exploring alternative energy sources such as solar energy.

3. We also urge all our members and agencies to assess their own energy consumption, finding ways to conserve, to eliminate waste, to revise transportation patterns, and to simplify lifestyles as a model for sound stewardship of the limited resources entrusted to us.

4. We support increased government funding for research and development of renewable energy sources,

especially solar energy, and government incentives to speed the application of the resulting technologies to our energy needs, wherever appropriate. The greatest national effort should be made in the areas of conservation and renewable energy sources.

5. We oppose any national energy policy which will result in continuing exploitation of Native American lands without the consent of the persons who control those lands. The despoiling of Native American lands and the increased health problems which have resulted among Native Americans because of the mining of coal and the milling of uranium must cease.

6. We support a national energy program which will not increase the financial burden on the poor, the elderly, and those with fixed incomes. If a rapid rise in the price of fuel is necessary to smooth out distortions in the energy economy, as many economists believe, then legislative means should be found to cushion the impact of such price increases on the poor.

7. We support full U.S. cooperation in international efforts to ensure equitable distribution of necessary energy supplies and rapid development and deployment of appropriate technologies based on renewable energy resources such as solar, wind, and water energy generation.

8. We strongly encourage The United Methodist Church at all levels to engage in a serious study of these energy issues in the context of Christian faith and the values of justice and sustainability.[19]

Equal Justice

It must be remembered that the advice, "Let every person be subject to the governing authorities" (Romans 13:1), is preceded by: "Live in harmony with another, do not be haughty, but associate with the lowly, never be

[19]*See* Social Principles I-B.

conceited. Repay no one evil for evil, but take thought for what is noble in the sight of all" (Romans 12:16ff).

The admonition is directed to the authorities who govern as well as those who may be subject.

The Social Principles of The United Methodist Church state that, "The Church should continually exert a strong ethical influence upon the state, supporting policies and programs deemed to be just and compassionate and opposing policies and programs which are not." "We support governmental measures designed to reduce and eliminate crime, consistent with respect for the basic freedom of persons. We reject all misuse of these necessary mechanisms, including their use for the purpose of persecuting or intimidating those whose race, appearance, lifestyle, economic conditions, or beliefs differ from those in authority, and we reject all careless, callous, or discriminatory enforcement of law."

The Police

In our democratic society, the police fill a position of extraordinary trust and power. Usually the decision of whether a citizen is to be taken into custody rests solely with the police. For these reasons, law enforcement officers must be persons who possess good judgment, sound discretion, proper temperament, and are physically and mentally alert.

Unusual care must be exercised in the selection of those persons to serve as police officers. We recommend psychological testing prior to employment of police officers and periodically thereafter. During the period of training and continually thereafter, police must be instilled with the knowledge that the rights of many will never be secured if the government through its police powers is permitted to prefer some of its citizens over others. The practice of citizen preference in the enforcement of our criminal laws must not be tolerated. Our laws must be fairly enforced and impartially administered. No one is immune from the requirements of the law because of power, position, or economic station in life. Further, the power of the police must never be used to harass and provoke the young, the poor, the unpopular, and the members of racial and cultural minorities.

Where there is heavy pressure upon police officers by police departments to make regularly a large number of arrests as a demonstration of their initiative and professional performance, we urge that such practice be discontinued.

In a democratic society, however, a large majority of police work encompasses peacekeeping and social services rather than crime control functions. Police routinely use more than 85 percent of their duty time in giving assistance to citizens and making referrals to other governmental agencies. It is important for police to be recognized and promoted for their effectiveness in such roles as diverting youths from disorderly activities, peacefully intervening in domestic quarrels, anticipating disturbances through the channeling of grievances, and the building of good community relationships.

The United Methodist Church recommends that police departments publicly establish standards of police conduct and policies for promotion. To this end congregations should encourage the police to conduct public hearings among all classes of citizens, giving adequate weight to peacekeeping, life-protecting, and other service roles, as well as the bringing of criminal offenders to justice. The standards must include strict limits on the police use of guns.

We further recommend that police officers live within the jurisdiction in which they are employed.

We make these recommendations not only in concern about the frequent abuses of people by the police, but also because we are concerned for more effective control of crime. We observe that only about one half the victims of serious crime and a far smaller proportion of witnesses report to the police. If offenders are to be apprehended and convicted, police and law-abiding citizens must work closely together. Such cooperation can occur only when the police are fair and humane and when they are publicly known to be sensitive and considerate.

The United Methodist Church urges that communities establish adequate salary scales for police officers and develop high standards for recruiting both men and women, and members of all ethnic groups. Recruitment must be followed by adequate training in social relations and dispute settlement as well as in law and the skills of crime detection investigation, and the apprehension of offenders. As police officers continue to meet those improved qualifications, we will recognize law enforcement as a profession with status and respect.

Criminal Laws and the Courts

Where the law recognizes and permits plea bargaining, and in those instances where the ends of justice dictate that a negotiated plea be considered, we recommend it should be permitted and approved only after full disclosure in open court of the terms and conditions of such plea bargaining agreement. Equal justice requires that all trials and the sentencing of those convicted under our criminal laws must be conducted in the public court room.

Since at present 90 percent of all criminal convictions are by guilty pleas—an unknown but large proportion of those by plea bargaining—this recommendation would mean a large increase in the work of the criminal courts. However, that work should be correspondingly eased by changes in the law such as the moving of most traffic offenses out of criminal court to administrative procedures, and by relieving the court of great numbers of civil cases through the adoption of genuine no-fault motor vehicle insurance laws. The courts must also organize their work efficiently, employing modern management procedures. Many improvements could be made by the use of administrative volunteers, including retirees who can furnish professional services at minimal costs to the court.

Other changes needed to obtain equal justice in the courts include:

1. The repeal of some criminal laws against certain personal conditions or individual misconduct. Examples are criminal prohibitions of vagrancy, personal gambling, public drunkenness, and prostitution. Together, these items alone account for more than half of all arrests in some jurisdictions. They result in little social good but great evil in class discrimination, alienation, and waste of resources needed for other purposes. Some related laws such as those against drunken driving and those limiting and controlling the operation of gambling establishments need to be tightened.

2. The adoption of systematic new penal codes prescribing penalties proportionate to the predictable damage done by the various kinds of crime, without regard to the class of the offender.

3. The training of judges of juvenile and criminal courts in the use of nonincarcerating community sanctions wherever the offense does not involve persistent violence.

4. The adoption of systematic new penal codes prescribing a range of penalties without regard to the class of the offender, but utilizing non-incarceration community sanctions wherever possible. The provision for court-fixed sentences, rather than mandatory ones, in order to draw upon the skill and the training of qualified judges.

5. Statement by the sentencing judge of the reason or reasons why he or she is selecting from the range permitted by the law the particular sentence being pronounced.

6. The development of appropriate jury selection procedures which would insure most inclusive representation including representatives of the socio-economic class and ethnic group of the defendants.

7. The adoption by all courts of: (a) speedy trial provisions which the constitution guarantees, and (b) that degree of personal recognizance and supervision which each defendant's situation warrants, in place of the present inherently discriminatory bail bond pre-trial release process that exists in some courts.

8. When fines are assessed, they should be scaled to the magnitude of the crime and the ability of the offender to pay. In suitable cases, fines should be made payable in installments.

9. Governmental regulated programs of compensation for reimbursement of financial loss incurred by innocent victims of crime should be encouraged.

We recommend that local churches consider setting up court monitoring panels to observe the court operations and proceedings. Such panels may well adopt a role of "friends of the court" or of advocacy on behalf of accused persons. They may adopt other appropriate procedures in the interest of criminal justice, including close scrutiny of plea bargaining and/or evidence of unequal imposition of sentences.

The Ft. Laramie Treaty

WHEREAS the 1868 Ft. Laramie Treaty was entered into by the United States of America, the Lakota Nation and other Indian nations, and was ratified by the Senate of the United States and proclaimed by its president in 1869;

WHEREAS this Treaty affirms the sovereignty of the people of all the nations involved;

WHEREAS treaties entered into by the United States Government are considered to be the supreme law of the land equal to its Constitution;

WHEREAS treaties cannot be unilaterally abrogated, according to international law;

WHEREAS the 1868 Ft. Laramie Treaty has never been legally abrogated;

WHEREAS the 1868 Ft. Laramie Treaty has been repeatedly violated and ignored by the United States Government;

WHEREAS these treaty violations have undermined both the moral integrity of the United States Government and the respect for its laws by U.S. citizens;

WHEREAS these treaty violations have resulted in the loss of land and loss of self-government which have contributed to poverty, ill-health, unresponsive educational institutions, loss of self-determination, and loss of life for the Lakota people;

Be It Resolved that we, the members of The United Methodist Church, recognize and reaffirm the sovereignty and independence of the Lakota people.

Be It Further Resolved that we, the members of the General Conference of The United Methodist Church call on our United States government to recognize the sovereignty and independence of the Lakota Nation through the 1868 Ft. Laramie Treaty. We call upon the President of the United States to form a Presidential Treaty Commission to meet with representatives selected by the Lakota people to redress the grievances caused by the U.S. violations of the 1868 Ft. Laramie Treaty to the mutual satisfaction of both nations, and to devise and implement specific steps to bring the United States into compliance with its treaty obligations with the Lakota Nation.[20]

Gambling

The Social Principles state that "Gambling is a menace to society, deadly to the best interests of moral, social, economic, and spiritual life, and destructive of good government. As an act of faith and love, Christians should abstain from gambling, and should strive to minister to

---

[20]*See* "The United Methodist Church and America's Native Peoples," 1980.

those victimized by the practice. Community standards and personal lifestyles should be such as would make unnecessary and undesirable the resort to commercial gambling, including public lotteries, as a recreation, as an escape, or as a means of producing public revenue or funds for support of charities or government."

One of the essential commandments, according to Jesus, is "Love thy neighbor as thyself" (Matthew 22:39-40). This, together with loving God with all of one's being, summarizes all of the law.

Gambling, as a means of keeping material gain only by chance and at the neighbor's expense, is a menace to personal character and social morality. Gambling fosters greed and stimulates the fatalistic faith in chance. Organized and commercial gambling is a threat to business, breeds crime and poverty, and is destructive to the interests of good government.

We oppose the growing legalization and state promotion of gambling.

Dependence on gambling revenue has led many states to exploit the weakness of their own citizens, neglect the development of more equitable forms of taxation, and thereby further erode the citizens' confidence in government.

We oppose the legalization of pari-mutuel betting, for it has been the opening wedge in the legalization of other forms of gambling within the states, and has stimulated illegal bookmaking. We deplore the establishment of state lotteries and their use as a means of raising public revenues. The constant promotion and the wide advertising of lotteries have encouraged large numbers of persons to gamble for the first time.

We express an even more serious concern for the increasing development of the casino enterprise in the United States, for it has taken captive entire communities and has infiltrated many levels of government with its fiscal and political power.

Public apathy and a lack of awareness that petty gambling

feeds organized crime have opened the door to the spread of numerous forms of legal and illegal gambling.

We support the strong enforcement of anti-gambling laws, the repeal of all laws that give gambling an acceptable and even advantageous place in our society, and the rehabilitation of compulsive gamblers.

The Church has a key role in fostering responsible government and in developing health and moral maturity which free persons from dependence on damaging social customs. It is expected that United Methodist churches abstain from the use of raffles, lotteries, Bingo, door prizes, other drawing schemes, and games of chance for the purpose of gambling or fund raising. We should refrain from all forms of gambling practices carried on in our communities and should work to influence community organizations to develop forms of funding which do not depend upon gambling.[21]

Grand Jury Abuse

Jesus' words, "Judge not that you may not be judged . . ." (Matthew 7:1) surely imply that all judgments are judged in the light of God's truth. The Social Principles of The United Methodist Church state boldly that ". . . governments, no less than individuals, are subject to the judgment of God."

Such a social principle causes us to appropriately view with concern the government's use of the Grand Jury to control dissent and harass those who act under the constraint of conscience.

The Grand Jury is envisioned in American law as a protector of citizens from unwarranted prosecutions. It is for this reason that its proceedings are secret and it has the power to subpoena witnesses.

Evidence indicates that in recent years the extraordinary

[21]*See* Social Principles IV-G.

powers of the Grand Jury often have been used—not for the protection of citizens—but in subjecting them to harassment and intimidation. Historically, political dissidents, anti-war activists, and leaders of minority groups and religious organizations have been particularly vulnerable to these abuses.

A government prosecutor can control the Grand Jury, thus distorting the Grand Jury's power to monitor and moderate the actions of the prosecution.

The prosecutor can use the subpoena powers of the Grand Jury to conduct investigations which are the responsibility of law enforcement agencies. As an example, Congress has never given the Federal Bureau of Investigation subpoena powers, yet agents routinely threaten uncooperative persons with subpoenas from a Grand Jury. In fact, subpoenas are often served at the request of the Federal Bureau of Investigation.

The use of the powers of the Grand Jury to harass and pursue political dissidents is a departure from its proper constitutional function, and is a threat to public order, lawful government, and true domestic security.

Witnesses called before a Grand Jury may be given little or no warning of their subpoenas, may be forced to travel to courts at distances from their homes, may not know whether they are targets of prosecution, may have little understanding of their rights, and cannot have legal counsel in the chambers.

Comprehensive Grand Jury reform legislation is needed to restore the constitutional guarantees of protection for citizens. The Fifth Amendment right against self-incrimination and false accusation must be re-established and reinforced.

The United Methodist Church, therefore, supports legislation designed to enhance the rights to due process of law, freedom of association, effective legal counsel, the presumption of innocence, and the privilege against self-incrimination of persons subpoenaed to testify before Grand Juries.

Guidelines for Interreligious Relationships
"Called to Be Neighbors and Witnesses"

Nations of the world are growing increasingly interdependent politically and economically, and the various world religious communities are also encountering each other in new ways. Religions of Asia and Africa are showing new life and power within their homelands and are spreading to other continents, creating new multireligious societies, especially in western nations. New sects, cults, and ideologies emerge and seek converts to their faith.

The emergence of these religiously diverse societies and the new dynamics in old religious communities have forced many faiths to reconsider how they relate to one another and to secular ideologies. There is danger that religious tensions will lead to oppression of religious minorities and curtailment of religious freedom with real potential for armed conflict. Worldwide problems of human suffering due to poverty, wars, and political oppression are so vast and pervasive that no one faith group can solve them, yet tensions between religious groups often prevent cooperation in solving these urgent human problems. As ancient religions demonstrate new life and power to speak to the deepest human concerns, questions are raised for Christians regarding their understanding these faiths and regarding their claims to a global mission to all people.

What are the implications of this religiously diverse situation for Christian theology? What does it mean to be a faithful follower of and witness to Jesus Christ? Can we of different faiths live together as neighbors, or will diverse religious loyalties result in mutual antagonism and destruction? What are the resources of United Methodist Christians for building constructive relationships between persons of different faiths?

The United Methodist Church provides this statement as guidance to its members and congregations in facing

171

these questions in their relations with persons of other faiths.

Called to Be Neighbors

For some Christians, it seems strange even to refer to "persons of other faiths." We are accustomed to calling them "non-Christians" or "non-believers." These attitudes have developed out of confidence in the ultimate truth of our own faith, and from ignorance of and insensitivity to other faiths, to the truth they contain, and to the profound meaning and purpose they give to the lives of people.

In conversation with a lawyer (cf. Luke 10:25), Jesus reminded him that his neighbor, the one to whom he should show love and compassion, included a stranger, a Samaritan. Today, our Lord's call to neighborliness (cf. Luke 10:27), includes the "strangers" of other faiths who have moved into our towns and cities. It is not just that historical events have forced us together. The Christian faith itself impels us to love our neighbors of other faiths and to seek to live in contact and mutually beneficial relationships, in community, with them.

What does it mean to be a neighbor? It means to meet other persons, to know them, to relate to them, to respect them, and to learn about their ways which may be quite different from our own. It means to create a sense of community in our neighborhoods, towns, and cities and to make them places in which the unique customs of each group of people can be expressed and their values protected. It means to create social structures in which there is justice for all and in which everyone can participate in shaping their life together "in community." Each race or group of people is not only allowed to be who they are, their way of life is valued and given full expression.

Christians distinguish several meanings of "community." One definition expresses their relationships as members of one another in the body of Christ, the Church, a people called together by Christ, a "communion of saints" who look to the reign of God. A broader definition points to the

172

relationship that is shared with others in the wider human community, where Christians are concerned for peace, justice, and reconciliation for all people. Other faiths also have their understanding of "community." The vision of a "worldwide community of communities" commends itself to many Christians as a way of being together with persons of different faiths in a pluralistic world. That suggests that we United Methodist Christians, not just individually, but corporately, are called to be neighbors with communities of other faiths (Buddhist, Jewish, Muslim, Hindu, and others), and to work with them to create a human community, a set of relationships between people at once interdependent and free, in which there is love, mutual respect, and justice.

Within this religiously diverse community, Christians, trusting in Jesus Christ for their salvation, are called to witness to him as Lord to all people, (cf. Acts 1:8). We witness to our Lord through words which tell of his grace, through deeds of service and social change that demonstrate his love, and through our life together in the Christian community, exhibiting God's power to heal, reconcile, and unite.

As relationships with persons of other faiths deepen, Christians discover how often their witness has been unneighborly, how much we have talked and how little we have listened, and how often insensitive and unappreciative approaches have alienated sincere truth seekers and persons who already have strong faith commitments. We become aware that we frequently communicate attitudes of superiority regarding our own faith and inferiority toward that of others, and that in so doing, we perpetuate walls and hostilities between us as human beings which lessen chances that our witness will be received.

As we United Methodist Christians reflect anew on our faith and seek guidance in our witness to and encounter with our new neighbors, we rediscover that God who has acted in Jesus Christ for the salvation of the whole world, is also Creator of all humankind, the "one God and Father of all men, who is Lord of all, works through all, and is in all," (Ephesians 4:6 TEV). The God to whom we point in Jesus

Christ is the God who is at work in every society in ways we do not fully understand and who has not left himself without witness in any human community. Here Christians confront a profound mystery, the awareness of God who is related to all creation and at work in the whole of it, and the experience of God who has acted redemptively for the whole creation in Jesus Christ. Christians witness to God in Jesus Christ in the confidence that here all people find salvation and in the trust that because of what we know of God in Jesus, God deals graciously and lovingly with all people everywhere.

Dialogue: A Way to Be Neighbors and Witnesses

"Dialogue" is the word which has come to signify a different approach to persons of other faiths, one which takes seriously both the call to witness and the command to love and be neighbors, and sees witnessing and neighborliness as interrelated activities. Rather than a onesided address, dialogue combines witnessing with listening. It is the intentional engagement with persons of other faiths for mutual understanding, cooperation, and learning.

"Dialogue" may be as informal as a conversation in the marketplace, or as formal as the leader of one religious group explaining to others its philosophy or worship life. Dialogue is more than an individual or academic enterprise. It also involves groups or communities of people holding different faiths, who reach out to one another. This community orientation gives a practical bent to interreligious dialogue.

In dialogue, one individual or group may seek a relationship with another in order to expose misunderstandings and stereotypes, and to break down barriers that separate and create hostility and conflict. Ethnic or religious communities may approach each other in dialogue in order to resolve particular problems or to foster cooperation in dealing with a local, national, or even global situation of human suffering. At its deepest level, dialogue is both learning about and sharing our respective faiths. Each partner learns from the rich store of wisdom of the other, and each expresses his or her own deepest conviction in the faith that it has a truth worth sharing with the other.

Through dialogue with persons of other faiths, new insights are received regarding God's activity in the world today and the divine purpose for humankind as a whole, and the place of the Christian community within these purposes. It is also a common experience for Christians to feel the need to express their own faith with greater clarity. We can expect the Holy Spirit to make known new and different insights through our encounter with persons of other faiths.

Because the Jewish community is the largest community of another faith in the United States, Jews will be a major partner in dialogue for United Methodists. Christians need Judaism lest their faith in God be compromised and truncated in a rootless Christianity. For many United Methodists, especially in Asia, Buddhists, Hindus, or Muslims will be their natural partners in dialogue. Dialogue with persons in these faith groups is increasingly important for United States Christians as well, since their numbers there are increasing. Muslims and Christians also share a close but often unrecognized relationship, since both have roots that go back to Abraham. In many nations, long histories of separation between Buddhist, Hindu, and Christian communities have yet to be bridged, while in the United States many youth have been attracted to the deep spirituality of Buddhist and Hindu adherents. Dialogue offers the possibility of sharing mutually beneficial insights, as well as overcoming past hostilities.

Dialogue frequently has been misunderstood. Some see it as limited to the commonalities between persons and communities of different faiths. It is important to discern and explore those commonalities and to utilize them to strengthen relationships. But there is more! Dialogue offers to both partners the opportunity of enriching their own faith through the wisdom of the other. In the process it helps overcome the deep mistrust, hatred, hostility, and conflict that characterize so many intercultural and interreligious relations. Each religious community asserts that its faith offers a way to resolve conflict in positive ways and has resources for building community among diverse peoples. Dialogue seeks to provide an environment which allows space for differences and to build on the positive affirmations of each faith and to bring them into relationship with each other.

The only precondition for dialogue is a willingness to enter a relationship of mutual acceptance, openness, and respect. Effective dialogue requires that both partners have deep convictions about life, faith, and salvation. True dialogue requires that Christians *not* suspend their fundamental convictions concerning the truth of the Gospel but enter into dialogue with personal commitment to Jesus Christ and with the desire to witness to that faith. Effective dialogue also requires that Christians be open to persons of other faiths, to their convictions about life, truth, and salvation and to their witness, as others also feel called to witness to their faith and teachings about the meaning of life.

Dialogue: An Exchange of Witness

Is not this urge to witness an obstacle to interreligious dialogue? It often has been but it need not be. Where there is listening as well as speaking, openness and respect as well as concern to influence, there is dialogue *and* witness. Indeed, dialogue at its most profound level is an *exchange of witness*. Participants share with each other their perceptions of the meaning of life, of ultimate reality, salvation and hope, and the resources of their faith for enabling community. In genuine "dialogue," we "witness and are witnessed to." The most effective dialogue takes place when both sides really do care that the other hear, understand, and receive their wisdom. Part of our witness is our openness to hearing the witness of the other.

Dialogue at these depths holds great promise. Long cherished convictions may be modified by the encounter with others. Misunderstandings may be clarified, potential hostilities reconciled, and new insights regarding one's own faith may emerge in contrast to that of another. The depths of another's faith may be so disclosed that its power and attractiveness are experienced. Dialogue is a demanding process, requiring thorough understanding of one's own faith and clear articulation of it to the other person.

Dialogue is *not* a betrayal of witness. Dialogue and witness are wrongly placed in opposition to each other. They need each other. Dialogue creates relationships of mutual understanding, openness, and respect. Witness presses dialogue to the deepest convictions about life, death, and hope.

Many persons of other faiths are suspicious that dialogue is a new and more subtle tool for conversion. In some ways this is inevitable since Christians do want others to learn of and receive the truth and grace we know in Jesus Christ. The difference between dialogue and other forms of witness is that it is a context for learning from the other the truth and wisdom of the other faith as well as sharing with the other the truth and wisdom of our own. We leave to the Holy Spirit the outcome of our mutual openness. Our concern is to be obedient to our own call to witness and to the imperative to be loving and neighborly to persons of other faiths. In dialogue, these deeply held truths encounter each other in witness and love, so that larger wisdom and larger understanding of truth may emerge which benefit all parties in the dialogue. As we exhibit courtesy, reverence and respect, and become neighbors, our fears of each other are allayed, and the Holy Spirit works within these relationships.

Neighbors and Witnesses

The command to love one's neighbors and the call to witness to Jesus Christ to all people are inseparably linked. The profound challenge which this represents for United Methodist Christians can be seen most sharply in the new religious movements which have arisen in recent years. These movements have become a source of concern for many Christians. Some groups seem to utilize methods that are manipulative and coercive. However, many people have found new vision, meaning, and hope in some of these new faiths. These new religious movements are very diverse and they should not be lumped together indiscriminately, condemned and dismissed. Neither should they automatically be embraced as valid expressions of human dignity and freedom.

Careful study and contact will enable Christians to distinguish those which are manipulative and coercive and which are to be challenged for reasons of faith. Questions of basic human rights are raised both by tactics sometimes employed by some religious movements and by acts of opposition against them. In particular, enforced deprogramming represents a violation of the personality of individuals and their rights of free choice. The question of what means are justified in trying to win back persons who have joined cults is a difficult one, and one to which Christians will respond differently. Where children of church members are involved, the parents are in special need of pastoral counseling and support. The best preparation for meeting these groups is the development within families and through the educational program of the Church a deeper understanding of and commitment to Jesus Christ and his claims, especially the costliness of following our "suffering servant" Lord. This commitment is deepened through the experience of acceptance and personal relationship within the fellowship of the Christian community.

As we take seriously this calling to be witnesses and neighbors, to people of all faiths old and new, we become aware of the biblical caution not to bear false witness (cf. Matthew 19:18) and the admonition to live at peace with all people (cf. Hebrew 12:14). How are we to avoid bearing false witness unless we know our neighbors and understand their faith commitments? How can one truly love a neighbor and hold back what to Christians is the greatest of all gifts—God becoming present to people in Jesus Christ? How can we live peacefully together, unless we are willing to be neighborly? How can we say we love our neighbor if we are unwilling to be attentive to the message and the gifts which God has given him or her? Love of neighbor and witness to Christ are the two primary attitudes of United Methodist Christians in their relationship with persons of other faiths. And when we become this kind of neighbor, we discover that God has given us another gift—people of different faiths.

Guidelines for Interreligious Relationships

The following guidelines will assist United Methodists to be faithful to their call to witness and to the call to be neighbors with persons of other faiths.

1. *Discover and find out about the persons of other faiths in your town or city and educate your congregation about them.*

a. Plan experiences that bring Christians into contact with persons of other faiths. Whenever possible initiate these experiences ecumenically. In the absence of cooperative efforts to develop relationships and explore tensions and difficulties, United Methodist initiative is encouraged.

b. Visit the services and meeting places of other faiths, but respect their sacred times and places and do not treat them as "tourist" attractions.

c. Study the new religious movements carefully and develop attitudes of courtesy towards them.

Support efforts in the community to insure that their human rights are not violated. Seek assistance in cases where efforts are being made to insure the human rights of members of a group by testing their freedom to leave it, and in developing perspectives on Christian witness to these new religious movements.

2. *Initiate dialogues with other faith communities.*

a. Seek relationships with Jews. Muslims, Buddhists, and Hindus, and their respective organizations. Initiate conversations, programs, and dialogues leading to: understanding of each faith, appreciation of their particular gifts, discovery of commonalities and differences, and areas of mutual cooperation.

179

b. With the Jewish community seek an awareness of both our common roots and the tragic interlocking of our histories, sensitivity to anti-Semitism among Christians, and an understanding of the significance of the Holocaust and the importance of Israel for Jews.

c. With the Muslim community, explore the negative stereotypes which perpetuate misunderstanding and continue to hinder the establishment of positive relationships, and seek an understanding of the role of the Islamic faith in various Middle Eastern societies.

d. With the Buddhist and Hindu community, explore their spiritual practices and understandings which have attracted many people in the west.

Prepare for dialogue through reflection on the following:

(1) Clarity regarding your understanding of and commitment to your own faith is absolutely essential.

(2) Each partner must believe the other is speaking in good faith.

(3) Each partner must strive for a clear understanding of the faith of the other and be willing to interpret it in its best light rather than its worst.

(4) Each partner must forthrightly face the issues that cause separation as well as those that create unity.

3. Share in common enterprises with persons of other faiths in practical ways.

a. Work together to resolve economic, social, cultural, and political problems in the community. Together become sensitive to infringements of the human rights of groups within the community and threats to their cultural values and heritage and initiate steps to protect them.

b. Jointly plan community celebrations with an interreligious perspective.

c. Participate in interreligious associations.

d. Seek to generate interreligious educational efforts in the community. This could include enlisting the aid of school authorities in the examination of texts used in schools to see that the various religious groups are depicted fairly and accurately. Other educational ventures might include providing courses in adult schools and for people who are planning trips abroad; or developing special programs for media such as television and radio to reach a wider audience.

4. Prepare carefully before sharing in celebrations, rituals, worship, and meditation with persons of other faiths.

It will not be possible for Christians to participate fully in another faith's rituals and worship, nor should they expect it. However, it is appropriate, where invited, to share in such occasions. Some may wish to share in joint prayer services. On such occasions, care should be taken not to relativize all religious symbols and practices to make religious differences unimportant. It is unwise to juxtapose symbols of different religions. Each partner must approach such occasions out of the integrity of his or her own faith.

Intent

The intent in developing interreligious relationships is not to amalgamate all faiths into one religion. We Christians have no interest in such syncretism. To engage in interreligious dialogue is not to say that any religion is all right just so you have one. Far from requiring a lessening of commitment to Christ, effective dialogue is only possible when one's own faith is strong.

We Christians are seeking to be neighbors with persons of other faiths whose religious commitments are different from our own, and to engage each other about the deepest convictions of our lives. In our assurance of and trust in God's grace in Jesus Christ, we open ourselves to dialogue and engagement with persons of other faiths and to other Christians whose understandings may be different from our own.

This interreligious engagement challenges United Methodist Christians to think in new ways about our life in the broader human community, about our mission, evangelism, service, and our life together within the Christian church. We seek to promote peace and harmony with persons of other faiths in our various towns, cities, and neighborhoods.

Yet we do not hide our differences, nor avoid conflicts, but seek to make them constructive. In each place we share our lives with each other, we witness and are witnessed to, we invite others into the Christian community and we are invited into theirs. Our prayer is that the lives of all in each place will be enriched by the differences of others, that a new sense of community may emerge, and that others may receive the gift of God in Christ, while we receive the gifts which have been given them.

Health Care Delivery
Policy Statement

I. *Introduction*

The United Methodist Church understands itself as called by the Lord to a holistic ministry of healing—spiritual, mental, emotional, and physical. Persons created by God are called to the abundant life—life in its wholeness—for which Jesus of Nazareth came. Health in this sense is something beyond, but not exclusive of, biological well-being. In this view, medical care is inadequate when it fixes its attention solely on the body and its physiological functions, as is any religion that focuses its interest entirely on the soul.

Although medical care represents a very important and expensive part of health care, it does not include the whole. More medical care does not always equal better health. Medical care in much of the world has evolved too much as disease care rather than health care. Disease prevention, public health programs, and health education appropriate to every age level and social setting are needed to supplement today's curative care.

Environmental factors—clean air, pure water, effective sanitary systems for the disposal of wastes, nutritious foods, adequate housing, safe and non-toxic work places—are essential to health. The best medical system cannot preserve or maintain health when the environment is disease-producing.

Personal habits are also crucial to health. Overeating, or eating non-nutritious foods, drug abuse (including alcohol, tobacco, barbiturates, sedatives, etc.) are clearly destructive of health. Failure to exercise or to rest and relax adequately are also injurious to health.

Still, illness and disease remain mysterious to us. Human suffering is caused by a variety of factors—personal, social, environmental, genetic, and others which remain unknown to us.

From these perspectives, The United Methodist Church urges that medical and health care services of good quality should be made available to all persons and should be so organized as to be readily accessible to all, subject only to necessary limitations of resources. Services should be provided in a compassionate and skillful manner on the basis of need, without discrimination as to financial status, mental or physical handicap, race, color, religion, sex, age, national origin, or language.

II. *Principles and Goals*

We view health holistically, and are fully aware of the shared responsibilities among individuals, families, communities, and the society at large for the impact of life style and environmental factors on health status. We affirm the following principles and goals as necessary for effective and responsible delivery of health services:

A. All people should be entitled to a basic benefit package of preventive and health care services. We reject any notion of dual standards of care.

B. The package of health care benefits should be comprehensive including preventive, therapeutic, and rehabilitative services.

C. New emphasis should be put on preventive care for all ages.

D. Adequate programs and information should be available to assist people in accepting appropriate responsibility for protecting their own health and for seeking medical and health care as needed. Schools, community organizations and churches, as well as health care personnel and health care institutions, should be involved in a coordinated health education program.

E. Human wholeness and health have religious and spiritual components which should be considered in the planning for and provision of comprehensive health care services. Religious and spiritual counseling should be available to all patients.

F. Structures and procedures for effectively evaluating the appropriateness and comprehensiveness of health services should be established.

G. Regional planning processes should coordinate the services rendered by all health care institutions, to create a more effective system of health services in every area. Priorities should be established for the provision of health services such as preventive care, mental health services, home care, and health education.

H. Consumers, broadly representative of the whole population, should serve on boards and groups who, with health care professionals and public officials, are given the responsibility to plan, administer, and evaluate the effectiveness of every level of the health care system.

I. We do not believe that one single way or organizing health care services can be developed for application to all communities. The system should display the requisite diversity and adaptability to meet differing social and community circumstances.

J. Professional health care personnel should be recruited and trained appropriately to meet the health care needs of all persons. Special priorities should be established to secure among the professional groups at least proportional representation of persons who are now seriously under-represented.

K. Where medical services are not available, or are in undersupply, it is essential that public or private sources provide the full range of needed services.

*Health Care Delivery
in the United States*

I. *The Medical Care Delivery System and Its Problems*

Excellent quality medical services exist in the U.S., but poor quality services are also found here. In some cases the medical care system consists of unrelated and uncoordinated health-providers who are heavily reimbursed by third parties—private or government insurance plans. Incentives for the more economical delivery of services have been dulled or frustrated by financial considerations. In spite of its real accomplishments, the medical care delivery system in the U.S. comes under criticism for weaknesses and failures. Among them are the following:

A. In some cases the current health delivery system is not well planned or coordinated.

B. Medical costs have been rising at a pace much faster than the general inflation rate.

C. There are serious gaps of coverage in private insurance, Medicaid, and Medicare.

D. Physicians and other professional medical care personnel are generally over-concentrated in urban, suburban, and affluent communities, and under-concentrated in rural, small-town, inner-city, and poverty areas. Physicians are also generally over-concentrated in the specialties and are in undersupply in primary care.

E. There is not proportional representation among physicians and management personnel by gender, race, and ethnic origin.

F. Overall there is some shortage and maldistribution of hospital beds, of intermediate care and nursing home care, of home delivered care, of neighborhood health centers and community mental health centers, of emergency care networks, and of prepaid group practice plans.

G. Significant deficiencies are found in some cases, including such problems as unnecessary and inappropriate drug prescribing, unnecessary surgery, superfluous testing, and inappropriate or unnecessary institutionalizing of patients.

H. Some patients are treated impersonally or even callously, and in too many cases the spiritual and psychological needs of patients are ignored.

II. *Alternative Health Care System*

Our present health care "system" consists of largely unrelated and uncoordinated health care providers who are largely reimbursed by third party payers on a fee-for-service basis. We urge that alternative systems, offering comprehensive services to an enrolled membership for a fixed premium, should be made available in all health service areas. All individuals and groups should have the option of enrolling in such plans, which are generally referred to as Health Maintenance Organizations (HMO's).

III. *Health Insurance*

For all persons in the nation to have equitable access to needed health care services, public financing must be a significant part of an overall health insurance plan. Public funding is necessary to pay for insuring those who cannot pay part or all of the necessary premiums required. This group includes, among others, the poor and the near-poor, most of the elderly, the unemployed, the disabled, and those whose care is extremely costly. Government should ensure that the providers of health care services are adequately and fairly remunerated for services rendered. Any overall plan and program for insuring the financing health care services should meet, at the minimum, the following tests:

A. The plan should support the provision of comprehensive health care services of high quality to all persons.
B. The plan should establish equitable cost sharing among all payers, and should remove the burden of excessive medical expense from any single individual or family.
C. The plan should provide for control of the overall cost of health care, with financial incentives for the provision of

quality care in cost efficient settings and modes, and with financial disincentives for waste, inefficiency, and inappropriate care.

D. The plan should be integrated and coordinated with all key elements in the health care system, including the health delivery system, the financing mechanisms, and the regulatory and administrative mechanisms.

E. The plan should allow sufficient time between enactment of legislation and actual implementation of its provisions to make possible the establishment of adequate delivery systems and appropriate regulatory structures. Any proposed regulation under such legislation should be analyzed and evaluated for long term consequences prior to promulgation.

IV. *Health Ministry: Our Responsibility*

We United Methodists are called to a ministry of healing. We must continue to support direct health services where needed and continue to provide, as we are able, such services in hospitals and homes, clinics and health centers. In addition, we have a responsibility to support public policies and programs which will ensure comprehensive health care services of high quality to all persons on the principle of equal access.

We urge individual United Methodists to:

*Recognize the need for certain fundamental changes in the way health care services in the U.S. are presently organized, delivered, and financed; and

*Choose those individual and family life styles which are conducive to good health.

Beyond this, we call upon United Methodists in their local churches, districts and annual conferences, in organizations and agencies, to work to enlarge the health care service choices available to people everywhere, by supporting:

1) adoption of a health policy which will provide comprehensive health care according to the principles and goals set forth in our health care statement;

2) alternative plans for financing health care delivery systems;

3) community health programs which assess health needs and provide preventive, primary, and home care services;

4) educational efforts and programs which help people understand the spiritual, emotional, mental, and physical components of health in their personal lives and circumstances;

5) development of holistic health centers within the context of the Church's ministry; and

6) appropriate national and international efforts and programs aimed at providing basic and necessary health care services to the people of other nations of the world, particularly in those places of greatest need.

7) a response to the mandate of the gospel, within United Methodist Church-sponsored health care institutions, to provide care for the poor and oppressed;

8) participation by Blacks and other minorities in representative numbers in all United Methodist Church efforts directed toward the implementation of its health care policy. Every effort should be made to ensure that actions directed toward the formation of recommendations and policy statements by United Methodist boards and agencies include representative numbers of black persons and other minority persons with professional skills commensurate with the task to be performed in the formulation of those recommendations and policy statements.

History of Blacks
in The United Methodist Church

WHEREAS, an examination and reassessment of America's church history reflects a significant omission of the contribution of black people outside and within The United Methodist Church; and

WHEREAS, this history now lies almost dormant and uneventful in the life of the Church; and

WHEREAS, a serious effort should now be made to flush this

history out of the religious milieu in order to dispel the myths that have accumulated over the years, and to place in proper perspective black witnessing to Christ.

Be It Resolved, that the commission intentionally seek out those Blacks who have historical records in their possession as well as those who can contribute to the facts from an oral tradition.

Housing

The Scriptures look ahead to that ideal day when all persons will enjoy pleasant, peaceful, and secure shelter under their own vines and fig trees and "none shall make them afraid" (Mich 4:4).

In many portions of the gospel, we find Jesus seeking out homes for retreat and renewal, for fellowship and hospitality. All persons are entitled to dwelling places that provide for privacy and recreation.

The Social Principles statement of The United Methodist Church declares: "We hold governments responsible for . . . guarantee of the right to adequate . . . shelter. We reaffirm this right as well as the assertion of the 1972 General Conference that 'housing for low income persons should be given top priority. . .' "

There are 75 million occupied housing units in the United States. Of these seven million are seriously substandard; another 25 to 30 million are marginal for human habitation. Furthermore, four and one-half million U.S. citizens are paying more than half of their income for housing. The need for adequate housing at affordable costs abounds.

Love for neighbor demands that Christians care about how adequately their neighbors are sheltered. Christians should identify with those who suffer daily from a shortage of available, decent, safe, and sanitary housing. There are many levels and forms of deprivation. Nearly every American town and city has its "street people," those who live literally without any form of shelter, carrying their entire possessions with them in a few shopping bags.

Millions of families huddle together in densely over-crowded apartments, rural shacks, ancient house trailers, converted warehouses, and condemned or abandoned buildings. At least seven million of our fellow citizens are forced by our society to live in intolerable housing because the remainder of us fail to recognize their plight or simply do not care enough.

Yet hundreds of United Methodists are engaged in a heroic battle to change such intolerable housing conditions. We commend every such individual, local church, interfaith group, non-profit, for-profit, and governmental effort. We endorse with gratitude and appreciation the thousands of dollars and untold hours of voluntary service which United Methodists dedicate to this battle to improve human shelter in our country. We urge local churches, districts and annual conferences to strengthen every housing ministry within their communities by providing additional financial and technical counseling and spiritual resources.

Many specific activities deserve greater United Methodist support.

A. *At the local level:*

Local churches, individually or in cooperation with other churches, can identify specific housing needs existing in their communities. Often bringing people in need of shelter to public consciousness is the first step toward alleviation of such need. Sometimes the use of existing church buildings can graphically demonstrate both the need and a solution which then can be developed more fully through the use of other facilities and financial resources. Examples of effective housing ministries include emergency housing, ministries of acceptance to "street people," various housing counseling services, location of available apartments and housing for rental or purchase, supporting tenants by providing meeting places and leadership, and providing technical expertise for organizing more susbstantial efforts to meet various specific housing needs.

Formation of non-profit and limited-dividend housing corporations or housing cooperatives is a viable approach in many situations. There are excellent opportunities for

190

establishing housing contruction, management, and advocacy programs. However, expert consultative and technical services generally are needed from the very earliest concept onward. We commend the Board of Global Ministries, National Division, for the provision of such services for the past decade and a half (Par. 1529.14, 1980 Discipline), and urge United Methodists to seek out such services at every stage of development of any housing ministry.

B. *At the regional level:*

We deplore the atmosphere of conflict which infects the relationship between cities, towns, suburban areas, counties, and states throughout our nation. Too often competition for use of land clothes subtle racism. Economic profit, likewise, often is used to justify a lack of concern for the impact of taxation measures. Uncoordinated planning and development results in jobs being located beyond the reach of those most in need of work. The "trickle down theory" of housing occupancy masks a selfish motivation, and results in maintaining and expanding existing ghettos, causes the formation of new ghettos, and enforces negative attitudes that support class and racial segregation. We urge United Methodists to challenge all such practices of, and to engage in every activity which can eliminate, such vestiges of discrimination from our nation.

Every urbanized area in our country is required to have some form of a regional planning agency. Most rural areas have some similar agency, such as an area development district. Generally these political structures have considerable influence upon housing patterns, planning, production, and usage. Most can have citizens' advisory groups which develop strategy proposals and monitor private and governmental housing activities. We urge United Methodists to become knowledgeable of, and involved in, such planning agencies. Whether serving as political appointees, elected representatives, professional staff, or designated "citizen advisors," United Methodists can make a substantial contribution toward developing realistic and morally just housing conditions by active participation in such regional agencies.

191

C. At the national level:

Since the enactment of the National Housing act of 1949 it has been the goal of this country that every citizen should be housed in "decent, safe and sanitary housing." Yet the reality is that we are farther from that goal today than ever before. In part this is due to growth of population and the ever increasing gap between those who are economically well off and those who are not. But in large measure the disparity is due to an unwillingness of our elected representatives to use tax revenues in ways which would achieve the goals more fully. Generally legislators feel they represent the views of their electorate, and receive very little support for using tax dollars to build more housing for low and moderate income families. The moral commitment first stated in 1949, and restated in every subsequent Housing Act by Congress (1959, 1968, 1974, 1978) has gone greatly unheeded. If "decent, safe and sanitary housing" is to be a citizens right, a much greater moral outcry must be heard.

Therefore, we call upon United Methodists to undertake a concerted effort to impress upon their elected representatives a profound concern over the continuing housing deficiencies existing in our cities, towns, and rural areas. Much more effort needs to be made to influence the legislative processes which affect housing issues: improving existing law, developing more imaginative approaches where possible, and providing adequate funding for housing designed to meet the needs of the ill-sheltered.

1. Subsidized Rental Housing (Section 8) and Public Housing

Under the Section 8 Housing Assistance Payments Program, normally renters pay a percent of their income for rent and the federal government makes up the difference between that and the HUD-established Fair Market Rent. We support this program for subsidizing rents as one way of opening up more housing units to low-income families and yet expecting such families, when possible, to provide their fair share of costs. We ask that this program be substantially expanded to include at least 600,000 units annually, which is the minimum needed to house our poorest citizens.

We support use of a wide variety of subsidized housing approaches in order to meet a greater demand to house needy people.

Public housing continues to be a vital necessity in both urban and rural areas. Every incorporated city, town, and county can, and should, use this means of providing well-constructed and well-managed rental housing for those who can not obtain it on the open market. Nearly 50 percent of all public housing now is occupied by the elderly. Since the church has traditionally expressed concern and provided care of the aging, it is especially crucial that this program be continued, expanded, and adequately funded.

2. Fair Housing

We support the Social Principles statement asserting "the right of members of ethnic minorities to equal opportunities . . . in housing purchase or rental."

Fair housing in our nation has progressed at a plodding pace. Because housing remains segregated in most places in the United States, schools tend to be segregated and jobs tend to be located at inconvenient distances from ethnic minority neighborhoods.

We therefore call upon the U.S. Congress to provide the Department of Housing and Urban Development with "cease and desist" enforcement powers and we encourage HUD to apply these powers evenly and with relentless determination to assure equal access to affordable housing in all markets.

Also, we are well aware that there can be no fair housing if the overall stock of housing is in short supply. Equal access to no available housing represents an unrealizable right. Therefore, to fulfill equal opportunity objectives we urge that much more housing be built and offered at prices most ethnic minority persons and the poor can afford to pay.

3. Redlining

We deplore the practice of "redlining" as it occurs in many urban areas. This generally means that financial institutions, insurance companies, and mortgage brokers collectively make it difficult for homeowners to secure adequate financing and insurance at reasonable rates in a certain neighborhood of a given urban community. Such questionable business practices inevitably hasten the decay of targeted neighborhoods. Thus they are marked for death. We ask that all steps necessary be taken, through negotiation and legislation, to eliminate this heartless practice and that churches take the lead in encouraging financial support arrangements that rejuvenate neighborhoods instead of destroying them. Vigilant monitoring by the religious community can forestall such unhealthy practices.

We support existing laws, such as the Home Mortgage Disclosure Act, which provides public information on where banks and savings and loans make their loans, and the Community Reinvestment Act, which mandates that banks and savings and loans have the responsibility to serve the credit needs of the moderate and lower-income communities.

We urge assessment of whether the institutions in which the Church deposits funds comply with the Home Mortgage Act; and we support such additional regulations and laws that will assure reinvestment in currently redlined communities in a way that will not result in unjust displacement of elderly, poor, ethnic minority, and other persons.

4. Housing for the Elderly

The Section 202 federal program is a bright spot in the otherwise dismal picture of housing for the elderly. Restricted to sponsorship by non-profit groups (the majority of which are related to some religious group), the 202 program continues to offer a direct ministry opportunity. Since it is a loan guarantee program and has limited impact upon the federal budget, it should be funded at much more realistic levels than in the past. The steady increase in age of our population argues for expanding the 202 program until the need for this type of rental housing for the elderly has been met.

We are greatly concerned over the rapidly increasing trend toward converting rental housing to condominiums for sale. Too often in practice this means pushing elderly people out of housing they can afford to rent but can't afford to buy. We therefore, recommend that the rate of condominium conversion of rental units be slowed. Further, we urge local housing authorities to offset this bind by encouraging increased housing stock of subsidized rental units for the elderly under Section 202.

5. Housing for Native Americans

As in the case with regard to other aspects of our national policy and practices toward Native American tribes and the continued isolation of our fellow citizens on reservations, implementation of housing programs to benefit our reservations population has been woefully inadequate. We call for substantial increases in programs at the federal level, and the use of state and local housing programs in every possible way, so that the shocking level of reservation housing conditions can be changed quickly. Special efforts by United Methodist programs and funds for ethnic minorities should be supportive of such efforts.

6. Increasing Housing Production

Outmoded materials and procedures required by building codes often force housing costs up. Also, because of a wide variation in building codes in different communities, it is difficult to utilize mass-produced building units and components. Therefore, we recommend that city and country governments and the trade unions review building codes with the prospect of revising them to reasonable restrictions which will not stand in the way of utilizing factory-built housing. We also recommended there be instituted state or national standardization of building codes so that system-built homes and apartments can be produced on a substantial scale. Nevertheless, quality workmanship and materials must be guaranteed.

Building codes should encourage use of adequate insulation and passive solar or other innovative fuel saving technology. Zoning codes should protect solar access for new construction, and allow for the possibility of converting existing residential units to solar technology.

Substandard lot sizes and topography often are deterrents to constructing housing units on available urban lots. In such instances, because manual labor must be used

195

instead of machine labor, it is difficult for builders to earn a profit, and quality must be compromised to break even. Therefore we recommend that the federal and state programs compensate for such site deficiencies through subsidies, and thus enlarge the housing stock by using lots that would otherwise add to the deterioration of a neighborhood. However, such use should not deny other possible needs, such as air space, recreational grounds, or other community amenities.

7. Financing of Housing

Traditionally, the vast majority of housing in our country has been financed through the private money lending business. There is little likelihood that this would need to change if the traditional principles against usury are followed. But more attention needs to be given to developing ways mortgage money can be made available to low income persons for homeownership, to provide rental housing for homeownership, and to provide rental housing for low income people. Federal and state programs benefit the moderate and upper income segments of our population quite well, but there are not equally helpful programs for the lower income sector of the population. Such government subsidized mortgage programs need to be further developed. New methods of private financing need to be developed so that traditional money sources do not abandon the housing field for other more profitable forms of investment.

Where feasible, generous tax credits and loan subsidies should be made available from various political entities to builders, owners, and renters for the installation and use of solar energy equipment.

8. Neighborhoods and Communities

An emphasis upon neighborhood revitalization is sweeping the urban scene. It may also be offered as a panacea for deteriorating suburban areas. Even rural communities and cross-road towns face the temptation to use a "Fix-up" approach to housing deterioration problems. There is much to be valued in retaining and restoring housing which is soundly constructed and can be expected to continue to be usable for years to come. Not only could it be somewhat less expensive, but such a process is a needed supplement to reduce pressures for the costs of new construction. But several pitfalls should be recognized. Changing types, sizes, and age levels of family units often make rehabilitation of existing housing more expensive than is justified by either the age of the building or the economic capability of the family. Often neighborhood revitalization is a less offensive term for displacement of families presumed to be less desirable, and so it becomes another type of class, racial, or ethnic discrimination. Likewise, maintaining "community" may often be little more than a cover for continuing various forms of ethnic and racial exclusiveness. We urge all citizens to be honest and realistic in assessing the value of any neighborhood or community development program and then proceed with caution and objective responsiblity in implementing rehabilitation and revitalization programs.

D. *Role of the Church*

A number of federal programs as well as some state programs exist today to make it possible for church groups to participate meaningfully in providing adequate housing in a wholesome environment. We encourage churches to join in such programs which require only a minimum of capital investment but a substantial commitment of time and energy. Churches should be aware that these programs are available to both urban and rural people. More church groups ought to 1) be concerned about the conditions of housing; 2) use the tools available to provide better housing; 3) develop a sense of mission and assure responsibility as stewards to meet these needs with no expectation of monetary reward.

In implementing any housing ministry, church people must maintain great sensitivity to community needs and work to achieve community participation and control. Needs of tenants for adequate, reasonably priced, and energy-efficient housing should be recognized. Care always must be exercised to assure our involvement as Christians as "enablers" rather than "controllers." Our goal must always be to enable those who benefit to be in control of their own

197

lives, future, and destiny. Whatever the form of community organization, housing production, management, or ownership, every effort should be made at each developmental step to insure that those who are being aided are afforded, indeed required to take, every action necessary to self-direct the undertaking. Wherever possible, we must train rather than service, transfer power rather than decide, empower rather than control. In this as in all other aspects of housing ministries, United Methodists should seek the best technical guidance, and provide the greatest professional competence for such a ministry. Let us equip ourselves and provide the widest possible range of supportive assistance to individuals, congregations, districts, conferences, and all forms of cooperative groups sharing similar goals and policies, so that our fellow citizens may achieve as their right "decent, safe and sanitary housing" at the earliest possible time.[22]

Human Rights

Mindful of the tradition in which we stand, we see the struggle for human rights for all people of God to be a continuous unfolding of the gospel. It is an unfinished task. Our participation in this struggle means that we must identify those principalities and powers that militate against the worth of persons and groups, that seek to devalue life by denying basic rights, or that claim an ultimacy for themselves rather than for the persons they are designed to serve.

We affirm that all persons and groups are of equal worth in the sight of God. We therefore work toward societies in which each person's or group's worth is recognized, maintained, and strengthened. We deplore all political and economic ideologies that lead to repression or totalitarianism, that pit persons against each other, that deny hope, that seek to enhance privilege and power of the few at the

[22]*See* Social Principles V-A; "Support of the Fair Housing Act," 1984.

expense of the well-being of the many. We condemn violations of human rights in all political and economic structures. The Church, while proclaiming the gospel message of a God of love and justice, must be wary lest it compromise its own witness and unwittingly become an uncritical ally of repressive power and privilege in society around it.

As United Methodists throughout the world give more attention to human rights, we must constantly examine or change our own practices in every locale where the basic rights of persons or groups may have been denied. The church in each community should be the means for removing the blindness from our eyes so that we perceive rights denied and redress imperfections.

Often the relationship of one country to another has been dictated by military and economic interests which tend to shape foreign policy and override moral imperatives to defend human rights. The Church should not sanction nor should foreign governments support those governments or regimes that deny people the right of speech, assembly, dissent, education, health, worship, or other rights.

Therefore we urge:

1. That The United Methodist Church on all levels continually examine the biblical and theological bases which call us to our own commitment to human rights.

2. That The United Methodist Church urge governments to cease all financial, military, open, or covert support of those governments or regimes that systematically violate the rights of their citizens.

3. That The United Methodist Church urge governments—nationally, regionally, and locally—to accord basic human right to all persons residing within their boundaries regardless of citizenship. These rights include the right to an education, adequate health care, due process and redress of law, and protection against social and economic exploitation.

4. That United Methodist agencies join in efforts—ecumenical, denominational, or international—on behalf of human rights, informing our people of developments in the

199

struggles and offering them means of constructive responses.

5. That The United Methodist Church designate human rights as a continuing study emphasis to be carried on in every local church, utilizing in part the Social Principles and materials published in 1979 by the National Council of Churches and the Board of Global Ministries for the study theme, "Human Rights and the International Order."[23]

Human Rights in Korea

The human rights of the people of South Korea have been seriously violated since the establishment in 1972 of the repressive Yushin ("revitalization") Constitution. In the period since the death of President Park Chung-hee in October, 1979, there seems to be some genuine movement toward the formulation of a democratic constitution. It is, nevertheless, a regrettable fact that freedoms of speech, press, and assembly, the very basis of democracy itself, continue to be denied the Korean people by means of martial law and many persons contine to be incarcerated or restricted for political reasons.

It is true that in the past twenty-five years, Korea has achieved significant economic growth. The standard of living of the population has increased substantially. These achievements, however, were made at the expense of workers and those who are not in the privileged economic class.

The United States, as the primary nation involved in the formation of the Republic of Korea, has a unique responsibility for the flourishing of genuine representative government there, and has supported Korea's governments with military and economic aid ostensibly in order to perserve democracy. However, the U.S. government has been reluctant to pursue a strong course of human rights in Korea in deference to perceived American national security interests.

[23]*See* Social Principles V-A.

Our religious faith calls us to affirm the dignity and worth of every human being and to struggle with our oppressed brothers and sisters for justice in order "to preach good news to the poor . . . to proclaim release to the captives . . . to set at liberty those who are oppressed."

Therefore, Be It Resolved that we, the General Conference of The United Methodist Church:

1. Express our continuing support for our brothers and sisters who struggle and suffer for the sake of social justice in Korea;

2. Call on the United States government to insist on the immediate end to martial law in Korea and the withdrawal of military officers from civilian governmental affairs, making it clear that the continued distortion of their proper defense role by the ROK military threatens the basis of the United States' commitment to the security of Korea.[24]

Study Document on Human Sexuality

God's love as promised in the Covenants and revealed in Jesus Christ is the norm for our relationships with each other. Relationships which call forth wholeness, caring, openness, and dignity between persons affirm God's covenant. God's love, expressed in covenant, calls us and strengthens us to live faithfully in human community. The crucial questions of life center on understanding who we are, on how we relate to one another, and on our response to the love of God. This is the Gospel's message.

Current discussions in our churches concerning sexuality indicate much fear, misconception, ignorance, hostility, or indifference, making evident the need for the Gospel's message of forgiveness and renewal in this crucially important area of human relationships. We are not as caring for each other as the Gospel calls us to be. Too often single persons feel outcast from church activities because pro-

[24]*See* Social Principles V-A; "Korea," 1984.

grams are designed for nuclear families or for married couples, or because the singles groups seem designed for "match-making." Too often the Church has not provided a supportive climate for the widowed and divorced. Too often teenagers and adults search for adequate sex education resources only to have the churches respond by saying the subject is "too controversial." Too often men and women who are genuinely struggling with problems in their sexual relationships or with ambivalences in their sexual orientation have had their concerns met with rigidity and simple moralisms, if met at all. Open and helpful dialogue is blocked, and personal needs are ignored. For many individuals this lack of openness results in their leaving the church in search of more supportive communities.

Why do we do this to one another? What is it about our view of sexuality that causes us, more often than not, to approach it negatively rather than positively? Are our expectations and experiences about human sexuality bound up with a culturally restricted view of humanity, full of "holy negatives"? Often we are subject to distorted and misinterpreted biblical, theological, and ethical interpretation. We are called to examine the biblical and theological roots of our understanding of human sexuality. Careful consideration should be given to the context in which Scripture was written. The emphasis on sexuality as limited to procreation is particularly in need of examination. Additionally the biblical teachings must be related to understandings provided by the human sciences and both should be applied to personal and corporate experience of contemporary Christians.

We recognize that for Christians across the United States and the world there is a profusion of voluntary and involuntary living patterns, caused by social, economic, cultural, and political factors. There is no one life pattern for all Christians. We are called to discipleship and to nurture the quality of our faith and life together.

To speak of our sexuality is to speak of all that it means to be male and female. It is a gift of God to each human being and it is a fundamental means by which we realize our individual life-in-community. It is not limited to nor even primarily expressed by genital behavior. All expressions of sexuality affect the emergence of genuine personhood and should reflect a concern for personal integrity, faithfulness in relationships, and the equality of men and women.

A full consideration of sexuality will require study of life's total reality. Each aspect of our sexuality needs full study and discussion. The following are examples of some aspects:

a) health care and health education related to sexuality;
b) psychological dimensions of sexuality;
c) the institutional practices in society that have kept women in an inferior role or status;
d) legal justice, including efforts to assure civil rights for homosexuals;
e) legal rights relating to contraceptives, abortion, rape, and incest;
f) economic exploitation of sexuality and dehumanization of persons, such as is evident in advertising, pornography and prostitution, with particular concern for the growing misuse of children in pornography and prostitution;
g) the tremendous increase in teenage pregnancy, its causes and implications.

These are not totally new areas to our Church's life and concern, but they do represent areas where much more open, rational, and loving dialogue must occur. These issues are not options for Christians to discuss. They are issues of basic human dignity and Christians must affirm the roots for establishing that dignity. We should not stereotype any person, or make certain persons or life situations the object of cruel jokes or flippant comments. Each person must be free to speak about these issues without fear of being labeled or excluded by others in the church.

We recognize at least five mistaken ways of viewing sexuality. They are: 1) to worship it as an ultimate concern; 2) to sacramentalize sexuality as so holy, so extraordinarily divine that it becomes threatening and dominating over our lives; 3) to debase sex and sexuality, viewing these aspects of life as essentially evil; 4) to trivialize sex and sexuality, denying the deep meanings of human relationships; and 5) to abuse sex and sexuality by using it as a means of manipulating and controlling others.

Profound changes in marriage, divorce, child-rearing, and living arrangements have occurred in the U.S. in the past decade. Family types are extremely diverse as a 1978 breakdown revealed:

Father as the sole wage earner, a mother as a full-time homemaker, and at least one child—15.9 percent.

Both the father and the mother as wage earners, plus one or more children at home—18.5 percent.

Married couples with no children, or with children living at home—30.5 percent.

Women who are single parents, with one or more children at home—6.2 percent.

Single-parent males, with one or more children at home—0.6 percent.

Unrelated persons living together—2.5 percent.

Single-person households—20.6 percent.

Female- or male-headed households that include relatives other than spouses or children—5.3 percent.

Statistics are from the U.S. Statistical Abstract, 1977. Children are defined as persons under 18.[25]

U.S. government sources indicated that the marriage trend, along with the continued increase in divorce, has made for stunning increases in the ranks of people living alone. Although most of such people are still elderly widows, big increases are evident among young men first and then young women. A corollary trend is the family headed by a woman.[26] The Church must address its word of love and hope to people in all these myriad conditions.

Data from the 1978 census reveals that one out of every five American households consisted of just one person, a staggering 42 percent increase over the 1970 census

[25]"Who Is the Real American Family?", *Ms.*, August, 1978, p. 43.
[26]"Marital Status and Living Arrangements; March 1978," Series P-20, No. 338, U.S. Government Printing Office, Washington, D.C. 20402.

statistic. Census experts tell us that nearly half of all children born today will spend a significant portion of their childhood with only one parent. The number of unmarried persons living together more than doubled in this eight-year period, although this does not necessarily imply a sharp rise in lifelong singleness.

The Church in its advocacy of human worth must take seriously the validity of singleness for clergy and laity, women and men, and incorporate this understanding into its program. Single women and men at all ages need expressions of physical affection and emotional support from both women and men. Widowed and divorced persons speak of this need. As long as one lives, there is need for loving support expressed physically and emotionally. The Church must search out ways for all persons to fulfill this basic human need for warmth, closeness, and affection.

Single parents need support groups within the Church for sharing concerns or for assistance in times of particular needs. Churches need to recognize single-parent families in their usual family life activities which tend to assume the nuclear family as the norm.

The nuclear family, which is defined as wife and husband and offspring living together in a common household, comprises 34.4 percent of all households in the U.S.[27]

Regarding the nuclear family, we recognize that the changing understandings of one's own sexuality result in new awareness of the dynamics of intimacy, meaning, and power. What is to be shared, or what is kept private? Where can married couples find support for their needs? Power within family units can no longer appropriately be exercised through an authoritarian style of life, or by automatically assigning power on the basis of gender. The varying stresses and opportunities affecting the nuclear family provide the Church with unique challenges for ministry and participation.

Some women, in coping with a changing society, turn even more strongly to concepts of femininity whereby they

[27]"Who Is the Real American Family?", p. 43.

regard themselves as sex objects and basically as inferior to men. Some persons have exploited this notion through organizations, book sales, political movements. The exploitation of sexual issues by playing upon the fears of people in order to gain a political following is a serious issue within the Church as well as within local, state, and federal governments. Narrow biblical teaching has been used to undergird this philosophy.

We believe that these concepts of females as sex objects exploit both men and women and seriously distort the basic gospel message of respect for persons. For the many women who are not married and for many who are, such methods perpetuate cruel illusions about sexuality and relationships. In contrast we believe that these times call for the active incarnation of the gospel example of mutual love and commitment to one another's well being in the midst of change.

In discussions about human sexuality, persons often reveal fear of the ambiguities inherent in life's experiences and relationships. Confronting this fear is part of the risk of living life fully, trusting the gospel message that mercy and grace come with the risk of faithfulness to God.

Sexuality is commonly associated with sin. The very notion of sin has a distinctly sexual suggestion in the popular mind. However, the basic form of sexual sin lies precisely in our alienation from our sexuality. At its root sin always involves alienation in three interwoven directions: separation from self, from neighbors, and from God.[28]

The Bible reflects the ambiguities we experience in our human sexuality. Yet its message about creation, sin, judgment, and redemption is that God is good, loving, and just and will sustain us in our brokenness as well as in our strength.

Nowhere in the Church's considerations of human sexuality is there more confusion, embarrassment, and even self-hatred evident than in the current discussions about

[28]The United Church of Christ, *Human Sexuality—A Preliminary Study* (New York: United Church Press, 1977).

homosexuality. It is not simply a matter of differences of opinion among church members or between clergy and laity. Homophobia, the fear of homosexuality in oneself or another, is one of the sexual fears which must be faced.

Homophobia has caused the waste of many human lives whose full talents have never been available to the churches because known homosexual men and women have been labelled and set apart. But a heavy cost is also paid by those who suffer from such a phobia. The resulting inhibitions spread to a whole range of behavior related to the feared activity.

We urge the Church to resist easy moralisms or dogmatic views which set up different views regarding the "normalcy" in sexual behavior of heterosexuality and homosexuality. Promiscuity, the idolatry of pleasure, the absence of fidelity, attack, seduction and violence, the exploitation of people, are characteristics found among persons of all sexual orientations. On the other hand, gentleness and warmth, compassion and strength, commitment and fidelity are human qualities which are found in persons of all sexual orientations.

What is the Church's mission? Are we commissioned to love and minister to all persons as sexual beings, or just to some? What is an inclusive Church? Is sin a state of being or an act? Is there less love, respect, and fidelity among homosexual followers of Christ? Is there only one sexual norm to which all must or can be converted.

In summary, we believe that the Church must concern itself with the reality of human sexuality in all its aspects, including:

—the needs of single persons in all categories;
—the needs of persons with physically or emotionally handicapping conditions;
—changes and needs facing the nuclear family;
—sex-stereotyping which results in inferior status for women;
—the needs of older persons;
—sexual orientation including heterosexuality, bisexuality, homosexuality;

207

—the meaning of sexuality and the fear of sexuality;
—the theological and biblical issues which would enlighten all the above.[29]

In Support of the United Nations

This General Conference affirms its historic support for the United Nations. Today we rejoice in the fact that for the past thirty-five years the United Nations has been a functioning organization working for international peace and justice. In that time it has:

• Provided mechanisms for the peaceful settlement of disputes.

• Provided an arena for promotion of a just and equitable world economic system.

• Provided assistance through United Nations Educational Scientific and Cultural Organization, United Nations Development Program, United Nations Children's Fund (UNICEF), World Health Organization, and its other agencies to persons who are usually neglected.

• Established peacekeeping forces in troubled areas.

• Defused big power confrontations.

• Provided a forum for discussion of difficult issues, such as decolonization.

World public opinion has affirmed the growing importance of the United Nations in the search for world peace. However, the respect for the organization which has developed among most of the world's peoples is paralleled with a growing apathy toward it in a few countries of the world, including the United States. This apathy jeopardizes the understanding and reduces the effectiveness of the work of the United Nations. We pledge ourselves to work to broaden citizen awareness in those countries in order to enable persons to evaluate accurately the work of the United Nations.

[29]*See* Social Principles II-F.

Despite the desire of the world's peoples, the United Nations has been unable to act in many important arenas. This inability is caused primarily by lack of political will on the part of member states. We have long declared selfish nationalism to be a primary enemy of peace. Although some change in the structure of the organization may, in the future, be desirable or necessary, structural problems do not prevent success in areas of action; it is instead the unwillingness of member states to act cooperatively. We ask United Methodists to urge their governments to utilize the United Nations and to provide leadership which will extend international cooperation and create world community. By this means the United Nations will be enabled to act constructively with regard to the major areas of concern to the world's peoples.

The pursuit of peace is thwarted when misunderstandings about the purpose and possibilities of the United Nations are widely promoted and believed. Therefore, we commend to the churches a wider study of the United Nations in order that Christians might be enabled to work in unity for peace and justice in the world.

To that end:

1. We reaffirm decisions of the General Conference beginning in 1944 to establish "an international office of education and publicity for peace." These decisions resulted in establishment of the Methodist Office for the United Nations and, in 1963, in construction of the Church Center for the United Nations.

2. We particularly commend the program "United Methodist Seminars on National and International Affairs" to local church, district, and Annual Conference groups as a way to experience first hand the work of the United Nations as it grapples with the work for peace.

3. We also reaffirm the importance of celebrating the signing of the Charter of the United Nations on October 24, 1945, with an emphasis in local churches on World Order Sunday, observed on that date or the Sunday preceding it.[30]

[30]*See* Social Principles VI-D; "The United Methodist Church and Peace," 1980.

In Support of Women, Infants, and Children's Supplemental Food and Nutrition Education Program (WIC Program)

WHEREAS, the Women, Infants, and Children's Supplemental Food and Nutrition Education Program (WIC Program) provides nutrition education and food coupons for needy high-risk pregnant women, lactating women, and children under five years of age, and

WHEREAS, the WIC food coupons are available to high-risk needy pregnant women such as those who are anemic, overweight or underweight, teenage or over 35, or those who have had problems with a previous pregnancy, and

WHEREAS, the WIC coupons, costing an average of $27 per month per person on the program, can be used only for milk, cheese, eggs, juices high in Vitamin C, iron-fortified cereal, and iron-fortified formula and not for high caloric junk foods that are low in certain essential nutrients, and

WHEREAS, malnutrition is a primary cause of low birth weight babies, and

WHEREAS, low birth weight babies get off to a slow start in life at great emotional expense to the parents and financial hardship to families, insurance companies, and the taxpayers, and

WHEREAS, the cost of putting weight on a newborn baby in a "premie nursery" is about $600 per day and about $5,000 per pound of weight gain, and

WHEREAS, inadequate diet in the formative years is a major cause of some types of mental retardation, and

WHEREAS, 60 percent of the total number of brain cells are already developed at the time of birth, the other 40 percent are developed by the age of 3, and from 3 to age 5 the brain cells increase in size, but not in number, and

WHEREAS, the cost of institutional care of a mentally retarded child is $1,400 per month or more, and of a mentally retarded adult is $700 to $1,400 per month for life;

Now Therefore Be It Resolved, that The United Methodist General Conference go on record as supporting the Women, Infants, and Children's Supplemental Food and

Nutrition Education Program, Public Law 95627 of the Child Nutrition Act, as a positive, cost-effective, malnutrition prevention measure.[31]

Inflation

Be It Resolved:

That the leadership and members of The United Methodist Church recognize inflation as a major domestic issue facing our nation, and that all United Methodists have a moral obligation and duty to seek to curb the damaging effects of inflation on the welfare of our people.

1. Inflation provides means whereby the strong and the well-organized can effectively exploit the weak, unorganized, and aged.
2. It provides methods of promoting changes in our economic, social, and political institutions that circumvent the democratic process.
3. It encourages deceitful promises in politics by allowing the government to validate its promises by the creation of money that becomes worth less and less.
4. It robs the pensioner and all people living on fixed incomes and causes suffering and want.
5. Its long-term consequences are unpredictable and thereby it makes all long-term planning of financial and economic matters—including those of our Church and its related institutions—colleges, hospitals, orphanages, and homes for the elderly—meaningless.

We therefore pledge ourselves to corporate and individual restraint in activities that are inflationary. We believe that inflation, at its present rate, can only lead to chaos in this country and that the only sane way to deal with inflation is to stop it. We urge the political leaders of our country, and all others in positions of public trust, to take immediate and corrective action in dealing with this problem, to which action we pledge our support.[32]

[31]*See* Social Principles V-A.
[32]*See* Social Principles IV-Preamble.

Juvenile Justice

Our Lord particularly identified with children and illustrated the loving care which they need to grow and mature (Mark 9:36-37, Mark 9:42).

The Social Principles of The United Methodist Church calls for special attention to the rights of children and youth. From these perspectives we are concerned that in many states children are arrested and incarcerated for truancy, incorrigibility, stubborn altercations with parents, and other conduct which would not be criminal if performed by an adult. Such status offenses should not be considered as grounds for involving a juvenile in processes of criminal procedure or even of delinquency procedures. Rather, a child in trouble should be helped by agencies for domestic assistance.

There is considerable evidence that the methods of dealing with the child have a major part in developing criminal tendencies. Most violent adults persistently repeating crimes began their conflict with law and order as children ten to fourteen years old. If treatment by the state or local agencies leads the child to think of himself or herself as a tough young criminal, he or she is likely to act out that role.

The United Methodist Church urges that all status offenses be eliminated from the juvenile codes and from the processes for determining juvenile delinquency. We urge further that all offenses by children and youth be handled with extreme reluctance to incarcerate the offender. We especially oppose solitary confinement of children and youths in official detention. Institutions where juveniles classified as delinquent often are segregated from the general population often become schools of crime. As an alternative, we encourage greater use of supportive services for parents and children in their home settings; foster child care; neighborhood group homes, Parents Anonymous, and other alternatives.

There are communities within the states in which children are routinely locked up in jails because of a lack of temporary shelter care or an unwillingness to use home detention. We urge the prohibition of placing dependent and neglected children in jails or facilities for juvenile delinquents.[33]

The Law of the Sea

We recognize that "All creation is the Lord's and we are responsible for the ways in which we use and abuse it." (1980 Statement of Social Principles.)

We are called to repent of our devastation of the physical and non-human world, because this world is God's creation and is therefore to be valued and conserved.

Nowhere is this need greater than in relation to the sea. In 1970 the United Nations agreed that those areas of the seabed beyond national boundaries were the "common heritage" of humankind. This means that the resources belong to everyone.

But this ideal is not yet expressed in international treaty. So the race is one to see who will be able to exploit and control the resources of the seas. The question facing the peoples of the world is whether global cooperation or global anarchy will prevail.

The best hope for global cooperation is through the United Nations, where representatives of the nations of the world are at work in the conference on the Law of the Sea.

The conference hopes to produce a fair and just law for the ocean, in which all nations will benefit. No one nation will have all of its interests satisfied, but mechanisms will be set up to maintain order and peace, and both developed and developing countries will have worked on the regulations.

The United Nations, concerned with protecting this "common heritage" of humankind, is negotiating international agreements to:

—guarantee unimpeded access to over 100 straits, facilitating commercial transportation;

[33]*See* Social Principles V-F; "Criminal Justice," 1984.

—prevent conflicts or "cold wars" like the one between Iceland and England over fishing waters;

—enforce environmental regulations forbidding countries to dump harmful wastes which spoil the ocean waters;

—share equitably the ocean resources, oil, fish, minerals, and prohibit unjust exploitation of these resources by the powerful;

—regulate access to the waters of coastal countries to permit research of the marine environment;

—limit the continuing extension of national sovereignty over international waters and settle legal disputes arising therefrom;

—prevent the division of the world into competing camps depending on powerful navies;

—create an international agency to cooperatively manage the international seabed resources.

We also affirm our support for the evolution of effective "commons" law, such as treaties now under development for the Antarctic and outer space, which supports our obligations of stewardship, justice, and peace.

Therefore, we urge all United Methodists to become informed about all of the aspects of "Law of the Sea," one of the most critical and least understood issues of our day.

Further, we urge all United Methodists to call upon their governments to commit themselves to the development of a just and equitable treaty through the United Nations Conference on Law of the Sea, and to ratification of the treaty by our respective governments.[34]

The Local Church
and the Local Jail

The writer of the Letter to the Hebrews, in suggesting conduct consistent with the new covenant brought through the mediation of Jesus, advises, "Remember those who are in prison as though in prison with them" (Hebrews 13:3).

[34]*See* Social Principles I; "Common Heritage," 1984.

214

The Social Principles of the United Methodist Church urges that the love of Christ be translated into "new systems of rehabilitation that will restore, preserve, and nurture the humanity of the imprisoned." This concern must be expressed in local communities by local congregations, for most of those imprisoned in the United States are in city and county jails.

Citizens pay millions of dollars for the support of jails in their local communities each year; yet, for the individuals who are detained in them, jail life is a particularly dehumanizing experience accompanied by the loss of freedom, the loss of contact with family and friends, and the loss of self-determination.

According to recent studies, most local jails provide inadequate food services, minimal medical care, no libraries or recreational facilities, no educational programs, and only a limited religious ministry. These conditions are physically injurious, mentally deteriorating, and spiritually destructive to those who are confined.

Most of the persons detained in local jails are being held for trial and actually are serving sentences prior to their conviction.

Since incarceration is by its very nature dehumanizing and destructive, The United Methodist Church states its belief that every responsible means should be used to reduce the present jail population and to use methods (such as release on recognizance, bail, probation, etc.) to keep persons out of jail.

All citizens have a fundamental right and obligation to know how the jails in their communities are being administered, how prisoners are being treated, and under what conditions they are being confined.

They should have further concern for the losses in human relationships and personal welfare which are suffered by those who are held in local jails.

The United Methodist Church urges its members to inform themselves about local jails through participation in citizen inspections; to establish programs of regular volunteer visitation with both individual staff members and

215

confined residents of jails; to support chaplaincy programs within jails; and to diligently seek the alleviation of the present inhumane conditions while working for the eventual elimination of jails, except as necessary places of detention for dangerous criminals. Members of churches are further urged to support and fund organizations in their local communities which advocate the protection of the rights of all citizens. Where conditions are found to be substandard, United Methodist Church members are urged to request formal inquiry procedures.[35]

National Academy of Peace and Conflict Resolution

WHEREAS, the Congress of the United States has approved the Commission on Proposals for the National Academy of Peace and Conflict Resolution; and

WHEREAS, the Congress has appropriated funds for the work of the commission; and

WHEREAS, the three members have been named by the President, the Senate President *pro tempore,* and the Speaker of the House:

Be It Resolved, that the General Board of Church and Society identify areas of work of the commission, publicize the work and findings of the commission, and educate the United Methodist membership as to the implications of the task of the commission for them.[36]

Opposition to a Call for a Constitutional Convention

As United Methodists, we are grateful that for almost 200 years the Constitution of the United States has provided a

[35]*See* Social Principles V-F; "Criminal Justice," 1984.
[36]*See* Social Principles VI-C; "The United Methodist Church and Peace," 1980.

basis for cherished religious and civil liberties. The document, drawn up by persons, including many descendants of those who fled to America because of persecution for their religious beliefs, has served as the cornerstone of our freedoms. The Social Principles statement of The United Methodist Church "acknowledge(s) the vital function of government as a principal vehicle for the ordering of society." With the rules for governing, a constitutional convention would become a vehicle of disorder rather than order.

We are therefore deeply concerned about state efforts to mandate that Congress call a convention which would re-open the Constitution and possibly jeopardize its provisions.

I. Background

Unknown to most citizens of the United States, state legislatures have petitioned Congress for a constitutional convention. Only seven more are needed to make up the three-fourths required by the Constitution. This would be the first constitutional convention since 1787 which was called to amend the Articles of Confederation. There are two forces behind the movement. One desires to add an amendment declaring a fetus a human person at the moment of conception, thus prohibiting abortions for any reason. Another force seeks an amendment to require a balanced federal budget.

The Constitution provides two methods for proposing amendments. One is the familiar route used to adopt all of the twenty-six present amendments. Five others were approved by Congress but not ratified by the states. Two are still pending. Both methods are described in Article V of the Constitution:

The Congress, whenever two-thirds of both Houses shall deem it necessary, shall propose amendments to this Constitution, or on the application of the legislatures of two-thirds of the several states, shall call a convention for proposing amendments, which, in either case, shall be valid to all intents and purposes of this Constitution, when ratified by the legislatures of three-fourths of the several states, or by conventions in three-fourths thereof, as the one or the other mode of ratification may be proposed by the Congress.

Since 1787 there have been over 300 applications for a constitutional convention but no single proposal has ever been endorsed by two-thirds of the states at the same time. The closest approach occurred in the mid-1960's when thirty-three state legislatures petitioned Congress to call a convention to overrule the "one person, one vote" decision of the Supreme Court dealing with equitable apportionment of state legislatures.

II. Reasons for Opposition to a Constitutional Convention

We state the following concerns as our reasons for opposing a constitutional convention.

1. There are virtually no guidelines regarding the specific rules for calling a convention and, if it were called, for determining how it would be run.

Since the language of the Constitution is vague, serious questions have been raised which constitutional scholars and jurists are unable to answer. What constitutes a valid application to Congress by a state legislature for an amending convention? Do all state petitions have to have the same wording, the same provisions, and the same subject matter? If the two-thirds of the legislatures do adopt a resolution, is Congress obliged to call a convention? Must all applications for a convention on a given issue be submitted to the same Congress, or is an application adopted in 1975, for example, still valid? If an amending convention were called, could it be limited to a single issue or might it open the entire constitution for change? How would delegates be selected and how would votes in the convention be allocated? What would Congress' role be in this amending method? Would disputes over calling a convention and over its procedures be reviewable by the courts?

The complexity of the questions, and the fact that

218

"experts" have no answers, illustrates the seriousness of attempting an uncharted route for changing the most fundamental document of our government.

2. This Constitutional convention process of amendment has been a less democratic procedure than the traditional means of amendment.

The fact that in almost 200 years there have been only twenty-six amendments to the Constitution attests to the fact that the traditional amendment route is constructed to assure wide national debate on each amendment and careful consideration by a three-fourths majority of the legislatures.

The process of calling for a constitutional convention has not been marked by careful consideration and democratic procedures. Of the twenty-seven states which have adopted the resolution, only six legislatures held hearings where the public was able to testify on the implications of the convention. In most instances there has been only cursory debate before adopting the resolution. In two states no committees considered the petitions before they were passed by the two bodies of the legislature. Committee reports were issued in only six states, explaining the proposed action. In one state, the senate committee discussed the petition for thirty minutes; the house committee discussed it six minutes.

Further, the people of the United States would have no direct vote on the results of the convention. State constitutional conventions, which are quite common, submit the proposed state constitutional changes to the voters. This has prevented the passage of changes pushed by small pressure groups, frequently over highly emotional issues. But the voters would have no ability to vote on a national constitutional revision, a matter affecting their most precious liberties.

3. Forces behind the call for a constitutional convention are dealing with highly emotional and highly complex issues which should be dealt with in the established manner for amending the Constitution.

"Right to Life" advocates, frustrated by their inability to succeed in their goals of eliminating all abortions through

219

the normal legislative process are now trying the constitutional convention route. Yet such an amendment, declaring the fetus a person from the moment of conception, would be, in effect, to write one theological position into the Constitution. Various faith groups, including the United Methodist Church, do not share that theology. Such a position would be tantamount to declaring an abortion for any reason a murder. It would also inhibit the use of contraceptives such as the inter-uterine device (IUD). This would be contrary to the doctrine of separation of church and state embodied in the Constitution, and would impinge on freedom of religion, guaranteed in the First Amendment.

While the idea of a balanced federal budget has wide popular support, economists are highly uncertain of its effect on the economy. Many believe that it would not cut spending, as the public believes, but instead might require higher taxes and higher revenues. Both Republican and Democratic leaders oppose such an amendment because of its inflexibility. The budget and the economy are closely interrelated. When unemployment goes up only one percentage point, the deficit swells by some $20 billion due to lost tax revenues and increased social welfare costs such as unemployment compensation. A constitutional amendment would make it impossible to deal with such situations. Congressional leadership also points to the fact that the federal budget could be balanced fairly easily—by eliminating the current $82 billion in aid to state and local governments. But the same states calling for an amendment do not want the budget balanced at the cost of lost revenue to their states.

In summary, the present move towards a constitutional convention is ill-conceived and is being promoted by persons looking for easy solutions to complex problems. The Constitution should not have to suffer at the expense of frustrations that should be dealt with in the normal procedural manner which has served us well for two centuries.

Therefore, Be It Resolved, that the General Conference:

1. Oppose efforts of state legislatures to petition Congress to call a constitutional convention;
2. Inform local congregations regarding the factors involved in proposing a constitutional convention; and
3. Urge United Methodists to communicate their opposition to such a convention to their state legislatures and, in states that have adopted such a resolution, to urge its withdrawal.

Penal Reform

Our Lord began his ministry by declaring "release to the captives . . . " (Luke 4:18) and he distinguished those who would receive a blessing at the last judgment by saying, "I was in prison and you came to me." The Christian, therefore, naturally has concern for those who are captive, for those who are imprisoned, and for the human conditions under which persons are incarcerated.

The Social Principles of The United Methodist Church asserts the need for "new systems of rehabilitation that will restore, preserve, and nurture the humanity of the imprisoned."

There is not one, but many correctional systems in the United States which bear the responsibility for the confinement or supervision of persons convicted of crimes. For the most part the systems are capable neither of rehabilitating criminals nor of protecting society. They are, in fact, institutions where persons are further conditioned in criminal conduct and where advanced skills in crime are taught. More often than not correctional institutions have created crime rather than deterred criminals. They represent an indescribable failure and have been subjected to a gross neglect by the rest of society.

The Church has participated in the neglect of the correctional system by being blind to the inhumanities which the system perpetuates and being silent about the social ills that it intensifies. The Church has challenged neither society nor itself to accept responsibility for making those critically needed changes in the penal system which would permit it to motivate improvement and offer hope to those detained within it.

Major changes are needed in the nation's correctional systems in order for them to become positive factors in the restoration of persons and the stabilization of society. Support needs to be given to alternatives to incarceration to reduce mounting costs, by using additional rehabilitative resources.

The United Methodist Church calls upon its members to express a practical faith in redemptive love through the supporting of:

1. The greater use of alternatives to pretrial detention for persons accused of crimes such as: (a) release on recognizance; (b) the setting of reasonable and equitable bail; (c) the payment of a modest percentage in cash of the designated bail.

2. The use of alternatives to prosecution such as dispute settlement services and conflict resolution programs and the diverting of persons formally subject to criminal prosecution for drunkenness, vagrancy, and juvenile "status offenses" into those organized programs which furnish noncriminal justice services.

3. The use of alternatives to incarceration for those convicted of crimes such as: fines, payments of restitution to victims of offenders' crimes, social service sentences, and probation.

The United Methodist Church further urges its congregations and members to support those penal policies which:

1. Promote social rehabilitation of convicted persons in preference to punitive confinement.

2. Develop and support a range of community-based alternatives to institutional incarceration such as work release programs.

3. Establish and maintain prisons and jails which have healthful and humane surroundings and a climate conducive to human growth and development.

4. Guarantee and maintain the rights of offenders to legal and medical services. Guarantee the freedom of

expression, association and religion, protect the lives and persons of offenders from abuse from staff and other inmates, and furnish effective procedures for the redress of grievances.

5. Establish uniform disciplinary procedures within correctional institutions.

6. Provide cooperation with community agencies.

7. Allow an optimal maintenance of relationships with the outside world, especially to preserve wholesome marriage and family ties; arrange for conjugal visits of husbands and wives following medical examinations and interviews for the purpose of insuring that mutual desire exists. Arrange visits of families with as much privacy as security will permit. Encourage friends and friendly counselors to make visits as well.[37]

Persons of Japanese Ancestry

WHEREAS, during World War II, the United States of America did forcibly remove and incarcerate, without charges, trial, or any due process of law, 120,000 persons of Japanese ancestry, both citizens and resident aliens of America and citizens from Latin America; and

WHEREAS, this action was initiated by a presidential order, enabled by Congressional legislation, and supported by the Supreme Court, thereby implicating the total government; and

WHEREAS, despite the government's claim of military necessity, this action proved to be made solely on the basis of race, there having been not a single case of sabotage or espionage committed by such persons and there having been no such sweeping action taken against Americans of German or Italian ancestry; and

WHEREAS, the American Convention on Human Rights, to which this country is signatory, states:

"Every person has the right to be compensated in

[37]See Social Principles V-F; "Criminal Justice," 1984.

accordance with the law in the event he has been sentenced by a final judgment through a miscarriage of justice;" and

WHEREAS, legislation has been submitted in the 96th Congress "to provide for payments to certain individuals of Japanese ancestry who were interned, detained, or forcibly relocated by the United States during World War II;"

Therefore, Be It Resolved:

That we urge a study of the facts surrounding the evacuation and incarceration without trial or due process of law of nearly 120,000 Americans of Japanese ancestry;

That this General Conference acknowledge the flagrant violations of human rights, and affirm the need for the United States of America for redress legislation;

That we call upon Congress to support legislation that would determine appropriate remedies; and

That the General Board of Church and Society be instructed to communicate this resolve to all members of Congress and to adopt support for redress as part of its program for this quadrennium.[38]

Population

The creation of the world out of chaos into order is the initial biblical witness. In this witness is the affirmation of the freedom and responsibility of humankind. We affirm God to be the Creator, the one who grants us freedom, and the one to whom we are responsible.

God's ongoing creative and re-creative concern for the universe was expressed through Jesus Christ, who has called us to find the meaning of our lives in dual love of God and neighbor. In this context we live responsibly before God, writing history by the actions of our lives. The imperative upon the individual Christian and the Christian community is to seek patterns of life, shape the structures of society, and foster those values which will dignify human life for all.

In this quest we must not "quench the Spirit" but allow the

[38]*See* Social Principles III-A.

spirit to lead us into God's new day for all people, a new day which calls for the compassionate and passionate desire to see a new birth out of justice.

We believe that history is not finished, but that we are engaged in a history. This is an age of possibility in which we are called under God to serve the future with hope and confidence. Christians have no alternative to involvement in seeking solutions for the great and complex set of problems which faces the world today. All these issues are closely interrelated: hunger, poverty, denial of human rights, economic exploitation and overconsumption by the rich, technologies that are inadequate or inappropriate, depletion of resources, and rapid population growth.

Hunger and poverty, injustice and violence in the world cannot simplistically be blamed on population growth, yet the rapidly swelling numbers of humankind are making it increasingly difficult to solve the other interconnected problems. There is much we do not yet know about the relationship between population size and the sustaining environment, but clearly we do know there can be too many people.

Programs aimed at reducing population growth should not be ends in themselves, not substitutes for other measures necessary to eliminate hunger and poverty. The Church supports population programs as needed to move toward its goal of a just and humane world order.

The population situation is different in different societies, and therefore nations must be free to develop policies in keeping with their own needs and cultures. These global and regional aspects affect all humankind and can only be solved by international cooperation.

At the individual level, our Church has long recognized the basic human right to have the education and means to plan one's family. For women, particularly, the ability to control fertility is a liberating force, making it possible to assume other roles and responsibilities in society. Men and women alike bear responsibility for family planning and contraceptives practices.

Today there are those who claim that some nations are

beyond help because of their rapid population growth. The Christian church cannot accept these voices of despair. Even as just means for achieving stabilization are urgently sought, the Christian church must reaffirm the sacredness of each individual and stand fast against attitudes and practices which treat people as mere numbers or masses.

We welcome the growing understanding of what just and desirable means for lowering fertility rates may encompass, and we affirm that the use of such means must take into consideration the critical importance and interrelated nature of these aspects: better education, and the opportunity for people to participate in decisions that shape their lives; the provision of basic economic security, including old-age security; upgrading the status of women; improved maternal and child health care; and finally, a strong birth control program, including the right to abortion and sterilization procedures which are both legally obtainable and voluntary.

The Church should take the lead in actions which can help focus on the problems caused by rapid population growth and to support measures to deal with them. We therefore call on the people and agencies of the Church:

1. To recognize rapid population growth to be a matter of great religious and moral concern, to develop education and action programs on the issues raised, and to increase understanding of the interrelationships between population growth and other world problems. Education must include sensitivity toward the existence of varying sociological patterns and religious philosophies.

2. To develop programs to increase understanding of the meaning in today's world of responsible parenthood. Churches can encourage acceptance of the idea that not everyone needs to be a parent and that those who choose to have children should accept the small family norm as responsible practice in today's world.

3. To help the affluent realize the devastating impact on the world and its people of wasteful consumption patterns and exploitative economic systems, and to develop re-

sources and curricula which encourage change in over-materialistic life-styles.

4. To urge that United Methodist medical and mission facilities and programs provide a full range of fertility-related and family-planning information and services. The Church should exert leadership in making possible the safe and legal availability of sterilization procedures for both men and women, and of abortion where appropriate.

The Church should offer informed counseling and support to both men and women on all options regarding childbearing. The Church bears a particular responsibility to stand guard against coercive use of birth control practices aimed at the poor and powerless.

5. To take the lead in measures to upgrade the status of women in societies and to include them in all development planning and processes, and give increased support to policies which will further the goal of equal rights for women, such as the Equal Rights Amendment in the United States.

6. To call on all governments to give priority to implementing the provisions of the World Population Plan of Action which the United Nations approved in 1974, and which called for population policies in a context of total social and economic development planning. We especially call on the United States government to develop a national population policy that would include the goal of stablizing the United States population, and recommendations on population distribution and land and resource use.

7. To call on the United States Congress and legislative bodies of the affluent nations to recognize the crucial nature of population growth, and to give maximum feasible funding to programs of population, health, agriculture, and other technological assistance programs for the poor nations. International assistance programs should be based on mutual cooperation, should recognize the diversities of culture, should encourage self development and not dependency, and should not attempt to require "effective population programs" as a prerequisite for other developmental assistance.

8. To call for government and private agencies to place a higher priority on research aimed at developing a range of safe, inexpensive contraceptives that can be used in a variety of societies and medical situations.

A high priority should also be given to research aimed at gaining greater understanding of attitudes, motivations, and social and economic factors affecting childbearing.

Even as we urge individuals and governments to intensify efforts immediately to achieve population stability as soon as possible, the churches need to keep before people the moral reasons why we need to be concerned with the population problem. Our goal in history is that everyone may have the conditions of existence necessary for the fulfillment of God's intentions for humanity. Our context in history is the preciousness of life and the love of God and all creation.[39]

Present Christian Approach
to Sex Education for All Youth

WHEREAS, the millions of teenage pregnancies that occur annually are a source of tragedy to the teenagers, to their offspring, to their families, and to society; and

WHEREAS, our youth are not uniformly educated in their sexual responsibilities and/or in the consequences of promiscuous sexual behavior; and

WHEREAS, the Christian church has the unique responsibility to reach out to the youths and provide them with a Christian perspective on sex;

Therefore Be It Resolved that The United Methodist Church implement programs to reach out to the young people, informing them of their responsibilities and providing them with a healthy and knowledgeable Christian perspective, including programs to reach pregnant teenagers, to reach all youth in formal and informal situations, and to inform those working with the young on sex education.[40]

[39]*See* Social Principles III-H.
[40]*See* Social Principles III-C.

Proper Use of Name:
The United Methodist Church

WHEREAS, The Methodist Church and the Evangelical United Brethren Church were united under the name The United Methodist Church in the year 1968 and that 1980 marks the 12th anniversary of the said union;

Be It Resolved that insofar as possible all materials used in correspondence, advertisements, and signs of the said churches and other organizations that belong to the Church, use the proper name The United Methodist Church.

Be It Further Resolved that the same lettering and style of letters be used in recognition of the great heritage that both groups brought into the union.

Puerto Rico and Vieques

The theme of human liberation is found again and again in the Bible, from Moses' leadership of the Hebrew people out of Egypt to Jesus in the synagogue proclaiming the acceptable year of the Lord.

The United Methodist Church has long stood for an end to colonialism and for the self-determination of all peoples. At the same time, the people of Puerto Rico have lived under the sovereignty of the United States in what can be described as a form of colonialism. Though plebiscites have been held and a degree of local autonomy granted, all of the island's political parties in recent years have expressed their dissatisfaction with Puerto Rico's political status. The situation has been aggravated by the U.S. Navy's bombing practice and related activities on and around two off-shore islands, at first Culebra and now Vieques.

The General Conference of The United Methodist Church:

1. Asks that the people of Puerto Rico be accorded full opportunity for self-determination of their future political status under conditions that assure a genuinely free choice

with generous provisions for adjustment to any new status chosen;

2. Expresses its solidarity with the people of Vieques in their most ardent desire that the United States Navy cease its military activity that adversely affects the citizens of Vieques, and that the United States Navy repair whatever damages it has caused to the people of Vieques.

To these ends the General Conference directs the attention of United Methodists and the general agencies of the denomination to the need for information and action.

Ratification of Human Rights
Covenants and Conventions

The General Conference of the United Methodist Church supports the ratification by the United States Senate of the International Convention on the Prevention and Punishment of Genocide, adopted by the General Assembly of the United Nations in 1948, and transmitted to the Senate of the eighty-first Congress by President Harry S. Truman. We deplore the protracted delay which continues in spite of the support of Presidents Kennedy, Johnson, Nixon, and Carter and urge its prompt ratification by this Senate as an affirmation of the elemental right of all human groups to exist and as a witness to United States' moral concern for all humanity.

In addition to this long-standing concern we support ratification by the United States Senate of the International Covenant on Civil and Political Rights, the International Covenant on Economic, Social, and Cultural Rights, and the International Convention on the Elimination of all Forms of Racial Discrimination which were transmitted to the Senate of the ninety-fifth Congress by President Jimmy Carter.[41]

---

[41]See Social Principles VI-D; "In Support of the United Nations," 1980.

Repression and the Right to Privacy

The Social Principles of The United Methodist Church affirms that "national security must not be extended to justify or keep secret maladministration or illegal and unconscionable activities directed against persons or groups by their own governments. We also strongly reject the domestic surveillance and intimidation of political opponents by governments in power, and all other misuses of elective or appointive offices."

The prophets of Israel denounced the repression of the poor, widows, orphans, and others of their society, and our Lord's ministry began with the announced purpose to set at liberty the poor and disadvantaged. In our biblical tradition we raise the following issues:

Repression

We have lived in a time when the accumulated hopes of racial and cultural minorities combined with a growing dissent in the United States were met by mounting fears and rising anxieties of the dominant group within the population. Seized with apprehension, many became obsessed with establishing a climate of security—even by sacrificing of creating and maintaining justice and protecting the rights and liberties of individuals.

The institutions of this society began to reflect the fears of the majority of the population and established policies and procedures that, in the short range, provided expedient control. These policies, however, were seen as repressive measures by those who sought legitimate rights and new opportunities.

In the immediate past, we sounded a call to concern because we recognized that society can become repressive in nature with hardly a trace of consciousness by the mass of the people, particularly if that people is feverishly fearful and has developed the readiness to accept any measure that seems to offer a new form of protection.

It is deplorable that in a society which is democratic in

231

theory and structure there are signs of increasing repression: dragnet arrests; police and the intelligence community's harassment of minority leaders; charges of conspiracy; summary acquittals of police accused of brutality; the rising militance of rank and file police; support for the use of preventative detention; the utilization of wire taps; censorship of journalism in educational institutions; heavy punitive action against dissidents; the confinement of those who protested within the military forces; the use of police to control dissent within the churches; utilizing grand juries for the purposes of harassment rather than indictment; and the use of church members, clergy, and missionaries for secret intelligence purposes by local police departments, the Federal Bureau of Investigation, and the Central Intelligence Agency.

We affirm the many civil, school, and church authorities who are working toward the elimination of these abuses through their work and example; and we note that many of the most flagrant of these acts of repression no longer occur. Congress, the press, and the American people have begun watching agency activities more closely and with a greater demand for public accountability.

This vigilance must not be relaxed, for if it is there may be renewed acts of repression and fresh attempts to curtail the rights of citizens whenever redress is sought for economic and social grievances.

Therefore, we urge that all Church members and leaders continue to be sensitive to this situation in their local community and in the nation by:

1. Seeking to understand and undergird responsible institutions and agencies of the community and being supportive of measurements that will improve them and upgrade their personnel.
2. Establishing programs in the community sponsored by local churches to: (a) educate church members and their wider community about the potential for repression in the institutions of society; (b) study and affirm the biblical and constitutional basis for justice under law; (c) work in state and federal legislatures to bring about just

and responsible criminal code revisions which do not reinforce repressive elements in our nation's life; oppose forms of legislation which would legalize repression; support legislation which would prohibit intelligence agencies from conducting surveillance or disruption of lawful political activities or otherwise violating constitutional rights; (d) develop an awareness of the rights and protection citizens should expect; (e) work for institutional change in situations where rights are not respected and protection is not furnished.

The Right to Privacy

The Christian faith stresses the dignity of and respect for human personality. Invasion of the privacy of an ordinary citizen of society negates this dignity and respect. Further, the Christian faith is supportive of a society which elicits hope and trust, not a society that foments fear and threatens with oppression.

The revelation that intelligence agencies, local police, and the United States Army have over a number of years developed a domestic espionage apparatus involving the gathering of information about the lawful political activities of millions of citizens is a cause for concern.

The Constituional Rights Subcommittee and the Privacy Commission Report provided substantial information which demonstrated that privacy lies in jeopardy as a result of the use of long, personal government questionnaires. Much government data is collected under the threat of jail or fine. As useful as such information may be to the government and to private agencies, the misuse of data banks is an imminent and serious threat to constitutional liberties.

We are concerned about the increased amount of government wiretapping and electronic surveillance which has taken place in recent years.

Although it is now illegal for any governmental unit to engage in any kind of wiretapping without a warrant of a court, we urge restraint in the use of wiretapping and electronic surveillance, for its prevalency creates an air of suspicion throughout the whole society and contributes to the insecurity of law-abiding American citizens.

Therefore, we respectfully request the Congress of the United States to:

1. Enact comprehensive charter legislation for all of the intelligence agencies which would prohibit them from engaging in surveillance, or disruption of lawful political activity. We oppose any charter provision which permits intelligence agencies to recruit and use as agents clergy or missionaries.

2. Place statutory limitations upon the demand by governmental bureaus and agencies for personal information about any citizen or family for statistical purposes. When such requests by agencies are for information not required by law, the respondent should be informed that compliance is voluntary. Restrictions should be placed by law on private agencies in gathering, storing, and disseminating personal information.

3. Retain the Freedom of Information Act as it is, in support of the right of all citizens to know the actions of their government.[42]

Ratification for District of Columbia Representation

The Scriptures tell us clearly that "God shows no partiality" (Acts 10:34). The Social Principles of The United Methodist Church cites "the full and willing participation of its citizens" as a key factor in the strength of our political system.

In keeping with the idea of impartiality and the call for citizen participation, we are concerned about the lagging issue of ratification of the Constitutional Amendment providing for full representation of the District of Columbia in the Congress. We are well aware that the population of

[42]See Social Principles V-C; "Domestic Surveillance," 1984.

the District of Columbia is powerless with respect to our national legislative body.

In October of 1971 a statement of the Board of Christian Social Concerns of The United Methodist Church asked the United States Congress to "provide the District of Columbia with two voting U.S. Senators plus the number of voting U.S. Representatives it would be entitled to if it were a State." This position was reaffirmed by the Board of Church and Society in October of 1978.

In 1978 The U.S. Congress passed a Constitutional Amendment providing for full voting representation of the District of Columbia in both the House and the Senate.

This amendment is now before the various state legislatures and, to become law, must be ratified by 38 states by 1985. A number of states have already ratified the amendment.

The District of Columbia contains about 750,000 residents. This represents a population equal to or greater than seven states—each of which has full voting representation in the Congress. Each year District residents pay more than $1 billion into the Federal treasury, yet they are not permitted to have voting representation in the Congress. Such a practice appears to violate our American heritage of "no taxation without representation."

In terms of simple justice we believe it is appropriate that District of Columbia citizens should have the right to elect national legislators who make the laws under which they, too, must live. Therefore, we urge all uncommitted state legislatures to ratify the Constitutional Amendment providing the District of Columbia with full voting representation in the Congress. We further encourage all United Methodists to support their state legislators in this endeavor.

Response to Cults Through Effective Evangelism

WHEREAS, it is estimated there exist some 400 or more cults in the United States. In general, a cult is a small religious

235

group outside the established churches, usually with a charismatic leader who is strong as an authority figure; and

WHEREAS, the cults see themselves as small enclaves in a hostile, secular world. Many current cults in the United States have their roots in Oriental, mystical religions. Most appeal primarily to whites in their 20s. The tragedy of the decade—Jim Jones and the death of nearly 1,000 at Jonestown, Guyana, mostly Blacks, indicate the cults' appeal to Blacks. About half the cults practice communal living. Nearly all tend to be family-like in orientation; and

WHEREAS, people moving out of the United States en masse should have been a matter of concern to our U.S. government; and

WHEREAS, life orientation for Blacks is listening to and following white people. So Blacks marched off to death following a person with a Messiah complex; and

WHEREAS, some ask, is this a failure of religion generally, the black church in particular? One of the things we teach in the black church is what to and what not to expect from religion, and

WHEREAS, the Jim Jones situation and People's Temple, where nearly 1,000 children, youth, and adults met death, cannot be taken lightly, and

WHEREAS, the inner-city is a haven for cults in our culture. Thousands of boys and girls, men and women give to the church a Macedonian call for help.

Therefore, Be It Resolved, that The United Methodist Church respond to this great army of people who have chosen cults and who feel rejected, enslaved, and ignored by the church and government.

Be It Further Resolved, that evangelism be continued as a major emphasis during the 1981-84 quadrennium.

Be It Further Resolved, that the General Board of Discipleship assist our churches to serve as service institutions with programs that aid when people are in need and hurting.

Safety and Health in Workplace
and Community

Just as biblical religion affirms that God is involved in the healing of individuals (Genesis 20:17; Matthew 8), so also does God's covenant with his people include the mandate to protect the community from dangers that threaten the health of the people (Leviticus 14:33–15:14). At the beginning of Methodism, John Wesley provided medicine and medical treatment at no cost to the poor in London and Bristol. In addition to pioneering free dispensaries in England, Wesley emphasized prevention of illness. In his book "Primitive Physic" he dealt with nutrition and hygiene, as well as treatment of the sick. The first Social Creed, adopted by the 1908 General Conference of The Methodist Episcopal Church (North), declared that workers must be protected "from dangerous machinery, occupational diseases, injuries, and mortality," and that working conditions must be regulated to safeguard the physical and moral health of the community. Today as well, the Church is called to declare that the health of every individual is part of community health, including safe and healthy conditions in places where people work. The Church has a responsibility to pronounce clearly the implications of God's law of love for human health. Where human life and health are at stake, economic gain must not take precedence.

A. *Public Health Hazards*

Public health hazards originate from a variety of sources, including organisms (e.g., bacteria, fungi, and viruses), physical conditions (e.g., hazardous machinery and excessive noise), toxic chemicals, and radiation. Some public health hazards, such as veneral disease and lead poisoning, were known to our biblical forebearers and to other ancient civilizations. Other hazards such as toxic chemical wastes are products of the past century's rapid technological development. Such hazards can produce infectious diseases, disabling injuries, incapacitating illnesses, and death. Toxic substances and related hazards such as ionizing radiation threaten the exposed individual to additional hazards such as cancer and sterility, and also threaten future generations with birth defects and gene mutations. A single toxic substance may have wide-range usage from the home to the workplace to the environment. It may persist for years in the form of dangerous wastes and residues. The human consequences of such public health hazards are vast. In 1977, work-related injuries claimed 5.3 million victims, 4,760 of whom died.[43] In 1976, compensation payments of $7.5 billion were made for work-related deaths, disease, and disability.[44] Environmental and occupational cancer are estimated to represent 20-38 percent of all cancer.[45] One substance alone, asbestos, is expected to claim the lives of 1.6 million of the 4 million individuals heavily exposed since World War II, including a substantial number of shipyard workers.[46] These deaths, diseases, and disabilities have an additional impact on the affected individuals and their families in terms of medical costs, lost earning capacity, pain, suffering, and grief. When long-term diseases such as cancer, birth defects, and gene mutations are involved, the human consequences extend far beyond the immediately perceived hazards of infection or injury.

B. *Declaration*

Public health is dependent on effective prevention and active protection before illness or injury have occurred. To

[43]Statistical Abstract of the U.S., 1978, U.S. Department of Commerce, 99th edition. Paperback, 1057 pp. P. 78, No. 112, 5,203 deaths from industrial type accidents shown for 1976.

[44]Ibid. P. 354, Table No. 558, "Workmen's Compensation Payments . . ."

[45]"Estimates of the Fraction of Cancer in the United States Related to Occupational Factors," prepared by National Cancer Institute, National Institute of Environmental Health Sciences, National Institute for Occupational Safety and Health, Mimeographed Report, September 14, 1978, p. 24.

[46]"Estimates of the Fraction of Cancer in the United States Related to Occupational Factors," prepared by National Cancer Institute, National Institute of Environmental Health Sciences, National Institute for Occupational Safety and Health, Mimeographed Report, September 15, 1978, p. 9.

fulfill God's commandment to love our neighbor as ourselves, we should support action to protect each individual's health and to preserve the health of the community. To this end we declare:

1. Every individual, including those with handicapping conditions and disabilities, has a right to a safe and healthful environment unendangered by a polluted natural world, a hazardous workplace, an unsanitary community, dangerous household products, unsafe drugs, and contaminated food. This human right must take precedence over property rights. Moreover, the necessary preservation of human life and health must not be sacrificed or diminished for economic gain. It is unconscionable that anyone should profit from conditions which lead to the disease, disability, or death of another. Furthermore, the essential protection of the physical and moral quality of human life must not be compromised by competing considerations of capital investment and return, or diminished by society's insistence on affluence, luxury, and convenience.

2. Public health hazards must be *prevented* in order to avoid the serious individual and community consequences of injury, illness, and untimely death, including disability, physical pain, mental anguish, lost human potential, family stress, and the diversion of scarce medical resources.

3. Public health hazards to future generations such as toxic substances and wastes which produce birth defects and gene mutations must be prevented in order to avoid a legacy of disease, disability, and untimely death. No generation has the right to assume risks that potentially endanger the viability of future life.

4. The public health risks of technological development must be fully and openly assessed before new technologies are introduced into the home, the work-place, the community, or the environment. Medical research should be required to give high priority to the identification of hazardous substances and processes.

5. The preservation and protection of human life from public health hazards is a fundamental responsibility of government which must be maintained by active public

support and adequate public funds. Efficient administration and effective enforcement of public health laws including those governing the use and disposal of toxic substances should be supported at all levels of government.

6. Preventive health care should be taught in educational institutions to persons in every age group at every level of society. Health professionals in all branches of medicine and public health, and those in related fields, should be educated in practicing preventive medicine, implementing community preventive health strategies, and assisting patients in the adoption of healthy lifestyles. Programs should be implemented that educate and inform consumers and workers about physical, chemical, biological, and radiological hazards of products, services, working conditions, and environment contaminants.[47]

The SALT Process

The Bible teaches us that ultimately there is no security in horses or chariots, or for that matter in tanks and planes. We are admonished to seek peace and pursue it. We are warned of the consequences of not knowing the things that make for peace.

Again and again, the essential unity of humanity is stressed, that God has made of one blood all nations to dwell together on the face of the earth. The nuclear threat to the whole world only serves to emphasize anew that we are our brother's and sister's keepers.

Our Social Principles reminds us "That human values must outweight military claims as governments determine their priorities; that the militarization of society must be challenged and stopped; and that the manufacture, sale and deployment of armaments must be reduced and controlled; and that the production, possession, or use of nuclear weapons must be condemned."

The Strategic Arms Limitations Talks (SALT) between

[47]*See* Social Principles IV-C.

the world's two superpowers constitute an important and necessary step toward this end. In view of the enormous destructive power and modern weaponry possessed by the U.S.A. and the U.S.S.R., it is absolutely essential not only that communication channels (hot line) be constantly open between these two countries, but also that negotiations continue in order to reduce the danger of war and take substantial steps toward elimination of nuclear arms.

We support the SALT process in the hopes that future agreements will reduce the level of world armaments. In the absence of such agreements, nations would not only retain their arsenals, but would increase them even more drastically and continue to devise new and more sophisticated weapons systems.

In view of the delay in the SALT negotiations, we call upon the governments of the U.S.A. and the U.S.S.R.:

1) To make strenuous efforts to reestablish the SALT process.

2) To strengthen SALT II, amending it to include a mutual moratorium on all further testing, production, and deployment of new nuclear strategic weapons, and to prohibit the deployment of additional nuclear arms beyond present levels.

3) To conclude agreements requiring large and continuing reductions in Soviet and U.S. nuclear arsenals; and

4) To seek similar reductions in the nuclear weaponry of all nations as others join in the talks.

5) To institute a moratorium on all research and deployment of nuclear weapons systems during the SALT process.[48]

Sexist Language and the Scripture

WHEREAS, we respectfully acknowledge the use of biblical imagery in shaping historic creeds and practice;

[48]See "The United Methodist Church and Peace," 1984.

WHEREAS, we acknowledge the need for language used among the people of God to be inclusive;

WHEREAS, we desire both to honor Holy Scripture and sound theological statements from the past and to move intentionally toward a future Church in which unhealthy distinctions are neither expressed nor implied in language and symbolism;

Therefore Be It Resolved:

1. That scriptural references used in approved publications of The United Methodist Church be faithful to accepted texts;

2. That unnecessary attempts to deny the validity of historic, biblical imagery be avoided;

3. That respect be accorded various members of the Church as they feel led to express valid Christian theology in worship and practice.

South Africa

Christian teaching stresses the heavy responsibility that rests upon the rich and powerful. Bible stories make clear the divine judgment upon those who fail to discharge their personal and social responsibilities. These should be read together with the injunctions concerning righteousness and peace to grasp the full imperative that rests upon the leaders of the nations of our world today.

For centuries the rich and powerful of this world have dominated, exploited, and segregated the peoples of Africa through colonialism, slavery, and apartheid. We celebrate the end of war in Zimbabwe and the peaceful transition into a new independent nation under the rule of all the people.

The government of South Africa continues to resist substantive change in its ruthless rule by apartheid. White South Africans have the highest standard of living in the world. Black South Africans live in poverty. Per capita income is more than ten times higher for whites than for blacks.

South Africa is completely segregated by law under the

242

apartheid system. 13 percent of the country is reserved for blacks, while 87 percent—including all the cities, industries, fertile farmland, and major mines—is legally the territory of the whites, who comprise only 16 percent of the country's population.

Blacks cannot vote or join political parties. By law the best jobs are reserved for whites. Black unemployment is well over 25 percent, while white unemployment remains at 1 percent. Education is compulsory and free for white children, while blacks must pay.

In recent years, the South African government has tried to crush all opposition to apartheid. In 1976, demonstrations spread throughout the country in which more than a thousand persons were killed by the police and the military. Thousands more were arrested. In October, 1977, all remaining organizations critical of the government were outlawed, including the Christian Institute. Steve Biko and many other leaders have been killed in prison. The government continues to ban persons such as Archbishop Tutu.

In 1950, U.S. direct investment in South Africa totaled $140 million. Since then the figure has grown to $2 billion, while indirect investment is mostly in the form of loans from large and small commercial banks throughout the U.S. Many of these loans have gone directly to the South African government and its agencies.

Another source of major support of the South African government is the "Krugerrand," a one-ounce gold piece minted and sold by the government to raise money. In 1979, Krugerrands accounted for 30 percent of South Africa's gold production and as of that year more than half of the world sales of the Krugerrand were in the U.S. Purchasers of such coins invest in poverty and oppression for the majority population of South Africa.

1. We call upon all nations, acting through the United Nations, to continue to press South Africa to eliminate the system of apartheid. Such pressure might include the adoption of economic sanctions by the United Nations Security Council.

2. We call upon all nations to work for the release of political prisoners in South Africa, to grant political asylum to South Africans who request it, and to extend such asylum to those refusing to serve in the armed forces.

3. We call upon the developed nations, including the United States, to end various forms of financial support to the government of South Africa.

4. We particularly call upon United States banks and corporations to make no new loans or investments and not to renew any previous loans to the South African government or government owned or related corporations.

5. We call upon all banks to stop promotion and sale of the "Krugerrand" coin.

6. We call upon legislatures, state and city government to pass legislation mandating the withdrawal of public funds from banks that continue making loans to the South African government or government owned or related corporations.

7. We call upon our Church at all levels—general boards and agencies, Annual Conferences, local churches, and individual members—to join in this effort to stop bank loans to South Africa, and to refrain from the purchase of the "Krugarrand" coin.

8. We call upon the financial officers of our Church at all levels to examine their banking and investment practices and to withdraw accounts from banks and financial institutions that continue to make loans to the South African government or government owned or related corporations. (Refer to Investment Policy, General Council on Finance and Administration, 1978). We do not engage in such efforts lightly, but with prayer and with the deep conviction that substantive change in South Africa will only come by a concerted effort of nations and peoples dedicated to justice for all, including the oppressed majority in South Africa.

The Status of Women

I

Christianity was born in a world of male preference and dominance. Practices, traditions, and attitudes in almost all societies viewed women as inferior to men, as having few talents and contributions to make to the general well-being of society aside from their biological roles. This was true of the Judaic society of which Jesus was a part.

But the life of Jesus, the redeemer of human life, stood as a witness against such cultural patterns and prejudices. Consistently he related to women as persons of intelligence and capabilities. He charged women as well as men to use their talents significantly in the cause of God's kingdom. His acts of healing and ministry were extended without distinction to women and men.

The central theme of Jesus' teaching is love for God and neighbor. Jesus embodied this message in his life and, in the early church, women held prominent positions of leadership. Christian love as exemplified in the New Testament requires that we relate to others as persons of worth. To regard another as an inferior is to break the covenant of love: denying equality demeans, perpetuates injustice, and falls short of the example of Jesus and the early Church.

II

The movement to improve the status of women is one of the most profoundly hopeful of our times. The United Methodist Church in various ways has sought to support that movement. Although change is taking place, in most societies women are still not accorded equal rights and responsibilities.

There is increasing awareness that we cannot solve world problems of hunger, population growth, poverty, and peace so long as the talents and potential of half the world's people are disregarded and even repressed. There are strong interrelationships between all these problems and the status of women.

The years from 1975 to 1985 have been designated the Decade for Women, a time for correcting these ancient injustices. For Christians, it is a time for repentance and for new dedication to Christ's ideal of equality. It is a time for examining specific areas which need to be addressed in societies:

ECONOMICS. Often the productive labor of women is ignored in economic statistics, reinforcing the impression that work done by women is peripheral, of secondary importance, even dispensable. For that reason, few studies have actually evaluated the importance of contributions by women. As one example, when women grow food to feed their families, they are "just" tending kitchen gardens, but when men grow cash crops like tobacco and coffee, they are engaged in agricultural and commercial enterprises. In more industrialized societies, the enormous amount of volunteer work done by women is not counted as adding to the nation's wealth.

In the United States, nearly half of all women are working outside the home in the paid labor force and there are well-publicized professional successes, yet actually the earning gap between men and women is greater than it was in the 1950's. Everywhere, women tend to be clustered in the lower-paying jobs and in certain stereotyped job fields.

LEGAL RIGHTS. In 1945, only 31 countries allowed women to vote; today women have the right in more than 125 nations. Only eight countries exclude women entirely from political processes open to men. Still, many areas of legal discrimination remain. In some nations, women are still considered the chattels of their husbands, with few rights in family law, landholding, inheritance, and guardianship of children.

In the United States some of the more glaring inequities are being corrected step by step. Nonetheless, a 1978 report of the Civil Rights Commission noted continuing discrimination on the basis of sex in the Federal Statutes.[49]

CULTURAL FACTORS. The perception of women as inferior and dependent is perpetuated through many institutions in society—the media, school textbooks and curricula, political structures, and often religious organizations. Education is one of the principal ways of opening doors to wider participation in society. Thus, it is distressing

[49]*Statement on the Equal Rights Amendment,* United States Commission on Civil Rights, Clearinghouse Publication 56, December 1978, page 5.

that, while the percentage of literate women is at an all-time high, the absolute number of illiterate women is greater than at any time in the past. The fact that two-thirds of the world's illiterates are female is evidence of continuing disparity in importance given to the education of boys and girls.

Traditional perceptions of female qualities also are a factor in the widespread domestic violence against women, now coming to be recognized as a tragically widespread occurrence.

HUMAN RIGHTS IN FERTILITY DECISIONS. Through the centuries, women have been little consulted or involved in the decisions regarding fertility-related laws or practices. For women particularly, the ability to make choices concerning fertility is a liberating force, helping to safeguard their health and that of their children, to plan for the future, to assume wider roles and responsibilities in society.

The United Nations has declared that education and access to means for determining the number and spacing of children is a human right, yet this is an ideal far from realization.

Coercion is still common, sometimes aimed at increasing births, sometimes at limiting them. Evidence now clearly shows that many poor, particularly ethnic, women have been sterilized without their understanding of what was being done to them and without their informed consent. In many places, safe and legal abortion is denied, in some cases even to save the life of the pregnant woman. In other cases, women are threatened that welfare payments or aid programs will be cut if the pregnancy continues. Such inconsistency reflects lack of value-centered decision-making, as well as sensitivity to the personhood of the woman involved.

While societal needs more and more should be considered in fertility matters, this should never be at the price of demeaning the individual or applying restrictive measures only to the poor. Women should be fully informed and fully involved in the decision-making.

DEVELOPMENT PROGRAMS. National and international development programs now often stress the need to "integrate" women into the development process. Full recognition is seldom given to the contributions women already make to economic and social progress. For example, women make up 60-80 percent of the agricultural workers of the world; in some parts of Africa women manage a third of the farms. Yet few programs of agricultural development seek to upgrade the skills of women, provide easier access to credit, assure them the right to land titles in their own names, etc. In some cases, modernization actually degrades the already low status of women.

III

Across the nations of the world, new movements are growing which address the serious handicaps and harsh realities of the lives of many women. In the context of this increasing momentum for a more just society, we call on local congregations and the agencies of the Church:

1. To exert leadership in working wherever possible for legal recognition of equal rights for women. In the United States, this means a strengthened determination to secure passage of the Equal Rights Amendment,[50] in line with the United Methodist General Conference affirmations of 1972 and 1976. We need to recognize that this measure has become a symbol of the drive for equality. It has meaning far beyond the borders of one nation in the search for equal rights in other societies.

2. To urge governments to ratify the Convention on the Elimination of Discrimination Against Women which was adopted by the United Nations, December, 1979.

3. To encourage support of studies by scientific and

[50]Proposed 27th Amendment:
Sec. 1. Equality of rights under the law shall not be denied or abridged by the United States or by any State on account of sex.
Sec. 2. The Congress shall have the power to enforce, by appropriate legislation, the provisions of this article.
Sec. 3. This amendment shall take effect two years after the date of ratification.

governmental bodies of the economic contributions made by women outside the formal economic sector, and to include this information in the Gross National Product of nations or compilations of national wealth.

4. To examine governmental policies and practices, including development assistance, as to their impact on women's lives; to work to ensure that policies upgrade the status of women, and that women are included in decision-making regarding development goals and programs. The key roles of women as workers and consumers and as transmitters of culture must be given adequate weight in national development activities.

5. To examine the impact of transnational corporations on women's lives, and to work to eradicate exploitative practices where identified. One such area is the promotion and selling of inappropriate products and technologies.

6. To encourage private charitable organizations, including churches, to initiate and support more programs of leadership education for women and other educational programs that upgrade the status of women.

7. To monitor printed and audio-visual media and other means of communication on their portrayals of the roles and nature of women and men, and to seek ways to eradicate narrow stereotypes which limit the possibilities of useful contributions by both sexes. The Church should encourage study of the impact of Western, particularly U.S., television, radio, and other media on cultural patterns and national development around the world, and should draw public attention to cases where such influence is destructive of other cultures.

8. To support programs providing knowledge of and access to services in the area of family-planning and contraception, and to involve women in planning and implementation of such services. This effort should include support for public funding for these programs; for access to safe, legal, and non-coercive contraception, sterilization, and abortion services; and for improved educational efforts on responsible sexuality and parenthood for both men and women. Attention should particularly be paid to ensuring

high standards for clinics performing abortions; to monitoring enforcement of regulations designed to ensure informed consent for sterilization procedures; to opposing profit-making referral agencies, which charge fees for providing information freely available elsewhere.

9. To examine the impact of judicial decisions at all levels upon the daily lives of women in such areas as child custody, employment, civil rights, racial and sexual discrimination, credit practices, estate settlements, reproduction and education, and socio-economic status.

IV

The words and acts of Jesus give the Christian a vision of what a just society should be. Discipleship to Jesus requires both men and women to measure their attitudes about themselves and all others by his values and to act in accord with those values. The full worth and dignity of each person is to be acknowledged and expressed. The church may help the vision of Jesus to be realized by proclaiming that women are persons created in the image of God, here to serve with men in the breaking forth of the Kingdom.[51]

The United Methodist Church and America's Native People

Most white Americans are isolated from the issues of justice for the United States' native people by the lapse of time, the remoteness of reservations or native territories and the comparative invisibility of natives in the urban setting, the distortions in historical accounts, and the accumulation of prejudices. Now is the time for a new beginning and The United Methodist Church calls its members to pray and work for that new day in relationship between native peoples, other minorities, and white Americans.

The United States has been forced to become more sharply aware and keenly conscious of the destructive

[51]*See* Social Principles III-F; "Equal Rights of Women," 1984.

impact of the unjust acts and injurious policies of the United States government upon the lives and culture of U.S. American Indians, Alaskan, and Hawaiian natives. In the past the white majority population was allowed to forget or excuse the wrongs which were done to the indigenous peoples of this land. Today, U.S. American Indians, Alaskan, and Hawaiian natives are speaking with a new and more unified voice, causing both the government and the American people to re-examine the actions of the past and to assume responsibility for the conditions of the present.

A clear appeal is being made for a fresh and reliable expression of justice. The call is being made for a new recognition of the unique rights which were guaranteed in perpetuity of U.S. American Indians by the treaties and legal agreements which were solemnly signed by official representatives of the United States government. A plea is being raised regarding the disruption of Alaskan and Hawaiian natives who were not granted the legal agreements protecting their culture and land base.

The time has come for the American people to be delivered from beliefs which gave support to the false promises and faulty policies which prevailed in the relations of the United States government with U.S. America's native peoples. These beliefs asserted that:

1. White Europeans who came to this continent were ordained by God to possess its land and utilize its resources.
2. Natives were not good stewards of the environment, permitting nature to lie in waste, as they roamed from place to place living off the land.
3. The growing white population tamed nature and subdued the natives and thus gave truth to the assumption that the white race is superior.
4. The forceful displacement of the natives was a necessary and justifiable step in the development of a free land and a new country.
5. The white explorers and pioneers brought civilization to the natives and generously bestowed upon them a higher and better way of life.

251

Rarely are these beliefs now so blatantly set forth, yet they are subtly assumed and furnish the continuing foundation upon which unjust and injurious policies of the government are based.

These beliefs, in former times, permitted the government, on the one hand, to seize lands, uproot families, break up tribal communities, and undermine the authority of traditional chiefs. On the other hand, the beliefs enabled the government to readily make and easily break treaties, give military protection to those who encroached on native lands, distribute as "free" land millions of acres of native holdings which the government designated as being "surplus," and systematically slay those natives who resisted such policies and practices.

In our own time these beliefs have encouraged the government to:

1. Generally asume the incompetence of natives in the management and investment of their own resources.
2. Give highly favorable leasing arrangements to white mining companies, grain farmers, and cattle ranchers for the use of native lands held in trust by the federal government or historically used as supportive land base.
3. Use job training and other government programs to encourage the relocation of natives from reservations or native territories to urban areas.
4. Utilize government funds in projects which are divisive to the tribal or native membership and through procedures which co-opt native leadership.
5. Extend the control of state government over native nations which are guaranteed federal protection.
6. Terminate federal services and protection to selected native nations and further deny federal recognition to others.
7. Engage in extensive and expensive litigation as a means of delaying and thus nullifying treaty rights and aboriginal land claims.
8. Pay minimal monetary claims for past illegal confiscation of land and other native resources.

9. Lump together United States natives with other racial minorities as a tactic for minimizing the unique rights of native peoples.

10. Punitively prosecute the native leaders who vigorously challenge the policies of the federal government.

The Church is called to repentance, for it bears a heavy responsibility for spreading false beliefs and for unjust governmental policies and practices. The preaching of the gospel to America's natives was often a preparation for assimilation into white culture. The evangelizing of the native nations often effected the policies of the government.

The Church has frequently benefitted from the distribution of native lands and other resources. The Church often saw the injustices inflicted upon native peoples but gave assent or remained silent, believing that its task was to "convert" the heathen.

The Church is called through the mercy of Almighty God to become a channel of the reconciling Spirit of Jesus Christ and an instrument of love and justice in the development of new relations between native nations, other minorities, and whites, in pursuit of the protection of their rights.

The United Methodist Church recognizes that a new national commitment is needed to respect and effect the rights of American Indians, Alaskan, and Hawaiian natives to claim their own identities, maintain their cultures, live their lives, and use their resources.

The United Methodist Church expresses its desire and declares it intention to participate in the renewal of the national responsibility to U.S. America's native people.

The United Methodist Church calls its congregations to study the issues concerning American Indian, Alaskan, and Hawaiian native relations with the government of the United States; to develop an understanding of the distinctive cultures and the unique rights of the native people of the United States; to establish close contacts wherever possible with native persons, tribes and nations; and to furnish support for:

1. The right of native people to live as native people in this country.

2. The right of native people to be self-determining and to make their own decisions related to the use of their lands and the natural resources found on and under them.

3. The right of native people to plan for a future in this nation and to expect a fulfillment of the commitments which have been made previously by the government, as well as equitable treatment of those who were not afforded legal protection for their culture and lands.

4. The right of American Indian nations to exercise the sovereignty of nationhood, consistent with treaty provisions.

5. The right of Alaskan natives to maintain a subsistence land base and aboriginal rights to its natural resources.

6. The right of native Hawaiians to a just and amicable settlement with the United States through federal legislation related to aboriginal title to Hawaiian lands and their natural resources.

The United Methodist Church especially calls its congregations to support the needs and aspirations of America's native peoples as they struggle for their survival and the maintenance of the integrity of their culture in a world intent upon their assimilation, westernization, and absorption of their lands and the termination of their traditional ways of life.

Moreover, we call upon our nation, in recognition of the significant cultural attainments of the native peoples in ecology, conservation, human relations, and other areas of human endeavor, to receive their cultural gifts as part of the emerging new life and culture of our nation.

In directing specific attention to the problems of native peoples in the United States, we do not wish to ignore the plight of native people in many other countries of the world.

*Note: This statement was reaffirmed by the 1984 General Conference.[52]

---

[52]*See* Social Principles III-A; "The Black Hills Alliance," "The Fort Loramie Treaty," 1980. "Select Committee on Indian Affairs," 1984.

The United Methodist Church and Conscription

The United Methodist Church since its inception in 1968 has consistently opposed peacetime conscription. In doing so, it has heeded its Lord's injunction to know and to seek the things that make for peace. The vision of peace portrayed so graphically in Isaiah and Micah concludes with the expectation that the day will arrive when men and women shall no longer learn the ways of war.

Despite the fears of some, we do not believe that military conscription is essential to the security of nations in times of peace. In fact, evidence indicates that conscripted armed forces can be used to conduct unpopular unauthorized wars for which volunteers would be unavailable.

Some countries require that all young people perform national service, military or civilian, and other countries are proposing to do the same. The cost and bureaucracy of such massive undertakings are enormous; the opportunities for indoctrination pose a constant threat to peace and freedom; the invasion of personal liberty and privacy is alarming; and the value of such involuntary service is dubious.

We urge all United Methodists (1) to oppose induction of persons into any system of military or civilian conscription except in times of war or national emergency, and (2) to work toward the elimination of existing conscription systems in times other than those of war or national emergency. Further, we declare that registration of persons should not be undertaken for psychological reasons nor designed to affect only a limited age group.

1984

Advocacy for the Poor

WHEREAS, we recognize the harsh reality of the serious crisis facing a large segment of our society, and are confronted with the fact that there have been billions of dollars in federal cutbacks borne by the poor, which have resulted in tremendous suffering and hardship for millions of women, men, children, elderly, and families in the United States; and

WHEREAS, the pastoral letter from the Council of Bishops, November 14, 1982, said: "As Christians we acknowledge that implicit in the faith of the church is a mandate for action. It is not enough to experience deep distress over the plight of the hungry and hopeless victims of the economic crisis." The gospel demands that we manifest our love for Christ through our efforts to relieve the suffering of those who are without food and shelter, who live under the burden of the current economic catastrophe and increasing social injustices; and

WHEREAS, the private sector has been unable and/or unwilling to respond effectively to the needs of the poor and oppressed people in our communities;

Therefore, in solidarity with the pastoral letter from the Council of Bishops, we call upon The United Methodist Church, at all levels, to be a reconciling force in this time of economic distress and to be an advocate for the poor and oppressed people of all nations, acting with a sense of justice, compassion, understanding, and God's presence.

We furthermore call upon members and congregations of The United Methodist Church to work to influence public policies which will bring about greater economic justice.[1]

Affirmation of the Leadership of Joseph E. Lowery

WHEREAS, Dr. Joseph E. Lowery, president of the Southern Christian Leadership Conference, and pastor of Central United Methodist Church, Atlanta, Georgia, has shared with the Church, the nation, and the world his courageous prophetic gifts and his commitment to racial and social justice; and

WHEREAS, we take pride in the fact that Dr. Joseph E. Lowery is a United Methodist;

Be It Resolved, that the 1984 General Conference of The United Methodist Church express its appreciation and affirmation of the leadership of Dr. Joseph E. Lowery.

Affirmative Action

The concept of "affirmative action" emerged and developed during the period of the 1960's along with many other programs designed to address the inequalities and discriminatory practices within our society. It was defined as measurable efforts by employers and educational institutions to hire and admit those who had traditionally been excluded. While it has been actively resisted in many ways, especially where it has meant change from long existing patterns, significant though small gains for women, ethnic and racial minorities, and persons with handicapping conditions have been achieved, but much more needs to be done.

Gunnar Myrdal reminded us in his book, *An American Dilemma* (published in 1944), the race problem in America is basically a moral dilemma, not a legal problem. The premise

[1] *See* Social Principles, III-E; "Concern for Persons in Poverty," 1980.

upon which affirmative action is built is essentially moral and spiritual in nature. Concern for the disadvantaged, the disinherited, and the oppressed is a major feature of both the Old Testament prophets and the message and ministry of Jesus. According to biblical teaching, what is required is a redress of grievances and a sincere effort to make amends. Strong leadership from the religious community is demanded when efforts to correct the injustices and evils of the past and present are under attack.

The characterization of affirmative action as "unfair" often appears to rest on the dubious assumption that conditions for women, minorities, and persons with handicapping conditions have improved so radically that further special efforts on their behalf are unnecessary. On the contrary, minority unemployment remains much higher than the national average, and women workers continued to earn less than male workers. Affirmative action has not yet even begun to reverse these trends; it may be merely serving to prevent a bad situation from becoming even worse.

Affirmative action recognizes the need to broaden the definition of compensatory, protective and preferential programs that now exist in our society such as tax breaks and the traditional preferential treatment given to nonminority groups and males. It also attempts to provide goals designed to achieve an inclusive society in a time when competition for jobs and educational opportunity is intensifying. The discrimination of the past, which automatically excluded certain groups of people—by color, by sex, by age, and because of handicapping conditions—is being corrected with due regard for the compensation necessary for the disadvantages of the past to be transformed into equality of opportunity in the future. Affirmative action plays an important role in "releasing captives" and "setting the oppressed at liberty." The Church has an important role to play in ministering which is designed to effect reconciliation and healing for those who suffer the pain cased by societal change, as well as in supporting the continuation of those changes.

259

We therefore call upon individuals and institutions, including United Methodists individually and as congregations, to:

1. Forthrightly and clearly affirm their support of affirmative action legislation and programs.

2. Reaffirm and increase their support of those efforts that seek to insure effective representation of minorities and women.

3. Continue to provide a much-needed role model for others in society by affirming, strengthening, and practicing their own affirmative action policies.

4. Affirm and proclaim the Judeo-Christian heritage of restitution, inclusiveness, justice, and grace as the best possible support for affirmative action.

5. Affirm the equal consideration of lay people in church-related positions where not prohibited by the Book of Discipline of The United Methodist Church.

6. Seek to interpret the true purpose and meaning of affirmative action against claims of reverse discrimination.

7. Support actively church-related programs such as Project Equality which seek to support equal opportunity and to promote an inclusive society.

8. Insist that agencies of The United Methodist Church follow affirmative action policies.

Affirmative Action Reaffirmed

Be It Resolved, that the 1984 General Conference of The United Methodist Church reaffirm its 1980 resolution in support of affirmative action and recognize the need to utilize all the talents of minorities and women to strengthen the health of the whole society;

Be It Further Resolved, that the 1984 General Conference mandate intentional implementation of affirmative action programs and procedures in general church boards and agencies, conferences, districts, local churches, and church-related institutions;

Be It Finally Resolved, that the Commission on Religion and

Race through its leadership in the area of affirmative action in elimination of racism and sexism in structure, continue to monitor affirmative action program processes in an effort to lead The United Methodist Church toward a more inclusive society.[2]

Agricultural and Rural Life Issues

I. *Theological Statement*

In the beginning, the Creator formed light and darkness, energy and matter, space and time, and the earth with all that is around, on and within it. Primal life forms were brought forth, and finally human beings were made in the Creator's image and likeness. The Creator looked over this work and called creation good. Thus could the Psalmist sing, "The earth is the Lord's and the fullness thereof, the world and those who dwell therein" (Ps. 24:1 RSV).

Several basic biblical themes repeat themselves regarding nature and the land: God is the owner of the land (Lev. 25), thus it is a gift in covenant which involves the stewardship of keeping and tending the land for present and future generations; as God's creation it has rights and needs, the need to be regenerated that it may sustain life and be a place of joy; and it is a corporate gift to all of humanity requiring just patterns of land use.

These basic biblical themes have not always been observed by present-day owners and managers of the lands. In the past 50 years, U.S. agriculture has changed dramatically in terms of organization and interdependence with the domestic and international economies. These profound changes include the concentration of land ownership into fewer hands and the continued loss of the family farm; the mining of the soil resulting in quickened land erosion; water aquifers contaminated and depleted; the loss of prime farmland to other social uses; the highest number of farm

---

[2] *See* Social Principles, III-A, G.

foreclosures since the 1930s; the vertical integration of the agricultural economy resulting in new forms of bondage; and the wasting of community, that sense of belonging to each other within common purposes and values. These trends have accelerated in the past 10 years.

Faith mandates that the stewardship of earth's resources must be a central concern of all God's people. We must allow our personal and social salvation in Jesus Christ and the leadership of the Holy Spirit to guide us into attitudes and actions appropriate to the management of agricultural and rural resources as God's servants. This central theological point is matched by the needs of all God's people for food, clothing, shelter, justice, and caring. We are called to be especially concerned about poor and powerless people and those who are starving or barely subsisting. We must make Scripture, tradition, experience, and reason central Wesleyan doctrinal forces as United Methodists face agricultural and rural life issues in the United States and around the world.

II. *Historical Involvement*

The United Methodist Church has long had an interest in rural life issues. Each General Conference since 1940 has given guidance to The United Methodist Church and/or its predecessor bodies and to society for improving the opportunities of rural people.

Since 1972, each General Conference had adopted major resolutions on agricultural and rural issues. The Social Principles speak to the need for building national support for the improvement of rural life, for meeting the special needs of migrant workers, the encouragement of industry to locate in non-urban areas, and the rights of women and children.

III. *Roots of United Methodist Rural Church*

As the United States developed westward, The United Methodist Church moved with the frontier and developed a lifestyle that met the needs of community, establishing churches, schools, hospitals, homes for persons in need, and welcome for the immigrants. The dynamic spiritual motivation, the circuit pattern, the lay preacher, and the traveling elder furnished the flexibility necessary for ministering to a people on the move. Rural churches became significant centers for community life; they still serve this vital function.

Today, approximately 88 percent of our members are located in population areas of 50,000 or less; 78 percent of our churches and 51 percent of our members are located in population areas of 10,000 or less; 58.3 percent of our churches and 24 percent of our members are located in population areas of 1,000 or less. Ours is a denomination of small membership churches, 64.6 percent of our churches have fewer that 199 members and 41.4 percent have fewer than 99 members. The multiple church charge is the primary pattern of pastoral assignment. Our 38,231 churches are lodged deep in the fabric of rural America. During the decade of the 1970s, rural areas grew 15.8 percent—a rate not seen since the early 1800s. This presents a unique opportunity to the church for a continuing and expanded ministry.

IV. *Issues in Town and Country America.*

Rural and urban America live in a necessary relationship of mutual aid. Less than 3 percent of the nation's population furnishes food and fiber sufficient for domestic and export needs. On the other hand, the cities and factory system furnish many of the necessary inputs for agricultural production. We affirm this interdependence and note that the survival needs of all our people are dependent upon the social relationships that exist between rural and urban areas. Vibrant rural communities based on a widely dispersed, owner operated agriculture serves the interests of all. Our concern with rural issues does not blind us to the problems of urban areas; we see them in dynamic relationship to each other.

1. The Family Farm. The family-type farm has provided an environment conducive to the growth of human personality, the enrichment of family life, the well-being of rural communities and institutions, and the protection of natural resources. This pattern of agriculture has also contributed notably to the development and preservation of democratic attitudes and practices as well as to economic efficiency, productivity, and stability. The family farm continues to be one of the most productive agricultural units in the world.

However, the viability of the family farm is being eroded by powerful domestic and international social forces. These factors include the rising cost of farm production due to energy cartels, erratic markets resulting from political crises, the increase in non-family corporate farming, inflation, lack of capitalization, farm consolidation, high start-up costs for new entry farmers, tax laws, and absentee ownership.

These trends must be reversed if the common good is to be served by family-type farming, that system which has produced abundance at affordable prices within a sense of community where important human benefits arise.

2. Land Use. Each year in the United States, over 1,000,000 acres of prime farmlands are taken out of production. They are lost to highways, airports, reservoirs, strip-mining, power plants, factories, housing developments, and other uses. This represents a half-mile-wide strip of land from New York to California. The predictable result is lower production of food and fiber and rising food prices. Immediate effects are felt on the ecological system.

The exploitation of land without thought to the effect on future generations is incompatible with the biblical understanding of the stewardship of creation. Our attention and advocacy must be in the following areas of concern: the encouragement of reforestation programs; the inclusion of farmland protection as part of a comprehensive growth management program; the control of toxic waste disposal so as to avoid the poisoning of the land and aquifers; monitoring the use of eminent domain for land acquisitions; the use of appropriate and sustainable technology at home and abroad to enhance the land for future generations; the conservation and protection of our parks and wildernesses from exploitation; the support of treaty rights of Native Americans to land and water; and the monitoring of lending policies of federal and state agencies which have the effect of concentrating land ownership into fewer hands.

As Christians we participate in a convenant relationship with God and creation as stewards of the land, and we call for just and sustainable patterns of land use so that present and future generations may enjoy nature, be fed, and be renewed in their lives.

3. The Quality of Rural Life. The census of 1980 reveals rapid change in the towns and communities of rural America. While overall U.S. population grew 11.4 percent, rural and small-town America grew 15.8 percent during the 1970s. New industrial development, changing priorities in lifestyles, urban spillover, and the migration of older people to the country account in part for this increased growth. Out of the past and recent changes, some urgent issues emerge concerning the quality of life in rural areas.

a) *Income and Poverty.* In 1950, the median income of rural residents was two-thirds that of city dwellers. Governmental programs (mostly transfer payments) and overall economic development helped to close the income gap in the next two decades. By 1973 rural income had reached 80 percent of urban income. Since then, there has been some slippage, and rural income is about 78 percent of urban. Contrary to popular belief, the cost of living is rising faster in rural America than in urban areas.

Today some 34,000,000 Americans live in poverty (as defined by government criteria). While this number is down from the high of 40,000,000 in 1959, more people are living in poverty in the mid-1980s than in 1965. Poverty is disproportionately rural. Although only 26 percent of the total U.S. population lives outside urban areas, some 40 percent of the 34,000,000 poor live in rural America. Within the Black rural population, 71 percent of the children living in families headed by women are poor.

265

b) *Employment.* While farming is vital to rural America, it is no longer the primary source of employment. Only 10 percent of all rural residents are directly involved in agriculture. Agriculture creates other jobs by its demand for production inputs (seeds, energy, pesticides, machinery, household goods, etc.) Even then, there has been a steady decline in the number of agricultural counties (20 percent of income from agriculture). In 1950 there were 2,000 such counties in the United States; in 1980, only 680. During the 1970s, employment increased in nearly all sectors of the rural economy—manufacturing, retail, government, and human services. The exception was a decline in agricultural employment. Sixty percent of all farm families have off-farm employment and income.

Still, job opportunities are hard to find in rural America. Hourly wages tend to be low. In 28 percent of the poor families in rural areas, the head of the household works full time. Unemployment is higher than in urban areas, and those holding part-time jobs because they can't find full employment is higher.

c) *Education.* Public education policies tend to ignore the unique features of rural life. Schools tend to be smaller; budgets are strained because of a smaller tax base; fewer courses are offered; they have fewer supplemental resources; and less is spent per pupil. In vocational education, where improvement would affect job opportunities and new plant location, rural counties receive $14.80 per capita; urban counties receive $44.80 (203 percent difference). Of those persons 25 years of age and older, 11.5 percent more urban persons graduate from high school than do rural persons. Formulas for federal and state aid to education should be based on a fairness doctrine (equality) rather than to some ratio related to present inputs from the local community. This simply institutionalizes the budgetary problems in some counties and school districts that already exist.

d) *Health Services.* Rural Americans have difficulty obtaining health services. Physicians prefer to practice in the cities, closer to research facilities and more fully equipped hospitals. The numbers of physicians, dentists, and registered nurses per 10,000 resident population for urban areas are 19.3, 6.0, and 38.0 respectively; for rural areas, the numbers are 8.0, 3.7, and 27 respectively. Infant mortality rates are higher in the rural areas. Also, rural citizens are not as well covered with medical insurance as are urban dwellers. The basic problem centers in the fact that sparsely populated areas do not create the necessary economic base for adequate medical services. It is necessary to integrate these services within a larger medical care system which will include cooperative efforts with urban areas. Church-related medical school could contribute to rural health by influencing a new generation of physicians to practice family medicine in towns and the countryside.

e) *Housing.* Rural housing starts slowed significantly during the early 1980s' economic recession just as increasing rural population was putting pressure on available housing. The rural and town sector has one-third of the nation's population but over one-half of the nation's substandard housing. There is great need for weatherization in order to control energy costs and to promote the health of families. The elderly, ethnic minorities, and migrant workers are the most vulnerable to the scarcity of adequate housing.

f) *Justice and Legal Services.* Sparsely spread populations do not create an adequate tax base for budgets that attract trained law enforcement officials and judges. Legal services tend to concentrate in the large and small cities. Public interest law practices offering legal aid to rural communities have lost government funding in recent years. The pursuit of justice and law enforcement is often inadequate in the rural United States.

g) *Water Resources.* There is a present and growing crisis in water resources in rural America. The quality of water resources is closely related to land use. In order to control the quality of water recharged into the nation's aquifers, it is necessary to control the use of the land above it. Since aquifers do not observe state boundaries, no political unit has developed a coherent public policy protecting the quality of water resources. Ground water use has grown from 21 billion gallons per day to 82 billion gallons in 1975, and it is projected to reach 100 billion gallons by the year 2000. A recent study revealed that 2,830 wells in 20 states have been contaminated in recent years from the leaching of toxic wastes. Adequate monitoring systems are not in place. The growing demand for water for irrigation, mining, industrial use, recreation, and home use requires a national policy for protecting water resources and for their fair allocation.

h) *Transportation.* The last two decades have seen a steady decline in transportation modes available to town and country people. Some areas have no rail service, bus service, nor air service at all. Yet many of the rural poor own no family vehicle and many of the elderly have no license to drive. This decline has also made it more difficult for farmers to move their produce to market.

Rail and bus systems can reach into our rural communities and be a valuable transportation source for rural people, a source that is energy efficient. It is essential that a national transportation policy be developed that takes into account the needs and rights of those in the town and country to have access to transportation for themselves and transport for their products.

i) *Rural Women.* Historically, women play a signficant role in the development of rural communities and the agricultural economy. They continue to do so on farms, in the professions, in schools and factories, in government, in the home, and throughout the social structure of rural America.

There are more than 34,000,000 women in rural America. Rural women, like non-rural women, suffer from inadequacies and inequities in the economic and political system. Sexual discrimination is experienced in the job market, before the law, and in social services. Distances, isolation, and lack of visibility constitute the social context out of which many problems arise. The lack of public transportation to needed medical and other services intensifies the problem. Isolation and loneliness may lead to depression. The economic vulnerability of the family farm may result in marital strain and discord and in some cases, domestic violence. Incest is often associated with isolation. Many rural women are single heads of households but child-care for working mothers is almost non-existent. At retirement, farm women do not receive social security benefits comparable to those received by their husbands, even after performing a lifetime of comparable work. Laws regulating a widow's inheritance of farm assets are changing, but equitable solutions must continue to be sought.

Among the poor, particularly ethnic minorities, the problems of women are intensified. The efforts of rural women to receive justice are severely handicapped by the lack of adequate data describing social conditions and problems in rural settings.

j) *The Rural Elderly.* People 65 years old and older account for 11 percent of the total population. In a major belt of predominantly rural counties running through the midwest and extending down into Texas, 16 percent of the population is 65 or older. The 1970s saw a rapid increase in immigration of older persons from urban to rural America.

Poverty is more commonplace among older people in rural areas than in the cities. About 20 percent of the rural elderly are poor, compared to 12 percent of the elderly in urban areas. Nearly 25 percent of the rural women 65 years old and older live in poverty. For older Black women, the precentage is almost twice as high. Among older women in rural areas living alone, 82 percent are poor.

This change in population mix is placing strain upon health services and voluntary agencies which attempt to cope with the needs for jobs, companionship, transportation, homemaking, and food.

V. *The Call to the People of the United Methodist Church.*

The United Methodist Church urges its congregations and annual conferences, rural and urban, to:

1. Engage in careful study and the practice of prayer in

order to deepen our understanding and motivation for the caring of creation.

2. Strengthen small and moderate-sized family farms by affirming resident land ownership, monitoring private and government lending policies to farmers, and disposing of church-owned lands in a way that demonstrates a continuing stewardship of the land.

3. Influence community decision-makers to introduce improvements in the delivery of social services that increase the quality of life in rural areas.

4. Seek solutions to the special problems of rural ethnic people so as to assure their access to land ownership. (Special attention is required for the treaty rights of Native Americans and the rights of Blacks in their land claims.)

5. Remember with thanksgiving the contribution of farm workers to our food supply; affirm the ministry of the churches among seasonal and migrant farm workers; and continue support for the organizing efforts of farm workers into unions of their own choosing.

6. Cooperate with each other in lay and clergy exchanges; develop comprehensive equitable salary plans; and plan adequate ministries for small membership churches and cooperative parishes.

The United Methodist Church directs all its board and agencies to:

1. Develop appropriate programs which educate on the interrelatedness of urban and rural interests.

2. Engage in ministries to rural America which will aid in resolving the issues outlined in this resolution.

3. Devote their best scholarship to a theology of the land.

4. Redress the unjust imbalance in the distribution of funds between rural and urban ministries.

The United Methodist Church calls upon its leaders and pastors to:

1. Undertake cooperative and ecumenical models of ministry to rural America, including adequate orientation and training of pastors serving rural churches.

2. Discover and utilize all available resources for community renewal programs aimed at the improvement of rural life.

VI. *The Call to United States Social and Economic Institutions.*

The United Methodist Church:

1. Calls upon farmers, agribusiness, and other corporations to be responsible stewards of the earth and to find sustainable ways of sharing the benefits of food, fiber, and energy with poor and hungry people in this country and around the world.

2. Urges agribusiness to recognize the rights of farm workers to organize into unions of their own choosing, receive adequate wages and benefits, and be protected from occupational hazards.

3. Encourages land-grant colleges to develop technologies and services appropriate for the small and moderate-sized family farm. (Special attention is needed for the protection of seed genetic variability so as to avoid the hazards of inbreeding.)

4. Urges urban social institutions to become more aware of the interrelatedness of interests and welfare between rural and urban America.

5. Encourages social institutions to be sensitive to the need and the values involved in local participation in planning and development of community based projects and services.

6. Urges farmers to give primary use of the land to the production of food and fiber rather than for non-essential products which are injurious to the nation's health (tobacco and beverage alcohol).

VII. *The Call to Federal, State, and Local Governments.*

The United Methodist Church calls upon the U.S. federal, state and local governments, and their appropriate agencies to:

1. Make grants and low-interest farm loans available to small and moderate-sized family farms for the preservation of farmland and to encourage labor intensive agricultural production.

2. Restructure investment and tax policies to promote small and moderate-sized family farm operations; discour-

age growth in large corporate and corporately controlled farms; and minimize foreign investment in farmland.

3. Promote farm ownership and management by Blacks, Hispanics, Native Americans, Asians, Pacific Islanders, and other ethnic minority persons.

4. Establish procedures and programs to ensure small and moderate-sized family farmers fair and equitable return on labor and products.

5. Develop land use and land reclamation policies, undergirded by adequate funding, to preserve productive farmlands, on local option or county option basis.

6. Expand the amount of funding and program resources available to rural schools and educational institutions administered on a local or state basis.

7. Support health care programs that provide for the medical needs of rural people.

8. Provide financial assistance and training to rural law enforcement officials and rural legal service agencies.

9. Expand energy efficient mass transporation programs in rural areas.

10. Upgrade housing programs in rural areas.

11. Respect the guaranteed land and water rights of all minority peoples.

12. Develop a national water and energy policy which assures participation of local residents in decisions about rural and agricultural resources.

13. Recognize and protect the right of farm workers to organize into unions of their own choosing, be covered by minimum wage laws, receive adequate benefits, including Social Security.

14. Redirect comprehensive employment and training programs to also meet the needs of rural unemployed persons.

15. Increase funding of food and nutrition programs in rural areas.

16. Expand programs that serve the needs of rural elderly.

17. Fund and conduct research and extension designed to increase production of food wherever it is needed.

All of the above governmental actions must be accomplished through processes that include all persons residing in the rural areas that will be affected by such decisions.[3]

Alcohol as a Health Problem

"In Western society alcohol is killing people faster than the deadliest wars of all history. Alcohol causes 60 percent of teenage deaths and 50 percent of all highway deaths."[4] Of the 6,000,000 known alcoholics in the United States, 350,000 will be buried before the year is out. In contrast, Vietnam killed 5,000 yearly.

Alcohol is the number one drug problem of American youth. Evidence suggests that problem drinkers start drinking at a younger age than others which may increase the potential for developing alcoholism later. There are 3.3 million young people under the age of 18 who are alcoholics, or serious problem drinkers. One of every 10 social drinkers will become a problem drinker, or an alcoholic. Besides all the obvious physical and psychological damage, even to the unborn, the "known" cost to the nation is $43 billion a year due to absenteeism, health and welfare services, property damage, and medical expense.

WHEREAS, in our country 65 percent of the murders, 40 percent of assaults, 35 percent of rapes, 30 percent of other sex crimes, 30 percent of suicides, 55 percent of assaults in the home, and 60 percent of the cases of child abuse are attributed to the use of alcohol; and

WHEREAS, alcohol is a major cause of family breakup in our culture; and

WHEREAS, according to the National Council on Alcoholism, Inc., alcoholism is the most neglected health problem in the United States and ranks with cancer and heart disease as a major threat to the nation's health;

[3] *See* Social Principles, III-K, IV-F; "Special Needs of Farm Workers," 1976; "Self-help Efforts for Poor People," 1976.

[4] Drescher, J. M. "Alcohol: A Witness Against Itself," in *Ministry*, March 1982.

Therefore, Be It Resolved, that the 1984 General Conference direct the General Board of Church and Society and the General Board of Discipleship to affirm in an intentional way and with renewed zeal "the support of abstinence from alcohol as a faithful witness to God's liberating and redeeming love for persons" and also as stated in the *Discipline* (¶ 72-I) "support educational programs encouraging abstinence from such use" by doing the following:

1. Develop materials for use in The United Methodist Church, reflecting in their content our support for abstinence, as stated in the *Discipline.*

2. Assist the local churches with materials and guidelines in the establishment of counseling services and self-help groups for members of the church and community who are alcoholics or problem drinkers and their families.

3. Make available materials for use in the local church in programming educational seminars concerning alcohol-related problems.

4. Emphasize annually the need for education and consciousness-raising in the area of alcohol-related problems through the conference, district and/or local structure of the General Board of Church and Society and the General Board of Discipleship.

5. Educate members about ways in which they can support current groups already organized by their concern for alcohol-related problems such as MADD (Mothers Against Drunk Driving), National Federation of Drug-free Youth, American Council on Alcohol Problems, et al., and legislation that seeks to deal with the problem.

6. Report to the 1988 General Conference their efforts to implement this resolution.

7. Give special attention to promoting a life style on college campuses that encourages "wellness" without alcohol.[5]

[5] *See* Social Principles, III-1; "Drug and Alcohol Concerns," 1980. "Health and Wholeness," 1984.

Appreciation of Certain Organizations

WHEREAS, the Southern Christian Leadership Conference, National Association for the Advancement of Colored People, Urban League, Operation People United to Serve Humanity, the Congressional Black Caucus, and many other religious, civic, social, and fraternal organizations are doing much to improve the social and economic conditions of Blacks and all persons of this land,

Be It Resolved, that the 1984 General Conference of The United Methodist Church offer congratulations and appreciation for the significant accomplishments of these organizations.

The Arab-Israeli Conflict

The Middle East continues to be the location of some of the most serious international conflicts facing the world today. Though the area includes the birthplaces of three historically linked religions—Judaism, Christianity, and Islam—its problems are not primarily religious but ones of conflicting national and class interests.

Iran and Iraq are at war; the Kurdish people's aspirations to national self-determination remain unfulfilled; Lebanon, already torn by years of civil strife and the presence of Syrian and Palestine Liberation Organization (PLO) forces now suffers from the effects of invasion by Israel. It is still occupied and its territorial and national integrity remain threatened. Any timely or effective proposal for peace must take seriously the complexity of the entire Middle East.

For two quadrennia the General Conference of The United Methodist Church has given attention to the serious problems of the Middle East. Two aspects demand the continued concern of the church: The Arab-Israeli conflict, and the homelessness of the Palestinian people.

The Historical Context

The long history of oppression suffered by Jews—especially in the Western world—prompted nineteenth century

275

European Jewish leaders to seek a Jewish homeland. Some urged return to the land which held so much historic national and religious significance. The oppression culminated in the Nazi holocaust and the extermination of millions of persons. Spurred by the holocaust and the unwillingness of nations to open their borders to Jewish refugees, the State of Israel was born. From its creation in 1948 as a result of the United Nations Partition Resolution to the present, Israel has lived in a state of war with Arab nations hostile to its existence. Continuing and resurgent anti-Semitism, together with fears of a second holocaust, have given "The Land" new theological, political and pragmatic meaning to many Jews around the world.

The Arabs of Palestine and the surrounding region, emerging from centuries of Ottoman colonial rule, aspired to independence which was thwarted by the establishment of British and French authority over the area in the wake of World War I. The 1947 U.N. Partition Resolution had also promised an Arab state in Palestine, but was rejected as inadequate by Arab leadership. The resulting conflict between the armies of Israel and the Arab states displaced and dispossessed large numbers of Palestinian Arabs. In the wake of the fighting, Israel occupied territory beyond that allotted to it by the partition plan, and Egypt and Jordan occupied what remained of the territory.

From 1948 to the present, the Palestinian Arab people, among whom are Christian brothers and sisters, have suffered in many ways. Those who were dispossessed and are in exile suffer from deprivation in refugee camps, violence and repression. In the Occupied Territories, the effects of military rule and the continuing establishment of Israeli settlements on expropriated Arab land have led to increased tensions between Palestinian Arabs and Israeli Jews. Palestinians remain in the state of Israel as citizens, but suffer political and economic discrimination, especially with regard to ownership of land and homes. These conditions have rendered reconciliation between the two peoples more difficult.

The signing of a peace treaty between Egypt and Israel in

1979 was welcomed by many as a sign of, and a first step toward overall peace. Others warned that this separate agreement would make comprehensive peace more difficult to realize. Similar hopes and fears exist as a consequence of the 1983 peace accord between Lebanon and Israel. However well-intentioned, peace initiatives so far have either ignored the Palestinians' aspirations to statehood, or have not had the opportunity to bear fruit. All such initiatives have been flawed by the refusal to allow Palestinians to speak on their own behalf. Thus, they have failed to achieve their objectives—security for Israel, self-determination for the Palestinians, and peace for the region. Consequently, both the Israeli Jews and the Palestinian Arabs still live under conditions of instability and insecurity.

The Search for Peace

Integral to the solution of the Middle East conflict is the recognition of the right to self-determination of both the Israeli Jews and the Palestinian Arabs. This recognition demands affirmation of the right of the State of Israel to exist, and support for the rights of the Palestinian people to self-determination within historic Palestine, including the option of a sovereign state apart from the Hashemite Kingdom of Jordan. Both entities would be expected to pursue non-discriminatory policies towards domestic minorities.

We call for peace initiatives which are comprehensive. We affirm the continuing efforts of the United Nations to maintain peace and resolve the conflict. We affirm the courage of leaders who are willing to take the risk for peace. We condemn persistent conditions which perpetuate injustice and armed conflict and recognize that true peace must meet the needs of both the Israeli and Palestinian peoples. We affirm those forces and voices in Israel, the Arab world, and the United States—Jews, Christians, and Muslims—who have been in the forefront of the struggle for a peaceful resolution of the conflict.

We call upon the Arab nations to commit themselves, singly and together, to a course of peace with Israel. And we call upon the PLO leadership to offer its own bold and creative initiatives toward peace through some combination of the following: cessation of hostilities against Israel, a public statement of its commitment to a peaceful solution, and an explicit recognition of the right of Israel to exist. We also call upon the government of Israel to commit itself to a course that will lead to a just and peaceful resolution of Palestinian aspirations, through some combination of the following: cessation of policies of annexation, land expropriation, expulsions, collective punishment, and a freeze on settlements in the Occupied Territories, especially in the West Bank; a willingness to be in discussion with the PLO as a representative voice for the Palestinians; and a public openness to a democratic process by whch the Palestinian people can move toward national self-determination.

With an urgency for the sovereignty of Lebanon, both its territory and its government, we affirm Israel's stated intention to withdraw from Lebanon and call for a similar disengagement of Syria and the disarming of remaining PLO forces. A similar ugency about the integrity of the Lebanese-Israeli border demands that we call upon Israel to respect it and to refrain from the use and support of seccessionist forces within Lebanon. We urge the government of Lebanon to ensure that southern Lebanon no longer be used as a base for attacks upon Israel. We call for the exchange or release of prisoners seized during and since the 1982 invasion of Lebanon, particularly the thousands held by Israel, the Lebanese army and various private militias.

As territorial compromise is a necessary factor in any peaceful settlement, we affirm Israel's return of the Sinai to Egypt as part of the Egyptian-Israeli peace process, we urge the demilitarization of the Golan Heights, and we consider the realization of Palestinian self-determination on the West Bank and Gaza Strip vital to a comprehensive peace.

278

The United States and the Arab-Israeli Conflict

The United States, the U.S.S.R., and other nations have become increasingly involved in the Middle East politically, economically and militarily, and it is incumbent upon the churches and their members to examine critically the reasons for and implications of such involvement. The Middle East, as a whole, remains an arena of a furious arms race. The supply of weaponry provided to Israel and its Arab neighbors continues to escalate and makes true and lasting peace more difficult to achieve. There is a danger that the arms race in general will have an adverse effect on the possibility of achieving an overall solution. The use and re-export of U.S. weapons in violation of treaty regulations that specify that these arms are not for offensive use and not for re-export raise concern about the continued U.S. supply of weapons.

Therefore, we urge the President of the United States through his reports to Congress and his executive powers to ensure that the U.S. laws governing the sale or grant of weapons be effectively and immediately applied in light of the extensive use of U.S. supplied arms throughout the region. We further urge the President to initiate a U.S. embargo on arms to the entire Middle East, and to seek similar action from the U.S.S.R., the United Kingdom, France, and other suppliers.

We urge U.S. citizens and the U.S. government instead to support increased levels of funding for programs in the Middle East designed to meet basic human needs.

We call on the U.S. government and others, in line with the precedent established by the U.N. Security Council in 1976 and the general tone of the Soviet-American statement on the Middle East in 1977, to engage in discussions with the PLO with the aim of furthering the peace process.

We reaffirm the need for governmental officials to seek an overall solution within a multilateral context, rather than pursuing narrow self-interest which may set states against one another and increase the isolation of the insecure and dispossessed.

The United Methodist Church

We urge that United Methodist members, local churches, and agencies take the following specific actions:

1. Pray for peace in the Middle East—in personal and corporate worship.

2. Request that the governments outside the region not fund the militarization of any state in the Middle East, but rather improve levels of funding to meet basic human needs, and organize action programs at all levels to oppose the continuing flow of arms from all sources to the Middle East.

3. Affirm and continue the support of United Methodist members, local churches, and Annual Conferences of church-related programs of relief to refugees, reconstruction and development through U.M.C.O.R., World Division, and the programs of the National Council of Churches, the World Council of Churches, and the Middle East Council of Churches.

4. Resist simplistic theologies, both in the Middle East and the U.S., which would either support uncritically Israeli policies on the grounds of exclusive claims to "The Land" or seek to deny the living covenantal relationship of God with Jews through its supposed supersedence by a new covenant.

5. Reject stereotypes of both Jews and Arabs as racist and instead seek opportunities to heighten sensitivity and increase awareness, out of which can grow a greater appreciation for the beliefs and values of Jews, Muslims, and Christians of Middle Eastern churches.

6. Participate in and promote educational programs aimed at helping United Methodists understand the intricacies of the Arab-Israeli conflict. Specific action should include:

a) Initiation of programs involving contact with and among Christians, Muslims, and Jews from the Middle East.

b) Encouragement of all leaders of and participants in "Holy Land tours" to contact indigenous Christian leaders in the Middle East, and to hear the concerns of both the Israelis and Palestinians who live there, as well as visit the biblical and historical sites.

c) Evaluation of the treatment of the conflict in United Methodist curricula and media.

d) Collaboration of appropriate boards and agencies to develop a packet of educational program materials.

e) Development of denominational participation in ecumenical and interreligious networks to raise consciousness, provide information about the Middle East, and to stimulate action to promote peace in the Middle East.[6]

Assistance and Sanctuary for Central American Refugees

WHEREAS, at various times in history the Christian Church has been called upon to give concrete evidence of its commitment to love and justice even when it seems contrary to public opinion; and

WHEREAS, according to the terms of the Refugee Act of 1980 the United States accords refugee or asylum status to persons who cannot return to their countries of origin because of persecution or fear of persecution, for reasons of race, religion, nationality, membership in a particular social group or political opinion; and

WHEREAS, refugees from Central America and other areas of Latin America and the Caribbean are fleeing to the United States to escape the persecution, torture, and murder of their civil-war-torn homelands; and

WHEREAS, many of these refugees have been tortured and murdered when forced to return to their homelands; and

WHEREAS, Scripture says not to mistreat foreigners who live in your land (Lev. 19:33) because sojourners and strangers have a special place in the heart of God.

Therefore, Be It Resolved, that The United Methodist Church strongly:

1. Urges the President of the United States, the Department of State, and Department of Justice, and the Congress, to grant "extended voluntary departure" legal

[6] *See* Social Principles, VI.

status to refugees from El Salvador and Guatemala, and other areas of the Caribbean and Latin America.

2. Requests that Annual Conferences and local churches assist in ministries to Central American, Caribbean, and other Latin American refugees by providing them with legal assistance, bail bond funds, food, housing, and medical care.

3. Encourages congregations who take seriously the mandate to do justice and to resist the policy of the Immigration and Naturalization Service by declaring their churches to be "sanctuaries" for refugees from El Salvador, Guatemala, and other areas of the Caribbean and Latin America.

4. Urges the United States to follow the United Nations definition of refugees.[7]

Baptism, Eucharist, and Ministry, Responses and Reception

WHEREAS, The United Methodist Church celebrates the formulation of the historic theological convergence of the World Council of Churches' document, *Baptism, Eucharist and Ministry;*

WHEREAS, The United Methodist Church thanks God for the privilege of participating over the course of more than five decades in the preparation of this document with Christians throughout the world;

WHEREAS, The Commission on Faith and Order of the World Council of Churches "invites all churches to prepare an official response to this text at the highest appropriate level of authority by December 31, 1985"; and

WHEREAS, The General Commission on Christian Unity and Interreligious Concerns of The United Methodist Church is mandated in the 1980 Discipline "to advocate and work toward the reception of the gift of Christian unity in every aspect of the Church's life and to foster approaches to

---

[7] *See* "Concern for Human Rights in Central America," 1984.

ministry and mission which more fully refects the oneness of Christ's Church in the human community" (Par. 2002.1);

Therefore Be It Resolved,

1. That the General Conference of The United Methodist Church urge local churches and other units at every level of the denomination to explore the incorporation of the theological convergence into its worship, educational, ethical, and spiritual life and witness; and

2. That the local and conference responses to *Baptism, Eucharist and Ministry* to be sent to the General Commission on Christian Unity and Interreligious Concerns for transmittal to the Council of Bishops; and

3. That the Council of Bishops be requested "to prepare an official response" to *Baptism, Eucharist and Ministry* by November, 1985.

Black Colleges and the Black College Fund

WHEREAS, higher education, uniting humane learning and vital piety, is indispensable to the life, character, mission, and responsibility of the Church of our Lord as embodied in The United Methodist Church; and

WHEREAS, for more than a century, the twelve black institutions of higher learning related to The United Methodist Church have been faithful to the church's commitment to the life of the mind, to the joy and beauty of learning, and to the Wesleyan tradition and heritage in higher education, and have made profound and enduring contributions not only to the black community but also to the quality of life and experience in the whole New World; and

WHEREAS, these colleges are essential to the richness, vitality, stability, health, and variety of life and culture in America; and

WHEREAS, the twelve black colleges related to The United Methodist Church offer high quality education to their students and have a profound commitment to academic excellence. We serve a wide variety of students and their needs. We respond creatively and realistically to their needs at every level. We have designed programs for the exceptionally gifted and superior student as well as for the academically deficient student; and

WHEREAS, these institutions have never been either segregated or segregating, and have always been open to and welcomed all qualified students regardless of race, creed, color, ethnicity, or nationality, and will continue to do so. Our colleges have been models of democracy, integration, quality and humanism in higher education; and

WHEREAS, our colleges perform a special service to black young men and women in particular and to the black community in general, in response to unique historical circumstances and needs; and

WHEREAS, these institutions have been the main source of black professionals—teachers, lawyers, scholars, physicians and dentists, engineers, writers, ministers, military officers, governmental officials, business executives, architects, etc.; and

WHEREAS, these colleges provide a nurturing, caring, concerned, and supportive environment for learning and a passion for academic excellence for disadvantaged students and a healthy respect for the dignity and worth of every person as made in the image of God; and

WHEREAS, these institutions of higher education have been the chief source of black leadership, the major preservers of black culture, and the principal instrument of black upward social mobility; and

WHEREAS, the twelve black colleges related to The United Methodist Church richly deserve generous and sustained financial suppport in order to continue their great services and contributions to American life, and black community, and the whole of humankind;

WHEREAS, the twelve presidents who comprise the Council of Presidents unanimously request of The United Methodist Church, through the General Council on Finance and Administration, a minimum of $34,849,606 (about 10 percent of their budgets) over the next quadrennium for current and capital expenses;

Be It Resolved, that the General Board of Higher Education and Ministry request through the General Council on Finance and Administration a minimum of $33,093,288 for the twelve institutions in the 1985-88 quadrennium, based on the World Service percentages as follows:

1985	$7,551,567	4% year of 1984
1986	$8,066,329	7% year of 1985
1987	$8,522,065	6% year of 1986
1988	$8,953,327	5% year of 1987

Be It Further Resolved, that one-sixth of the annual request be distributed over the next quadrennium for capital improvement.

Be It Further Resolved, that the total amount be distributed by the Division of Higher Education of the General Board of Higher Education and Ministry of The United Methodist Church based on a formula approved by the Division and the Council of Presidents.

Be It Finally Resolved, that this resolution be recorded in the Book of Resolutions of the 1984 General Conference.

Black Colleges and Goals for the Black College Fund

WHEREAS, the Methodist Episcopal Church organized the Freedmen's Aid Society in 1866 for the purpose of providing educational opportunities for the newly freed Blacks; and

WHEREAS, the Freedmen's Aid Society and the Methodist Episcopal Church, South, established nonsegregating and unsegregated colleges for the primary purpose of educating black people; and

WHEREAS, the black colleges have made a significant contribution to racial progress in America and have played a unique role in advancing democracy; and

WHEREAS, black colleges are the repositories of black history, culture, and research by which black heritage has

285

been, and is preserved, interpreted, and articulated in North America and the world; and

WHEREAS, private black colleges continue to serve a vital role in the education of Blacks and other students who are attracted to these institutions because of their academic programs, their geographic locations, their intimate sizes, their ability to motivate intellectually promising students and nurture educationally and economically disadvantaged youths, and their deliberate provisions for financial assistance; and

WHEREAS, these colleges provide carefully planned opportunities for developing talents and leadership skills through active involvement in all phases of campus life; and

WHEREAS, United Methodists have reaffirmed their long-standing commitment to these institutions by establishing the Black College Fund; and

WHEREAS, that at no time in the history of the church has the financial support of these colleges reached its maximum potential; now

Be It Resolved, that $33,093,288 be established as the goal for the 1985-88 quadrennium; and

Be It Further Resolved, that the University Senate, through its Commission on Black Colleges, continue to assist these institutions in fulfilling their missions.

Christian Faith and Disarmament

The prophecy of Isaiah to Ahaz, King of Judah, declared that security cannot be gained in foreign alliances, intensified hatreds, or strengthened defenses. Isaiah's action program was for the king to "Take heed, be quiet, do not fear, and do not let your heart be faint . . ." (Isa. 7:4).

Isaiah had named his son, "A remnant shall return" which offered God's hope for those who remained faithful, a foretelling of the failure of those who rely on force of arms to survive (Isa. 7; II Kings 17; II Chron. 28).

We affirm Isaiah's words as a standard for today. They are consistent with our denominational history and our contemporary stance. We remember the words of the bishops of the Evangelical Association who said in 1816, "War and the shedding of blood are incompatible with the teachings and example of Christ." Thus we place ourselves with those who reject planning for war as a path to peace. We also affirm Isaiah's words of hope. We are not called to despair. The landmark study *The Christian Faith and War in the Nuclear Age,* directed by the 1960 General Conference of The Methodist Church and given to the church in 1963, said: "The Christian Church and the individual must accept responsibility for the creation of a climate of opinion in which creative changes can occur." It called work for these creative alternatives, "Our mission field as we live as disciples of the Prince of Peace".[8]

We recognize the current situation which is described as a "nuclear dilemma," presents the possibility that, referring to Isaiah's prophecy of a faithful remnant, there may not be a remnant left.

But we also recognize our own responsibility to act, on the basis of our faith, to establish alternatives to war as outlined in the Social Principles and "The United Methodist Church and Peace."

In that mission, we recognize certain events and rejoice in the work that is being done:

• We stand with and affirm our bishops as they lead us through their ministry for peace, especially as it was represented by their Pastoral Letter of April, 1982. We rejoice in their challenge to all United Methodists to join together in seeking an end to the arms race and dedicate ourselves to accept their challenge to be peacemakers.

• We praise the American Conference of Catholic Bishops for their Pastoral Letter, *The Challenge of Peace: God's Promise and Our Response.* We are strengthened in our understanding and actions through their studied bibilical/theological analysis as well as by their analysis of our global situation.

• We rejoice that a challenge to the escalating nuclear

[8] *The Christian Faith and War in the Nuclear Age,* p. 105.

arms race has been developed by the National Movement for a Nuclear Freeze in the United States, and has been affirmed internationally in the United Nations. We commend and encourage our congregations and members who are leaders in that movement at all levels. We support a mutually verifiable freeze of nuclear weapons as a politically viable first step toward achieving our goal of the elimination of the production, possession, or use of nuclear weapons.

• We also rejoice that many United Methodists throughout the world participate in various other movements designed to seek alternatives to armaments. In these actions, they are joining together corporately to fulfill the request of the 1963 study which says the Christian must act and must "not sit on the sidelines while momentous decisions are being made."[9]

In order to fulfill our obligations to witness to God's hope for the future we pledge ourselves to these actions:

• We, as United Methodist Christians, must build the conditions for peace through development of confidence and trust between peoples and governments. We stand unalterably opposed to those who would instill hate for one people and nation in the people of another nation. As a worldwide church, we recognize in Christ the unity of all humanity. There must be no hatred between sisters and brothers. We will seek out and struggle against any attempt to instill hatred of any, whether a country, people, or national symbol.

• United Methodists and other Christians must recognize that conflict can be alleviated by accepting the validity of political and economic systems in other countries, and by pledging to work to eliminate attempts to impose systems developed in countries other than their own. That recognition is a necessary first step toward stopping the threat to one system by the government of the other.

• Our goal of world disarmament must be achieved through intermediate steps of arms reduction. We reject deterrence as a permanent basis for the securing and

[9] *Ibid.,* pp. 100-101.

maintenance of peace. It can only be tolerated as a temporary expedient and while real measures of disarmament are set in motion. We affirm measures, particularly between the U.S.S.R. and the United States which develop trust in negotiating postures, and deplore words and actions of one or the other of the major nuclear powers designed to threaten the other.

• We seek to include "no first-strike" pledges in disarmament agreements. We oppose development of weapons systems which lead to automated, hair-trigger responses or pre-emptive strikes. Such systems radically shorten time available for rational response to presumed nuclear attack.

• We continue to urge ratification by all nations of international treaties designed to curb the spread of all types of weapons, both on earth and in outer space. We pledge ourselves to aid in the development of situations where non-nuclear countries do not feel compelled to seek nuclear weapons. We ask governments to structure appropriate political and economic relations with such countries that will encourage them in their non-nuclear path.

• We encourage our local churches and members also to engage in other actions that lead to a disarmed world, including prayer services, vigils, petition drives, and contacts with public officials. To these ends we support those Christians who feel called upon by God to participate in acts of non-violent civil disobedience.

• Disarmament and peace depend upon all nations discovering a prophetic vision of justice and tranquility, as well as the intentions of the Preamble of the U.S. Constitution. We, therefore, call upon The United Methodist Church to establish justice ministries committed to spreading scriptural holiness and reforming the land. Justice requires the end of racism, poverty and violence, and the emergence everywhere of reconciliation. For that reason we reaffirm the program emphasis of Peace With Justice.[10]

[10] *See* Social Principles, VI-C; "The United Methodist Church and Peace, I-"Disarmament."

The Christian Family—Becoming Transformed and Transforming

A Call to the Churches Concerning Families

Summary Statement

Because We Understand That God . . . calls the church to proclaim the gospel to all the world, to teach the gospel to all who will hear, and to nurture persons in their growth as faithful followers of Christ,

And Because All Persons . . . respond to God and relate to each other out of their own past and present family experiences, use family images as parables of God and the world, and make decisions that either affirm or destroy persons in their many other relationships,

We Therefore Call Our Churches To . . .

1. Become more aware of the pervasive powers of families as creators of persons, proclaimers of faith perspectives, and shapers of both present and future society.

2. Study families and marriages, their resources, possibilities, and needs.

3. View families as fundamental human communities that socialize their members for citizenship in society and can nurture and support their members from conception to death.

4. Support marriage as a major voluntary family commitment that creates families and shapes the quality of family life.

5. Understand families as Christian communities of faith, hope, and love, like the larger church, that witness and minister to each other and to the world.

6. Act in their churches and communities to strengthen families as centers of creative power, redemptive love, and sustaining nurture through ministries the church can provide.

7. Influence governments and their agencies to enact and enforce laws and provisions that enable families to do their nurturing and socializing tasks well.

8. Urge educational institutions, businesses, and all other groups in society to enable families to do their nurturing and socializing tasks well.

And We Call Our Church Boards and Agencies . . . To create study and action resources that enable congregations to implement this call in every way possible.

As a church our central task is to proclaim the gospel of Jesus Christ and to participate in the Holy Spirit's transforming work in persons, families, communities, nations, and the world. Because of our commitment to Christ, we seek a world of healthy, happy, productive persons who, through God's loving grace, live in peace, justice, and love with each other. God creates us for relationships through which we give and receive mutual care and love (among many examples are Gen. 1:27; 2:18; Matt. 18:20).

Sin distorts and breaks our relationships with God and other persons. Some family experiences lead individuals to develop harmful patterns such as alcohol and other substance abuse, crime, prejudices, intolerance, spouse and child abuse, selfishness, indifference, manipulation, and many other characteristics that express our sin before God. Some are tempted to withdraw within their families and ignore the needs of others. Jesus has a harsh word for this temptation: "He who loves father or mother more than me is not worthy of me . . ." (Matt. 10:37-39). Some are tempted to ignore or hurt their families in their pursuit of career or other goals, and the fifth commandment reminds us of our family relationships (Deut. 5:16; Mark 7:9-13).

At its best, the transforming Christian family is an agent of change and improvement in its community and world, bringing the values of life in Christ to bear upon all relationships of life, in anticipation of the kingdom.

We do not take our fundamental criteria for family life from culture, social sciences, or mass media. To do so would be to conform to societal standards that often conflict with the gospel. "Do not be conformed to this world but be transformed by the renewal of your mind, that you may prove what is the will of God, what is good and acceptable and perfect" (Rom. 12:2).

Marriages and families inevitably shape individuals and communities. Whether recognized or not, God is at work in every family to redeem, sustain, and nurture it toward healing and wholeness. We point toward the power of Christ to redeem families as households of faith and renewal centers of transforming love.

Family relationshps such as child, sibling, spouse, and parent, help us to understand and experience God's Spirit at work in us and through our families to others in the world. We lift up Christian marriage, parenthood, and other family relationships as parables of the relationship between God and persons. We affirm marriages in which both spouses are co-equal partners with God (I Cor. 7) and which express many facets of God in relation to women and men (among many examples: Prov. 31: Hosea 1-3; Eph. 5:21*f*).

We press on toward an understanding of Christian personhood and perfection in love based upon life in Christ which can enable families to be in creative dialogue with culture, not conformed to it (Romans 12). At its best, the transforming Christian family is an agent of change and improvement in the community and world.

We believe in the power of Christ to redeem, sustain, and empower families as centers of transforming love, and we call on every congregation to proclaim this power in word and work. We seek Christian families who identify themselves as God's own people (1 Peter 2:9-10), a community of the faithful living "in but not of the world" (John 17:6-19), as units of the body of Christ (I Cor. 12:12-27).

Every Family is Unique and Special

The United Methodist Church recognizes the myriad forms of "family" in our time, affirms all those that serve as centers of guidance, nurture, and love—and calls every congregation to ministries with various families at their diverse points of need.

All families are important. Family refers to those persons

who are related by blood or marriage and live in the same household, and also to family members who live elsewhere, such as at school, in the armed forces, or in an institution. Family includes our families of origin and ancestry, to whom we relate as children and grandchildren: Family also refers to the homes we create through marriage, and, if children come, to our own children and grandchildren. Family can also mean the larger groups of marriages and families who are linked together by bonds of blood, law, adoption, and choice.

Family focuses on a specific group of persons in a specific residential household, yet also transcends both time and space in drawing its members to each other through common commitments and concerns. We recognize that family structures are quite varied and different, yet we emphasize that family experiences are the basic foundation for love, justice, and peace in all our other human relationships.

Toward Christian Families

It is not the prerogative of The United Methodist Church to lay down some concrete ideal of what the Christian family "ought" to be. Christ has freed us from such legalism. But it is the mission of the church to support its families in discovering and enacting a style of being in the world that is both transformed and transforming—and to this mission every congregation is called.

We can describe characteristics of "the Christian family" that produce love and the many other fruits of the Spirit (Gal. 5:22). Some of the goals of the Christian family are:

1. Family members increasingly identify themselves as Christians through baptism and active commitment to Christ.

2. As a center for faith development, family members are growing in love and traveling their own life journeys in response to God's calls and leadings.

3. Family members are actively involved in the supportive fellowship of a local congregation as part of the universal church.

4. For married couples, Christian marriage increasingly forms the central bonds in the family, as wife and husband voluntarily covenant together as co-equal spouses before God and with the support of the Christian community.

5. Since the Christian family is a body of whom Christ is the head, each family member brings needed gifts to the body, and members respect each other as unique persons under God.

6. The Christian family is a priesthood of believers. They act as incarnations of Christ to one another, each doing for the others what Christ does for him or her, in order to generate and confirm in one another an abiding faith in Jesus Christ, and to provide a sanctuary for family members as a haven to help heal the stresses and storms of life.

7. Through family worship, Bible study, prayers at meals and other times, stories of personal faith, conversations, and other means of grace, "by precept and example," members use a variety of family rituals to celebrate their faith.

8. The family's ministry is directed to all persons, including "the least of these"—the weak, the ill, the very young, the very old, the disabled, the rejected—and this is expressed through their relationships with diverse people and their political and community activities.

9. The Christian family practices a responsible lifestyle committed to a just and sustainable future for all peoples. They act out this commitment in their stewardship of all their money and other resources, and their tithing and proportionate giving.

10. As a community being transformed by God's grace, the Christian family serves and acts in society through careers, recreation, and lifestyle to transform the world.

11. Christian family members give redemptive, forgiving love to restore persons to wholeness with each other as expressions of God's grace, but inevitably all family members sin and fall short of their possibilities when relationships are broken, commitments forgotten, and guilt weighs heavily.

Good News for Today's Families!

The United Methodist Church rejoices in God's gifts of love and freedom by which persons around the world are finding new joy and fulfillment in family life—and urges every congregation to share this good news with the families of its community.

While there is much bad news about family life, we do not despair for the family. We proclaim that in our time there is more good news than bad. There are more signs of promise than ever before. The liberating power of the gospel, working in families both in the church and in the secular world, continues to open bright new frontiers for family life.

Merely proclaiming this good news does not make it so for families. Millions have not even heard this liberating message, and millions more have heard it but are still trapped by old expectations, habits, and other limitations. Indeed, there are forces in society intent on preserving the old stereotypes of power and privilege for some families and some family members.

Affirmations

The Spirit of God works in very human lifestyle and circumstance to bring healing and renewal (some examples: Job; Rom. 8:28-39). No lifestyle should be idolized, and all lifestyles must be evaluated by Christ's standards of love, justice, and mercy. We affirm the right and responsibility of every individual to choose lifestyles that are consistent with the highest Christian ideals of spiritual character, excellence of mind, purity of body, and responsible social behavior.

We affirm the United Methodist Social Principles that directly and indirectly supports individuals, marriages, and families as channels for nurturing persons by God's creating Spirit.

In addition to those Social Principles, we therefore affirm:

1. Both singleness and marriage as valid lifestyles for Christians (I Cor. 7).

2. Human sexuality as a good gift of God for responsible procreation (Gen. 1:27-28) and for joyous re-creation and communion (Song of Solomon; Prov. 5:18-19; 1 Cor. 7:9) ("Male and female he created them. . . . And behold, it was very good") (Gen. 1:27; 31).

3. Our liberation from limiting roles for male and females ("There is neither male nor female; for you are all one in Christ" (Gal. 3:28b). Characteristics and tasks we once called masculine or feminine are now seen as simply human.)

4. Shared responsibilities in a family in which all are equal before God.

5. Every life stage, from birth and infancy to old age and death, as equally part of God's plan for our growth into the fullness of his creation in us (No age or stage is less important, nor more important, than another age or stage in our life journey to Christ.)

6. The distinctive lifestyles of ethnic minority families, and respect the validity of every family tradition and heritage that expresses God's ways of peace, justice, freedom, and love.

7. Marriage and parent preparation, education, counseling, therapy, and other means for helping families to learn new ways to live with each other in mutual love and support.

8. Persons in a disintegrating family involving divorce must be helped to learn ways to restructure their lives in more constructive ways, keeping before us Jesus' words against divorce (e.g., Matt. 5:31-32; Mark 10:2-12) and acknowledging that it falls short of God's intention for marriage.

Marriage and Family Ministries in Our Third Century

As people of faith we know that the realm of God is "already," but still "not yet." The day of righteousness, wholeness, peace, and justice is now "in the midst of us" (Luke 17:21b), and yet we work and pray that it may "come on earth" (Matt. 6:10) in its fullness. Families are a major channel of this gracious activity of God. Family ministries are equally as important as and require the same levels of local church and denominational resources as our efforts in discipleship, educational institutions, world and home missions, and social concerns.

Marriage and family ministries include our ministries to individuals and family households, programs that enable family units to minister to others, and efforts that seek to shape the larger social orders, such as business and government, that establish the living conditions and possibilities for families.

God challenges us to strengthen and expand our current ministries, to develop many needed additional marriage and family ministries, and to enable families to be ministers to the world. To this end we must create much stronger family ministries structures at the national, conference, and local church levels to enable these ministries to be done.

We therefore call local congregations and the various administrative structures of The United Methodist Church to four major types of family ministries:

1. Ministries Within Families and Between Family Members. These ministries are the caring, nurturing, and supportive acts that family members provide to each other, so essential to mainaining healthy families. Among these many ministries of love (Rom. 12, I Cor. 13) are:

Celebrations such as meal time prayers, family worship, birthdays, holy days, holidays, and other affirmations of faith in God and support of each other.

Support for meaningful family traditions and ethnic cultures that link family members to their heritage as a foundation for living and relating to other traditions in the community, nation, and world.

Support for authentic marriage commitment of fidelity between spouses, marriage preparation and enrichment, parent education, understanding sexuality, family finance, work and leisure, communication of trust and forgiveness, and the many other attitudes and behaviors that form the structures and lifestyles of families.

Continuing Christian nurture, discipline, and faith development appropriate to each family member's life stage, experience, and journey.

2. *Ministries to Families in Need.* All families need help from others at times of normal transitions of growth and change. Among these ministries are:

Worship, church school, and home visitor services.

Preparation for transitions such as births, baptism, leaving home, career and job changes, moving, and marriage.

Care in endings when members of the family leave through death, divorce, or other departures.

Intergenerational activities in which persons of all ages can relate to other members of the larger church family.

All families also face times of crisis and unwanted changes. We must maintain and increase our ministries to families in times of difficulty. Among these ministries are:

Marriage and family counseling and therapy, divorce counseling, and related educational programs.

Therapies and other rehabilitative care for alcohol and other substance-addicted persons and families, physical or sexually abusive spouses and parents.

Counseling and guidance to persons involved in unmarried cohabitation, problem pregnancies, or criminal offenses.

Support to families with chronic health conditions, catastrophic illnesses, or unemployment.

3. *Ministries from Families to Others.* Through these ministries families celebrate and share the benefits they have received—time, abilities, funds, the natural world— care for them wisely, and decide how they will use them in accord with God's will in ministry to others. Among these ministries are:

Emergency shelters, foster parenting, hospice care, and other ministries to persons in need.

Tithing and proportionate giving through church and community channels to aid others in need.

Paid and volunteer work as expressions of God's calling and vocation in society, and family support of their members who serve in these ways.

Participation in neighborhood, community, school, and other programs that assist individuals and families.

Friendships and informal contacts with others through whom family members can witness to the gospel.

Family lifestyles that respect God's creation, conserve natural resources, and express stewardship of God's world.

4. *Ministries on Behalf of Families.* Families are directly affected by war, peace, education, governmental policies, economic factors, and other conditions in the larger societies of nation and world. We need to expand our efforts and develop additional ministries to policymakers and other leaders whose decisions shape the structures that often set the limits and provide the possibilities for families. Among these ministries are:

Efforts toward the empowerment of the weak, protecting and being a voice for persons and groups who are poor, powerless, battered, abandoned, disabled, dispossessed, or imprisoned.

Active involvement in political processes and efforts to improve living conditions for families, provide marriage and family education, and be alert to the many effects of government and business actions on families.

Undergird ethnic minority families in their effort to find a place in a diverse society, and, where needed, their struggle against unjust social and economic pressures.

Continuing support of programs that enable all persons to have adequate food, clothing, housing, medical care, and other basic necessities that empower them for their own self-determination.

Guided by the Holy Spirit, we can do marriage and family ministries. We need the firm conviction that these ministries are fundamental and essential ministries of our congregations and of The United Methodist Church at conference and national levels. With this conviction, let us apply our genius for disciplined organization, planning, and implementation to serving the families of our churches and communities

The United Methodist Church is committed to ongoing ministries within families, ministries to families, ministries through families, and ministries on behalf of families—both within and outside the church, as central to the mission of the

church at local, regional, and national levels. We call on every congregation and every leader to take up this ministry prayerfully, thoughtfully, enthusiastically, and effectively.[11]

The Church and Persons with Mentally, Physically, and/or Psychologically Handicapping Conditions

We call United Methodists to a new birth of awareness of the need to accept, include, receive the gifts of and respond to the concerns of those persons with mentally, physically, and/or psychologically handicapping conditions, including their families.

Because the experience of handicapping conditions is included in all racial, social, sexual, and age groupings, and this experience is common to every family and at some time in every life;

And because a large part of the ministry of our Lord focused on persons with mentally, physically, and/or psychologically handicapping conditions;

And because the Body of Christ is not complete without people of all areas of life;

And because we cannot afford to deny ourselves fellowship with these persons and must intentionally develop more healthy attitudes and behavioral responses to persons with handicapping conditions;

And because there exist inadequacies in the church and in society with regard to concerns for the rights of persons with handicapping conditions, utilization of talents, and their full participation within the life of the church and society;

And because more suffering and exclusion from the fellowship of the church of persons with mentally, physically, and/or psychologically handicapping conditions;

And believing that the church is most faithful to the teachings and example of Jesus when it expresses love in concrete ways in a mutual ministry with those who are outcasts, neglected, avoided, or persecuted by society,

[11] *See* Social Principles, II-A.

And believing in the legacy of John Wesley, Phillip Otterbein and Jacob Albright who held that vital piety flows into compassionate ministry;

And knowing that prevailing societal norms unduly glorify the conditions of youthful beauty, mental alertness, and material affluence to the exclusion and avoidance of those whose handicapping conditions put them outside these norms.

Therefore, we pledge ourselves to:

Accessibility

● Renew and increase our commitments as a church to the development of a barrier-free society, especially in the many facilities of the church. To indicate the seriousness of our intent we must set time limits to assure the greatest physical accessibility in the shortest feasible periods and extend our policy of not providing funding through or approval by United Methodist agencies unless minimum guidelines are met which include but are not limited to:

A. Providing adequate access to sanctuary pews, altars, classrooms, and restrooms.

B. Providing curb cuts, ramps with at least a 1:12 inclination or platform lifts.

C. Providing facilities with equipment and supplies to meet the needs of persons with seen and unseen handicapping conditions including persons with vision and/or hearing impairments.

● All meetings of The United Methodist Church, beyond the local church, be accessible to persons with handicapping conditions. As general church agencies, jurisdictions, annual conferences, and districts nominate persons with handicapping conditions to their boards and committees, it is necessary for these boards and committees to accommodate these persons.

● All United Methodist Churches are asked to conduct an audit of their facilities to discover what barriers impede the full participation of persons with handicapping conditions.

Steps should then be taken to remove those barriers. **The accessibility audit for churches** is a recommended resource available from the General Board of Global Ministries.

Awareness

• Sensitize and train local church pastors to the needs and opportunities for those who are handicapped and their families to better minister to and with them.

• Lead the local chuches in attitudinal change studies to the end that the people called United Methodists are sensitized to the gifts, needs, and interests of persons with handicapping conditions, including their families.

• Take advantage of the great opportunities for our church to work cooperatively with other denominations who also are addressing these issues and extend an active invitation to work jointly where possible.

• Suggest one Sunday a year as Access Sunday to sensitize people to our accessibility concerns.

Adequate Resources

• Provide resources through the church at all levels, including curricula, for persons with various handicapping conditions, such as those who are blind, deaf, para or quadriplegic, mentally retarded, psychologically or neurologically disabled, etc., so that each individual has full opportunity for growth and self-realization with the community of faith and the society at large.

• Strongly recommend that all curriculum material be so designed that it can be adapted to meet the needs of persons with handicapping conditions. That curriculum material portray persons with handicapping conditions in leadership roles within church and society. That curriculum material reflect the guidelines for the Elimination of Handicappist Language as produced by the General Council on Ministries.

Affirmative Action

• Include in all our efforts of affirmative action the concerns and interests of persons with handicapping

302

conditions, particularly in the active recruitment and encouragement of these persons for leadership roles, both clergy and lay, within the church and its agencies, in hiring practices, in job security, housing and transportation.

That the General Board of Higher Education and Ministry monitor Annual Conference Boards of Ordained Ministry so that persons with handicapping conditions are given equal treatment in the steps to ordained ministry.

• Strongly urge that our schools of higher education and theological training provide specialized courses for faculty and students in the awareness of and appreciation of gifts, needs, and interests of persons with handicapping conditions. This must include the emphasis of accessibility and equal employment in these institutions as well as in those in the larger society. Accreditation by the University Senate should be withdrawn where handicapped persons are excluded, either from attendance, services, or employment.

• Strongly urge local churches to conduct needs assessment surveys. Such a survey would suggest to a local church what particular actions must be taken to include fully persons with handicapping conditions within the life of the church.

Advocacy Within the Church

• Implement within each Annual Conference methods of recruiting, sensitizing, and training persons as advocates to work with and on behalf of persons with handicapping conditions on a one-to-one basis and to enable them to achieve their human and civil rights as well as to assume their rightful place in the life of the church and community. Each Annual Conference should also develop the larger concern of advocacy for persons with handicapping conditions to enable them to achieve appropriate housing, employment, transportation, education, and leisure time development.

Advocacy Within the Society

While there is much to be done within the church to make real the gospel of inclusiveness with regard to persons with

303

handicapping conditions, yet there is a world society which also must be made aware of the concerns and needs of these persons. We admonish the church and its people to stand alongside persons with handicapping conditions and to speak out on their rights in society. These rights include access to jobs, public transportation, and other reliable forms of transportation, adequate housing, and education. We are people under orders to minister to and with all God's children. We are all a people in pilgrimage! We have too often overlooked those of God's children who experience life in different ways than ourselves. We pledge ourselves to an inclusive, compassionate, and creative response to the needs and gifts of persons with mentally, physically, and/or psychologically handicapping conditions.[12]

The Church in a Mass Media Culture

The world is moving from an agricultural and industrial dominance into the information and communication age. In the United States, more persons are employed in information-related industries than in all other types of work combined. Public governments and private industries control the technology and flow of information, wielding great power over the lives of billions of people.

All people are affected by the information revolution. Persons in developing countries may receive most of their news from First World news services while their crop development and natural resources may be surveyed by foreign satellite. Some Third World nations are leapfrogging past the wired nation into the satellite era.

In First World countries such as the United States, persons are spending more and more time in communication activities: viewing more television programming as cable and direct signals from satellites increase, using the home computer and playing video games.

This new development in world history is driven by

[12] *See* Social Principles, III-G.

quantum leaps in basic information management technology and can be described as a revolution because of its pervasive effects at several levels:

• The centralization of control and ownership of information in First World countries.

• The socializing acculturating effects of world media bringing the same messages and information to diverse audiences.

• The increasing amounts of time persons are interacting with media rather than with other persons and the passive nature of much media viewing.

• The incentive for a mass audience leads to dominant content of the entertainment and information media categorized by escapism, consumerism, violence and exclusion of minorities.

• The increasing involvement of the work force and capital investment in information technology-related endeavors in the developed and developing world.

As United Methodists, we have "emphasized God's endowment of each person with dignity and moral responsibility" (¶ 69, page 76, 1980 *Book of Discipline*). We recognize that "faith and good works belong together" (¶ 69, p. 77). We have a long history of concern for social justice, so it is within both a biblical and historical context that we as United Methodists speak to the communication and information revolution.

The goals of The United Methodist Church, based on our understanding of the gospel, are clear.

• Persons everywhere must be free in their efforts to live meaningful lives.

• Channels of communication must operate in open, authentic and humanizing ways.

• Christians should be involved seriously and continuously in the communication systems of their societies.

In the implementation of these goals, we must be aware of the power of the mass media. All media are educational. The mass media—especially radio, television, cable TV, motion pictures, newspapers, books and magazines—are pervasive and influential forces in our culture. The new media of video games, direct broadcast satellite, video recordings for home use and computers are increasing. Whether they deal with information, opinion, entertainment, escape, explicit behavioral models or subtle suggestion, the mass media always are involved, directly or indirectly, in values. Furthermore, all media messages speak from some theological assumptions. Therefore, we as Christians must ask such major questions as:

• Who controls the media in a country? Who determines the structures of and the public's access to the mass media? Will deregulation of radio, television and cable in the United States result in greater diversity, freedom and justice, or less? Who controls international technologies of communication?

• Who determines message content and within what guidelines of responsibility?

• Who uses the media and for what purposes?

• What rights do users have in determining media structure and content? What is the user's responsibility in bringing critical appraisal and judgment to the messages received?

• What is the appropriate response to the growing demands of developing countries that there be new and more just world information systems which meet their needs?

As Christians, we affirm the principle of freedom of expression as both an individual and corporate right. We oppose any laws or structures which attempt to abridge freedom of expression and we state our concern about the numerous incidents of repression of freedom of expression occurring in the United States and around the world. We believe:

• Freedom of expression—whether by spoken or printed word, or any visual or artistic medium—should be exercised within a framework of social responsibility. The church is opposed to censorship.

• The principle of freedom of the press must be maintained and must receive full support from the church and its constituents, even when the cost is high.

● The electronic spectrum is a limited natural resource. The airwaves should be held in trust for the public by radio and television broadcasters and regulated in behalf of the public by government. While the broadcaster has great discretion for the program content this does not abridge the public's "right to know," to be fairly represented and to have access to the media.

● Public broadcasting as it continues to develop should be supported by both public and private sectors of the society to help further the diversity of programming and information sources.

● All persons of every nation should have equal access to channels of communication so they can participate fully in the life of the world. We encourage United Methodist members and agencies to participate in the study and continuing dialogue across national boundaries concerning the development of fair and just communication and information systems within nations and between nations.

● No medium can be truly neutral. Each brings its own values, limitations, criteria, authoritarian or democratic structures and selection processes with it.

● Appropriate agencies of The United Methodist Church should keep abreast of new communication technologies and structures, helping the church to stay informed so it may respond to developments which affect the human condition.

While we acknowledge the practicality of the necessity of media professionals to determine the societal and moral content of mass media, we must continue to oppose the practices of those persons and systems which use media for purposes of exploitation. Exploitation comes in many forms:

● Emphasizing violence.
● Showing pornography.
● Appealing to self-indulgence.
● Presenting consumerism as a way of life.
● Offering easy solutions to complex problems.
● Favoring the mass audience to the exclusion of individual and minority needs.

- Withholding significant information.
- Treating news as entertainment.
- Presenting events in isolation from the larger social context.
- Stereotyping characters in terms of sex roles, ethnic or racial background, occupation, age, religion and economic status.
- Failing to deal with significant political and social issues objectively and in depth.
- Exhibiting an overriding concern for maximizing profit.
- Discriminating in employment practices.
- Presenting misleading or dangerous product information or omitting essential information.
- Failing to educate adequately and inform the public about the nature and processes of these media themselves.

We call upon the mass media industries and their leaders to recognize their power and to use this power responsibly in enabling persons to achieve their fullest potential as members of the family of God. We urge Christians and church members involved in the media industries to utilize their faith in their decision-making and in their work place, to find others with moral and ethical commitment, and to discuss ways of enabling their industries to exercise their power for the good of humankind.

We urge the church to devise ways of responding to the mass media, including the following:

- Participating in research on the effects of media and information technologies.
- Developing criteria and resources by which church members can evaluate and interpret what is being communicated to them through the mass media.
- Recognizing that all information and entertainment programs can be used for learning, thereby making use of mass media programming in the church's ministry.
- Recognizing that communication professions offer opportunities for ministry and service.
- Working with the mass media at local and national levels, linking the life of the church with the life of the community.

● Participating in the development of the regulatory requirements of media.

We urge our churches to communicate, minister, and serve their communities through the public media. This will require them to:

● Discover the needs of persons in the community and determine how the church can minister to those needs through the media.

● Work with other churches in an ecumenical spirit of service and ministry.

● Commit time, budget, and talent to ministry through the media.

● Recognize the variety of purposes the church can fulfill in communicating through mass media, such as education, witness, evangelism, information, social service, and ministry.

● Be advocates for those shut out of the media; the poor, less powerful, and those on the margins of society.

In our own communication structures and processes within the church, we need to establish models of communication which are freeing, which respect the dignity of the recipient, and which are participating and non-manipulative. We need to democratize our own media to allow access and open dialogue. As a major institution within our society, we can demonstrate to other institutions the power of a connectional church which structures its communication patterns not by concentrating media power but by emphasizing the values of the gospel which recognize the sanctity of every individual.[13]

Church-School Curriculum
for Small Membership Churches

Be It Resolved that the General Boards of Discipleship and Publication, through the Curriculum Resources Commit-

[13] *See* Social Principles, V-A; "Free Flow of Information Among All Peoples of the Earth," 1984.

tee, develop church curriculum materials appropriate for churches which have only one children's, one youth, and one adult class, including clear instructions for use by teachers; and

Further Be It Resolved that such curriculum materials take into account the cultural/social life experiences of town and rural, urban, ethnic, and other such groupings of the United Methodist churches of small membership, including illustrations, photographs, and language that will reinforce learning experiences in these small membership churches; and

Further Be It Resolved that these materials be intentionally biblically centered, appeal to the pluralism of The United Methodist Church, and present in a clear and positive manner the role of small membership churches within the ministry and mission of The United Methodist Church; and

Finally Be It Resolved that the committee(s) responsible for preparation of curriculum materials consult with representatives from the town and country, urban, and ethnic networks.

Common Heritage

Common Heritage Concept

The common heritage is a pioneering concept in actual international cooperation and sharing of the benefits of the world's resources. This concept stems from the underlying premise that resources outside control of different nations should be under a just and equitable system of management. Several principles are a general guide to what a common heritage area may be. These include the need for full participation in decision-making for all nations; the use of the resource area only for peaceful purposes; no nation allowed an exclusive claim; the transfer of technology; and development of the resources for the benefit of all humanity while insuring future generations the use of the area and resources as well.

Past, Present, and Future Implementation

The international community has been developing the concept of common heritage through the United Nations Law of the Sea Treaty and the Agreement Governing the Activities of States on the Moon and Other Celestial Bodies. The system that has evolved in the Law of the Sea is one to which most countries have agreed, although no one nation has been totally satisfied. Nations are continuing in the process to complete the implementation of the concept through the ongoing Law of the Sea process. The concept of the common heritage is being expanded to include, but is not limited to, the air we breathe; water which sustains all life; the genetic variability of plants and animals upon which future agriculture and medicine may depend; Antarctica; the moon and other planets; and outer space.

Biblical and Theological Base

The common heritage concept has its roots for people of faith in the biblical understanding that all creation is under the authority of God and that all creation is interdependent. Our covenant with God requires us to be stewards, protectors, and defenders of all creation. The use of natural resources is a universal concern and responsibility of all as reflected in Psalm 24:1, "The earth is the Lord's and the fullness thereof."

The New Testament confronts us with the implication of the Old Testament understanding when it asks us how we use our resources in relation to our brothers and sisters. John the Baptist prepared us for Jesus' ministry by stating "Those who have two coats let them share with those who have none; and those who have food let them do likewise" (Luke 3:11). This philosophy was carried forth into the early church by incorporating the belief that the way in which one shares one's goods is a reflection of how one loves God. This is stated in I John 3:17; "But if anyone has the world's goods and sees his brother in need, yet closes his heart against him, how does God's love abide in him?"

311

Our Denominational Witness

The Social Principles of The United Methodist Church applies these basic biblical perceptions to how we use the resources of creation when it says: "We believe that Christian faith denies to any person or group of persons exclusive and arbitrary control of any other part of the created universe. Socially and culturally conditioned ownership of property is, therefore, to be considered a responsibility to God."

The Social Principles also reminds us that "upon the powerful rests responsibility to exercise their wealth and influence with restraint." Furthermore, the statement says that as United Methodists "we applaud international efforts to develop a more just international economic order, in which the limited resources of the earth will be used to the maximum benefit of all nations and peoples."

United Methodists have affirmed the common heritage since 1976 and have worked to see the common heritage become codified into international agreements for Law of the Sea, the moon, and Antarctica.

Statements of Understanding

In light of the uneven patterns of utilization of the world's resources and in light of our own understanding of the gospel and United Methodist tradition, we affirm these principles:

1. Specific natural resources belong to all humanity, and therefore must be developed and preserved for the benefit of all, not just for the few, both today and for generations to come.

2. All people have the right to enough of the resources of the universe to provide for their health and well-being.

3. God's creation is intended to be used for the good of all as a precious gift, not for warfare or economic oppression of others.

Recommended Actions

Therefore as United Methodists we are called to:

1. Work for and support the process of legal implemen-

tation of the common heritage concept as understood in the Law of the Sea Treaty and the Agreement Governing the Activities of States on the Moon and Other Celestial Bodies, as vehicles to address a more just and responsible use of God's creation.

2. Request that the appropriate general agencies of The United Methodist Church study and develop a broad biblical and theological understanding of the common heritage concept, which should include but not be limited to Antarctica, outer space, plant and animal genetics, air and water.

3. Request that the appropriate general agencies of The United Methodist Church develop and distribute resources for education about, and become advocates for, the common heritage concept.

4. Study these materials on the common heritage as individuals, local congregations, general program agencies, and other groups.[14]

Concern for Human Rights in Central America

All persons and groups are of equal worth in the sight of God. We, therefore, work toward societies in which each person's or group's worth is recognized, maintained, and strengthened. We deplore all political and economic ideologies that lead to repression or totalitarianism, that pit persons against each other, that deny hope, that seek to enhance privilege and power of the few at the expense of the well-being of the many. We condemn violations of human rights in all political and economic structures. The church, while proclaiming the gospel message of a God of love and justice, must be wary lest it compromise its own witness and unwittingly become an uncritical ally of repressive power and privilege in society around it. (Human Rights, *Book of Resolutions*.)

As members of the Body of Christ we affirm: ". . . that there may be no discord in the body, but that the members may have the same care for one another . . . if one member is honored, all rejoice together" (I Cor. 12:25-26).

[14] *See* Social Principles, I; "The Law of the Sea," 1980; "Environmental Stewardship," 1984.

313

In the last few years we have been pained by the suffering of our sisters and brothers in Central America. We have witnessed the unending persecutions, kidnappings, rapes, and assassinations of the people in most countries in Central America, while natural disasters, diseases, and grinding poverty continue to aggravate the sharp social stratification which divides their societies. We have witnessed the plight of Indian communities in Central America and in some instances genocidal practices against them. In addition, the countries and people of the region have been plagued with a history of relationships characterized by economic, political, military, and religious domination by Europe and the United States. We have been shocked by the testimonies coming from the people in each of the countries where human rights are grossly violated.

In Nicaragua, in 1983, the Evangelical Committee for Relief and Development (CEPAD) pleaded with Christians in the United States with the following statement:

As Christians, committed to justice and to love, we can no less than denounce before all of you and before the world, the atrocities committed by the counter-revolutionaries attacking our country, of which our brethren are victims.

These groups are clearly trained and financed by the government of the United States, which the press of the United States has on various occasions exposed, and as they invade our country they are planting death, panic, and desperation among our people.

In El Salvador, in 1983, Archbishop Rivera y Damas of San Salvador, noting that 30,000 Salvadoran non-combatants had been murdered in the past four years, declared:

Curiously, in the case of (the deaths of) North American citizens, elements belonging to the security forces have been detained, while in the case of thousands of assassinated Salvadorans, very rarely has justice been done. Where are the perpetrators of these crimes. . . ? Those murders continue, in many cases with victims pulled from their houses in the middle of the night.

314

Archbishop Rivera y Damas also framed an eloquent Christian response to the violence in Central America in his November 13, 1983 homily. He said the violence against clerics in Guatemala, El Salvador, and Nicaragua "makes us understand that the Church is and will continue to be a hindrance and an object of persecution when it does not accommodate the whims of a totalitarian system of government, be it of the right or of the left."

In the case of Guatemala, the Inter-Church Committee on Human Rights in Latin America (ICCHRLA) reported, in the latter part of 1982: "that human rights violations including torture, disappearances, assassinations and massacres have not only continued but, in many areas, have increased since the March 1982 coup which brought General Jose Efrain Rios Montt to power."

In the wake of the coup in the summer of 1983 any hope for peace with justice dimmed since the new leader (Chief of Staff) General Oscar Umberto Mejia Victores, was the Minister of Defense under General Montt.

In Honduras, in 1983, Honduran Christians voiced their apprehensions to United Methodists from the United States. Dissent is repressed. Violence in the countryside is on the increase. Refugees from Nicaragua, El Salvador, and Guatemala pose enormous burdens on the people of Honduras. And, Hondurans are confused by a US policy, which, while claiming support of the civilian government, has greatly reinforced the power of the military through its increased aid in arms and training. A strengthened military is seen by some as a threat to civilian leadership.

In the last three years Christian Councils in Latin America have appealed to Christans in the United States. Representatives from the Council of Evangelical Methodist Churches in Latin America came to the United States in 1982 and were itinerated throughout The United Methodist Church. They urged their brothers and sisters in that country to pressure the United States government to change its policies toward the countries of Central America. And in 1983, the Executive Committee of Latin America Council of Churches voiced the same concern:

In the name of millions of indigenous farmers of Central America who have been thrown off their lands, whose right to life and personal safety has been taken away; in the name of the malnourished and sick children who die each day with no hope in their countries; in the name of political, student, union, and religious leaders who have been killed, or disappeared, or put in jail in this prolonged and growing struggle which seems to have no end; in the name of the innumerable refugees going through a dark night of exile and desolation; in the name of thousands of Christian martyrs (among them several Protestant ministers) who, especially in the life offering of Monsignor Romero, plead to heaven and earth for justice and for full and genuine liberation, and peace for our nations; but, above all, in the name of Jesus Christ, "the faithful witness, the first-born of the dead" (Rev. 1:5) and He who is present in the lives and sufferings of those our lesser brethren (Matthew 25:31-46) we beg you to take our plea upon your hearts and consciences, and to act now, before it is too late.

And most recently, following the announcement of elections by the Nicaraguan government, and the increasing aggression, overt and covert, by the government of the United States through the Central Intelligence Agency, the same council authorities sent in April, 1984, the following cable to the churches in the United States:

The mining of Nicaraguan ports and the constant aggression aimed against that nation by the United States government, is a cynical violation of the human rights of the Nicaraguan people and a threat to the future of Latin America.

In the name of the God of Truth and of History, in the name of the more than one hundred Churches of the Latin American Council, we condemn these colonialist actions, and call for firm reaction from and the solidarity of all genuine Christian and democratic forces of the North American people and of the entire world.

I

Because of the cries for justice and liberation of our brothers and sisters in Central America;

—because of our conviction that injustice and war do not lead to peace;

—and because of the participation of the government of the United States in this suffering;

316

We call upon the government of the United States to:

1. Recognize the conflicts in Central America as struggles for human rights and self-determination rather than confrontations between the superpowers of East and West.

2. Actively support the Contadora group (Venezuela, Mexico, Colombia, and Panama) in efforts to find a peaceful, non-military solution to conflict in the region and become a willing participant in the peace negotiation process being conducted by the Contadora group.

3. Refrain from any activity, military, economic, or of any other nature, covert or overt, directed against any sovereign state in Central America designed to destabilize existing governments.

4. Refrain from granting external economic aid without the credible means of ensuring its equitable distribution.

5. Apply human rights certification based upon data from Amnesty International and the United Nations Human Rights Commission as a criterion for military and economic assistance to governments in the region.

6. Respect and recognize each nation's sovereignty and rights to self-determination and cease imposing its own political and economic system on the countries of Central America.

7. Grant "extended voluntary departure status" for persons fleeing repression and war in Central America.

II

Because we believe that a political solution must be found on an international level, we call upon the United Nations to press for an end to all military intervention, overt and covert, in all of the countries of Central America.

III

Because of our commitment as United Methodist Christians to peace, justice and liberty we will begin a massive effort in education, mission and witness concerning

317

the plight of Central America. To carry out this endeavor we will:

1. Strengthen our ties of solidarity with the people of Central America by deepening our understanding of the history and cultures of the region.

2. Provide, through the general boards and agencies, curriculum materials, study guides and other resources prepared in consultation with Latin American Christians for local church usage.

3. Encourage Annual Conferences and Central American churches to take advantage of opportunities for mutual travel and dialogue.

4. Provide that exchanges of curriculum material and, whenever possible, exchanges of visitors between United States and Central American churches should be inclusive of various theological and political philosophies so that our peoples may better understand the diversity of the viewpoints that exist within our communions.

5. Continue to be supportive of Christians (Roman Catholic, Orthodox, and Protestant) who are participating in the struggle for liberation and self-determination including: freedom of association; freedom of expression; freedom of religion; open and competitive elections free from outside interference by any nation, institutions or corporations; and against dictatorships of the right and left.

6. Encourage and enable The United Methodist Church to increase its efforts to assist Central American victims and refugees.

7. Advocate and support policies and programs by The United Methodist Church directed to the protection, defense and promotion of the indigenous (Indian) communities in Central America.

8. While realizing the legal implications, be supportive of and encourage churches in the United States that provide sanctuary.

9. Pray that justice and peace prevail in Central America.[15]

[15] *See* Social Principles, V-A; "Assistance and Sanctuary for Central American Refugees," 1984.

Continuing Membership In the National Council of the Churches of Christ in the U.S.A.

WHEREAS, The United Methodist Church is a member, its predecessor Methodist and Evangelical United Brethren churches having been charter members of the National Council of the Churches of Christ in the U.S.A., and

WHEREAS, the National Council of the Churches of Christ in the U.S.A. provides a forum for the Christians of its members churches to offer mutual nurture and to join in Christian action on behalf of unity, mission and service, and

WHEREAS, the Council provides a unique opportunity for denominational representatives to share divergent traditions in matters of faith and practice, and

WHEREAS, the Council provides a channel for cooperation in Christian education, church and society issues, broadcasting television and film development, regional and local ecumenism, faith and order issues, production of Christian literature, stewardship and overseas ministries, and

WHEREAS, the Council provides leadership in Christian-Jewish and Christian-Muslim relationships and in dealing with justice, liberation and human fulfillment, and

WHEREAS, through the Council, member churches share their faith, life, ministry and mission together, and

WHEREAS, The United Methodist delegates who come from each of the jurisdictions provide distinguished leadership to the Council and consistently have expressed the concern for Christian unity that has been a mark of The United Methodist Church:

Be It Resolved, that the 1984 General Conference of The United Methodist Church reaffirms our membership in and support for the National Council of the Churches of Christ in the U.S.A., in accordance with ¶ 2402 of the 1980 Book of Discipline.

Criminal Justice

Justice is the basic principle upon which God's creation

319

has been established. It is the necessary ingredient required for the achievement of humanity's ultimate purpose.

Justice is an integral and uncompromising part in God's redemptive process which assures wholeness. It is a quality relationship based on God's love and the human response motivated by love.

Justice is the theme which permeates the history of God's people as participants in the ongoing human drama of their daily existence.

The gospel, through the example of Jesus Christ, conveys the message for Christians to be healers, peacemakers, and reconcilers when faced with brokenness, violence, and vengeance. Through love, caring, and forgiveness, Jesus Christ was able to transform lives and restore the dignity and purpose in those who were willing to abide by his principles.

Jesus Christ was opposed to vengeance as the way to administer justice (Matt. 5:38-44).

As Christians we recognize that each person is unique and has great value before God. Human worth does not diminish when a person violates laws made by human beings, for human worth has been guaranteed even when God's law has been violated.

The Christian Church as an institution is charged with the responsibility to ensure that a system of justice safeguards the inherent right that human beings possess as God's creatures and objects of the love and care which derive from that relationship.

The primary purpose of the criminal justice system and its administration is to protect individuals and society from any violation of their legal and constitutional rights.

The criminal justice system in this country has been adversely affected by economic and social conditions which have resulted in discrimination against the poor, minorities, and women.

Too often prisons are places where dehumanizing conditions reinforce negative social behavior. This contributes to the high incidence of recidivism and perpetuates the cycle of violence, crime, and incarceration.

The administration of the criminal justice system has reached a level of saturation which leads to expediency rather than the even-handed application of justice and punishment.

As United Methodist Christians we are called to sensitize those institutions which operate within the criminal justice system to be responsible, more humane and just, to ensure the full participation in society by those who have deviated from laws established as normative guidelines for behavior. Therefore, we will:

1. Minister to prisoners, offenders, exoffenders, victims, and to the families involved. (This includes working toward the goal of restoration and reconciliation of victims and offenders.)

2. Develop and offer competent ministries of mediation and conflict resolution, within the criminal justice system.

3. Nurture members of The United Methodist Church and the general public in the insights of the faith as they provide guidance in expressing redemption and reconciliation for those persons embroiled in the criminal justice system.

4. Develop attitudes of acceptance in the community and opportunities for employment for those persons who are released from imprisonment or who are participating in programs that assist them to re-enter community life.

5. Monitor governmental policies and programs in the field of criminal justice and respond to them from our faith perspective.

Law Enforcement and Courts

Because we believe in reconciliation and redemption, we will work for a criminal justice system that is just and humane and has as its goals restoration rather than vengeance. Toward this end we will support the following:

1. Provision of safeguards to ensure that the poor, minorities, and the inexperienced have available the legal assistance and other advantages available to the rich, powerful, and the experienced.

321

2. Elimination of influences and practices of discrimination based on race, ethnic, or cultural background, political identification, age, class, or sex.

3. Staffing of the criminal justice system at every level by persons who represent a diversity of backgrounds in our society and who meet high standards of training and experience, including cultural understanding and care about the persons who come under their jurisdiction.

4. Separation of juvenile offenders from adult offenders with correction given to them outside the traditional courts and correctional system.

With specific regard to law enforcement officials and the courts, we as United Methodists:

1. Support efforts to develop alternative methods to the use of deadly force by law enforcement officials.

2. Insist that accused persons should have competent legal assistance and be ensured a speedy trial.

3. Recognize that organized crime has corrupting power over the racial, political, and economic life of our nations and support efforts to oppose it through effective legislation, strong law enforcement, and the development of public awareness.

Sentences

The primary purpose of a sentence for a crime is to protect society from future crimes by the offender, the deterrence of offenders from committing a crime, restitution of the victim, and assistance to the offender to become a law-abiding citizen.

Believing in the love of Christ who came to save those who are lost and vulnerable, we urge the creation of a genuinely new system and programs for rehabilitation that will restore, preserve, and nurture the total humanity of the imprisoned. We believe that sentences should hold within them the possibilities of reconciliation and restoration. Therefore we assert that:

1. In the sentencing by the courts and in the implementation of the sentences, the criminal justice system should use all resources and knowledge available to ensure that

sentencing embodies the possibility of rehabilitation and reconciliation.

2. Imprisonment should be imposed only when the continued freedom of the offender poses a direct threat to society and when no acceptable alternative exists.

3. Capital punishment should be eliminated since it violates the concept of sacredness of human life and is contrary to our belief that sentences should hold within them the possibilities of reconciliation and restoration.

4. Sentences to restitution, community service, and other non-imprisonment alternatives provide economical, rational and humane systems of justice for non-dangerous offenders and provide justice for the victim.

5. Community involvement and concern is needed to monitor the policies and practices of the criminal justice system.

6. The criminal justice system must be accessible to all persons.

7. Accused persons must not be prejudged for detention before trial on the basis of their character, race, culture, gender, or class.

8. Percentage-of-sentence limitations on "good behavior" paroles violate the Christian mandates for redemption and reconciliation.[16]

Declaration from the Second
International Christian Youth Conference

Be It Resolved, that The United Methodist Church endorses the statement of The Second International Christian Youth Conference as adopted by its 1,200 delegates from 44 countries at its meeting August 8-15, 1983, which reads as follows:

[16] *See* Social Principles, V-E, F; "Local Church and Local Jail," 1980; "Equal Justice," 1980; "Grand Jury Abuse," 1980; "Juvenile Justice," 1980; "Captial Punishment," 1980; "Penal Reform," 1980; "Gun Control," 1976; "Police Firearms Policies," 1976; "Ministries in Social Conflict," 1976.

The Second International Christian Youth Conference meeting in the Bahamas declares:

That God created and sustains the world in love.
That Jesus Christ is Lord of the World and the Church.
That God continues to call the Church to its task of liberation and reconciliation as the expression of love for our world.
That we who are part of the Church are determined to discover the role that God has for us within the life of the Church and its ministry in the world.

The following issues (not prioritized) emerged from the conference as the most pressing human rights problems to which all of humanity must respond.

Disarmament, peace, and justice are some of the most urgent and pressing problems in the world today. Humankind must unite to prevent world destruction.

Unemployment, particularly youth unemployment, which erodes human dignity and worth, demands the attention and action of the church and society.

Hunger and poverty are life and death realities that cannot and must not be ignored by the church.

Moral crisis. The world faces a moral crisis as people struggle to cope with the ethics of sexuality, drugs, alcohol, and the value of human life.

Racism/discrimination eliminate human rights and dignity causing oppression that must be countered by the Gospel of the Kingdom which breaks down the dividing walls of race, class, sex, ethnicity, and abilities.

Social pressures brought by media, adults, and peers make it difficult to maintain a Christian lifestyle.

We accept that each of these problems touch the lives of people at every level.

Therefore, as young Christians convinced of the power of God which overcomes all evil, sin, and death, through the Holy Spirit at work in this, God's world, and recognizing the responsibility that each of us must carry to be faithful in both action and word, we commit ourselves:

1. To the Lordship of Jesus Christ over all the world.
2. To the church as God's servant family committed to

reconciling people to God, people with people, and people with their whole ecological environment.

3. To join with the church in the task of evangelism—claiming all people for Christ and enabling them to grow in faith and discipleship.

4. To demand and to work toward all forms of disarmament, peace, and justice as God's will for our world despite the conflicts and mistrust that exists.

5. To work with social and political systems to bring about policies which will provide opportunities for all people to have productive employment.

6. To work for the elimination of poverty and hunger by insisting on a more equitable economic order which allows for a just distribution of the earth's resources. We call upon governments to eliminate economic inequities and to reconsider the stewardship of our world's resources. We will live more simply so that others may simply live.

7. To act as agents of change in a world in which sexual permissiveness, drug abuse, and alcoholism are norms, and which by their degrading nature, stifle the wholesome development of the human life.

8. To a lifestyle which becomes the Gospel of the Kingdom where moral values are rooted not only in what is pleasing to self, helpful for others, but most importantly acceptable to God.

Dependent Care

The Problem

Almost all families at one time or another need assistance from persons outside the immediate family structure. Increasing numbers of families require some degree of help in the day-to-day care of family members who, because of age or disability, need constant supervision. With a growing number of women entering the paid labor force and with the increased mobility of families away from communities where elderly parents and relatives reside, more and more families need some kind of supportive care.

1. Need for a Safe Environment for Children. Children are often victims at an age when they should be developing trust and confidence in persons and in life itself. Children determine neither what food they will eat nor who will care for them in the absence of parents. Adults make these and other life-affecting decisions for them.

The church has a special responsibility to children and their families to demonstrate concern for and responsiveness to human need. The Christian faith proclaims that children are to be valued not as potential adults but as persons in their own right—persons deserving of dignity, joy, and a protected environment. Because of their vulnerability, children need defenders and guardians, both within the family circle and in the larger extended family of the community. They must be protected from prejudices that may victimize them because of their racial, ethnic, and socio-economic backgrounds.

In many communities are large numbers of latchkey children—children who are unsupervised during parts of the day or night because their parents are at work and no one is available to care for them. Unfortunately these children are often victimized by persons who prey on the unprotected. To avert potential problems, the U.S. Department of Agriculture and the 4-H community clubs have initiated a nationwide program to teach latchkey children various techniques for survival and self-protection. But these children also need to have someone reach out to them, sharing love, care, and security.

2. Need for Long-term Dependent Care. The ability of families to remain intact is severely strained when a child, a spouse, or an older relative is disabled and needs constant health-monitoring or supervised care. Families often need help with these situations in the form of in-home health care or custodial care. In many cases, a small amount of assistance could enable these families to function well and maintain healthy relationships with minimal stress. But without aid, stress related to these circumstances can result in divorce, separation, or institutionalization of loved ones—eventualities neither wanted nor necessary.

The need for long-term dependent care frequently arises from several trends in modern society. Among them, the increased mobility of persons worldwide and the movement from rural to urban areas often result in the isolation of family units from their network of relatives. Older relatives then find themselves separated by long distances from other family members.

Too, the need of many families to rely on the cash economy has moved more women—traditionally the care-givers for family members with long-term needs—into the paid work force, rendering them no longer available to provide free care. Recent statistics show that in the United States:

- Eighty percent of home health care is provided by female relatives whose average age is 55. Forty-four percent of these care-givers are also in the paid work force.
- Two-thirds of the women in the paid work force are either sole providers or have husbands who earn less than $15,000.
- Forty-six percent of all preschool children and 46 percent of all school-age children have mothers in the paid workforce.

A myriad of problems—ranging from inadequate facilities to the high cost of securing persons who can provide care—is placing an unnecessary strain on many modern families who have limited resources and nowhere to turn for help.

The Call. The Christian faith mandates us to recognize and respond to the value of each human person. Our task as the church is to minister to the needs of all persons and to insure for them a caring community where all may be nurtured in a dignified and loving manner. This mandate is to be seen not as a burden, but rather as an opportunity. We are called to participate in the creative, redemptive work of God. Jesus, who provides our example, said: "The Spirit of the Lord is upon me, because he has anointed me to preach the good news to the poor. He has sent me to proclaim release to the captives and recovering of sight to the blind, to set at liberty those who are oppressed, to proclaim the acceptable year of the Lord" (Luke 4:18-19).

Christians who take their commission seriously will accept the challenge to become responsive to the needs of families for external support systems. God has given each person an element of sacredness by the very nature of having been born into the world. This blessing carries the need for a commitment by families, church, and community to help enable persons to live life in the fullness that Jesus proclaimed.

We have answered the call in the past by building hospitals, homes for the elderly, and institutional settings for children who need them. This has been done on a worldwide basis. Now we must take seriously the opportunity to create and support responsive systems of child care and long-term care for those persons who are elderly or who have handicapping conditions (in independent living situations or within family settings).

The Task. In matters of public concern, the church has a responsibility to make its voice heard. Since dependent care (such as child day care, senior day care, home health handicaps) is important to the present and future well-being of various segments of our society, the church's position on the system of dependent care delivery constitutes an appropriate public policy concern. The role of dependent care in its various forms should be seen as a support system for families. Such services enable rather than usurp the traditional role of families.

A national survey of church-based child care discovered that in the United States, churches are the major providers of out-of-home child care. These child care workers listed as a priority task the provision of care that benefits the emotional, social, and learning needs of children. Within this context, persons sponsoring or overseeing church-based programs and churches with special ministries to families have a responsibility to be involved in policy discussions on the form and function of dependent care.

It becomes the obligation of churches to urge and promote coherent, inclusive, and equitable policies that affect families. There is a temptation to separate dependent care from the various programs designed to support and aid families in their life in the church and community, but it must be recognized that most families, at some time or another, rely on formal or informal support systems relative to the care of children, the elderly, or persons with handicapping conditions.

As it approaches public advocacy for dependent care, the church must be guided by the variety of forms of its ministry. The church must acknowledge the importance and implement the provision of affordable and high-quality family support systems that are equitably distributed to those who need them.

Toward this end, the church on all levels is called to advocate the following policies:

1. Public policies that enhance the availability of dependent care in its varied forms to meet the needs of families by providing:

a. Adequate financial aid (such as private foundation grants, tax credits, tax reimbursement, sliding fees) to allow families to care for loved ones at home rather than having these persons institutionalized when that option is not desired, needed, or economically possible.

b. Sufficient information on the availability of dependent care services as well as on methods of evaluating the care provided.

2. Church policies and ministries that enhance the spiritual and psychological needs of families who care for dependent members.

3. Community services that help families/individuals who are under psychological and psycho-social pressures resulting from the responsibilities of caring for dependent family members.[17]

[17] *See* Social Principles, III-C, E; "The Christian Family," 1984.

Domestic Surveillance

Openness is a redemptive gift of God, calling for trust and honesty between various segments of the community. Justice is the cornerstone of that trust we have come to expect in our elective and appointive representatives of the community. Communal wholeness is attained through the concerted use of these elements.

Domestic surveillance is an issue which, without adequate safeguards of civil rights, threatens the moral and legal fiber of our society.

Domestic surveillance is the gathering of information pertaining to the intent, capabilities, and activities of individuals and/or groups involved in criminal activities for a foreign agent or power. The intent is to root out elements that threaten or harm the national security of a country. Yet, congressional hearings, over time, have revealed that intelligence agencies often misuse and abuse surveillance activities: "Domestic intelligence has threatened and undermined the constitutional rights of Americans to free speech, associations, and privacy. It has done so primarily because the constitutional system for checking abuse of power has not been applied" (1976, Senator Church's Committee Report on Intelligence).

Examples of abuse include:

1. The use of grand jury investigations to harrass American citizens and groups exercising their freedom of speech under the First Amendment. Those under subpoena to grand juries have been incarcerated after exercising their rights under the Fifth Amendment.

2. The surveillance, disruption, infiltration and harassment of, and thefts from peace groups during the Vietnam era, and later, anti-nuclear, anti-war groups.

3. The active surveillance and infiltration of church and missional programs, environmental groups, civil and constitutional rights groups, etc.

Governmental directives and policies have been formulated that provide the intelligence agencies with a wider latitude in initiating domestic investigations. Recent directives expand the role these agencies play in conducting surveillance, and use techniques that heretofore had been considered violent and extreme. These directives legitimize abuses by giving the intelligence agencies the power to:

1. Conduct warrantless searches and seizures, in direct violation of the Fourth Amendment of the Bill of Rights, including electronic surveillance, unconsented physical surveillance, and mail surveillance.

2. Direct intelligence techniques toward anyone who comes in contact with a foreign person or organization, i.e., "foreign" friends, members of the United Nations, church and related support agencies.

3. Infiltrate and influence the activities of law-abiding organizations in the United States, without valid reason to suspect or allege illegal activities.

4. Use journalists, missionaries, students, business-persons, and teachers as undercover agents, oftentimes without their expressed knowledge.

5. Conduct secret campus research, if authorized by undefined "appropriate officials."

As United Methodists, the issue of domestice surveillance and its misuse and abuse deserves a renewed focus. As stated in the Social Principles:

> We also strongly reject domestic surveillance and intimidation of political opponents by governments in power, and all other misuse of elective and appointive offices. Citizens of all countries should have access to all essential information regarding their government and its policies. Illegal and unconscionable activities directed against persons or groups by their government or governments must not be justified or kept secret even under the guise of national security.

We therefore call upon The United Methodist Church at all levels to:

1. Affirm the rights of individuals and groups to address governmental policies that reject the freedom to associate and the freedom of speech, especially to the beliefs that enhance the political, social, economic, and spiritual quality of life.

2. Recommend revocation of directives and policies that reduce public review of executive, judicial, and legislative procedures.

3. Support the continuing need for the present Freedom of Information Act. Actions to weaken FOIA and to restrict public access to local, state, and federal documents violates the principles of trust and openness, elements that enhance human development.

4. Affirm the responsibility of governments to ensure the national security of its people. We reject the use of "national security" as a guise for illegal and unconstitutional actions of governments. Invocation of the term "national security" for unjust reasons undermines the credibility of governments and threatens the safety of its citizenry at home and abroad.

5. Support local, state, and federal actions and policies that respond adequately to the needs of the citizenry and ensure their fundamental moral and legal rights. Local, state and federal agencies should work together with community representatives in formulating policies that account for these needs.[18]

Environmental Stewardship

I. *A Theology of Stewardship and the Environment*

Many of today's "environmental problems" have their roots in humanity's short-sighted use of God's creation. While focusing on the stewardship of monetary resources, we forget that the source of all wealth is God's gracious creation.

In the Bible, a steward is one given responsibility for what belongs to another. The Greek word we translate as steward is *oikonomos*, one who cares for the household or acts as its trustee. The world *oikos*, meaning household, is used to describe the world as God's household. Christians, then, are

[18] *See* Social Principles, V-C; "Repression and the Right to Privacy," 1980.

to be stewards of the whole household (creation) of God. *Oikonomia,* "stewardship," is also the root of our word "economics." *Oikos,* moreover, is the root of our modern word, "ecology." Thus in a broad sense, stewardship, economics, and ecology are, and should be, related. Indeed, a "faithful and wise steward" (Luke 12:42) must relate them.

The Old Testament relates these concepts in the vision of *shalom.* Often translated "peace," the broader meaning of *shalom* is wholeness. In the Old Testament, *shalom* is used to characterize the wholeness of a faithful life lived in relationship to God. *Shalom* is best understood when we experience wholeness and harmony as human beings with God, with others, and with creation itself. The task of the steward is to seek *shalom.*

Stewards of God's Creation. The concept of stewardship is first introduced in the creation story. In Genesis 1:26, the Bible affirms that every person is created in God's image. But this gift brings with it a unique responsibility. Being created in God's image brings with it the responsibility to care for God's creation. God chose to give human beings a divine image not so we would exploit creation to our own ends, but so we would be recognized as stewards of God. To have dominion over the earth is a trusteeship, a sign that God cares for creation and has entrusted it to our stewardship. Our stewardship of all the world's resources is always accountable to God who loves the whole of creation and who desires that it exist in *shalom.* The intention of creation was that all should experience *shalom,* to know the goodness of creation. In the Old Testament, "fullness of life" means having enough, sufficient, to experience the goodness of creation. By contrast, our age has come to define "fullness of life" as more than enough. The desire of many for excess begins to deny enough for others, and *shalom* is broken. That all should participate in creation's goodness is a fundamental of stewardship.

Another theme of *shalom* is that in creation we are all related. Humans are not self-sufficient. We need God, others, nature. The story of the garden (Genesis 2) attempts to picture the complete and harmonious interrelatedness of all creation. There is *shalom* only when we recognize that interrelatedness and care for the whole. When we violate the rules of the garden, we are dismissed. In ecological terms, when we violate the principles of ecology, we suffer environmental damage.

As the story of the garden shows, God's intention of *shalom* was not carried out. Sin intervened, and the *shalom* was broken. But God offered a way to restore *shalom*—redemption. And as God's stewards we have a role in that redemption. Stewardship, then, is to become involved wherever wholeness is lacking and to work in harmony with God's saving activity to reconcile, to reunite, to heal, to make whole. Stewardship has to do with how we bring all of the resources at our disposal into efficient use in our participation in the saving activity of God. Environmental stewardship is one part of our work as God's stewards. As stewards of the natural environment we are called to preserve and restore the very air, water, and land on which life depends. Moreover, we are called to see that all persons have a sufficient share of the resources of nature. The environmental crises that face us need not exist. With new hope rooted in Christ and with more obedient living as stewards of the earth, the creation can be healed.

II. *United Methodist Historical Concerns*

Since the beginnings of the Methodist movement, there has been a concern with what we today call "environmental concerns." Wesley's emphasis on "cleanliness" came as he observed a land of open sewers, impure water, unplanned cities, and smoke-filled air. In the mines and mills, squalor and filth were everywhere, as was disease. The substantial decline in the death rate in England from 1700 to 1801 can be traced to improvements in environment, sanitation, and a wider knowledge of concepts of basic health such as those advocated by Wesley.

The first Social Creed, adopted by the 1908 General Conference of The Methodist Episcopal Church (North) focused on the environmental and health hazards facing workers.

As the problems of soil erosion and dwindling reserves of natural resources became more obvious, General Conferences in the 40s, 50s, and 60s called for the development of programs stressing careful stewardship of the soil and conservation of natural resources. In 1968, a United Methodist Church concerned with continuing pollution of the environment insisted that community rights take precedence over property rights and that "no individual should be permitted to degrade the environment . . . for the sake . . .of profit."

In the mid-1980s, the environmental problems of the world are no less acute than they were in the 1960s and 1970s. While some parts of the industrialized world have less pollution of some sorts, polluting factories have been relocated to the industrializing nations. Hazardous chemicals have been banned in one nation, while their use increases in another. In the United States, children have been poisoned by toxic wastes under their schools; in Central America children have been poisoned when the fields they have worked in have been sprayed with pesticides banned in other countries.

Sometimes our solutions create new problems. Some thought higher smokestacks would help disperse air pollutants; instead we have more acid rain. Herbicides, used in "no till" agriculture, while helping to control soil erosion, have begun to pollute aquifers. The environmental problems of the next few decades will require more effort and more initiative to solve than the problems of the past.

The Christian church should actively support programs to implement principles which will safeguard the environment. Some of the areas we now recognize as key are: responsible use of resources, toxic and hazardous substances, air quality, pesticide use, use of wild and agricultural lands, water quality, the military and the environment, and the impact of new technologies on the environment.

III. *Principles for Christian Stewardship of the Environment*

A. *Responsible Use of Natural Resources.* We support measures which will lead to a more careful and efficient use of the resources of the natural world. We encourage programs which will recycle solid materials of all sorts—paper, glass, metals, plastics, etc. We urge United Methodists to participate actively in community recycling programs and urge the establishment of such programs in communities without these programs.

B. *Toxic and Hazardous Substances.* We advocate that governments devote sufficient monetary and human resources to assessing the extent of possible toxic and hazardous waste disposal problems within their jurisdictions. We believe that the entity or entities responsible for the problem should pay the costs related to the site's cleanup and for any health damages caused by the improper or inadequate disposal of such substances. We call upon those agencies responsible for enforcing existing laws to adopt a more aggressive strategy in responding to violators. We support strong penalities for those convicted of illegal disposal of hazardous and toxic materials. We oppose the practice of exporting materials banned in one nation for use in another nation. We advocate that all parties with information on the health effects of a potentially toxic or hazardous substance make these data available to users of the substance. We support the right of those groups that would be affected by a nuclear, toxic, or hazardous material waste repository to be involved actively in all decisions to locate such repositories in their neighborhoods or jurisdictions.

Finally, in order to preclude serious environmental threats to the world population, we urge a discontinuation of the dumping of nuclear waste at sea and support the monitoring of waste disposal of a toxic nature in the soil.

C. *Clean Air.* We believe all persons have the right to breathe clean air. Where the air quality is now poor, steps should be taken to improve its quality including the elimination of toxic pollutants, the limiting of pollutants from cars, trucks and buses, the clean-up of smokestack emissions. Where the air is now good, every effort should be made to maintain such good air quality. We advocate the adoption and strict enforcement of adequate standards to control indoor air pollutants, including toxic substances and tobacco smoke. Special attention should be given to such long-range air quality problems as the depletion of the ozone layer, the heating of the atmosphere, and acid rain. We support international and bilateral efforts to eliminate the cause of such long-term problems.

D. *Chemical Use.* Many chemicals are used for agricultural purposes. These include pesticides, herbicides, and fertilizers. These are required to maximize yields in feeding a hungry world, but their use may be detrimental to the crops or to the environment if improperly selected and/or applied.

We recommend the concept of integrated pest management (IPM), natural control systems, and crop rotation. We urge that greater restrictions be placed on the export of restricted agricultural chemicals from the United States and that the U.S. development agencies encourage the use of agricultural techniques which rely less heavily on agricultural chemical use.

A wide variety of chemicals is used for the processing and preservation of food products. There is growing suspicion, and some scientifically confirmed knowledge, that some of these chemicals are harmful to animals and humans. We recommend that continual aggressive investigation and study be made on the long-range effect of these chemicals by industry, consumer groups, and governmental agencies. We urge policies that retard the indiscriminate use of chemicals, including those used for growing, processing, and preserving food.

E. *Land Use.* All agricultural productivity relies on our careful stewardship of a few inches of topsoil. We encourage economic and farming practices which conserve and promote the improvement of topsoil. We urge that governments provide farmers with incentives for more careful management of this precious resource.

Just as the best farm land is lost through erosion, so too is it lost when it is used for purposes other than farming (e.g., highways, reservoirs, housing, industrial uses and surface mining). Likewise, land that has become poisoned with salt through poor irrigation practices or with pesticides may become less productive as an agricultural resource. We urge that the careful maintenance of the productivity of the land be the central goal of all management of agricultural lands. We urge governments to preserve the most productive soils for agricultural purposes. Careful management of agricultural lands can help discourage the so-called "reclamation" of forests, wetlands, and wild areas. These areas are valuable in their own right and should be preserved for the contribution they make to ecological balance, wildlife production, water, and air quality, and the human spirit.

F. *The Diversity of Life.* We believe that the wondrous diversity of nature is a key part of God's plan for creation. Therefore, we oppose measures which would eliminate diversity in plant and animal varieties, eliminate species, or destroy habitats critical to the survival of endangered species or varieties.

G. *Water.* We live on what has aptly been called the "Water Planet." More than 70 percent of the surface of the earth is covered with water; yet only a small part of that water can be used for drinking, industrial, and agricultural purposes. Our careless use of water in the past means that it will cost more in the future. Decisions over how to allocate increasingly costly supplies of pure water for drinking, industry and agriculture will be among the most contentious resource policy questions of the next decades. We urge that steps be taken by all concerned parties to ensure more careful management and preservation of existing ground-water sources. We support the right of native peoples to the first use of waters on their lands. We urge that industrial, municipal, agricultural and individual consumers of water find ways to use more efficiently the water we now have. We believe that conservation of an area's existing water supplies, not costly transfers of water from basin to basin, or other large-scale projects, usually offers the most efficient and environmentally sound source of new water. Finally, we believe that all persons have a right to a sufficient supply of high quality water free from toxic chemical or pathogenic impurities.

H. *Impact of Technology.* We urge that the ethical and environmental effects of new technologies be fully examined before these technologies are used on a widespread basis. We acknowledge the constantly imperfect state of our knowledge of the effects of our creations and urge the development of those technologies most in accord with God's plan of wholeness for all creation.

I. *The Military and the Environment.* We oppose the military's imperious claim to our planet's resources and its willingness to risk massive environmental contamination through accidental or intentional release of nerve gas, preparation for biological warfare, or continued testing and possible use of nuclear weapons for the sake of claimed offensive and defensive needs.

We also oppose the production of nuclear weapons and the resultant production of tremendous amounts of nuclear waste that endangers the environment.

IV. *Involvement*

We urge all United Methodists to examine their roles as stewards of God's earth and to study, discuss and work to implement this resolution.[19]

Equal Rights of Women

The gospel makes it clear that Jesus regarded women and men as being of equal worth. Nowhere is it recorded that Jesus treated women in a different manner than he did men. Although the gospel writers recorded little in the way of verbal statements of Jesus *about women,* they have preserved for us many incidents in the life of Jesus which

[19] *See* Social Principles, I.

indicated that he understood the equality of all people, male and female alike, to be a significant element of his message.

While Jesus called only males to be part of the 12, biblical evidence indicates that others, including women, were considered disciples or followers of Jesus. In open defiance of the customs of his society, Jesus taught women, spoke to them in public, and refused to confine women to the traditionally accepted roles. Moreover, women were the first witnesses to the resurrection and were directed to go and tell their brothers.

While both the Old and New Testaments came out of male-centered cultures and necessarily reflect that culture, interpretations of the Scriptures by the church have unduly emphasized male "superiority." For example, popular interpretations of the two creation stories often assume the women as "help mate" or "helper," which implies female inferiority or subordination. In the original Hebrew, however, the word translated "helper" described a person of at least equal status to the one helped. Indeed, the majority of times this word appears in the Old Testament it is speaking of God as "helper." Rather than defining women as secondary to man, each creation story points to the equality of the male and female, both of whom are made "in the image of God."

A number of statements attributed to Paul have frequently been cited to support the idea of feminine subordination and submission. However, when these statements are taken in context and balanced against the rest of the New Testament, especially against the message of Jesus, there can be no doubt that women are of equal value with men and should enjoy the same rights, privileges, and obligations as men.

The support of The United Methodist Church for equal rights of women derives from our traditional concern for justice, human dignity, and equality of all persons.

Examples of courageous action throughout our history inspire us as we move into our third century. Grounded in our biblical understanding, experience, and tradition, equal rights for women in church life, public institutions, and personal relationships have been, and will continue to be, fundamental in our call to be faithful as United Methodists.

Since 1972 this commitment was focused through our denomination's effort to support ratification of the Equal Rights Amendment to the United States Constitution. Three successive General Conferences, with practically unanimous votes, supported involvement in the ratification effort for the proposed 26th amendment which would have guaranteed equity in the formation and implementation of the legal statutes in the United States. Yet, the deadline for ratification occurred in 1982 with only three states lacking the necessary approval. Thus, in the United States citizens continue to live in a situation where the laws at the local, state, and federal levels discriminate against persons. Social policies which view women as dependents continue to the extent that many women reach mature adulthood and their senior years to find themselves in poverty. Trends indicate that women, children, and other dependents living in families headed by women will compose almost all the persons living in poverty in the United States by the year 2000 if current social policies continue. These social conditions include social services cutbacks, unemployment, salary discrimination, inequality of opportunity, and the weakening of affirmative action and Equal Employment Opportunity regulations. For women of racial or language minority groups or women who are older, the burden of these conditions is the most extreme.

Be it therefore resolved, that we, as United Methodists will continue:

1. To lift up our historic concern for the equality of women and men, to confess those times when we have failed to confront discrimination, and to rejoice in efforts to support human dignity.

2. To work through local churches, councils of churches, conference committees, general agencies, and appropriate coalitions to research laws and policies that discriminate on the basis of gender and to advocate changes that enable equality of rights and opportunities (This work will continue to require strategic focus and coordination on every level.).

3. To support the passage pf the Equal Rights Amendment to the U.S. Constitution; to educate United Methodists and others to its history, meaning and purpose, and to work through all appropriate channels for its passage.

4. To monitor those public policies and practices which affect unemployment, pay inequity, inequality of opportunity, and in the United States the weakening of affirmative action (with special concern for the interlocking impact of discrimination on the basis of gender, race, age); to support those public policies and practices that create new jobs, that encourage women to move into non-traditional jobs and that alleviate competition between women and minorities for jobs.

5. To encourage United Methodist general program agencies and annual conferences to develop creative approaches for the development of governmental social policies that will eliminate the burden of poverty on women and children; to offer opportunities for service and action to United Methodists who want to be involved in eradicating those conditions; and to work for economic justice.[20]

Formosan Churches (Presbyterian) Under Persecution

WHEREAS, Formosa has been under official martial law since 1949, under Chiang's Nationalist government (Kuomintang); and

WHEREAS, the largest Protestant church (250,000 members) in Formosa has never been party to opposition riots and demonstrations, but is now being severely persecuted; and

WHEREAS, on April 24, 1980, 9:15 p.m., the Rev. Dr. C.M. Kao, general secretary of the Presbyterian Church of Formosa was arrested by military police garrison personnel for alleged crimes of connections with subversive organizations and harbouring of a fugitive; and

---

[20] See Social Principles, III-F; "Treatment of Women in the United States Regarding Social Security," 1984; "The Church's Ministry to Women in Crises," 1980; "The Status of Women," 1980.

WHEREAS, the Rev. Dr. C.M. Kao is still in jail serving his seven-year sentence; and

WHEREAS, on December 3, 1983, there was an election in Taiwan (Formosa) for the seats of the Legislative Yuan ("court" or "college"), but most of the members (275 out of 373 to be exact) were elected in 1947 in Nanking, before Chiang Khai-shek's regime fled to Formosa; and

WHEREAS, the Legislative Yuan, as a branch of the government, has the power to legislate law and oversee government spending, and according to the Constitution, a general election is supposed to be called once every three years to elect the members of this Yuan; and

WHEREAS, after the application of the martial law in formosa in 1949, which is still in effect, Chiang declared that there would be no election and there was no election; and

WHEREAS, Chiang maintained his "no-election" policy, the old members of his government kept dying, even at a rate of two or three per month in recent years, and from the 400 members in the Legislative Yuan in 1947, there were 275 left last November; and

WHEREAS, the government was forced to hold a partial election to make up for the number of the dead, and the first such election was held in 1977, after Chiang's death in 1976; and

WHEREAS, the 275 members, out of 373, who were elected in 1947 do not have to run for re-election, there were 98 seats to be filled, but among these 98 seats, the government reserves the right to appoint 69 of them and these appointments are to be made among overseas Chinese groups, pro-Chiang's regime groups; and

WHEREAS, the real election held last December was to elect those 29 seats left, but even if all 29 seats were won by the non-party candidates, they would still be a minority in the Legislative Yuan; and

WHEREAS, in Formosa, under the present regime, the opposition party is not allowed and those who do not run under the banner of the Kuomingtang are generally called "non-party candidates;" and

WHEREAS, there were six non-party candidates elected in the December 3, 1983, election out of over 20 running; and

WHEREAS, these candidates and the Presbyterian Church in Taiwan have called for Formosa's future to be decided by the residents of Formosa; and

WHEREAS, the Presbyterian Church in Formosa (Taiwan), under the leadership of Dr. Kao, issued statements in 1971, 1973, and 1978 urging the government in Formosa and the superpowers to respect the God-given human rights for the people of Taiwan in deciding their own future; and

WHEREAS, for the first time in Formosa, the matter of self-determination was mentioned publicly in a campaign, even though the government tried to censor it; and

WHEREAS, the general public in Formosa have come to realize that what the church has been doing is simply trying to fulfill its role as the prophet of the time and the conscience of the society and has spoken out for the welfare of the people in Formosa;

Therefore, Be It Resolved, that The United Methodist Church strongly support the struggle of the Formosan people for their human rights and religious freedom and their right to participate fully in the political processes of their country, and that the General Conference write to President Chiang Ching-Kuo of the Republic of China, and to the American Institute in Taipei to urge a stop to such brutal oppression of the Formosan Presbyterian Christian brothers and sisters.

Be It Also Resolved, that The United Methodist Church register its disappointment over the government's treatment of the church and arrest of their leader and express its support for the Formosa Presbyterian Church's desire to recover its ties with the internal and ecumenical body of the WCC.

Be It Further Resolved, that all the General Conference delegates be requested to communicate with their respective government officials to vote their concerns for the right of the Formosan people to dissent and to have the right of religious freedom, and that all delegates support the church in Formosa with their prayers because the church there is still suffering.

Foundation Statement for Christian Stewardship

Introduction

This foundation statement for stewardship is presented to The United Methodist Church for the following reasons:

1. To provide a working definition of Christian Stewardship.

2. To provide a basic outline of stewardship which could serve as a guideline for writers of curriculum materials and other literature in which stewardship is being treated.

3. To interpret stewardship broadly so that it deals with more than finance, and more concretely than from a viewpoint which classifies all phases of Christian thought as "the stewardship of something," with the result that the identity and significance of the concept are thereby lost.

4. To encourage the membership of the church to incorporate the philosophy of Christian stewardship into their daily lives and into all phases of the church's program.

5. To help the local church understand the importance of stewardship for its total year-round program.

6. To challenge The United Methodist Church to place stewardship at the very center of its life, and to function itself as a responsible steward.

7. To provide a theological foundation for the work of the various dimensions of The United Methodist Church as they work with all aspects of Christian stewardship.

What Is Christian Stewardship?

Christian stewardship is the recognition of God's sovereignty through creation and is a grateful response to God's manifold gifts. Human response is expressed by a dedicated and creative use of all these gifts toward fulfillment of Christ's mission in the world.

345

Christian stewardship is a response to the love of God as revealed in Christ and is expressed in terms of the worthy management and care of all resources available for the sustenance and enrichment of life.

The only appropriate response that persons can make to the grace of God is to cooperate with God in fulfilling the divine will and purpose. This is done as persons recognize that what they receive from God is to be developed and invested in enterprises of the kingdom. All that is committed to the fulfillment of God's purposes is sanctified. The Christian steward whose life and abilities and resources are totally committed to God's purposes is thus totally sanctified. Such a commitment to vocation brings the Christian's life into the stream of God's purpose so that the spirit of God flows through such a person in a blessing to the world.

Christian stewards accept life, including abilities, power, influence, and money as special trusts from God and relationship with God. These persons will seek to develop these to the fullest, and endeavor to use body and mind and abilities for the purposes of God. Christian stewards also feel a responsibility for the well-being of all people, giving them the opportunity to develop their full potential as well.

Christian stewards accept the family as a trust from God and seek to provide the atmosphere in which each member can realize his or her fullest potential. Every person is accepted as a child of God, worthy of dignity and respect. In all personal relationships, others are valued as of equal worth and the exploitation of any person by other individuals, groups or systems is rejected.

Christian stewards accept the church (as the fellowship of the committed ones) as a trust from God, and seek to assure through this fellowship the extension of God's mission into the community and into the world.

Christian stewards accept the gospel as a trust from God, seek to understand it fully, and endeavor to be faithful custodians of its liberating and reconciling truth. They endeavor to transmit it to others so that they may see its relationship to the whole of life.

Christian stewards accept material resources as a trust from God to maximize the use of these resources. They use the power of this wealth from the purposes of God. Stewards strive to increase the productivity of the world without exploitation and to make it possible for others to share in his bounty.

Christian stewards accept power and influence as a trust from God and endeavor to administer them according to the purposes of God. They encourage others to do likewise.

Christian stewards accept this world with its tremendous resources as a trust from God, seeking to understand what God is doing in the events of history and through technological developments, and endeavoring to be involved in the decisive issues facing society. They strive to penetrate the arena of secular society with the good news of the kingdom.

Christian stewards are hopeful about the ultimate outcome of history, accepting their personal destiny as a trust from God, and endeavoring to invest life and abilities and resources as partners with God and others in shaping one's personal destiny as well as the world's future.

Biblical and Theological Foundations

An examination of the origin and background of the word stewardship enriches the understanding of the concept. In classical Greek, the word used is *oikonomia*, which is derived from two words: *oikos*, meaning "house," and *neimein*, meaning "to distribute." These words combined set forth the idea of the administration of a house.

In addition to the meaning, "a place of residence," the word *oikos* in the scriptures also implies a bond which unites all who belong to the household. While the household begins with the immediate family, it is extended to include relatives, servants, and guests.

The biblical concept includes the idea that God is the architect of an entirely new household. To be included in this household means to participate in new life which emerges from God's constant process of creation. A place in the family of God means becoming a member of the body of Christ in which all Christians are included. The growth, nurture and attainment of maturity on the part of the Body depend on God's continuous acts of grace and love in creation and on the faithful response of all who are involved.

Free Flow of Information Among All Peoples of the Earth

In the international arena there is widespread discussion of what is known as the "new world information and communication order." The discussion involves the world-wide flow of information in the light of such factors as governmental restraints, multinational commercial communication enterprises, and the modern technology of communication. The church has a witness to bear upon these issues.

1. *The Scriptural Base*

Scripture is replete with demands for freedom, truth, justice, and fair treatment of others.

The Old Testament records how, in the early history of the Hebrew people, God's law demanded truth, honesty, and equity. In the great nineteenth chapter of Leviticus God calls for equal treatment of the powerless (v. 15), for love and fair dealing toward the sojourner or stranger (v. 33-4), and for truth and honesty in all dealings (v. 35-6). The Ten Commandments forbid false witness (Deut. 5:20).

The prophets called for justice and righteousness. Amos gave God's word: "Let justice roll down like waters" (5:24). Micah declared that the Lord required of humans "to do justly and to love mercy" (6:8).

In the New Testament Jesus both demands and promises truth and freedom. In John's Gospel he says, "If you continue in my word, you are truly my disciples, and you will know the truth and the truth will make you free" (8:31-2). In the synoptic gospels he commands respect for others, especially those who are weak. Each person's responsibility

348

toward the "little ones" (Matt. 18:5-6; Mark 9:42; Luke 17:2) may be seen also as a responsibility toward the powerless. By example he was an advocate for persons on the margins of society.

Paul, as he wrote the Galatians about freedom in Christ, called his readers to enjoy and use their freedom, but to use it as an opportunity to serve others (5:13-15).

As Christians of today we seek to apply these biblical concepts to the opportunities and problems of the modern media.

2. *Our Historic Witness*

The United Methodist Church and its predecessor denominations have a long history of defending freedom of religion, freedom of expression, and the rights of persons who are powerless because of political or economic conditions. This concern found expression in the original (1908) Social Creed and successor documents down to the present Social Principles, including today a specific call for freedom of information and protection of the people's right for access to the communication media (Section V). The concern is raised in actions of the 1980 General Conference as recorded in The Book of Resolutions. The resolution on Church-Government Relations urges Christians to participate meaningfully in public affairs. The resolution on the Church in a Mass Media Culture declares that channels of communication "must operate in open, humanizing ways." In the resolution on Open Meetings the church demands of itself the high standard of openness that it commends to others. The Book of Discipline instructs one of the church agencies to "work toward promotion and protection of the historic freedoms of religion and the press" (¶ 1106.5).

3. *Problems in the Flow of Information*

Nowhere in the world do people have full and free access to information about people and events elsewhere. Even in the United States, with a tradition of press freedom and

349

constitutional guarantees, our view of the world is circumscribed by what is selected for us by newspaper and news magazine editors and radio/television news producers. A study of datelines in newspaper stories quickly reveals that most of the news pertains to our own country or Europe, and that news from countries elsewhere is likely to be filtered through Western conduits.

Persons in many countries, especially in developing nations, feel that they seldom have the opportunity to express themselves, or even describe themselves, in their own words and on their own terms. They feel that they are seen mainly through the eyes of foreigners—usually reporters for the commercial news services of Europe and North America.

Many persons live in countries where newspapers and broadcast news are controlled by governments. In many countries there is outright censorship. Some governments use the mass media for political purposes.

Modern technology, especially computer-based communications and transmission by satellite, makes global comunications possible on a scale and with an immediacy never possible before. But the cost is beyond the reach of all but the most affluent countries or corporations. Those who control communication technology have the power to determine what is known about others. The same technology makes it possible to treat information as a commodity to be bought and sold, to be shared or withheld for payment or consideration.

In the United States the broadcast and print media increasingly have turned viewers and readers into a product to be delivered to the sponsors. As a result, the media's goal becomes to reach and hold the largest possible audience, regardless of other journalistic objectives.

These, and other related concerns, demand serious thought in all countries, especially those countries that have the power to create and control the media of communication. The light of the Christian gospel must be applied to these questions.

4. *Statement of Principles*

In view of inequities in the flow of information among the peoples of the world, and in the light of our own understanding of the gospel, we state these principles:

● All peoples of earth have a right to free flow of information.

● Peoples have a right to originate information and make statements about themselves in terms of their own culture and self-view.

● Journalists must be given access to information within their own countries and across international frontiers.

● Journalists have a responsibility for accuracy and fairness in all that they write, photograph, edit, publish or broadcast. Part of this responsibility includes cross-cultural sensitivity and awareness as well as freedom from language bias.

● The licensing of publications or of journalists violates freedom.

● Information is a human right and not only a commodity to be bought and sold. (However, those who gather, edit and transmit information are entitled to fair rewards for their efforts.)

● Every citizen has a right to be informed in order to participate in politics intelligently.

● Censorship by governments or by those who control news media is abhorrent and should not be permitted; neither should there be legal restrictions to the free flow of information. The withholding of information for security reasons must be limited by publicly-stated guidelines.

● Readers and viewers in every land have a right to a broad view of the world, drawing upon multiple sources of information.

● The churches should be primary advocates for a free flow of information and diversity of sources. The churches should oppose the practice of those persons and systems which use media for purposes of human exploitation, political control, or excessive private profit.

351

5. *Recommended Actions*

This resolution is commended to the churches and to individual United Methodists for study and action, such as monitoring local and national media and legislation and instituting appropriate follow-up. Dialog with journalists, publishers and broadcasters is recommended.

The United Methodist Church must ensure that, in its own communications, persons of other countries and cultures speak for themselves.

Individuals, local churches, and local church groups are urged to join with other Christians in their communities in study and action on the issues and principles stated in this resolution.

The results of local study may indicate suggestions to local media. Recommendations may be made to representatives in local, state or national government. Viewpoints may be registered also with governmental agencies, such as the Federal Communications Commission, and with intergovernmental or international agencies.

General agencies of the church, particularly United Methodist Communications, the General Board of Church and Society and the General Board of Global Ministries, are directed to provide coordinated resources and guides for study and action.[21]

Global Racism

God through creation has established a mode whereby, through a reconciling process, human beings can achieve the full potential of their existence.

The worth of every human being resides in the intrinsic value which God has given to each individual. This affirmation is echoed in Jesus' parables where each human being is valued according to God's special love for that person.

[21] *See* Social Principles, V-C; "The Church in a Mass Media Culture," 1984.

Any person who places another person, by thought or deed, outside of the possibility of human growth and development violates God's sacred mandate to humanity: "Love your neighbor as yourself."

This mandate sets the conditions for human existence through justice, mutual respect, and trust. Our failure to fulfill this mandate has resulted in oppression and racism.

Racism is a system of domination in which one racial group claims superiority and oppresses other groups for economic, political, cultural, psychological and/or religious reasons. Racism confers certain privileges on a small group of people who benefit from the resultant inequities. It is the creation and defense of these privileges that underlie and maintain the systems of racial domination. For this reason, racial domination is exceedingly complex. It is enforced and maintained both consciously and unconsciously by the legal, cultural, educational, economic, political, and military institutions of a society. This oppression is a pervasive, worldwide phenomenon, not confined to certain countries or continents. No economic system—socialism, capitalism or any other—is immune to it.

Racism is encountered whenever:

1. Persons, even before they are born, are assigned to a group, severely limited in freedom of movement, choice of work and places of residence because of their race.

2. Groups of people, because of their race, are denied effective participation in the political process and are compelled, often by physical force, to obey the edicts of governments which they were not allowed to have a part in choosing.

3. Racial groups within a nation are excluded from the normal channels available for gaining economic power, through denial of educational opportunities and entry into occupational/professional groups.

4. Policies of a nation ensure benefits for that nation from the labor or racial groups, migrant or otherwise, while at the same time denying to such people commensurate participation in the affairs of the nation.

5. The identity of persons is defamed through stereotyp-

ing of racial and ethnic groups in textbooks, cinema, mass media, interpersonal relations and other ways.

6. People are denied equal protection of the law, because of race, and when constituted authorities of the state use their power to protect the interests of the dominant group at the expense of the powerless.

7. Groups or nations continue to profit from regional and global structures that are historically related to racist presuppositions and actions.

The Social Principles states that:

Racism plagues and cripples our growth in Christ, inasmuch as it is antithetical to the gospel itself. Therefore, we reject racism in every form, and affirm the ultimate and temporal worth of all persons. We rejoice in the gifts which particular ethnic histories and cultures bring to our total life. We commend and encourage the self-awareness of all racial and ethnic minorities and oppressed people which leads them to demand their just and equal rights as member of society. We assert the obligation of society, and groups within the society, to implement compensatory programs that redress long-standing systemic social deprivation of racial and ethnic minorities. We further assert the right of members of racial and ethnic minorities to equal opportunities in employment and promotion; to education and training of the highest quality; to nondiscrimination in voting, in access to public accommodations, and in housing purchase or rental; and positions of leaderhsip and power in all elements of our life together.

Confession of Racism in Today's Church

As a religious community, both as United Methodist congregations and individuals, we often have failed to proclaim and live out the gospel message of love toward our neighbors in terms of salvation and liberation for all of God's people. Too often we have not recognized the struggle against racism as central to our church's missions to the world.

Confession of Racism in Today's Society

Within the larger secular society, it is the economic and political manifestations of racism that are the most obvious.

Usually, it is people of color, women and children, and those people in developing countries who suffer most from the priorities of racist policies and attitudes.

As United Methodists we recognize the need to:

1. Examine our direct and indirect roles in retarding the self-determination and development of racially oppressed people.

2. Critique immigration patterns and promote nonracially determined immigration policies.

3. Recognize the exploitation of the world's resources and people by many transnational corporations who place profit before people.

4. Demand greater corporate responsibility and accountability.

5. Demand greater responsibility from the communications/media industry in their role of attitude formation and perpetuation of racist stereotypes and mythology.

6. Assess the continued exploitation inherent in the dichotomies of north/south, rich/poor, industrialized nations/world of color.

7. Critique and reform legal and judicial systems which disproportionately jail, imprison, and execute people of color.

8. Support the restructuring of the educational systems to enable all children to learn to their fullest potential under conditions of maximum opportunity.

9. Support the enforcement of affirmative action in employment, housing, health care institutions, and governmental system, even in the face of laws which compel such behavior.

10. Support changes in laws and practices which doubly discriminate against women of color.

As United Methodists in the United States we recognize the need to:

1. Condemn the Ku Klux Klan, the Nazi Party, the Posse Comitatus and similar militantly racist movements.

2. Assess the increasing militarism of the United States, which is based on racist enlistment patterns growing out of economic forms of racism; the ultimate wrong of U.S.

355

minorities fighting in the Third World on behalf of an elitist group of economic interests.

3. Understand the implications of bilingual and multicultural experiences in relationship to racism.

4. See our actions on racism in the light of histories and issues of Black Americans, Hispanic Americans, Native peoples, Asians, and Pacific Islanders.

5. Examine the domination by the United States of Puerto Rico's development, particularly the Island of Vieques.

6. Examine the racist actions involving Haitian, Vietnamese, Kapuchean, Mexican, Salvadorean and other refugees in the United States.

7. Halt racist actions directed at Native peoples, related to broken treaties, land rights and national resources questions

8. Give high visibility to U. S. immigration policy and the plight of undocumented persons.

9. Examine the racism of the welfare system in the United States.

Therefore, as United Methodists, Committed to Understanding and Eliminating Racism:

We affirm the use of non-violent action and resistance as alternatives to human abuse, injustice, war, and exploitation, and that non-violence become one of the strategies for a new international coalition to combat racism.

We recommend the following actions:

1. That the Commission on Religion and Race, in cooperation with other program boards, develop a program for the implementation of the "Charter for Racial Justice Policies in an Interdependent Global Community" throughout the entire church and progress report be given to the 1988 General Conference.

2. That the Commission on Religion and Race, in cooperation with the Council of Bishops and other program boards, call for a national convocation of United Methodists to be held early in the quadrennium and then followed by five jurisdictional conferences that would examine:

a) Explicit racism in The United Methodist Church's relationship with its employees.

b) How to call to accountability those groups and/or individuals who maintain and encourage discriminatory practices within their congregations, districts, and conferences.

c) Develop a process to evaluate present and future strategies toward the elimination of racism within The United Methodist Church.

3. The general boards and agencies, the Council of Bishops and local congregations affirm and encourage the sue of theologies of ethnic peoples which will free all people from the domination of Anglo-European theologies and make ethnic faith relevant to their own communities.

4. Individuals and local congregations be encouraged to explore how their invested money is being used and to question the racial practices of those companies in which they invest.

5. The General Boards of Church and Society and Global Ministries work through the political process in the United States to:

a) Urge the U. S. Government to cease all collaboration with the government of South Africa until it abandons its policy on apartheid.

b) Encourage the U.S. Senate to ratify and become an advocate for the International Convention on the Elimination of All Forms of Racial Discrimination.

6. The General Board of Global Ministries and the General Board of Discipleship promote study and use of interpretive materials for local churches on the World Council of Churches' Program to Combat Racism.

7. The Commission on Religion and Race and the General Board of Global Ministries make a careful analysis of the perspective of indigenous and aboriginous peoples vis-a-vis racism, especially in those cases were genocide is being practiced.

8. The appropriate United Methodist agencies sponsor a convocation in the United States for members of the mass media to:

a) Examine racism in reporting both in the United States and outside.

b) Examine racism in advertising.[22]

Health and Wholeness

Introduction

All human beings have been created in the image of God and are called to the abundant life. In the biblical story of the woman with the hemorrhage, Jesus provides an example of his healing ministry that includes the spiritual as well as the physical status of the person.

"And behold, a woman, who had suffered from a hemorrhage for twelve years came up behind and touched the fringe of his garment; For she said to herself, 'If I only touch his garment, I shall be made well.' Jesus turned and seeing her, he said, 'Take heart, daughter; your faith has made you well.' And instantly the woman was made well" (Matt. 9:20-22).

The United Methodist Church, as an entity, believes that its mission is to continue the redemptive ministry of Christ, including teaching, preaching and healing. Christ's healing ws not peripheral but central in his ministry. The church, therefore, understands itself as called by the Lord to the wholistic ministry of healing: spiritual, mental and emotional, and physical.

Health in this sense is something beyond, but not exclusive of, biological well-being. In this view, health care is inadequate when it fixes its attention solely on the body and its physiological functions, as is any religion that focuses its interest entirely on the spirit. Taking the gospel mandates seriously, United Methodists are called to work toward a healthy society of whole persons. Part of our task is to enable

[22]*See* Social Principles, III-A; "A Charter for Racial Justice Policies in an Interdependent Global Community," 1980; "Resurgence of the Ku Klux Klan," 1984; "The United Methodist Church and Race," 1976.

people to care for themselves and to take responsiblity for their own health. Another part of our task is to ensure that people who are ill whether from illness of spirit, mind, or body are not turned aside or ignored but given care that allows them to live a full life. We see this task as demanding concern for spiritual, political, ethical, economic, social, and medical decisions that maintain the highest concern for the condition of society, the environment, and the total life of each person.

Human suffering is caused by a variety of factors, the environmental, social and personal factors mentioned as well as others which remain unknown to us.

Environmental Factors. Clean air, pure water, effective sanitary systems for the disposal of wastes, nutritious foods, adequate housing and hazard-free work places are essential to health. The best medical system cannot preserve or maintain health when the environment is disease-producing.

Social Factors. Inadequate education, poverty, unemployment, lack of access to food, stress-producing conditions, and social pressures reinforced by marketing and advertising strategies that encourage the use of tobacco, alcohol, and other drugs are detrimental to good health.

Personal Habits. Overeating or eating non-nutritious foods, substance abuse (including alcohol, tobacco, barbituates, sedatives, etc.) are clearly destructive of health. Failure to exercise or to rest and relax adequately are also injurious to health.

Although medical care represents a very important part of health care it does not include the whole. More medical care does not always equal better health.

Medical care in much of the world has evolved too much as disease care rather than health care. Disease prevention, public health programs, and health education appropriate to every age level and social setting are needed globally. Services should be provided in a compassionate and skillful manner on the basis of need; without discrimination as to economic status, mental or physical handicap, race, color, religion, sex, age, national origin, or language.

A Just Health System

Within a just society every person has a right to:

1. Basic health services that are accessible and affordable in each geographic and cultural setting.

2. An environment that promotes health.

3. Active involvement in the formulation of health care activities that meet local needs and priorities.

4. Information about his or her illness and to be an active participant in treatment and rehabilitation.

5. Receive compassionate and skilled care.

6. A health care system sensitive to cultural needs.

7. Access to funding sources where necessary for basic health services.

Health Insurance

For all persons to have adequate access to needed health care services, public financing must be a significant part of an overall health insurance plan. Public funding is necessary to pay for insuring those who cannot pay part or all of the necessary premiums required.

Health Maintenance

Many health problems and illnesses are preventable if we accept the fact that health maintenance requires understanding of the unity of the human body, mind and spirit. The whole person needs proper nutrition, exercise, the challenge to learn and grow, and an acknowledgement that this is a life-long process. We recognize that these needs are difficult to meet when environmental factors contribute to ill health. But we must acknowledge the fact that we have separated spiritual health from physical health. In Western Protestant interpretation of health and healing, the union of the body and spirit are often dismissed. Cultures that respect and revere that union are often disregarded or looked upon in a condescending manner. The early church did not make these distinctions, nor did Jesus in his healing ministry. We must, if we are to obtain good health, unite the body and spirit in our thinking and actions.

Therefore, as Christians we accept responsibility for modeling this wholistic, preventive style of health maintenance. We commit ourselves to examining the value systems at work in our society as they impact the health of our people and to working for programs and policies that enable people to breathe clean air, drink clean water, eat wholesome food, and have access to adequate education and freedom that enable mind and spirit to develop.

Medical Services

We support the following principles of access to health services:

1. In a just society all people are entitled to basic maintenance and health care services. We reject as contrary to our understanding of the gospel the notion of differing standards of health care for various segments of the population.

2. Health care should be comprehensive, including preventive, therapeutic, and rehabilitative services.

3. Religious and other appropriate forms of counseling should be available to all patients and families when they are called upon to make difficult medical choices, so that responsible decisions, within the context of the Christian faith, may be made concerning organ transplants, use of extreme measures to prolong life, abortion, sterilization, genetic counseling, institutionalization, and death with dignity.

4. We encourage development of community support systems that permit alternatives to institutional care for such groups as the aging, the terminally ill and mentally ill, and other persons with special needs.

5. Professional health care personnel should be recruited and appropriately educated to meet the health care needs of all persons. Especially urgent is the need for physicians trained in geriatric medicine. Special priorities should be established to secure among the professional group at least

proportional representation of women and minorities who are now seriously underrepresented.

6. In areas where medical services are not available, or are in undersupply, we urge private or public funding to provide the full range of needed services. To meet these goals, we recommend the reallocation of funds from armaments to human services, both nationally, and internationally (Social Principles ¶ 75c).

7. Regional planning processes should coordinate the services rendered by all health care institutions, including those funded by governments, to create a more effective system of health services in every area. Priorities should be established for the provision of health services, such as preventive care, mental health services, home care, and health education.

8. Corrective measures should be taken where there is maldistribution or unavailability of hospital beds, intermediate care and nursing home care, home-delivered care, neighborhood health centers, community mental health centers, and of emergency care networks.

9. We encourage medical education for laypersons that will enable them to evaluate effectively medical care they need and are receiving.

10. We support the medical community in its effort to uphold ethical standards and to promote quality assurance.

Health and Wholeness Ministry

As United Methodists we are called to a ministry of health and wholeness. Therefore, we challenge our membership to:

1. Make health concerns a priority in the church with special emphases that include but are not limited to women's health concerns; appropriate, unbiased, informed diagnosis and treatment of older adults; preventive care (incuding health education); special health concerns and needs of children and youth; and establishment of networks for information sharing and action suggestions.

2. Support the provision of direct health services where

needed and to provide, as we are able, such services in hospitals and homes, clinics, and health centers.

3. Accept responsibility for educating and motivating members to follow a healthy lifestyle reflecting our affirmation of life as God's gift.

4. Become actively involved at all levels in the development of support systems for health care in the community including: dependent care (respite and 24-hour care, in-home and short-term out-of-home care), meals, programs for women in crisis, halfway houses, support systems for independent living, and family support systems.

5. Become advocates for: a healthful environment, accessible, affordable health care, continued public support for health care of persons unable to provide for themselves, continued support for health-related research and provision of church facilities to enable health related ministries.

6. Become involved in a search for Christian understanding of health, healing and wholeness and the dimensions of spiritual healing in our congregations and seminaries.

7. Encourage colleges, universities, hospitals and seminaries related to The United Methodist Church connectional units to gain an added awareness of health issues and the need for recruitment and education of persons for health-related ministries who would approach such ministries out of a Christian understanding and commitment.

8. Support public policies and programs that will ensure comprehensive health care services of high quality to all persons on the principle of equal access.

In the United States, we affirm the findings of The President's Committee on Medical Ethics of 1983. While noting the importance of cost containment, the committee wrote: "Measures designed to contain health care costs that exacerbate existing inadequacies or impede the achievement of equity are unacceptable from a moral standpoint."

A positive response to these challenges within the Christian context will help assure to all persons an abundant mental, emotional, and spiritual life.[23]

Health for All by the Year 2000

WHEREAS, The United Methodist Church is global in its outreach and has a strong commitment to work with other churches and secular organizations which are concerned about the health of the world's people; and

WHEREAS, The United Methodist Church has had a long history of medical missions, training of health personnel, support of health facilities, involvement of local churches in health education and direct service programs; and

WHEREAS, The United Methodist Church affirms health as a condition of physical, mental, social, and spiritual well-being to be desired and worked for by all persons, and that all pesons are entitled to basic health care, while at the same time having a responsibility to care for their own health and to protect the health of others; and

WHEREAS, it is recognized that more than anything else people's health is affected by the circumstances of their lives including living and environmental conditions, education and employment opportunities, resources and life style, political and socio-economic realities, spiritual nurture, and supportive relationships; and

WHEREAS, it has been a part of the prophetic, redemptive and healing ministry of The United Methodist Church to identify always with those persons whose needs are not being met; to focus clearly on those factors which impede individuals and communities in their search for health and wholeness; and to point to what must be done if people are to be freed from those powers and practices which stand in the way of healthy development, physically, mentally, socially and spiritually; and

[23] *See* Social Principles, V-A; "Mental Health," 1976; "Health for All by the Year 2000," 1984.

364

WHEREAS, the member states of the World Health Organization, including the United States, affirmed in 1977 at the 30th World Health Assembly that one of the most important social goals of the world community in the coming decades should be the attainment by all people of the world by the year 2000 of a level of health that will permit them to lead a socially and economically productive life; and

WHEREAS, the Director General of the World Health Organization has affirmed that cooperation between sectors of society, with an emphasis on religious as well as secular bodies, is essential toward the goal of health for all by the year 2000; and

WHEREAS, The United Methodist Church through its seven central conferences, 73 annual conferences, 38,000 local churches, 9,500,000 members, and its involvement with health ministries around the world, has a unique opportunity to protect and promote health; minister with persons who have illnesses of body, mind and/or spirit; create opportunities for individuals and communities to participate in determining local health priorities and methods for delivery of needed services, identify unmet needs and advocate that those needs be met; and address those political, economic and social factors which contribute to ill health and the unequal distribution of those opportunities, goods, and services which are essential to attaining and maintaining health;

Therefore be It Resolved, that The United Methodist Church: *Joins* with the international community affirming health for all by the year 2000 as one of the most important social goals of the 20th century;

Asks its annual conferences, central conferences, their related institutions, local churches, and all church members to be informed about the goal of health for all by the year 2000, and to work with other groups to develop means of promoting and protecting health, giving particular attention wherever possible to the needs of mothers and infants; children, youth and families; older persons; persons with handicapping conditions; and immigrants and refugees;

being aware of how ageism, sexism, racism, handicappism, poverty and other forms of discrimination impede persons and communities in their achievement of health and wholeness; and

Encourages each Annual Conference and central conference to focus on health for all by the year 2000 through its health and welfare unit, or other most appropriate unit; and

Assigns responsibility to the Health and Welfare Ministries Program Department of the General Board of Global Ministries to develop and make available interpretive material about health for all by the year 2000 and to suggest ways in which the various units of The United Methodist Church can be involved in this goal.[24]

Historical Site

Resolved that the General Conference designates Baltimore as the American Methodist Bicentennial City.

Human Hunger

I. *Introduction*

At the last Judgment, the question is asked, "When did we see thee hungry and feed thee?" (Matt. 25:37). The answer follows, "As you did it to one of the least of these my brethren, you did it to me" (Matt. 25:40). St. Paul, interpreting the new ethic of the Kingdom, instructed the early church to satisfy the hunger and thirst of enemies (Rom. 12:20).

From the earliest times, the Christian community, in response to these teachings, has expressed compassion and care for those in need. In recent years this has been expressed in the giving of millions of dollars for direct food distribution. More systemically, the church has deployed

---

[24] *See* Social Principles, V-A; "Health and Wholeness," 1984.

agricultural missionaries, supported demonstration farming and development programs, challenged unjust social and economic systems which condemn people to poverty, and witnessed for just public food policies at state and federal levels.

In the last decade, scant progress has been made in meeting the food needs of the hungry on a continuing basis. Too often, the attention span of church leaders and those who follow is curtailed by institutional interests and program fads. Our involvement as the owners of lands and buildings, our identification with social, economic, and political establishments, and our approval of those values which limit productive and distributive justice work together to limit our ministries "to the least of these."

II. *The Situation*

Interest generated by the World Food Conference (Rome, 1974) led to research which has resulted in a better understanding of the world food situation. The Food and Agricultural Organization of the United Nations has produced many studies and continues to monitor the status of world food production and distribution. The International Foundation for Development Alternatives, the Brandt Commission, and the Presidential (U.S.) Commission on World Hunger issued reports and recommendations for achieving world food security.

From a global perspective there is enough food to feed the present world population, at least at minimal levels. The extra food needed to provide adequate diets for the malnourished of the world is not large in relative terms. The deficit in calories is equivalent to about 37 million tons of grain per year—one fiftieth of the world's grain production and less than 10 percent of the grain fed to livestock in the rich nations. Even within most countries, food supplies would in general be adequate if they were evenly distributed. People are hungry, not because there is no food available, but because they are unable to buy.

In the early 1980's, by a conservative estimate, one billion persons are undernourished. Approximately one-half of this number is chronically undernourished, representing one-ninth of the earth's population. It is estimated that 40 percent of these are children. These malnourished persons are found mainly in a group of 45 developing nations that were most seriously affected by the economic and food crises of the 1970s plus the world-wide recession of the 1980s.

Even in the United States, with its enormous productive and distributive capacity, the progress in eliminating hunger in the 1970s has been stalemated. Indeed, those living in poverty have increased in numbers. This is especially true of families where the primary earner is a woman. The gross number of persons living in poverty in 1983 was larger than in 1965, the beginning of the war on poverty. From 1978 to 1982, there was an increase of 9.9 million persons living in poverty in the United States, an increase of 40 percent.

World population is increasing by approximately 77 million per year. Although the increase in world food output continues to exceed world population growth and food consumption patterns, the shortfall in grain production in the developing countries by 1990 will be on the order of 100 to 140 million tons per year. Currently, one-half of the African countries are producing less food than is being consumed and are net importers.

III. *Causes of the World Food Crisis*

The fact that one-ninth of the earth's population is chronically malnourished (70 percent few calories than necessary for health) has both precipitating causes and much deeper systemic causes.

A. *Precipitating Causes.* Among the many precipitating causes, three stand out: the weather, political decisions, and economic recession.

During the early 1970s an erratic weather pattern developed in a wide band across the tropics bringing with it drought. Scenes of starvation were televised to a world audience. More normal weather patterns returned and a few good crop years followed. However, drought struck again in the early 1980s affecting the countries of sub-Sahara Africa, parts of Europe, Asia, Oceania, and some of the richest grain growing areas of the United States. In the 1970s six nations were affected in Africa; in the 1980s 18 countries were especially hard hit.

Some of the political decisions most deleterious to food production and prices center in the management of surplus grain held by the rich countries. In an attempt in 1983 to lower production and decrease the amount of grain in storage, U.S. farmers were paid in grain to reduce acreage planting. By happenstance, this was accompanied by a drought in many areas of the midwest. At the same time, a decision was made to sell nine to 12 million tons of grain annually for the next five years to the Soviet Union. Grain prices responded sharply in the future's markets, raising the price of grain to the importing developing nations.

The world economic recession of the early 1980s seriously affected the ability of developing nations to meet the problem of undernourishment. Their balance of trade was seriously affected. The recession depressed commodity prices, lowered demand, restricted access to markets, and promoted protectionist policies. The world index of commodity prices for developing countries dropped as much as 30 percent. The result was lessened income of international currencies for the purchase of foodstuffs.

B. Systemic Causes. Beyond the immediate causes of malnourishment lie more fundamental structural constraints of which hunger and poverty are but symptoms.

1. *Unjust economic systems, a legacy of colonialism.* Almost without exception, the poor countries were at one time colonies of imperial powers. Colonialism developed them primarily for the export of raw materials, mainly mining products and agricultural crops (coffee, tea, sugar, rubber, cocoa, etc.) To achieve this the colonial powers restructured traditional social and legal customs, land distribution and tenure, food production, political power, regional and international economic relations, and the economy. The

369

colonial system depended upon depressed wages and local elites. Two economic sectors resided side by side, unintegrated: the traditional (subsistence farming and artisanal products) and the modern (export enclave). These unintegrated models of development continue to exist and more of the malnourished are related to the traditional sector. Military regimes and wealthy elites continue to cooperate with foreign powers in resisting the structural changes required for full development, justice, and the sharing of power.

2. *Insufficient food production in developing nations.* A principal result from colonial policies has been the insufficient development of food production in many lower income countries. This distortion occurs through market forces and tax policies which encourage the cultivation of a single crop for export rather than the balanced production of food for domestic use. For example, Africa's food problem is virtually continent wide and has been chronic for 20 years. Per capita food production, which declined by 7 percent from 1960 to 1970, declined by 15 percent from 1970 to 1980. Even then, when food production is insufficient for a healthy diet, African nations have experienced a sharp increase in their annual production of agricultural goods (coffee, tea, cocoa, flowers, etc.) for export to the rich nations. The urgent need for land and credit reform is ignored. A higher priority is given to industrial development, tourism, and military needs than to agriculture. In addition, urban unrest is often controlled through a public policy of cheap food, a disincentive for agricultural development.

3. *Population Growth.* Since the late 1960s, world population growth has declined from 2.4 percent per year to 2.0 percent. At that rate, the present world population of 4.7 billion will double in 35 years. The largest rate of increase will be in the less developed countries which will add 1.4 billion population by the year 2000. This increase is occurring in those countries which have a negative rate of growth in terms of per capita food production.

Rapid population growth and inadequate food supply have a common origin and a joint explanation. They both are symptoms of structural poverty—those economic and political frameworks in which poor people exist. The experience is worldwide. Wherever poverty gives way to a rising standing of living, the birth-rate declines. Wherever the security of the family increases, the birth-rate declines. Such family security depends on social and economic development which is based on the values of justice and shared power.

4. *Maldevelopment in the rich nations.* While inadequate and unbalanced development exists in the low-income countries, acute maldevelopment exists in the rich nations. This maldevelopment is characterized by growing militarism, waste of resources by the production of unnecessary goods and services, degradation of the environment, increasing structural unemployment, inflation, institutionalized consumerism, recession, persistence of poverty, rising nationalism, and a crisis in values especially felt in the lives of the young.

In 1980, the rich nations with 24 percent of the earth's population consumed 79 percent of the world's goods and services leaving 21 percent for the developing nations with 76 percent of the population. In public health expenditures, the rich nations consumed 92 percent of the goods and services; the developing nations received 8 percent. A policy of more of the same cannot lead from poverty to health and nourishment. Without radical change, the structural distortions will continue their toll on the human family.

IV. *Theological Bases for Hope*

As Christians, the central question we must ask ourselves in this situation is: What does God require and enable us individually and corporately to do? Some of our central affirmations of faith provide at least a partial answer.

God is Creator of all, and loves and cares for all Creation. Because every person is a creature loved of God, every person has a basic human right to food, a necessity for survival. Because all persons are creatures of God, equally subject to God's grace and claim, all are bound together in inseparable ties of solidarity. It is the task of God's people to show solidarity in support of adequate provision for basic human needs such as food.

In the incarnation, life, death, and resurrection of Jesus Christ, the promise and first fruits of redemption have been brought to our sinful and selfish humanity. Jesus' own concern for human need in his ministry is a model for the church's concern. His opposition to those who would ignore the needs of the neighbor makes clear that we grossly misunderstand and fail to grasp God's grace if we imagine that God overlooks, condones, or easily tolerates our indifference to the plight of our neighbors, our greed and selfishness, or our systems of injustice and oppression.

As Holy Spirit, God is at work in history today, refashioning lives, tearing down unjust structures, restoring community, engendering faith, hope, and love. It is the work of the Holy Spirit which impels us to take action even when perfect solutions are not apparent. Thus, we engage in the struggle for bread and justice for all in the confidence that God goes before us and that God's cause will prevail.

V. *Goals for Action by Christians*

In faithfulness to our understanding of God's good intentions for all peoples, we can set for ourselves no lesser goals than the abolition of hunger from the earth. Movement toward that ultimate goal requires commitment to such immediate and instrumental goals as the follow:

A. The transformation of persons and institutions which create and perpetuate strongholds of power and privilege for some at the expense of many, into new personal, social, economic and political environments which are more conducive to justice, liberation, self-development, a stabilized population, and a sustainable environment.

B. The development and implementation of agricultural and other policies which 1) provide incentives to farmers to produce abundantly, using appropriate technology, those crops needed to feed themselves, their communities and the world's population; 2) protect farmers from the harsh economic consequences which market-oriented economies

372

frequently visit upon producers of abundance; 3) more agricultural practices toward greater harmony with the diverse and fragile eco-systems of the planet; 4) enable all nations to become self-sufficient in the production or securing of food; 5) support plant improvement through traditional breeding and genetic engineering to ensure that genetic variability remains the common heritage of future generations.

C. The simplification of lifestyles in developed nations, one more congruent with the solidarity of humankind and the limitations of the world's resources.

D. The establishment of urgently needed "interim" measures and long-term distributive systems which, recognizing the unique status of food as a commodity essential for survival, assure to every human being access to food as a matter of right.

With such goals in mind, we turn to the more specific responsibilities of Christians and Christian institutions.

VI. *Responsibilities of Christian and Christian Institutions*

A. We call upon all Christians and other persons of humanitarian concern to join in a renewed commitment to the task of eliminating hunger from the earth. To this end we call for:

1. Re-examination and simplification of personal and family lifestyles with special attention to ways of reducing consumption and the waste of food and other limited resources.

2. Sensitivity to the existence of hunger in our own immediate communities and participation in efforts to correct the conditions which perpetuate that hunger.

3. Increased sharing of our resources with the hungry world through support of church-related and other agencies dedicated to emergency feeding, to agricultural and human development, for example, UMCOR, Advance Specials for National and World Hunger, and to the transformation of unjust systems.

4. Joining with concerned persons in local community,

373

area, and national covenant fellowships dedicated to increasing awareness and sensitivity about the problem of hunger; mutual commitments to lifestyle simplification; relevant action in specific situations of hunger locally and around the world; the participation in the political processes necessary to influence public policy in directions indicated in later sections of this statement.

5. Developing networks to influence public policy and engage in advocacy for direct food aid and more just social and economic systems which would lift persons from poverty, for example, in the United States, Bread For the World, IMPACT and Interfaith Action for Economic Justice.

B. In addition, we call upon United Methodist churches, boards and agencies to re-examine their respective institutional lifestyles. Included in such review should be church policies and practices in the following crucial areas:

1. *The widespread ownership by churches and church institutions of potentially arable land.* Could much of this land be utilized for food production, for agricultural demonstration purposes, or made available to the landless poor for farming?

2. *The church's use of its own economic power.* Substantial portions of church-owned investments are in food-related industries and in transnational corporations dealing in food and/or food production supplies and equipment. Have the holders of these church investments been sufficiently inquisitive and critical about the policies and practices of such companies in the use of corporate funds and power?

3. *The style of church response to hunger appeals.* With all respect for the compssionate response by the churches to emergency food needs, are the churches responding adequately to the longer-run issues of agricultural development, population stabilization, institutional reform, economic justice, human empowerment, and public food policy?

VII. *Recommended Public Policies*

In economic terms, food is a commodity, but it is a unique commodity. Food is the basic necessity of human existence.

One of the greatest needs of our time is the development by the world's sovereign states of a mutually-shared world food policy.

The United States, as a leading agricultural producer and trader in farm commodities, has a crucial role to play in the implementation of a sound and effective world food policy design. If the United States is responsibly to perform that vital international role, it will require a much more coherent and humane national food policy.

We call upon the governments of all nations and especially the United States Congress and Administration more promptly and vigorously to develop, adopt and implement national food policies which will include among their major components the following objectives:

A. *For the Transformation of Institutions*
1. *The goal of eliminating hunger.* The United States government should follow through on the major recommendation of the Presidential Commission on World Hunger (1980) and make the elimination of world hunger the primary focus of its relationships with the developing world. Because the United States has a special capacity it has a special responsibility to take the initiative in the campaign against hunger and malnutrition.

2. *Increased aid for social and economic development.* The developed nations should increase their response to the requests of developing countries for technical assistance and other forms of aid appropriate to their social and economic development needs. Aid is not only a small fraction of the gross national product of the developed countries, it is a declining fraction: from 0.52 percent in 1960 to 0.37 percent in 1980. The United Nations suggested a goal of 0.7 percent of GNP from the donor nations; the United States for example, responded with 0.27 percent, a decrease of 15 percent over the previous decade. This development assistance should be allocated increasingly through international and voluntary agencies and coordinated with the efforts of international institutions. Governments of developing nations should examine their coun-

375

tries' role in assuring a just production and distribution of food among the world's hungry.

3. *Justice for small farmers, tenants, and farm laborers.* Studies conducted in the 1970s indicate that the small farmer is more productive than the large farmer and makes more efficient use of resources, especially labor. This encouraged the World Bank to develop a new strategy for rural development, the central element being increased production by millions of small farmers.

Although the reform of oppressive systems of landholding, tenancy, and farm labor is difficult, the United States should encourage in every legitimate way the transformation of agrarian structures in the interest of justice for the small farmers, tenants, and farm labor.

4. *Family planning and population stabilization.* The developed nations should contribute to the stabilization of the world's population through development programs which reach the poorest and raise their standards of living. They should also support the efforts of developing countries and international agencies in their programs of family planning and population stabilization. To be effective, these programs must include more than direct techniques and incentives for limiting births. More importantly, they must provide programs to improve job opportunity and income security; reduce infant mortality; upgrade maternal and child health; advance basic education, especially for women; elevate the status of women; and improve the quality of life for the poor and the oppressed.

5. *Liberalization of international trade.* The United States should take the initiative in support of international efforts to create price-stabilizing commodity agreements. While trade is necessary, developing nations should produce primarily for domestic needs. Especially is this true for food. Expanding world trade and minimizing protectionism would increase growth, development, and employment in the total world economy. Developing countries could well examine the possibility of creating producers' associations and common procurement relationships.

6. *Arms limitation.* In those years which almost match the 1985-88 quadrennium of The United Methodist Church, the United States government is projecting a military budget of $1.5 trillion. In total, the world military budget is $600 billion per year. Thirty-two nations spend more for military purposes than for education and health services combined. If these trend lines continue, by the year 2000 national governments will have spent $15 trillion on military budgets. In the last decade, international contributions for aid and development in the lower income countries declined as a percent of gross national product. Morality demands an end to this frantic spending. We call on all governments, especially the United States and the Union of Soviet Socialist Republics, to reduce their military expenditures, curtail their sales of arms, and press vigorously for international treaties for arms control and reduction. Vast funds could thus be released to eradicate hunger and malnutrition through social and economic development wherever needed.

7. *Development of international germplasm repositories.* Aside from nuclear war, there is probably no more serious environmental threat than the continued decay of the genetic variability of crops. Once the process has passed a certain point, humanity will have permanently lost the coevolutionary race with crop pests and diseases and will no longer be able to adapt crops to climate change. Plant species are becoming extinct at the average rate of one per day, and may well reach an average of one per hour by the year 2000. Worldwide plant expeditions to document the remaining plant species are needed. Once located, the preservation of plants in their indigenous areas, primarily tropical regions to developing nations, is essential to the sustainability of the food producing capability of the planet earth.

8. *Multinational corporations.* Three major study commissions have found that effective national laws and international codes in such areas as technology sharing, restrictive business practices, tax policy, and labor standards are

needed to provide a framework in which multinational corporations could contribute better to development. Technical assistance should be provided to the poorest countries to improve their bargaining capacity with multinational corporations. The developed nations should support United Nations efforts to prescribe standards for MNC investments.

B. For the Increase of Food Production

1. *Self-reliant agriculture.* There will be a growing demand for food before populations stabilize. Also, it is predictable that emergency food supplies will be needed for the victims of drought, flood, disease, pestilence, earthquakes, and the variation in food production due to changes in weather patterns. Emergencies aside, most countries have the potential for meeting their full food needs. Many experts believe that an annual increase in food production of 3.5 to 4.0 percent is possible. This could be done by expanding and improving land resources, increasing yields through irrigation, use of fertilizers, and improved seeds, the use of non-conventional energy sources, and research. Studies indicate that in many instances yields could be tripled. The findings are that a sustainable source of food supply can best be developed locally and self-reliance in agriculture should be the goal of aid. The cost would be about 7 percent of what is being spent annually on world armaments. The result would be a giant step toward world security and the banishment of malnutrition from the earth.

Until then, there will be a continued need for the food rich countries to support the international agencies (government and voluntary) for distributing food to those hungry persons who cannot meet their food needs in world markets. Food should not be used by any nation as a bargaining tool for political purposes.

2. *Increased production and better use of fertilizer.* The early 1980s marked the first decline in world fertilizer use since World War II. There was a 15 percent drop in Latin America. The average use of fertilizer in kilograms per hectare of land in Africa is 5 kilograms; in the United States it is 80 kilograms; in Japan it is 400 kilograms. One-half of

378

the fertilizer used in the developing countries is on non-food crops. Since fertilizer is probably the most important physical input for raising yields, international programs for encouraging and underwriting its use should be developed. Natural fertilizers are an alternative. Over 103 million tons of organic waste are produced each year in the developing countries. The nutrient content is eight times all of the inorganic fertilizer currently being used. Such non-conventional sources of nutrients could make a major contribution to increased food supplies.

3. *Expansion of agricultural research.* Scientific research and technology appropriate to conditions in the developing countries are essential to the expansion of their food production. About 98 percent of world expenditures on research and development occurs in the rich nations. This raises the question of the proper role of governments, voluntary organizations, and multinational corporations in the transfer of knowledge and technology. To the maximum extent possible, this form of assistance should be deploycd through international institutions and those of developing countries. There is a need for research to be done on-site in the developing countries. Research is needed on such basic things as use of organic wastes as fertilizer, intercropping, improvement of acid soils, development of plants requiring less water and fertilizers, development of nitrogen fixing capability in non-legumaneous plants, irrigation, efficient water use, and others. The United Nations has found that the investment return on such ressearch over a 10-year period may be as high as 40 to 60 percent per year. More support for plant breeding at public institutions is needed in order to maintain public control of plant improvement.

4. *Irrigation.* Expanded irrigation has great potential for increasing crop yields. Irrigated lands represent only about 14 percent of land under cultivation worldwide, yet they produce (in value) almost as much food as non-irrigated land. The United Nations is emphasizing the improvement of existing systems. Expansion through the use of tubewells is financially feasible in some countries. This is an area

where voluntary agencies could concentrate efforts and receive a rapid return of efforts to develop innovative small-scale uses of wind, solar, and bio-gas for irrigation.

5. *Protection of the environment.* Attempts to solve the interrelated problems of food supply, population growth, and poverty raise the question of the further degradation of the environment. The key factor in the prevention of further degradation is the pattern of development. If the developing countries follow the pattern introduced by the rich nations, a greater maldevelopment will follow. This is not necessary. An adequate standard of living can be achieved in the less developed countries through an egalitarian strategy which stresses a broader distribution of the land, labor intensive agriculture on the best lands, and the introduction of appropriate technologies. Such growth would lead to a greater care of the land, less pressure on marginal land where desertification occurs, employment opportunities and a stabilization of the population. All governments and voluntary agencies should encourage programs which keep food production practices in harmony with ecosystems. Funding for agricultural conservation practices, technical assistance, and plant gene banks should be expanded.

C. For Changing Patterns of Consumption by the Affluent.

Malnutrition exists in the rich countries alongside the diseases associated with overeating. In the United States, for example, long food lines at the voluntary agencies testified to the increase in domestic hunger during the early 1980s. Public policy changes resulted in removing three million children from food programs. The general welfare calls for public programs which ensure an adequate diet for all citizens, especially the young and the elderly. A greater control of waste and a more careful use of food resources by the affluent would generate savings that could be reflected in public policies of food aid. In addition, the general health of the nation would improve along with decreased medical costs.

D. For Meeting Immediate Needs.

The difference in food production and consumption in the developing countries is made up by trade and aid. By

1990, the developing countries will need to import over 100 million tons of grain annually. Some of this will be in the form of aid. Efforts have been strengthened by the work of the United Nations in developing an early warning system for identifying food emergencies. Also, the World Food Convention makes a major contribution toward these efforts. What is needed is a system of international grain reserves which will even out the uncertainty associated with variations in crop year yields. Attention should be given to assisting less developed countries in establishing their own reserves. Food aid allocation should be based on need and with regard to political or ideological considerations through the planned channels of international agencies such as the World Food Program.

VIII. *Conclusion*

We call upon all nations, but particularly the developed nations, to examine those values, attitudes, and institutions which are the basic causes of poverty and underdevelopment, the primary sources of world and domestic hunger.

We specifically call for The United Methodist Church to:

1. Engage in an educational effort that would provide information about the scale of world and domestic hunger and its causes.

2. Challenge colleges and universities with matching grants to engage in research designed to increase food production in developing countries.

3. Develop TV and radio spots for national and regional broadcasts that depict the joy of sharing in overcoming world hunger.

4. Send delegates to the World Food Assembly of 1984.

5. Lead in influencing public policy to establish international germ plasm repositories.

6. Engage in study and effort to integrate the church's missional programs into a coherent policy with respect to just, sustainable, and participatory development.

Finally, as delegates to the 1984 General Conference we resolve and covenant with each other to do the following:

a) On the second Sunday of each month calculate the cost to us of the main meal of the day and use an equivalent amount of cash to help feed the hungry.

b) Encourage all other United Methodists and all other Christians to make the same covenant.[25]

Immigration

I. *Biblical/Theological Reflection*

The Old Testament is the story of a people on the move, often as immigrants and refugees, frequently as seekers of a better homeland. It is the story of suffering and repression and God's liberating action in the midst of that history. The sojourn of Ruth and the fleeing of Jacob and his sons to avoid famine are just two of the many stories related by the witness of the Old Testament. The Hebrew people, pilgrims themselves, were also reminded by their leaders and prophets: "Do not mistreat or oppress a foreigner; you know how it feels to be a foreigner because you were foreigners in Egypt" (Exod. 23:9), and "You are strangers and sojourners with me" (Lev. 25:23).

The New Testament story begins by reaffirming this heritage of uprootedness as the infant Jesus and his family fled to Egypt to avoid political persecution. Jesus' life from that beginning was marked by uprootedness: "Foxes have holes, wild birds have nests, but the Son of man has nowhere to lay his head" (Matt. 8:20). His friends and disciples were neither the "pillars of society" nor the holders of power, but those who were themselves homeless and often poor, powerless, despised, and rejected. His encounters were often with people who were direct challenges to the political and social sterotypes of his own nation-state.

Into a world of ethnic diversity, racial fears and nationalistic insecurities, Jesus brought a grace and power

---

[25] *See* Social Principles, III-K, IV-D, IV-E, V-A; "A Just World Order in an Age of Interdependence," 1976.

to overcome those fears. His new way was: "Love one another. As I have loved you, so must you love one another" (John 12:34-35). Love is fulfilled in the love of the stranger and sojourner. As stated in Heb. 13:1-2: "Let . . . love continue. Do not neglect to show hospitality to strangers for thereby some have entertained angels unawares."

II. Historical Background

Nearly all the citizens of the United States have come from other parts of the world. Since the 17th century, millions of immigrants came to the colonies and the United States, often to seek greater freedom and broader opportunities in a new land. No other nation has welcomed so many immigrants from so many parts of the world for so many centuries. Nevertheless, the history of immigration policy in the United States has been heavily influenced by public views on economics and racism. Since 1798 with the passage of the Alien Act until the present, the U.S. immigration policy has at times encouraged the presence of immigrants who could provide the cheap hard labor to build canals and railroads, help with the harvesting of crops, and supply industry with needed workers. At other times U.S. immigration has sytematically excluded immigrants because of racial, ethnic, religious, or other prejudicial reasons. Examples are the Chinese Exclusion Act of 1882, Immigration Act of 1924, designed to deport Mexican laborers, the Quota Law of 1921, and the Refugee Act of 1980, which denied Haitian, Ethiopian, and Latin Americans the classifications of refugees. While changes in immigration law and policy are necessary, we as the church need to be mindful of our tradition as stated in our Social Principles: "The church must regard nations as accountable for unjust treatment of their citizens and others living within their borders."

Therefore, we call the leaders of the United States of America:

1. To continue to strive to make the United States a model of social justice in its domestic immigration policies as well as

in its foreign policy and diplomatic relations with other nations.

2. To interpret broadly the immigration laws of the United States a) by providing sanctuary for those fleeing because of well-founded fear of persecution due to their political affiliation, religious orientation and/or racial origin; and b) by adopting reasonable standards of proof of eligibility as refugees for those seeking asylum.

3. To withhold support to governments with a documented recent history of abuses and disregard for human rights.

4. To eliminate within the Immigration and Naturalization Service (INS) all abuses of civil and human rights including such practices as the violation of due process, denial of bail, or hasty deportation of the undocumented and overstayed.

5. To strengthen the service arm of the INS by increasing availability of personnel at the administrative levels in order to process applications and diminish the backlog of immigration applications.

6. To monitor all attempted reforms on immigration policy to ensure fair and adequate process in regards to judicial review, quota systems, and family reunification.

7. To reject the use of an identification card as a measure to control immigrants.

We urge the leaders of all nations:

1. To alleviate conditions and change internal politics that create a momentum for the migration of people over the world. (This means working for agrarian reform, social justice, and an adequate measure of economic security of all peoples.)

2. To create international economic policies that use capital, technology, labor, and land in a manner that gives priority to employment and production of basic human necessities. (At the same time such policies should not give inordinate power to transnational corporations and should avoid displacing people from their land.)

3. To recognize and respond to the causes and consequences of internally displaced people.

4. To seek an end to hostilities and terrorism through the just resolution of the socio-political conflicts which spawn such activities and give rise to large numbers of refugees.

5. To ensure protection of the basic human rights of immigrants (such as the right to an education, adequate health care, due process and redress of law, protection against social and economic exploitation, the right to a cultural and social indentity, and access to the social and economic life of nations) for both documented and undocumented, permanent or transient refugees or immigrants.

6. To welcome generous numbers of persons and families dislocated by natural disasters, war, political turmoil, repression, persecution, discrimination, or economic hardship.

7. To stop all military and financial aid and certification of governments which disregard human rights.

We speak to the whole church, and specifically call upon United Methodist churches and agencies to devote special attention and resources to the care of the legal, social, and other needs of overstayed and of undocumented persons. We instruct the General Board of Church and Society and the General Board of Global Ministries to:

1. Continue explorations of solutions to the problems of the overstayed and of undocumented persons.

2. Serve as advocate on behalf of The United Methodist Church in support of the immigration principles of family unity and documentation for other cases of a hardship nature.

3. Monitor cases of possible human rights violations in the area of immigration and give guidance to United Methodists in responding to such cases.

4. Provide technical and financial assitance to local churches in active ministry to overstayed and undocumented persons.

5. Continue the task of educating United Methodists on the subject of immigration.[26]

[26] See Social Principles, VI; "Assistance and Sanctuary for Central American Refugees, 1984."

Infant Formula/The Church and Economic Boycotts

A. *Infant Formula*

WHEREAS, the problem of infant malnutrition and mortality continues to be a critical aspect of global hunger, thereby frustrating God's loving purposes for human children, and we recommend that the whole focus on the infants of the world, a helpless group of God's children who still need continuing attention and protection, continue to be lifted up for the church's attention; and

WHEREAS, the 1980 General Conference authorized appointment of a task force to establish dialog with four major companies in the infant formula industry, seeking modifications of advertising, promotion, and distribution methods which may contribute to nutritional harm of infants in areas of chronic poverty, illiteracy, and inadequate hygenic conditions; and

WHEREAS, this United Methodist Infant Formula Task Force has commended the Code of Marketing of Breastmilk Substitutes, adopted by the World Health Organization in 1981, as the best expression of informed worldwide professional consensus on guidelines needed for the marketing of infant formula; and

WHEREAS, the General Council on Ministries, upon recommendation of the task force voted not to bring The United Methodist Church into the Nestle boycott and voted to recommend that all who are involved in that boycott should suspend their participation and renew it only if the company breaks faith with its commitments to the church and to the public; and

WHEREAS, the Nestle Company, in response to the boycott and in dialogue with the task force, has agreed to comply with the WHO Code in all countries outside Europe, whether or not compelled to do so by specific legislation, even though this has made that company more vulnerable to competition from other, less restrained, companies; and

WHEREAS, the Nestle Company has also established an

effective auditing body to assure itself and the public of its compliance with the WHO Code; and

WHEREAS, the changes in Nestle Company policy have now been recognized by the decison of the International Nestle Boycott Committee by the suspension of the boycott; and

WHEREAS, the Nestle Company and the International Nestle Boycott Committee have entered into a public agreement to suspend the boycott; and

WHEREAS, the three major American companies in this industry, Abbott-Ross Laboratories, Bristol-Myers, and American Home Products, have now also committed themselves to compliance with the WHO Code in Third World countries, and are engaged in further dialog with the task force and ecumenical groups on details of implementation and monitoring;

Therefore, Be It Resolved, that the 1984 General Conference:

1. Record its appreciation to the four named companies for their willingness to engage in serious dialog with representatives of The United Methodist Church and for their resultant commitments to the WHO Code.

2. Celebrate with the General Board of Church and Society, General Board of Global Ministries, Annual Conferences, Interfaith Center on Corporate Responsibility, International Baby Food Action Network, Infant Formula Action Coalition and other ecumenical agencies, the successful suspension of the Nestle boycott and urge others in the church to take similar action.

3. Authorize transferral of the responsibilities of the current (1980-84) task force to a new task group under the aegis of the General Board of Church and Society, with the understanding that this task force would:

a) Operate in the spirit of current task force.

b) Utilize the accumulated experience recounted in the task force report.

c) Complete the dialogs with the companies.

d) Assure an adequate system of monitoring of compliances with the WHO Code by all infant formula companies.

e) Relate the church effectively to the on-going review of the WHO Code and to other aspects of the problem of infant nutrition.

4. Find it inappropriate for any of the general agencies to resume participation in the boycott of the Nestle Company unless authorized to do so by the General Council on Ministries upon recommendation by the General Board of Church and Society, it being understood that this is a specific and unique recommendation pertaining only to the now-suspended boycott of the Nestle Company.

5. Urge the four named companies and the rest of the infant formula industry to respect the universal applicability of the WHO Code by adopting its provisions in all countries except where prohibited from doing so by law.

6. Recommend that all health care institutions, including those historically related to The United Methodist Church, comply with all aspects of the WHO Code, noting in particular those provisions discouraging promotion through gifts of samples and supplies of infant formula.

7. Authorize as a Prior Claim amount from the World Service Contingency Fund in 1985-1988 quadrennium up to $25,000 per year for the work of the task force.

B. *The Church and Economic Boycotts*

WHEREAS, economic boycott of the products of companies engaged in unethical and socially irresponsible practices has sometimes proved to be an effective means of influencing reconsideration and change of such practices; and

WHEREAS, economic boycott is an ethically and legally permissible means of seeking such reform under some circumstances; and

WHEREAS, church bodies as well as individual Christians have sometimes joined in sponsorship of economic boycott; and

WHEREAS, economic boycott should be a method used by the church only when it is prepared to accept the burden of justifying its moral necessity in light of clear criteria and when it can be controlled responsibly; and

WHEREAS, the church is in need of a clear review of the criteria justifying the use of boycott methods as well as other factors pertinent to consideration of economic boycott;

Therefore Be It Resolved, that the 1984 General Conference:

1. Urge all United Methodist and organizational units of the church, when considering participation in economic boycotts, to study the circumstances carefully in order to determine whether such coercive methods are truly necessary and whether it will be possible to undertake them responsibly and in harmony with the Christian faith.

2. Direct the General Board of Church and Society to undertake, during the 1985-1988 quadrennium, a comprehensive study of the church's use of the method of economic boycott in consultation with other church agencies, and drawing upon the experience and wisdom of the whole church. This study should:

a) Survey the history of the use of economic boycotts in this and other denominations.

b) Secure expert opinion on the legal responsibilities of boycotting organizations.

c) Explore the theological and ethical ramifications of the use of economic boycott.

d) Develop a list of criteria to indicate when economic boycotts might be warranted ethically, taking into account the criteria proposed by the 1980-84 Infant Formula Task Force's report to the 1984 General Conference and other existing formulations of criteria by general agencies and other church bodies.

3. Request the General Board of Church and Society to summarize the findings of this study in recommendations to be considered by the 1988 General Conference. This statement of findings should be made available to the church no later than October 1986, in order to facilitate its review by other members and agencies of the church, with opportunity for comment prior to the 1988 General Conference.

4. Invite all United Methodists and their local churches, annual conferences, and agencies, to contribute their

suggestions for this study and respond to its conclusions by communicating with the General Board of Church and Society.

Korea

In 1984, two centuries of Catholic mission and one century of Protestant mission in Korea will be celebrated. This history of this period is filled with the heroic martyrdoms of scores of Korean Christians faithful to their God in the face of persecution and injustice, and the admirable witness of hundreds of missionaries under conditions of hostility, suspicion, and cultural isolation. The blood of these martyrs and witnesses has seeded a church firm and strong in the faith and active with evangelical and prophetic fervor to witness in today's world.

Yet the suffering of the church in Korea has not ended. The global confrontation between the United States and the Soviet Union has divided the land, the people, and the churches of Korea. Peoples in the north have been without the freedom to worship openly since the founding of the Kim II Sung regime in 1948. In the south a succession of dictatorial regimes has limited and divided the church by an anti-communist ideology that perverts its integrity and destroys its autonomy. Today, a military-dominated political system continues to persecute those who minister to the poor, the silenced, the imprisoned and the tortured, just as it persecutes others who speak out for the restoration of democracy and respect for human dignity.

The Korean Methodist Church has spoken about its "deep concern that the unjust powers of tyranny in our land must go no further in trampling upon the dignity of human beings who have been created in the image of God."[27]

We support this conviction and prayerfully join in this struggle:

[27] Statement, Board of Missions, Executive Committee, the Korean Methodist Church, June 30, 1983.

1. We call on United Methodists and other Christians throughout the world to join in prayerful reflection upon the centenary of Protestant mission and bicentennial of Catholic mission in Korea, celebrating God's presence with the church and people in Korea, expressing gratitude for the growth of the church in numbers and faithfulness, and imploring God's abiding sustenance to the people of Korea in their struggle to realize the justice and freedom which is their due as the sons and daughters of their Creator.

2. Because the United States, as the primary nation involved in the formation of the Republic of Korea, has a unique responsibility for the flourishing of genuine representative government there, and has supported its governments with military and economic aid, we call on the U.S. Government to increase diplomatic efforts to restore democratic government to Korea.

3. We call on the governments of both the Republic of Korea and the Democratic People's Republic of Korea to restore institutions of representative government as a basis for dialog leading toward the ending of hostility and mutual fear and the eventual reunification of Korea.[28]

Ministry to Runaway Children

The United Methodist Church calls its members to follow Jesus Christ in his mission to bring all persons into a community of love. The Social Principles upholds the potential of the community for nurturing human beings into the fullness of their humanity through its basic unit, the family. We as United Methodists acknowledge children as beings to whom adults and society in general have obligations; the rights to food, shelter, clothing, health care, and emotional well-being. We also recognize youth and young adults as those who frequently find full participation in society difficult.

The United Methodist Church, having accepted its com-

---

[28] *See* Social Principles, VI-A; "Human Rights in Korea," 1980.

mission to manifest the life of the gospel in the world within the context of hope and expectation, deplores the fact that in this nation 1,000,000 children are reported missing every year, that countless thousands are forced out or "thrownaway," and that homicide is one of the five leading causes of death among children between the ages of one and seventeen. We recognize the prevalence of physical, sexual or emotional abuse as the underlying cause for almost half of the behaviors classified as running away.

Running away is not unique to any social class. The average age for runaways is dropping and the majority are girls. We are alarmed that a whole new category of children known as street children are living degrading and dangerous lives in the streets of our towns and cities.

We believe these runaways should neither be a police problem nor processed through the legal system where they are usually incarcerated rather than protected and adjudicated rather than enlightened. Most such youths require temporary shelter and supervision instead of secure detention.

We commend those congregations and annual conferences already engaged in outreach to runaway youth, providing food, shelter, and protection from personal exploitation as well as referral to sources of help. We feel that the runaway crisis offers a further opportunity to help families when they want and are receptive to such help. Therefore, we support immediate crisis intervention and counseling for youth and their families with the primary objective of returning the youth to his/her home. When there is no possibility of it becoming a healthy environment, we support the development of alternate living arrangements that provide a nurturing environment.

We further urge that United Methodist agencies join in efforts to develop innovative ministries of support and protection for street children who would not usually come to a runaway shelter.

We encourage local church efforts toward prevention by programming to strengthen and support families within their congregations. We call Christians everywhere into service wherever God and a loving heart may call them; into the schools where poor school performance is often the precipitating crisis to running; into their own neighborhoods and community where there are countless opportunities to help troubled youth; into supporting programs in the community which deal compassionately with abusing parents.

"And the King will answer them, 'Truly, I say to you, as you did it to one of the least of my brethren, you did it to me'" (Matt. 25:40).[29]

[29] See Social Principles, III-C.

Mutual Recognition of Members

Introduction

The General Conferences of 1976 and 1980 adopted affirmations of the basic Consultation on Church Union principle of mutual recognition of memberships based on baptism. All other member churches have done the same. Now as the Consultation is moving forward on further implications of theological consensus, mutual recognition, convenanting together and eventual reconciliation, The United Methodist Church wishes to join with other churches in moving from affirmation to action.

The plenary of the Consultation on Church Union in November, 1984 will focus on the new theological statement of consensus, the implications of a developing covenant toward unity (that is expected to be before the General Conference of 1988) and liturgical expressions of both. These emphases are related to the new World Council of Churches statement on *Baptism, Eucharist and Ministry* currently being reviewed and responded to by United Methodists.

We have a stake in the faithful discipleship of other communions. Other churches have a stake in the faithful discipleship of The United Methodist Church. For it is the

Church of Jesus Christ that is called to share in mission and ministry for the world. God's covenant is with the whole People of God. A concurrent expression of United Methodist seriousness in the cause of Christian unity is needed. Clear visible evidence that we understand ourselves to be part of the Body of Christ is needed.

Be It Resolved, that participation with voice in United Methodist governing bodies and agencies and the joining in our liturgical celebrations by representatives from other communions are both symbols of the oneness of the Church of which we are a part and signs to others of our ecumenical seriousness.

To mainfest our integrity as part of the Church of Jesus Christ, several items of legislation are proposed to the General Conference, including the permissive inclusion (outside of quota requirements) of representatives from other communions in General Conference, Annual Conferences, General and Conference Boards and other agencies. This resolution supplements that legislation with specific recommendations which relate to annual conferences and local churches, namely:

1. That United Methodist Annual Conferences be empowered, encouraged, and enabled to invite official representatives from other denominations, especially from member churches of the Consultation on Church Union, to their sessions and committees with voice and that United Methodist judicatory leaders nominate representatives to the official church bodies of other denominations where invited to do so.

2. That representatives of other denominations be invited to participate in the laying on of hands in annual conference ordination ceremonies, symbolizing the catholicity of our ministry.

3. That Annual Conference Commissions on Christian Unity and Interreligious Concerns and Conference Councils on Ministry be alert to and consider carefully the development by the Consultation on Church Union of 1984 of: a) the principles and the text of an "Act of Covenanting"; b) development by them of enabling acts related to pos-

sible representation in "Councils of Oversight" that may be formed at middle judicatory levels of the COCU member churches; and c) encourage responsiveness to liturgical formulations developed by COCO which will be based on theological consensus and the covenanting processes.

4. That United Methodist local churches be encouraged to invite representatives from other denominations to participate in celebrations such as World Communion Sunday, baptism, and confirmation, and in special commemorative occasions in the congregation's life.

5. That local churches be urged to take initiatives in cooperation with congregations of other denominations in issues of racial and social justice, in mission and evangelism, and in occasions of special study and celebration (such as Advent, Lent, Easter, and Pentecost); and that special efforts be made to share persons with special skills, talents and imagination between denominations in order to strengthen the whole body of Christ in its nature and witness.

6. That local churches and Annual Conferences, aided by the General Commission on Christian Unity and Interreligious Concerns, study the COCU publication of a seven-chapter consensus on *In Quest of a Church of Christ Uniting* and respond to the GCCUIC.

Nuclear-Free Pacific

The United Methodist Church affirms its commitment to a Nuclear-Free Pacific. As Christian people committed to stewardship, justice and peacemaking, we oppose and condemn the use of the Pacific for tests, storage, and transportation of nuclear weapons and weapons delivery systems and the disposal of radioactive wastes. We further affirm the right of all indigenous people to control their health and well-being.[30]

[30] *See* Social Principles, I, VI-C; "Environmental Stewardship," 1984.

Organ and Tissue Donation

WHEREAS, selfless consideration for the health and welfare others is at the heart of the Christian ethic; and

WHEREAS, organ and tissue donation is a life-giving act, since transplantation of organs and tissues is scientifically proven to save the lives of persons with terminal diseases and improve the quality of life for the blind, the deaf and others with life-threatening diseases; and

WHEREAS, organ donation may be perceived as a positive outcome of a seemingly senseless death and is thereby comforting to the family of the deceased and is conducted with respect, and with the highest consideration for maintaining the dignity of the decreased and his/her family; and

WHEREAS, moral leaders the world over recognize organ and tissue donation as an expression of humanitarian ideals in giving life to another; and

WHEREAS, thousands of persons who could benefit from organ and tissue donation continue to suffer and die due to lack of consent for donation, due primarily to poor awareness and lack of an official direction from the church;

Be It Resolved, that The United Methodist Church recognizes the life-giving benefits of organ and tissue donation, and thereby encourages all Christians to become organ and tissue donors by signing and carrying cards or driver's licenses, attesting to their commitment of such organs upon their death, to those in need, as a part of their ministry to others in the name of Christ, who gave his life that we might have life in its fullness.

Papers of Bishop James Cannon Jr.

Resolved, that The United Methodist Publishing House release from its vault the papers, documents, and materials related to the investigation of Bishop James Cannon Jr. for permanent deposit with and administration by the General Commission on Archives and History.

Permanency of the Select Committee on Indian Affairs

WHEREAS, the Western Jurisdiction Native American Council of The United Methodist Church supports the permanency of the Select Committee on Indian Affairs—Senate Resolution 127—as part of the United States Senate structure; and

WHEREAS, the council (WJNAC) is made up of Native Americans who are active members of local Native American United Methodist Churches within the Western Jurisdiction, this resolution affirms and is in compliance with our goal to strengthen leadership, educate and see to the needs of our Indian communities; and

WHEREAS, this council (WJNAC) realizes the devastating impact on Native American Indian legislation if Senate committee jurisdiction is transferred or divided among the Senate Energy, Senate Labor and Human Resource Committee or Sub-committee; and

WHEREAS, immediate action from the Western Jurisdiction Native American Council and the regional and national United Methodist Church is necessary to convey, as constituents, to the U.S. government via local officials, state governments, U.S. House of Representatives, and the U.S. Senate the importance that the Senate Select Committee remain intact and permanent;

Therefore Be It Resolved, that the General Conference does hereby support the passage or enactment of S.R. 127.

Further, we direct the secretary of the General Conference to immediately communicate this position to the members of the Senate and to the chair of the Senate Select Committee on Indian Affairs;

Finally, we direct that the Board of Church and Society will follow up this resolution with continuing advocacy.[31]

[31] *See,* "The United Methodist Church and America's Native Peoples," 1980.

The Philippines

President Ferdinand Marcos declared martial law in the Philippines in September 1972. Democratic processes were dismantled. Opposition parties, free elections, Congress and the constitutional rights of citizens such as freedom of speech, press, and assembly were abolished. More than 60,000 persons have been unjustly arrested and detained. Most were held without charges and denied due process of law. Many were tortured or maltreated.

The Filipino people are being victimized by unjust and oppressive economic structures that benefit only a few and keep the vast majority of the people impoverished. They are ruled by a repressive political regime that has robbed them of their rights and human dignity. Although martial law was abolished in 1981, its most oppressive decrees were incorporated into constitutional law in 1976. Democratic processes to change those laws do not exist.

The Marcos government is supported by the U.S. government. Hundreds of millions of dollars worth of guns, tanks and bombs are paid by the United States in exchange for rental of military bases at Clark and Subic in Luzon. Under the guise of maintaining law and order, the Marcos government utilizes U.S. supplied weapons to intimidate and silence dissent, and to maim and kill others who oppose or resist it.

Workers in the Philippines are exploited and their rights severely violated while foreign transnational corporations amass wealth through this exploitation. Land is taken away from farmers for the benefit of transnational plantation corporations. Through support for the Marcos regime, the U.S. government subordinates the human rights of over 50 million Filipinos to the economic interests of a corporate few and to perceived U.S. strategic interests.

Many of our brothers and sisters in Philippines' churches have responded to the evangelical challenge to work for peace through justice in solidarity with the poor and the oppressed. These persons have been the targets of harassments, arbitrary arrests, illegal detention, false charges, torture, disappearances, and political killings.

We deplore the tragic political murder of former Philippine Senator Benigno Aquino within minutes after his return to the Philippines. The circumstances of the murder raise serious questions about the credibility of the Marcos government. Senator Aquino's death and others once again raise our awareness of the many human rights violations against those in the Philippines who are struggling for a more genuinely democratic and just society.

Our Christian faith calls us to affirm the dignity and worth of every human being. In our understanding of the above we:

1. Express our continuing support and solidarity with our Philippine brothers and sisters who are struggling for self-determination and a just and democratic society.

2. Call on the U.S. government, a. To uphold its historic concern for the right of self-determination of the Filipino people, b. To desist from all forms of military intervention, c. To develop diplomatic, business and banking policies that would discourage economic exploitation, and d. To oppose the dictatorial policies of the present Philippine government.[32]

Prevention and Reduction of Juevenile Delinquency

WHEREAS, the abhorrent ills of our society (child abuse and neglect, teenage pregnancy, suicide, veneral diseases, drug and alcohol abuse) that relentlessly assail children have a profound effect on the quality of their lives, and without proper intervention, are often manifested in destructive behavior within the school setting;

WHEREAS, these debilitating effects often become cyclical, appearing in generations after generations, and result in the loss to society of fully functioning and competent adults;

WHEREAS, our school systems emphasize remediation at the secondary level to prevent delinquency;

[32] *See*, Social Principles, V-A, VI-A.

Be It Resolved, that all United Methodists work through the appropriate structures and channels to provide guidance counseling at the elementary level of all schools in prevention of delinquency.

Be It Further Resolved, that United Methodist pastors are encouraged to develop cooperative relationships with persons doing such counseling.

Process for 1988 Statement on Agricultural Issues

WHEREAS, agriculture is a basic industry of our society;

WHEREAS, agriculture in the United States is diverse;

WHEREAS, The United Methodist Church is composed of a constituency that represents all the segments of U.S. agriculture;

Therefore, Be It Resolved, that any future statement by The United Methodist Church concerning U.S. agricultural issues for the 1988 General Conference use various existing networks to dialog with persons at the grass-roots level.

Be It Also Resolved, that a writing team for the 1988 position concerning The United Methodist Church and U.S. agricultural issues involve a staff person from the General Board of Church and Society, Office of Town and Country Ministries, General Board of Global Ministries, an active United Methodist agriculture producer from each jurisdiction; and a board member from both the General Board of Global Ministries and the General Board of Church and Society.

Be It Further Resolved, that the process begin early enough that the first draft of the resolution on agricultural issues be distributed to various persons and groups at the grass-roots level for their reaction.

And Be It Finally Resolved, that this statement be referred to the General Board of Global Ministries and the General Board of Church and Society for implementation.

Reaffirm Opposition to Capital Punishment

WHEREAS, there is a rising tide in the United States of America to reactivate capital punishment in all states; and

WHEREAS, in the last year there have been several executions of human beings by the penal system as punishment for crimes committed; and

WHEREAS, we are convinced that the rising crime rate is largely an outgrowth of unstable social conditions which stem from an increasingly urbanized and mobile population; from long periods of economic recessions; from a history of unequal opportunities for a large segment of the citizenry and from inadequate diagnosis of criminal behavior; and

WHEREAS, we believe the state cannot teach respect for human life by destroying human life; and

WHEREAS, the Holy Scriptures teach us that human life is both sacred and divine and that we bear the image of the incorruptible God; and

WHEREAS, Jesus Christ taught us love, forgiveness and reconciliation; and

WHEREAS, all Christians are under divine mandate to safeguard life and work for the salvation of all humankind;

Therefore Be It Resolved, that The United Methodist Church reaffirm strongly its position against capital punishment; and

Be It Further Resolved, that the General Board of Church and Society prepare and disseminate materials and work with each annual conference in developing a plan of action to impact capital punishment legislation in their state; and

Be It Finally Resolved, that the 1984 General Conference issue a national press statement which clearly states the church's opposition to capital punishment and its commitment to work for its abolition.[33]

Reaffirming Membership in the World Council of Churches

WHEREAS, The Constitution of The United Methodist Church points out that dividedness in the Church of Jesus

---

[33] *See* Social Principles, V-F; "Capital Punishment," 1980.

Christ "is a hindrance to its mission" in the world and has committed us to ecumenical involvement, and

WHEREAS, The United Methodist Church is a member, its predecessor Methodist and Evangelical United Brethren churches having been charter members and strong supporters of the World Council of Churches, and

WHEREAS, the World Council of Churches has provided a world-wide forum for Christians of its member churches to provide mutual nurture and to join in Christian action on behalf of unity, mission and service, and

WHEREAS, relationships with brothers and sisters who affirm "the Lord Jesus Christ as God and Saviour according to the Scriptures" are stronger than economic, ideological, political and theological differences that sometimes separate us, and

WHEREAS, the World Council of Churches has led all the churches to study anew such theological issues as baptism, eucharist and ministry; has provided channels for humanitarian service and aid to refugees; has made significant contributions to theological education the world over; has developed mission and evangelism in critical areas; has led in the interchange between scientific technology and the church's faith and in other ways made clear that Christian unity is related to the oneness of the total human community:

Be It Resolved, that the 1984 General Conference of The United Methodist Church reaffirm our membership and participation in the World Council of Churches, in accordance with ¶ 2403 of the 1980 Book of Discipline.

Recognition of Cuba

The United Methodist Church is linked in Christ with the Methodist Church of Cuba. We share a common heritage and mission. We are mutually responsible for the proclamation of God's love and the nurturing of neighbor-love.

"God's world is one world." The Social Principles requires us to make the community of God a reality as we "pledge ourselves to seek the meaning of the gospel in all issues that divide people and threaten the growth of world community." Such a world cannot exist when nations refuse to give diplomatic recognition to one another.

For over 20 years the government of the United States has not maintained diplomatic relations with the government of Cuba and has instead pursued an economic embargo prohibiting any kinds of trade with Cuba. This policy has resulted in the loss of an important commerical market and trade partner for the United States, and in the heightening of tensions in the Caribbean. The objectives sought by the proponents of this policy were to force a change in Cuban foreign policy and to halt the growth and development of Soviet influence in that country.

It is now clear that the embargo policy has not succeeded with those objectives. If anything, its most evident result has been to force Cuba to an even closer political and military reliance on the Soviet Union.

WHEREAS, the Methodist Church in 1964 made an historical statement entitled the "Re-examination of Policy Toward Mainline China, Cuba and other Countries," which said: "The Christian gospel involves reconciliation by encounter and by communication regardless of political considerations. Therefore, we cannot accept the expression of hostility by any country, its policies, or its ideologies as excuses for the failure of Christians to press persistently, realistically, and creatively toward a growing understanding among the peoples of all countries";

WHEREAS, the government of the United States is the only major Western country pursuing a policy of non-relations with Cuba, while Canada, France, Great Britain, West Germany, Japan, Mexico, Argentina, Bolivia and almost all other countries of the western alliance maintain normal diplomatic and/or economic relations with Cuba; and

WHEREAS, the government of the United States has in recent years strengthened its commercial and diplomatic relations with other Communist countries such as the Soviet Union itself, China, Hungary, Poland, and Romania, independently of their foreign policy which differs and often collides with that of the United States; and

WHEREAS, the Reagan administration declared that the United States will not use food as a foreign policy instrument when it lifted the grain embargo imposed against the Soviet Union by the Carter administration in order to protest the Soviet intervention in the conflict in Afghanistan; and

WHEREAS, the lifting of the economic embargo against Cuba would help relieve tensions in the Caribbean while creating a new and important market for American industry and agriculture, especially at a time of high unemployment in this country; and

WHEREAS, the Ecumenical Council of Cuba of which the Methodist Church of Cuba is a member, the Cuban Conference of Roman Catholic Bishops, and several other international as well as U.S. religious bodies such as the United Church of Christ, the Presbyterian Church (USA), and the American Baptist Churches have passed resolutions in favor of lifting the embargo;

Therefore Be It Resolved, that The United Methodist Church, from its Christian and humanitarian perspective, hereby petitions the government of the United States to lift its economic embargo against Cuba and to seek negotiations with the Cuban government for the purpose of resuming normal diplomatic relations.

Religious Freedom

We, the people of The United Methodist Church, believe that religious freedom is of fundamental importance. Human beings must be able to do freely that for which they were created—to worship God.

Religious liberty includes the following freedoms: (1) the freedom to worship and assemble and to establish and maintain places for these purposes; (2) to establish and maintain charitable, humanitarian, and social outreach institutions; (3) to make, acquire, and use necessary articles and materials related to the rites or customs of a religion or belief; (4) to write, publish, and disseminate relevant publications; (5) to teach religious beliefs to one's children; (6) to promulgate religious beliefs to others in the community and the world at large; (7) to solicit and receive voluntary financial and other contributions from individuals and institutions; (8) to speak to and influence the other social institutions of society, as one part of a pluralistic system; (9) to train, appoint, elect, or designate leaders and staff for the organized expression of religious belief, free from government interference or direction; (10) to observe days of rest, to celebrate holidays and ceremonies in accordance with the precepts of one's religion; (11) to establish and maintain communication with individuals in communities in matters of religion and belief at the national and international levels.

Threats to Religious Freedom

Freedom of religion involves much more than the right to worship quietly within the walls of a church. Religious institutions have the right—even the obligation—to offer moral testimony on the great issues of state and society. Prohibiting such social involvement is one form of denying religious freedom.

Religious freedom is also denied when one form of religion is allowed and encouraged by the state while others are disallowed and repressed—sometimes violently.

Religious freedom is denied in totalitarian societies, where all forms of voluntary association—even for the purposes of private religious worship—are seen as a threat to the all-encompassing dominance of the state.

Religious freedom is denied when governments or political movements seek to transform religious institutions into instruments of political power and ideology by means of manipulation, infiltration, or hidden control. Such misuse of religion poisons the one vessel of conscience and spirit that often remains to the subjects of a police society. It violates history's traditional place of consolation and sanctuary. It turns the refuge of the oppressed into another of the torments of the oppressor.

Church Action to Expand Religious Freedom

The United Methodist Church places a high priority on the struggle to expand religious freedom in the world. Our actions must include prayer, public witness, acts of mercy and, inevitably, protests against governments and political movements. It is precisely because church members in totalitarian societies are denied the right of protest that Christians who enjoy freedom have an obligation to speak out on behalf of those who do not.

In carrying out this responsibility, United Methodist agencies shall follow several important guidelines, and shall advocate these guidelines in the ecumenical groups in which our church participates:

1. We will apply a single standard of human rights and religious freedom to all societies, irrespective of their political coloration.

2. We will advocate freedom of association, speech, and free and competitive elections, as the best guarantee that people will have a say in structuring and maintaining their own political, economic, and cultural institutions, including religious institutions.

3. We will reach out to those people who seek genuine democratic change and speak against those around the world who would substitute a new form of repression in the name of change which would deny religious liberty and human rights.

4. Although "silent diplomacy" has its uses, we, as Christians, will also provide open testimony to help protect persecuted believers by focusing public attention on the actions of their oppressors.

5. We consider it a special obligation to minister to those brave souls who refuse to succumb to the state's efforts to control and subjugate them. Our contacts will not be limited to government sanctioned international religious conferences and institutions, but expanded to include the broad community of believers.

6. We understand why church representatives from totalitarian countries are at times forced to advocate the policies of their governments. But we will be forthright in criticizing the governments that impose such demands on our sisters and brothers. Such criticism will no doubt displease despotic rulers. But it will give oppressed religious leaders in such societies a useful tool for expanding the autonomy and interdependence of their organization.[34]

Resurgence of the Ku Klux Klan

WHEREAS,

● The resurgence of the Ku Klux Klan in recent months has been widely reported in the media;

● In many instances the impression has been conveyed that the burning of crosses and destruction of homes of Black residents may be simply an act of vandalism carried out by juveniles;

● The cross burnings and destruction of homes and desecration of synagogues and churches is an elaborate and premeditated act which cannot be dismissed as only the spontaneous expression of juvenile restlessness;

● The involvement of minors in such racist rituals means that tomorrow's generation of Whites is embracing as a virtue the racism of its elders;

Therefore, Be It Resolved, that the General Conference of The United Methodist Church expresses its sympathy to the victims of recent outbreaks of racial and religious violence and calls upon all United Methodists to:

1. Oppose the involvement of minors in paramilitary training sponsored by the KKK and other racist groups.

2. Embark on a serious program of education in the church and elsewhere on the current resurgence of the Ku Klux Klan and its challenge to the witness of the gospel and the dignity of all persons.

3. Continue to express their abhorrence at the claim

[34]*See* Social Principles, V-A; "Democracy and Religious Freedom," 1980.

of the Ku Klux Klan that its values and practices are compatible with Christian teaching and the faith and practice of The United Methodist Church.

4. Formulate and maintain caring systems to support and maintain parishes, churches and families harrassed by members and friends of the Ku Klux Klan.

5. Support and work in coalition with groups that are already working on this issue.

6. Call upon federal, state, and local governments to use resources to implement positive educational programs about the dangers and costs of racism in a democratic society.

7. Call upon federal, state, and local governments to exercise the utmost vigilance and bring to justice perpetrators of racial and religious violence and intimidation.

8. Express their minds and hearts in this coming electoral season and urge that candidates for government positions name the struggles against racism and injustice as a top priority.

9. Support the Greensboro Civil Rights Suit as an important and valid means of ascertaining the truth about the November 3, 1979, killings of five antiKlan demonstrators in Greensboro, N.C.

10. Support a congressional hearing on racist violence in those states where statistics reveal an increase in the activity of the KKK and such other groups, and on allegations of government involvement or negligence exacerbating such violence.[35]

Southern Africa

The Social Principles of The United Methodist Church states: "We hold governments responsible for the rights of the people to the freedoms of speech, religion, assembly, and communications media; to the rights to privacy; and to

[35] *See* Social Principles, III-A; "Global Racism," 1984; "The United Methodist Church and Race," 1976.

the guarantee of the rights to adequate food, clothing, shelter, education, and health care" (1984 Book of Discipline, ¶ 74-A).

While rejecting the use of violence, it states: "But governments, no less than individuals, are subject to the judgment of God. Therefore, we recognize the right of individuals to dissent when acting under the constraint of conscience and after exhausting all legal recourse, to disobey laws deemed to be unjust" (¶ 74-E).

We affirm the intent of past General Conference resolutions on Southern Africa (1976), South Africa (1980), and A Charter for Racial Justice Policies in an Interdependent Global Community (1980).

We affirm our commitment to the just struggle of the African people to establish societies in which all can enjoy basic human rights and fundamental freedoms.

We seek biblical and theological guidance in our concern regarding political and economic systems in our world. We seek to be true witnesses of Jesus Christ.

The *apartheid* system as practiced in Namibia and South Africa is legalized racism in its cruelest form. Inherent in the system is the negation of political, economic, social, and cultural rights for the majority Black population. (A current attempt is underway to grant partial rights to "Coloreds" and "Indians.") The inalienable rights of citizenship are based on race, color, and ethnic classifications.

The South African government has tried to further implement a policy of "separate development." Thirteen percent of the land has been allocated to the African majority. This land has been divided into 10 isolated and fragmented "bantustans" or "homelands." Four of these have been declared "independent" and their new citizens have been stripped of their South African citizenship. Eventually, all Black South Africans are to be citizens of these psuedo-independent countries which are recognized by no government except South Africa. Eventually, no Black South African is to have South African citizenship.

In pursuit of racist political, economic, and security goals for the White minority, the government of South Africa has continued on a path of harassment, oppression, killings, imprisonment without trial, detention and bannings. Though P. W. Botha, Prime Minister of South Africa, has said to White South Africa, "adapt or die," he and his government seem determined to follow a suicidal course rather than to make substantive changes in their oppressive system. Bishop Desmond Tutu, General Secretary of the South African Council of Churches (SACC), said in September 1982: "Just as the Nazis had final plans for the Jews in Germany, the White South Africans have their final plans for Blacks in South Africa."

In 1982 the General Council of the World Alliance of Reformed Churches stated that: "*Apartheid* is sin and . . . the moral and theological justification of it is a travesty of the gospel and, in its persistent disobedience to the Word of God, a theological heresy."

While we are heartened by improved relations between South Africa and Mozambique, we continue to be concerned with the international impact of the *apartheid* system. We are painfully aware of the past and present South African policy of destabilization in the neighboring countries of Angola, Botswana, Lesotho, Mozambique, the Seychelles, Swaziland, Zambia and Zimbabwe. We consider this policy a serious threat to world peace, especially since there are growing data which suggest that South Africa has nuclear capability.

Our concern is increased by the growing economic and strategic alliance between South African and other nuclear powers. These arrangements lend support not only to South Africa's nuclear potential, but also to its policies of *apartheid*.

We recommend that United Methodists and United Methodist agencies and institutions:

1. Reject as heresy any attempts to justify *apartheid* as an expression of biblical tradition.

2. Support the Namibian and South African persons, churches, movements and institutions which take courageous stands against *apartheid*.

3. Support the contributions of the Council of Churches

in Namibia (CCN) and the South African Council of Churches (SACC) for the prophetic role they play in Southern Africa and the world.

4. Support the courageous position of the Christian churches in South Africa in denouncing the continued forced removal and relocation of the Africans in South Africa. We further urge wide dissemination of available documentation from the South African Council of Churches and the Southern African Catholic Bishops' Conference throughout the denomination.

5. Pray for and support Namibian and South African political prisoners and their families, and all who are oppressed by the *apartheid* regime.

6. Support the creative role of trade unions in the struggle of South Africans for their liberation, and support the right of Namibian and South African workers to organize into unions of their own choosing, and to bargain collectively over wages, hours and conditions of employment free from government harassment.

7. Encourage study and financial support for the Special Fund of the World Council of Churches' (WCC) Program to Combat Racism.

We encourage United Methodist and United Methodist agencies and institutions to join with others in their communities to:

1. Close accounts with and withdraw funds from banks and divest from corporations doing business in South Africa.

2. Refrain from the purchase, sale and/or promotion of the "Krugerrand" coin.

3. Support efforts to boycott sporting events and cultural personalities which serve to affirm *apartheid*.

We urge United Methodists and United Methodist agencies and institutions to pressure their governments to support United Nations sanctions against South Africa and end any collaboration with South Africa by:

1. Preventing further expansion of South African consulates, airways and exploitative industries such as de Beers Consolidated Mines, Ltd. (a diamond concern).

2. Opposing expanded participation of corporations in the South African economy, especially such involvement which enables more efficient police oppression (through computerization) or which promotes the "homelands" policy.

3. Opposing South Africa's policy of destabilization of governments in neighboring countries.

4. Rejecting the withdrawal of Cuban troops from Angola as a condition for the independence of Namibia.

We further urge United Methodists and United Methodist agencies and institutions to pressure their governments to:

1. Support United Nations supervised elections in Namibia at the earliest possible date.

2. Support the role of the South West African Peoples' Organization (SWAPO) in its efforts to prepare its people for the national independence of Namibia.

3. Oppose covert and overt support to insurgent groups in Angola as blatant intervention in its sovereignty.

4. Encourage the United States and the Peoples' Republic of Angola to engage in diplomatic discussions which will lead to mutual recognition.[36]

Statement on Aging for the United States of America

I. *Preamble*

The elderly in the United States of America occupy a new frontier in a rapidly changing industrial society. A frontier has two aspects: its hazards, uncharted ways, unknowns, anxieties; its promises, hopes, visions, and fulfillments. A frontier becomes a promised land when guides chart the way, pioneers settle and builders develop the land. But this new frontier is yet to be charted for the aged. Existing institutions have not been able to adapt fast enough nor

---

[36] *See* Social Principles, VI-D; "A Charter for Racial Justice Policies in an Interdependent Global Community, 1980."

have new institutions been created to meet the new conditions. Some research, however, has recently begun to topple some myths and stereotypes about the aging process and older persons.

This statement is for study, discussion, and implementation and action by The United Methodist Church in the United States. It contains brief sections on the current situation of the older population, on a theological response and on calls to the society and to the church. There has, however, been no attempt to set priorities for ministries in this new frontier described within this statement; it is hoped that appropriate church agencies and units will set their own priorities.

II. *The Situation*

During the past 100 years, life expectancy in the United States has increased roughly 26 years, a fact to be celebrated. The numbers of persons 65 years of age and older have grown from 3,000,000 in 1900 (4.0 percent of the total population) to 25,000,000 in 1980 (11.2 percent of the total population). This number is expected to increase from 32,000,000 in the year 2000 (12.2 percent) to 55,000,000 in 2030 (18.3 percent). The older population includes a disproportionate number of women (100 women to 69 men) and persons with a wide range of capacities, from active and employed to fragile, frail, and chronically disabled. The fastest growing age group in the population is 85 years of age and over, and the second most rapidly growing is the 75 to 81 age group.

The trend in recent years has been for older persons to live alone rather than with family members or in a formal care setting (only 4 percent). Social Security provides some benefits to about 95 percent of the older adult population. However, about 15 percent or 3.3 million persons 65 and older had incomes below a subsistence poverty level in 1980. The median annual income for older men in 1981 was $8,173, for women $4,757. Since half of all older women have incomes below or within $4,000 of the official poverty level ($4,359), it is not surprising that 72 percent of the elderly poor are women and 30 percent of the total elderly minority population are considered marginally poor.

Clearly, the elderly are not a homogenous group. This data point out that not all subgroups fit into the normative situation of the larger population of the elderly. In addition, middle class persons with much higher incomes often find themselves reduced to poverty by the cost of health treatment and long-term care. The increased probability of widowhood and divorce also may produce economic instability for older women. For example, in the case of pensions, only 13 percent of older women receive pensions as a result of their participation in the labor force, and fewer than 10 percent receive benefits from their husband's pensions.

The current health system is more adequate for persons who are younger and have excellent insurance plans. Even though aging itself is not a disease, older people have more illness for a longer period of time than younger people do. Adequate health insurance coverage for millions of uninsured women has been identified as the most pressing health issue faced by older women today. Older women under 65 who are neither married nor in the work force often find health insurance so expensive that it is unaffordable or impossible to buy because of the exclusions for "existing conditions." This problem is made worse because they have no claim on employer-based group policies in which their husbands participated if divorce or death occurs; as well as having fewer job options with good insurance plans if they choose to work outside the home.

Medicare is a health insurance program primarily for persons over the age of 65. Medicaid provides a supplement to medicare as well as coverage for younger persons in poverty. Out-of-pocket costs not covered by medicare or medicaid amount to 19 percent of the annual income of those over 65.

In 1982, 80 percent of older men were married while 50 percent of the older women were widowed. There are almost six times as many widows as widowers. Women are likely to live 10 or more years as widows and half of them will live alone. A number of factors signal problems. For instance: because of traditional sex role socialization, older men are psychologically ill-prepared for living alone, and older women are often inadequately prepared for assertiveness in financial and other management decisions when they find themselves alone. Since most people have been socialized to live in families, they are not prepared to live alone in old age. We need to develop adequate responses to single persons in a society that is oriented toward family living.

Although most older persons live in urban places, they also comprise a large proportion of rural populations where facilities and resources for them are extremely limited. This condition is complicated further by a disproportionately low allocation of federal funds to meet the needs of the rural elderly.

Race and ethnicity are important determinants of the residential patterns of elderly people. While about one-third of all older persons lives in central cities, one-half of all Blacks and Hispanics over 65 is heavily concentrated in urban areas. The popular shifts in housing patterns brought about by urban renewal and gentrification (higher income persons buying property in formerly poor neighborhoods) and the resultant increase in homeowner taxes have a major impact on the elderly, especially minorities. Houses that have been paid for are lost because of the tax increases, or low rents rise astronomically.

We need to dispel the common misunderstanding that aging is senility and that older persons are unable or not motivated to learn, grow, and achieve. Opportunities for continuing education and growth have long been unmet by a system geared to the needs of the young. This demand for continuing education will become acute as better educated, younger generations grow older. We need to counteract the impact of racism and sexism on later life because of underemployment, no employment, inequitable access to education, and language or nationality barriers.

Some problems that beset older persons are the result of

415

the social and physical process of aging. These include change in work, family and community roles; the reduction of energy; and the increase in chronic illness and impairments. These conditions can lead to increased dependence on others for life's necessities. Other problems faced by the elderly are the result of social and political institutions that sometimes victimize the elderly through various techniques of both subtle and overt discrimination. Being old today is not easy, either in the church or society. If the situation of older persons is to be improved, the church must act.

III. *The Technological Response*

Aging is a process involving the whole life span from birth to death. A theological understanding of aging, therefore, must be concerned with the whole life process, rather than with only its final stages. The meaning of life, rather than death, is the central point from which to theologize about aging. In our pluralistic church, there is a certain legitimacy for several traditional, biblical and theological understandings of the meaning of life in its progression from birth to death. The position presented here is one attempt to express this meaning.

A. All of creation is God's work (Gen. 1). Human beings are only a small part of the totality of life forms. The aging process is universal in all life forms. Birth, aging, and death are all part of divine providence, and are to be regarded and taught as positive values. This does not, in any way, mean that such things as birth defects, disease or deaths at an early stage in life are the will of God.

B. As Christians, the mystery of God's involvement in the person of Jesus Christ provides us with a unique source of divine help (grace) in our passage through life's successive stages. This is especially significant in the later stages, when spiritual maturation and well-being can be experienced even in times of physical decline. The power of the cross is a special revelation of how suffering can be reconciling and redemptive. Faith in the resurrection provides us with an assurance of the abiding presence of the Risen Lord (Matthew 28:20) and the Holy Spirit (John 14:16-19; II Cor. 3:17-18; Rom. 8:9-11), and the permanence of our relationship with God beyond the mystery of death. In this spiritual presence we also find the source of the potential of all persons for self-transcendence. God's act in Christ was for life abundant (John 10:10) in all stages of life. Christ also gives us our traditional Wesleyan vision of the goal of ultimate perfection (Matt. 5:48). The grace of God in Christ is therefore important throughout life, including its last stages.

C. In response to this saving grace, we believe in the inevitable need to walk in the ways of obedience that God has enabled (Eph. 2:8-10). These ways are defined by love for God and neighbor (Mark 12:28-31; Rom. 13:8-9). It is therefore the privilege of Christians to serve all persons in love, including older persons with their special needs. Furthermore, since God's grace is not conditioned by any human standards of worthiness or usefulness (II Cor. 5:19), we should regard all persons as valuable to God (Matt. 6:25-30). In the larger pattern of human needs and rights, those of elderly persons must be consciously and intentionally included.

D. Older persons are not simply to be served, but are also to serve; they are of special importance in the total mission of the church. Since the Christian vocation has no retirement age, the special contributions of elderly persons need conscious recognition and employment. The experience of all older persons, and the wisdom of many, are special resources for the whole church.

E. The church as the Body of Christ in the world today (I Cor. 12:27) is God's method for realizing the reconciliation accomplished by Christ (Col. 1:16-20). As such, it intentionally sponsors institutional forms that help reconcile persons of all ages to each other and to God. This especially includes those institutions designed to meet the needs of elderly persons and to keep them fully incorporated into the Body of Christ. The church also is charged with an abiding concern for justice for all. It should work tirelessly for the freedom of all persons to meet their own fullest potential and to liberate those who are captive to discrimination, neglect, exploitation, abuse or poverty.

IV. The Call

A. To society at all levels

United Methodist people are called upon to engage in sustained advocacy for the elimination of age discrimination in personal attitudes and institutional structures. We should pursue this advocacy vigorously and in cooperation with appropriate private and public groups, including all levels of government. We recognize that there needs to be creativity in developing the proper cooperative mix of private and public programs to serve the elderly, but all our efforts should be based on the following assumptions:

1. Religious institutions can make a unique and significant contribution to the context of care provided for persons. Secular society involves ethical issues and value decisions; therefore, a religious presence in neighborhoods and institutions is important to the quality of total community life.

2. Government should play a critical role in assuring that all benefits are available to all elderly persons to improve their quality of life. Christians should support governmental policies that promote sharing with those who are less fortunate. This does not absolve either the institutional church or individual Christians from responsibilty for persons in need.

3. A standard of basic and necessary survival support systems should be accepted and established in our society and made available to all persons. These should include at minimum: health care, transportation, housing, and income maintenance. Church people need to identify and promote those facilities and services that assure opportunities for prolonged well-being. These services should be provided at a cost within the financial means of the elderly with appropriate public subsidy when necessary. They include the following:

a) Health resources systems special to the needs of the elderly which are comprehensive, accessible and feasible within available resources. (These must include long-term care, hospice care, home health care and health maintenance organizations.)

b) Health education systems that emphasize proper nutrition, proper drug use, preventive health care, and immunization as well as information about the availability of health resources within the community.

c) Training for medical and social service personnel concerning the special cultural, physical, psycho-social, and spiritual aspects and needs of the elderly.

d) Adequate housing, that is both affordable and secure, with protections that massive tax and rental increases will not create displacement, and transportation systems that meet the special needs of the elderly.

e) Basic governmental income maintenance system adequate to sustain an adequate standard of living affording personal dignity. (This system should be supplemented when necessary by private pension programs. Both public and private pension systems must be financed in a manner that will assure their ability to meet all future obligations, as well as guarantee equitable consideration of the needs of women and minorities.)

f) When basic pension systems benefit levels are not adequate to meet economic needs at least equal to the defined poverty level, supplementation by benefits from public funds.

g) Continuing educational and counseling opportunities for the elderly in pre-retirement planning, in work-related training, in interpersonal retirement relationships, and in personal enrichment.

h) Formal and informal community associations such as public and private centers that foster social, recreational, artistic, intellectual, and spiritual activities to help persons overcome loneliness and social isolation.

i) Continuing employment opportunities for those who desire them in flexible, appropriate work settings related to varying life styles.

j) Opportunities for volunteer work and paid employment that best utilize the skills and experiences of the elderly.

Finally, our society is called upon to respond to a basic human right of the elderly: the right to die with dignity and to have personal wishes respected concerning the number and type of life-sustaining measures that should be used to prolong life. Living wills, requests that no heroic measures be used, and other such efforts to die with dignity should be supported.

B. To the church at all levels

1. Each local church is called upon:

a) To become aware of the needs and interests of older people in the congregation and in the community and to express Christian love through person-to-person understanding and caring.

b) To affirm the cultural and historical contributions and gifts of ethnic minority elderly.

c) To acknowledge that ministry to older persons is needed in both small and large churches.

d) To assure a barrier-free environment in which the elderly can function in spite of impairments.

e) To motivate, equip, and train lay volunteers with a dedication for this important ministry.

f) To develop an intentional ministry with older adults which:

i. Assures each person health service, mobility, personal security, and other personal services.

ii. Offers opportunities for life enrichment including intellectual stimulation, social involvement, spiritual cultivation, and artistic pursuits.

iii. Encourages life reconstruction when necessary, including motivation and guidance in making new friends, serving new roles in the community and enriching marriage.

iv. Affirms life transcendence including celebration of the meaning and purpose of life through worship, Bible study, personal reflection, and small group life.

g) To recognize that older persons represent a creative resource bank available to the church, and involve them in service to the community as persons of insight and wisdom. (This could include not only ministry to one another, but also to the larger mission of the church for redemption of the world, including reaching the unchurched.)

h) To foster intergenerational experiences in the congregation and community including educating all age groups about how to grow old with dignity and satisfaction.

i) To assure that the frail are not separated from the life of the congregation, but retain access to the sacraments and are given assistance as needed by the caring community.

j) To provide guidance for adults coping with aging parents.

k) To cooperate with other churches and community agencies for more comprehensive and effective ministries with older persons including radio and television ministries.

l) To accept responsibility for an advocacy role in behalf of the elderly.

m) To develop an older adult ministry responsible to the Council on Ministries involving an adult coordinator or older adult coordinator, volunteer or employed. (An older adult council may be organized to facilitate the ministry with older adults.)

2. Each annual conference is called upon:

a) To provide leadership and support through its Council on Ministries for an intentional ministry to older persons in its local churches with special attention to the needs of women and minorities.

b) To develop a program of job counseling and retirement planning for clergy and lay employees.

c) To share creative models of ministry and a data bank of resources with the local churches and other agencies.

d) To define the relationship between the annual conference and United Methodist-related residential and non-residential facilities for the elderly, so that the relationships can be clearly understood and mutually supportive.

e) To relate to secular retirement communities within its boundaries.

f) To recruit persons for professional and volunteer leadership in working with the elderly.

g) To serve as both a partner and critic to local church and public programs with the elderly, promoting ecumenical linkages where possible.

h) To support financially, if needed, retired clergy and lay church workers and their spouses who reside in United Methodist long-term care settings.

i) To promote Golden Cross Sunday and other special offerings for ministries by, for, and with the elderly.

j) To recognize that other persons within the conference, both lay and clergy, represent a significant and experienced resource that should be utilized in both the organization and mission of the conference.

3. General boards and agencies are called upon:

a) To examine the pension policies of the general church and their impact related to the needs of those who are single (retired, divorced, or surviving dependents of pensioners).

b) To create specific guidance materials for ministry by, for, and with the elderly.

c) To prepare intergenerational and age-specific materials for church school and for other special studies in the local church.

d) To promote advocacy in behalf of all the elderly, but especially those who do not have access to needed services because of isolation, low income, or handicap. (This might include advocacy for health care, income maintenance and other social legislation.)

e) To assist institutions for the elderly to maintain quality care and to develop resource centers for ministry with and by the elderly.

f) To create a variety of nonresidential ministries for the elderly, such as Shepherd's Centers.

g) To coordinate general church training in ministry with the elderly.

h) To provide for formal coordination on aging issues.

i) To advocate the special concerns and needs of older women and minorities.

j) To utilize older persons as a creative resource bank in the design and implementation of these objectives.

4. Retirement and long-term care facilities related to the church are called upon:

a) To develop a covenant relationship with the church to reinforce a sense of joint mission in services with the elderly.

b) To encourage the provision of charitable support and provide a channel for the assistance of the whole church.

c) To encourage both residential and nonresidential institutional settings that emphasize the spiritual, personal, physical, and social needs of the elderly.

5. Seminaries and colleges are called upon:

a) To provide seminarians instruction on aging and experiences with older persons in the curriculum.

b) To prepare persons for careers in the field of aging.

c) To develop special professorships to teach gerontology, and to provide continuing education for those who work with the elderly.

d) To stimulate research on the problems of aging, special concerns of minorities, the status of the elderly, and ministries with the elderly, the majority of whom are women.

e) To enable the elderly to enroll in courses and degree programs and to participate generally in the life of educational institutions.

6. Finally, all levels of the church are called upon:

a) To include ministries for, with, and by the elderly as an essential component of the church and its mission.

b) To promote flexible retirement and eliminate mandatory retirement based solely on age.

c) To develop theological statements on death and dying that recognize the basic human right to die with dignity.

d) To develop ethical guidelines for dealing with difficult medical decisions that involve the use of limited resources for health and life maintenance.

e) To authorize appropriate research, including a

demographic study of members of The United Methodist Church, to provide greatly needed information on the socioreligious aspects of aging.

f) To establish a properly funded pension system with an adequate minimum standard for all clergy and church-employed laypersons and their spouses, including the divorced spouse.

V. *Summary*

Life in the later years has caused older persons to ask two questions: How can my life be maintained? What gives meaning and purpose to my life in these years? Both questions have religious implications.

Concern for older persons in the church is theologically grounded in the doctrine of creation, in the meaning of God's work in Christ, in the response to grace that leads us into service, in the continuing value of older persons in the larger mission, and in the nature of the church as an agent of redemption and defender of justice for all.

Older adults in the United States deserve respect, dignity, and equal opportunity. The United Methodist Church is called to be an advocate for the elderly, for their sense of personal identity and dignity, for utilization of experience, wisdom and skills, for health maintenance, adequate income, educational opportunities, and vocational and avocational experiences in cooperation with the public and private sectors of society.

The graying of America implies also the graying of The United Methodist Church. The church, however, is called to be concerned, not only for its own, but also for all older people in our society.

As the aging process is part of God's plan of creation, with the good news of Christ's redemption giving hope and purpose to life, United Methodist people are called upon to help translate this message through words and deeds in the church and in society.[37]

[37] *See* Social Principles, II-H, III-E.

Support Amnesty International

WHEREAS, Amnesty International has documented and verified political imprisonments, tortures, and killings over the last few years, involving government linked forces by governments of widely differing ideologies in more than 20 countries on four continents;

AND WHEREAS, Amnesty International has mounted a campaign to publicize such crimes against humanity which involve thousands of victims, and in this way to bring pressure upon the governments involved;

Be It Resolved, that The United Methodist Church adds its endorsement and support to Amnesty International, along with that already given by the Central Committee of the World Council of Churches, the National Council of the Churches of Christ in the U.S.A., and the American Baptist Churches, USA.

And Be It Further Resolved, that notice of this support be sent to Amnesty International, USA, to the Secretary General of the United Nations, and to the media.

Support for Conscientious Objectors to Registration

WHEREAS, President John Silber of Boston University has stated that it will be that university's policy to go beyond the limits of the Solomon Amendment and deny all financial aid, federal or otherwise, to students who conscientiously refuse to cooperate with draft registration; and

WHEREAS, Boston University has a historical and institutional link with The United Methodist Church and receives funds from the church and its institutions;

Therefore, the General Conference of the United Methodist Church encourages Boston University President John Silber and the Trustees to respect those students who conscientiously refuse to cooperate with the draft registration and provide them equal access to scholarships to which they may be entitled.[38]

[38] *See* Social Principles, V-G; "Concerning the Draft in the United States," 1980; "Certification of Conscientious Objectors," 1980; "The United Methodist Church and Peace," 1980.

Support of the Fair Housing Act

WHEREAS, discriminatory practices in the sale and rental of housing on the basis of race, sex, sexual orientation, national origin, religion, or handicapping conditions continue to restrict access to adequate housing for a significant portion of the population; and

WHEREAS, weaknesses in the enforcement scheme of federal, state, and local laws have made it difficult to achieve the fair housing goals of Title VIII of the Civil Rights Act of 1968;

Therefore, Be It Resolved, that the 1984 General Conference of The United Methodist Church affirms that the primary role of public housing policy is to build neighborhood stability by ensuring housing opportunity for all persons in the neighborhood of their choice; and

Be It Further Resolved, that the 1984 General Conference of The United Methodist Church reaffirms its support for the Fair Housing Act, and specifically supports congressional efforts to amend Title VIII to provide an effective judicial enforcement procedure for resolving fair housing complaints when conciliation efforts fail; and

Be It Further Resolved, that the General Conference of The United Methodist Church supports expanding the coverage of the Fair Housing Act to provide protection for persons with handicapping conditions against discrimination in housing; and

Be It Finally Resolved, that the General Conference of The United Methodist Church supports state and local legislation that would strengthen fair housing enforcement across the country and HUD and Farmers Home Administration funding assistance for states with laws that are substantially equivalent to federal law, and supports referral of fair housing cases for disposition at the state level where such equivalent enforcement mechanisms are in place or enacted.[39]

[39] *See* Social Principles, V-A; "Housing," 1980.

The Treatment of Women in the United States Under Social Security

The Old and New Testaments share prophetic-messianic traditions in which God stands with the oppressed against a dehumanizing and destructive social order. The emphasis on the protection of those in deepest need was a theme of the events of Exodus. And Jesus, drawing on intimate knowledge of the Hebrew Scriptures, inaugurated his ministry with a quotation from Isaiah: "The Spirit of the Lord . . . has annointed me to preach good news to the poor . . . to set at liberty those who are oppressed. . ." (Luke 4:18-19; cf, Isa. 61:1-2).

The early Christian Church in Jerusalem, following this tradition, established a community in which all things were held in common. Special attention was given to those who were the neediest: widows, the elderly, the disabled. Israel and the early church exemplify the role that a community of faith is called upon to play: concern for the welfare of the poor and establishment of a just social system.

In the United States, millions of aged and disabled persons, especially women, depend on the Social Security System for the necessities of life. For most Americans, especially aged women, the Social Security System is often the one program that stands between them and poverty.

Inequities in the system, however, also make it a program that tends to keep many women in poverty. Because of the important role of Social Security, people of faith have a special interest in ensuring that it is operated fairly and securely. Its benefits must be designed to overcome disadvantages of age, race, sex, or disability. And it must be regularly reviewed to assure that it is flexible enough to adjust to the changing needs of our society.

The Social Security System in the United States has historically functioned as a basic insurance program to provide income and medical expenses for those persons who are retired or disabled. It has helped to hold families together by maintaining income in times of personal hardship. It has relieved younger people of the necessity of

427

BOOK OF RESOLUTIONS

total care for aging parents while also allowing retired persons the independence and dignity of their own income by providing basic benefits. Since its enactment in the 1930s, the program has been a cornerstone of the social policy of the United States. However, U.S. society has radically changed in the intervening years and modifications in the Social Security System are now required to meet those social changes.

When the Social Security System was first established, only 17 percent of the paid work force was female. Today over half of all women in the United States work outside the home. However, the wage differential between women and men has been deteriorating during the last 25 years. It is now about 60 cents to $1. Changes in the labor force participation of women and the inequality of pay, combined with an increased divorce and remarriage rate and extended life expectancy of women have resulted in an oppressive situation for many women under Social Security.

In 1980, approximately 52 percent of all Social Security recipients were women, either as workers or dependents. Thirteen percent were children and remaining 35 percent were men. The average monthly Social Security benefit in 1982 for adult women was $308 compared to $430 for men. Retired female workers averaged $335 compared to $438 for men. Spouses of retired or disabled husbands averaged $196 and widows $351. The median annual income for all women over 65 from all sources was only $4757 as compared to $8173 for men in 1981. The figures for minority persons are painfully lower.

Clearly, the system needs attention. Widowed, divorced and never-married women account for 72 percent of all aged people living in poverty. Changes in the Social Security System are desperately needed in order to achieve equal and adequate treatment for all persons. Benefits are clearly inadequate for divorced women, widowed women, ethnic minority women, women who have never married, and women who are not citizens. The current benefit structure penalizes women who work regularly but who spend time out of the labor force to bear and raise children. Further,

428

couples with one wage earner receive larger benefits than do two-earner couples with the same total earnings. Structural unemployment results in increased numbers of unemployed American women and, therefore, less Social Security coverage. Also, the growing issue of undocumented workers who pay into the Social Security System but receive no benefits from their payments needs to be addressed.

The 1983 report of the National Commission on Social Security Reform did not deal with basic systemic change in the gender-based system. However, after the report was released, a majority of the commissioners declared in favor of "earnings sharing," a concept that affirms marriage as a partnership, dividing equally any earnings by either spouse for Social Security purposes. Following that report, the General Boards of Global Ministries and Church and Society affirmed "earnings sharing" as a way of bringing greater equality to the Social Security System.

The United Methodist Church, in its Social Principles, urges social policies and programs that ensure to the aging the respect and dignity that is their right as senior members of society; affirms the need to support those in distress; and calls for the equal treatment of men and women in every aspect of their common life.

Therefore, be it resolved:

1. That the 1984 General conference supports the effort to address the many inequities suffered by women in the Social Security System and urges that the governmental body established to consider these inequities should consult with older women, ethnic minority women and representatives of organizations dealing with older women's issues. Such a body should give special attention to:

a) The concept of "earnings sharing" with a "hold harmless" provision which would prevent persons now receiving benefits from being cut.

b) Social Security credits for the homemaker.

c) An allowance for more "child care" years spent out of the work force.

2. That the Secretary of the General Conference shall

communicate this support to the appropriate officials in the executive and legislative branches of the U.S. government.

3. That the General Boards of Church and Society and Global Ministries shall continue to document social security issues and shall inform their constituencies about the needs for reform.

4. That The United Methodist Church shall educate its constituencies so that churches and individual United Methodists can encourage their legislators to support needed reform.[40]

Unemployment

I. *Historic Commitments*

"Historically, The United Methodist Church has been concerned with the moral issues involved with the social problem of unemployment" (opening sentence, 1976 General Conference statement on "Unemployment").

Three key statements from the Social Principles provide the basis for the church's approach to this critical social concern:

● "Every person has the right and responsibility to work for the benefit of himself or herself and the enhancement of human life and community and to receive adequate remuneration" (¶73 c) "Work and Leisure").

● "We recognize the responsibility of governments to develop and implement sound fiscal and monetary policies that provide for the economic life of individuals and corporate entities, and that ensure full employment and adequate incomes with a minimum of inflation" (¶73, introductory paragraph, "The Economic Community").

● "We believe private and public economic enterprises are responsible for the social costs of doing business, such as unemployment . . . , and that they should be held accountable for these costs" (¶73, "The Economic Community").

[40] *See* Social Principles, III-F; "Equal Rights of Women," 1984.

The 1976 General Conference adopted the most recent statement on "Unemployment" (as part of a comprehensive resolution on "Human Relations") that built on the historic concern for translating these basic principles into " . . . governmental policies . . . that would ensure full employment in order that workers may fully participate in society with dignity, so that families may be economically secure, and so that the nation may achieve coherent high priority goals" (from introductory paragraph, 1976 General Conference statement on "Unemployment").

This 1984 resolution reaffirms and updates these historic commitments of our denomination.

II. *Present Situation*

In the intervening years since 1976, however, little has been done to resolve the issue of unemployment. In 1984 unemployment rates still remain at about 7.8 percent; underemployment results in large numbers of families living under the poverty level; and increasing numbers of people have become discouraged and have dropped out of the labor force altogether.

Furthermore, the levels of unemployment among Blacks, Native Americans, Hispanics and some other minorities have become a national disaster.

III. *Call to Action*

Once more it is necessary for the church to remind itself and the nation of this unhappy and unjust situation and to recommend, as it did in 1976, certain specific policy actions that will help move society towards full-employment.

A. The General Conference of The United Methodist Church calls upon the local, state, and federal governments in the United States to:

1. Develop policies and programs that will help achieve full-employment.

2. Cooperate with private business and labor to institute comprehensive job training programs. (These programs

must be devised to meet the special needs of minorities and women who bear a disproportionate share of unemployment and underemployment.)

3. Cooperate with private business and labor to create the jobs needed to secure employment for all who wish to work. (It is to be remembered that government has the right responsibility to invest in the public service sectors of transportation, health, education, and environment, all of which create many jobs. Some funds presently going to production of military weapons converted to these public service purposes could supply the needed investment funds.)

4. Cooperate with private business and labor to provide the unemployed workers with an income adequate to meet their families' needs.

B. The General Conference also calls upon the churches to:

1. Prepare the moral climate/understanding that would enable the nation to discover the resolving unemployment, by (a) educating its own constituencies and the general public about the causes, effects, and victims of unemployment and underemployment in the current and emerging American and global economy; (b) undergirding this educational effort with the biblical-theological basis of Christian responsibility for helping to resolve these issues; (c) incorporating in this education an emphasis on a biblical and social ethical analysis of the interrelationships between unemployment and racism, sexism, classism, militarism, and other forms of social violence.

2. Provide *direct services* to address unmet needs for employment, food, clothing, shelter, health care, and emergency financial assistance; and for counseling and support groups to meet the personal and family, economic and spiritual needs of the victims of unemployment.

3. Support *community-based economic development ventures* that provide local job opportunities and the recycling of money within local communities.

4. Encourage and support *local, state, regional, and national coalitions* that constructively address private and public

sector policies that relate to the issues of unemployment and underemployment, plant closings and economic dislocation, and other ancillary concerns.[41]

The United Methodist Church and Peace

"Peace is not simply the absence of war, a nuclear stalemate or combination of uneasy cease-fires. It is that emerging dynamic reality envisioned by prophets where spears and swords give way to implements of peace (Isa. 2:1-4); where historic antagonists dwell together in trust (Isa. 11:4-11); and where righteousness and justice prevail. There will be no peace with justice until unselfish and informed live is structured into political processes and international arrangements" (Bishops' Call for Peace and the Self-Development of Peoples).

The mission of Jesus Christ and his Church is to serve all peoples regardless of their government, ideology, place of residence, or status. Surely the welfare of humanity is more important in God's sight than the power or even the continued existence of any state. Therefore, the Church is called to look beyond human boundaries of nation, race, class, sex, political ideology, or economic theory, and to proclaim the demands of social righteousness essential to peace.

The following are interrelated areas which must be dealt with concurrently in a quest for lasting peace in a world community.

I. *Disarmament*

One hard fact must be stated bluntly: the arms race goes on, the momentum of the race never slackens, and the danger of a holocaust is imminent. Meanwhile, millions starve, development stagnates, and international cooperation is threatened. Increasingly sophisticated weapons

[41] *See* Social Principles, VI.

systems accelerate arms spending and heighten anxieties without adding to the security of the nations. Again and again, regional tensions grow, conflicts erupt, and great powers intervene to advance or protect their interests without regard to international law or human rights.

True priorities in national budgeting are distorted by present expenditures on weapons. Because of fear of unemployment, desire for profits, and contributions to the national balance of payments, the arms industry engenders great political power. Arms-producing nations seek to create markets, then vie with one another to become champion among the arms merchants of the world. Food, health, social services, jobs, and education are vital to the welfare of nations. Yet the availability of all of these is constantly threatened because of the overriding priority given by governments to what is called "defense."

If humanity is to move out of this period of futility and constant peril, the search for new weapons systems must be halted through comprehensive international agreements. Moreover, disarmament negotiations should include all nations with substantial armaments systems. The vast stockpiles of nuclear bombs and conventional weapons must be dismantled under international supervision, and the resources being used for arms must be diverted to programs designed to affirm life rather than destroy it. Serious consideration should be given by nations to unilateral initiatives which might stimulate the reaching of international agreement.

World public opinion justly condemns the use of chemical or biological weapons. Governments must renounce use of these particularly inhumane weapons as part of their national policy.

Where nations in a specific region band together to bar nuclear weapons from the area as encouraged by the international community, we commend such constructive agreements and urge other countries, particularly the great powers, to respect them.

We affirm peoples' movements directed to abolition of the tools of war. Governments must not impede public debate on this issue of universal concern.

434

The goal of world disarmament, demanding a radical reordering of priorities and coupled with an effective system of international peacemaking, must be kept constantly before peoples and governments by the church.

II. *Democracy and Freedom*

Millions of people still live under oppressive rule and various forms of exploitation. Millions more live under deplorable conditions of racial, sexual, and class discrimination. In many countries many persons, including Christians, are suffering repression, imprisonment, and torture, as a result of their efforts to speak truth to those in power.

Action by governments to encourage liberation and economic justice is essential but must be supported by parallel action on the part of private citizens and institutions, including the churches, if peaceful measures are to succeed. Unless the prevailing oppression and denial of basic human rights are ended, violence on an increasing scale will erupt in many nations, and may spread throughout the world. The human toll in such a conflict could be enormous and could result in new oppression and further dehumanization.

We are concerned for areas where oppression and discrimination take place, and specifically for Namibia and South Africa, where White minorities continue to oppress and discriminate against Black majorities through legal systems.

This concern extends to all situations where external commercial, industrial, and military interests are related to national oligarchies which resist justice and liberation for the masses of peole. It is essential that governments which support or condone these activities alter their policies to permit and enable people to achieve genuine self-determination.

III. *The United Nations*

International justice requires the participation and determination of all peoples. We are called to look beyond the "limited and competing boundaries of nation-states to the larger and more inclusive community of humanity" (Bishops' Call for Peace and the Self-Development of Peoples).

There has been unprecedented international cooperation through the United Nations and its specialized agencies as they have worked to solve international problems of health, education, and the welfare of people. The United Nations Children's Fund (UNICEF) is one of the agencies that has been successful in this area.

These achievements are to be commended. However, in other areas political considerations have diminished the support needed for the United Nations to achieve its goals. Many nations, including the most powerful, participate in some programs only when those actions do not interfere with national advantage.

We believe the United Nations and its agencies must be supported, strengthened, and improved. We recommend that Christians work for the following actions in their respective nations:

1. The Universal Declaration of Human Rights is a standard of achievement for all peoples and nations. International covenants and conventions which seek to implement the Declaration should be universally ratified.

2. Peace and world order require the development of an effective and enforceable framework of international law which provides protection for human rights and guarantees of justice for all people.

3. Greater use should be made of the International Court of Justice. Nations should remove any restrictions they have adopted which impair the court's effective functioning.

4. Development agencies should not be dominated by the industrialized world. Efforts to make controlling bodies of these agencies more representative should be supported.

5. International agencies designed to help nations or peoples escape from domination by other nations or transnational enterprises must continue to be created and strengthened.

6. Issues of food, energy, raw materials, and other

commodities are greatly affected by economic and political considerations. Efforts in the United Nations to achieve new levels of justice in the world economic order should be considered, reviewed, and supported.

7. Collective action against threats to peace must be supported. Wars fought in the search for justice might well be averted or diminished if the nations of the world would work vigorously and in concert in seeking changes in oppressive political and economic systems.

IV. *World Trade and Economic Development*

The gap between rich and poor countries continues to widen. Human rights are denied when the surpluses of some arise in part as a result of continued deprivation of others. This growing inequity exists in our own communities and in all our nations. Our past efforts to alleviate these conditions have failed. Too often these efforts have been limited by our own unwillingness to act or have been frustrated by private interests and governments striving to protect the wealthy and the powerful.

In order to eliminate inequities in the control and distribution of the common goods of humanity, we are called to join the search for more just and equitable international economic structures and relationships. We seek a society that will assure all persons and nations the opportunity to achieve their maximum potential.

In working toward that purpose, we believe these steps are needed:

• Economic systems structured to cope with the needs of the world's peoples must be conceived and developed.

• Measures which will free peoples and nations from reliance on financial arrangements which place them in economic bondage must be implemented.

• Policies and practices for the exchange of commodities and raw materials which establish just prices and avoid damaging fluctuations in price must be developed.

• Control of international monetary facilities should be

more equitably shared by all the nations, including the needy and less powerful.

• Agreements which affirm the common heritage principle (that resources of the seabed, subsoil, outer space and those outside national jurisdiction are the heritage of humanity) should be accepted by all nations.

• Multilateral, rather than bilateral, assistance programs should be encouraged for secular as well as religious bodies. They must be designed to respond to the growing desire of the "developing world" to become self-reliant.

• Nations which possess less military and economic power than others must be protected, through international agreements, from loss of control of their own resources and means of production to either transnational enterprises or other governments.

These international policies will not narrow the rich-poor gap within nations unless the powerless poor are enabled to take control of their own political and economic destinies. We support people's organizations designed to enable the discovery of local areas of exploitation and development of methods to alleviate these problems.

Economic and political turmoil within many developing nations has been promoted and used by other powers as an excuse to intervene through subversive activities or military force in furtherance of their own national interests. We condemn this version of imperialism which often parades as international responsibility.

We support the United Nations' efforts to develop international law to govern the sea and to ensure that the world's common resources will be used cooperatively and equitably for the welfare of humankind.

We urge the appropriate boards and agencies of The United Methodist Church to continue and expand efforts to bring about justice in cooperative action between peoples of all countries.

V. *Military Conscription, Training, and Service*

1. *Conscription.* We affirm our historic opposition to compulsory military training and service. We urge that

military conscription laws be repealed; we also warn that elements of compulsion in any national service program will jeopardize seriously the service motive and introduce new forms of coercion into national life. We advocate and will continue to work for the inclusion of the abolition of military conscription in disarmament agreements.

2. *Conscientious objection.* Each person must face conscientiously the dilemmas of conscription, military training, and service and decide his or her own responsible course of action. We affirm the historic statement: "What the Christian citizen may not do is to obey persons rather than God, or overlook the degree of compromise in even our best actis, or gloss over the sinfulness of war. The church must hold within its fellowship persons who sincerely differ at this point of critical decision, call all to repentance, mediate to all God's mercy, minister to all in Christ's name" (The United Methodist Church and Peace, 1968 General Conference).

Christian teaching supports conscientious objection to all war as an ethically valid position. It also asserts that ethical decisions on political matters must be made in the context of the competing claims of biblical revelation, church doctrine, civil law, and one's own understanding of what God calls him or her to do.

We, therefore, support all those who conscientiously object: to preparation for or participation in any specific war or all wars; to cooperation with military conscription; or to the payment of taxes for military purposes; and we ask that they be granted legal recognition.

3. *Amnesty and reconciliation.* We urge understanding of and full amnesty or pardon for persons in all countries whose refusal to participate in war has placed them in legal jeopardy.

VI. *Peace Research, Education, and Action*

We call upon The United Methodist Church in the light of its historical teachings and its commitment to peace and self-development of peoples to:

1. Seek the establishment of educational institutions

devoted to the study of peace (such as the National Academy of Peace and Conflict Resolution).

2. Develop alternatives to vocations that work against peace and support individuals in their quest.

3. Explore and apply ways of resolving domestic and international differences which affirm human fulfillment rather than exploitation and violence.

4. Affirm and employ methods that build confidence and trust between peoples and countries, rejecting all promotion of hatred and mistrust.

5. Continue to develop and implement the search for peace through educational experiences, including church school classes, schools of Christian mission and other settings throughout the church.

6. Encourage local churches and members to take actions that make for peace, and to act in concert with other peoples and groups of good will toward the achievement of a peaceful world.[42]

United States Church—China Church Relations

Our faith affirmations and historical understandings of a relationship with the church in the People's Republic of China. Throughout the history of the Christian church, changes in the social, political, economic and cultural environment have elicited new, different, sometimes creative, sometimes destructive, responses in the ministry and witness of the church.

The church which re-emerged in the People's Republic of China (P.R.C.) in 1979, having been officially closed during the Cultural Revolution in 1966-1976, is striving to shape a new church, a new ministry, a new witness in China. A fundamental task for United Methodists is to develop the perceptiveness and spiritual depth that will enable us to

[42]See Social Principles, V-G, VI; "Christian Faith and Disarmament," 1984; "Arab-Israeli Conflict," 1984; "In Support of United Nations," 1980; "A Just World Order in an Age of Interdependence," 1976.

enter into new relationships with the P.R.C. and with this new church. Entering this new relationship requires an honest examination of past patterns of work and relationships, a rethinking of our understanding of the task of the church, and an openness to new ways of being, relating and doing under the guidance of the Holy Spirit.

God's Church is called to mission. Individually and together, both the church in the People's Republic of China and the church in the United States are called to find their place in God's mission. This understanding, which forms the basic approach of the United Methodist China Program, is founded on certain affirmations drawn from biblical faith and shaped by our contemporary social and historical context.

I. Our faith is in God, who is one, the only transcending reality, who is creator of heaven and earth, who has made humankind one, and who continues to work in human history. God's love is expressed in great cosmic and human events; it is also very personal and individual. Created by God, each individual is loved of God, made for God, and drawn to God.

Faith in God as Creator affirms a common humanity with the Chinese people, a recognition that God relates to and has always been at work in Chinese history and culture and in individual persons. Persons in other cultures have much to learn from the Chinese people and from their experiences. Western values and assumptions cannot be projected as universal for all peoples.

II. God has called into being, through Jesus Christ, a particular people, the Church, and has made them one and has sent them into the world in mission and service to all humankind. Christians are linked to Christians in every nation and place through Jesus Christ. Living their daily lives in separate nations and cultures, Christians seek relationships which draw them into fuller expressions of unity while allowing for diversity and independence.

Churches within each nation have a primary link with one another and are the Body of Christ, the church in that place. They are also linked with churches, the Church, in every

441

other nation, and together are the one Body of Christ in the world. Their unity is a sign to the world of God's intention to reconcile and unite humankind. As God continues working in human history, creating, judging, reconciling and redeeming, so the Church, and the churches are called to share in this mission to the world.

Fundamental to the mission are acts of thanksgiving:

We give thanks for all those persons, both indigenous and expatriate, through whose lives and ministries the Church has come into being throughout the world.

We rejoice that God stands with all people, especially the poor and the oppressed of the earth.

Christians give thanks wherever the poor of the earth are receiving new life, and affirm this as part of God's work.

Fundamental to mission also are acts of repentance. We are aware of historic links between the missionary movement and Western influence. Christianity must not be used as a tool of Western penetration. While all are sinners and offered God's grace and forgiveness, the Church is called to stand especially with those who are "sinned against." As the Church renews its covenant of witness, ministry, and mission, it does so with deep repentance and humility, accepting God's forgiveness and seeking the forgiveness of those it has wronged. Trusting God's grace and guidance, the Church moves forward with courage to seek new relationships in mission and service.

III. Through the Holy Spirit the Christian community, within and outside the People's Republic of China, is being challenged to respond in new ways to a new China. Together, the Chinese government and people have brought about many improvements in basic physical needs. The attitudes of the people are also changing. Liberation from foreign domination has brought a renewed sense of pride and dignity in being Chinese. Growing self-reliance in overcoming seemingly insurmountable problems has underscored this feeling of self-respect and self-esteem.

In 1949 many Chinese viewed the church in China as a foreign institution, largely supported by foreign funds and personnel, and closely allied with those who opposed the

Revolution. While the Chinese Communist Party and Chinese church differ on their views of religious belief, the Constitution now provides for both the policy and practice of religious freedom.

Chinese Christians now reaffirm their responsibility to bear witness to the gospel in the People's Republic of China through Christian communities that are self-governing, self-supporting, and self-propagating. Responsibility for Christian mission in the People's Republic of China is with the Christians in the P.R.C. Their leaders want no assistance from outside organizations or individuals without mutual consultation and decision. The Chinese Protestant Three-Self Patriotic Movement and the China Christian Council are institutional expressions of these affirmations.

The life of the church in China, as in other countries, is a precious gift offering a powerful witness to the world. Part of the task of the churches outside China is to receive that witness and to allow time and space for it to grow.

In its centuries-old struggle for survival, China is an inspiration and a challenge to United Methodists. Where is God in the struggle and pathos of the Chinese people? How does the Church of Jesus Christ share in this history? Our historical involvement as United Methodists with the people of China offers a rare opportunity for us to look at the ambiguous relationships between the Chinese people and ourselves. It forces us toward a new understanding of faith in the gospel which seeks to unite all things in Jesus Christ. A new understanding is primary in all that we do in cooperation with the people of China, and the church in China. Christians in China have requested our new understanding and underlined this need by asking us to pray for them and for ourselves.

Recommendations on U.S. Church-China Church Relations

1. That The United Methodist Church provide information, guidance, and encouragement to help its constituency understand the struggles of the people of China, and to

pray fervently with informed sensitivity for the people and the church in China.

The church in the People's Republic of China has declared itself to be self-governing, self-supporting, and self-propagating. The primary responsibility for Christian mission in the People's Republic of China belongs to the church there. We must not act as if the church in the People's Republic of China does not exist, or as if only we are called in mission. We thank God that the church lives in China, and that it is a Chinese church.

2. That The United Methodist Church affirm the selfhood of, respect the autonomy of, and reaffirm our readiness to hear and interact with, the church in the People's Republic of China as together we shape future relationships based on mutuality.

Christians in the Peoples's Republic of China have declared themselves to be in a "post-denominational era." There are now no denominations in the People's Republic of China. There is no Chinese body of Christian believers having an agreed upon polity, creed, rites, etc. What future form of organization, doctrine, ritual the church will take is yet to be determined. Chinese Christians are now concerned that they be allowed to determine these issues within their understanding of the Holy Spirit's leading and without foreign interference. The de-emphasis on denominations in the church in the People's Republic of China is a reminder to United Methodists that the whole Church of Jesus Christ must manifest unity as a sign and sacrament of the unity of humankind.

3. That The United Methodist Church reaffirm its continuing commitment to work ecumenically with other Christian bodies in relating to the church in the People's Republic of China and with the Chinese people.

Christians in the People's Republic of China have made us sensitively aware of the imbalances of relationships between China and ourselves. They have also pointed out the growing disparities between the rich and the poor nations. They have challenged us to examine our involvement with the poor and oppressed in our own society.

4. That The United Methodist Church recommit itself a) to a sustained program for awareness of the disparities between the rich and the poor; and b) to work with faithfulness and integrity to create new attitudes and institutional structures which more perfectly manifest the gospel of Christ that all humankind be united. Such efforts include:

● Being sensitive to areas of our national life which exploit peoples of other societies as well as our own.

● Standing with the poor and the oppressed in the United States as well as in other countries.

● Examining and learning from the accomplishments and the mistakes in past and present missionary efforts in China and other parts of the world.

● Being available for mutual ministry with Christians in China, in the United States, and in other countries.

5. That The United Methodist Church also commit itself to a strengthened program of communication and dialogue within The United Methodist Church about the People's Republic of China and the church there.[43]

United States—China Political Relations

Our Political Understandings

In late 1978 the governments of the United States and the People's Republic of China (P.R.C.) reached agreement establishing full diplomatic relations. The United States ended official relations—diplomatic and military—with the authorities on Taiwan. (In March 1979 the U.S. Congress passed the Taiwan Relations Act putting U.S. relations with Taiwan on an unofficial basis). The United States recognized the People' Republic of China as the "sole legal government of China," but reserved the right over P.R.C. objections to sell "defensive" weapons to Taiwan. At the time of normalization the P.R.C. refused to rule out the

[43] *See* "United States-China Political Relations," 1984.

possibility of reunifying with the island of Taiwan by force, but offered to allow Taiwan to maintain the political, economic, and military status quo if Taiwan were to recognize P.R.C. sovereignty.

This normalization agreement ended a 30-year period in which formal American commitments to the authorities on Taiwan blocked closer relations with the People's Republic of China. It laid the foundations for framework of cooperation and exchanges which continue to develop. Highlights include:

● Government-to-government agreements covering consular relations and embassies, civil aviation, scientific and technical cooperation, educational exchange, trade and credit, fisheries and a wide range of other fields.

● Substantial expansion of tourism and specialized visits.

● Educational programs facilitating nearly 10,500 scholars and teachers (10,000 Chinese; 500 Americans) to be resident in the other country.

● Numerous governmental and private institutional exchange agreements in education, the fine and performing arts, cinema, publishing, etc.

● Sister state-province and city-to-city agreements calling for various kinds of cooperation.

● Increased two-way trade.

● Discussions at the highest governmental levels about strategic and military concerns and cooperation.

The rapid growth and elaboration of these bilateral relations have been unusual and, to many, unexpected. While the direction is generally positive and the initial results heartening, the relationship is still in its early stages. Because the P.R.C. and U.S. systems are so different, translating worthwhile goals into concrete practice has often been difficult.

Fundamentally, the two countries have yet to determine what kind of long-term relationship they want. Misperceptions and misunderstandings are all too commonplace on both sides, even on basic principles.

As a case in point, the two sides had sharp disagreements during 1981 and 1982 over the issue of continuing U.S.

arms sales to Taiwan. By August 1982, Washington and Beijing had clarified their understanding on this question: the P.R.C. stated that its "fundamental policy" was to "strive for peaceful reunification" with Taiwan. In that context, the U.S. government pledged not to increase and in fact to reduce its sale of arms to Taiwan. But this agreement only holds in abeyance a resolution of the Taiwan issue.

Recommendations on U.S.—China Political Relations

The United Methodist Church:

1. Affirms the establishment of full diplomatic relations between the United States and the People's Republic of China as an important step toward mutual cooperation and understanding and toward world peace.

2. Advocates that the U.S. government, in accordance with the Joint Communique of December 1978, should continue to deal with the people of Taiwan on an unofficial basis.

3. Recognizes the necessity for China to continue its economic and social development and urges U.S. cooperation to that end within the context of Chinese independence and selfhood.

4. Feels the long-term basis of U.S.-China relations should emphasize people-to-people, educational, social, and economic cooperation based on mutual understanding and benefit, not short-term or expedient military or strategic interests; expresses deep concern about the anti-Soviet rationale used to explain U.S.-P.R.C. relations; opposes the sale of U.S. military equipment to the P.R.C.

5. Endorses a peaceful approach to ending the long-standing conflict between the governments in the People's Republic of China and in Taiwan while recognizing that the resolution of the status of Taiwan is a matter for the Chinese people themselves, and in that context supports the continued reduction and early cessation of U.S. arms sales to Taiwan.

6. Declares our continuing concern regarding the human rights of all people on both sides of the Taiwan Straits.

7. Recognizes that U.S.-P.R.C. relations have an important influence on the peace and stability of the Asian region, particularly in Southeast Asia; and urges both the United States, and the People's Republic of China to seek peaceful means to contribute to the peace and stability of the region.[44]

The Use of Alcohol and Drugs on Campuses

WHEREAS United Methodist colleges should provide an environment suitable for pursuing a higher education in a Christian atmosphere;

THEREFORE, BE IT RESOLVED, that The United Methodist Church addresses this issue by (1) promoting an alternative life style that encourages "wellness" without drugs and alcohol, (2) seeking authentic advocates for this alternative life style, and (3) having these advocates promote this image on United Methodist campuses across the nation.[45]

---

[44] See "United States Church-China Church Relations," 1984.
[45] See Social Principles, III-I; "Drug and Alcohol Concerns," 1980.

Index

Notes

Notes

Notes

Notes

Notes

Notes

Notes

Notes

Notes

Notes

Notes